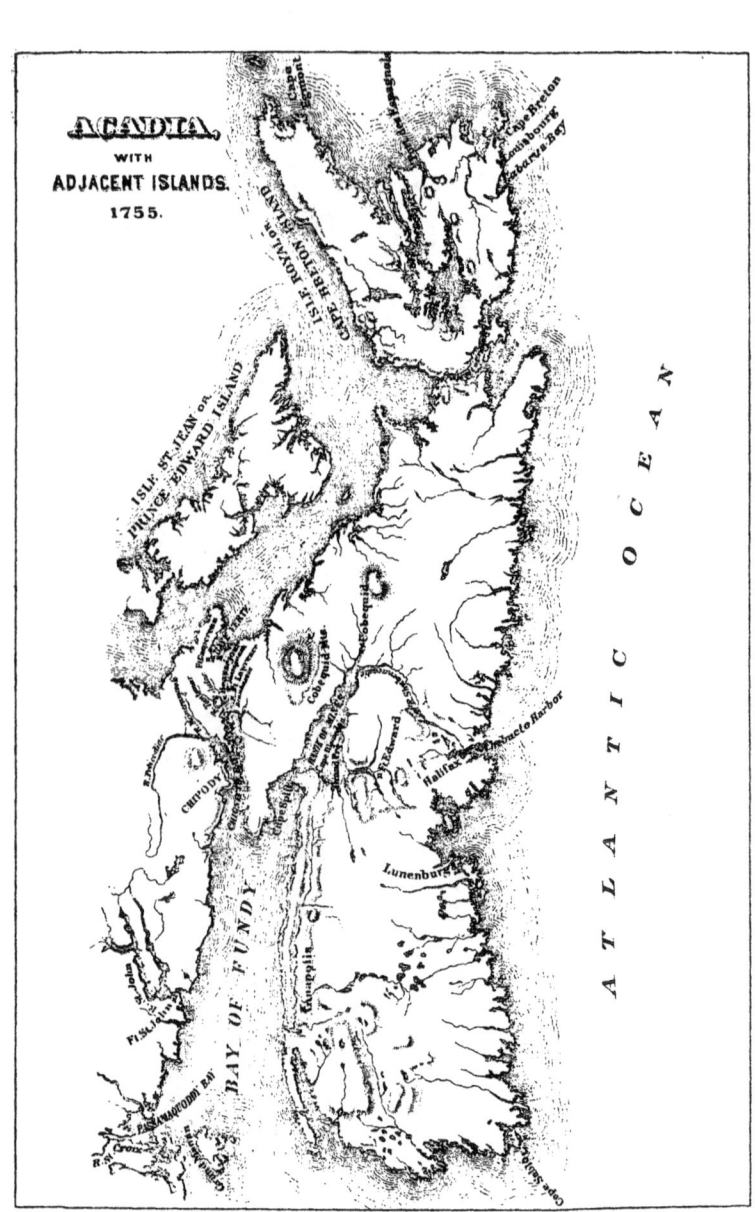

French and Indian War Notices
Abstracted from Colonial Newspapers
Volume 1: 1754-1755

Armand Francis Lucier

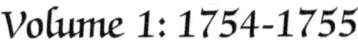

HERITAGE BOOKS
2007

HERITAGE BOOKS
AN IMPRINT OF HERITAGE BOOKS, INC.

Books, CDs, and more—Worldwide

For our listing of thousands of titles see our website
at
www.HeritageBooks.com

Copyright © 1999 (index) Heritage Books, Inc.

Published 2007 by
HERITAGE BOOKS, INC.
Publishing Division
65 East Main Street
Westminster, Maryland 21157-5026

Copyright © 1999 Armand Francis Lucier

Map of Acadia by Francis Parkman, reproduced from *Pocket Parkman, Vol. 1* © Little, Brown & Co., 1898. "The Braddock Massacre" by H. A. Ogden, 1896, © Jones Bros. Publishing, 1918.

All rights reserved. No part of this book may be reproduced or transmitted in any form or by any means, electronic or mechanical, including photocopying, recording or by any information storage and retrieval system without written permission from the author, except for the inclusion of brief quotations in a review.

International Standard Book Number: 978-0-7884-1085-7

CONTENTS

Foreward..v

February 1754..................................1
March 1754.....................................9
April 1754....................................37
May 1754......................................49
June 1754.....................................65
July 1754.....................................73
August 1754...................................83
September 1754................................91
October 1754.................................105
November 1754................................123
December 1754................................129

January 1755.................................143
February 1755................................153
March 1755...................................163
April 1755...................................173
May 1755.....................................179
June 1755....................................193
July 1755....................................215
August 1755..................................255
September 1755...............................287
October 1755.................................319
November 1755................................339
December 1755................................349

Index..355

FOREWORD

All the following articles contain the dates that they were published in the Weekly Colonial Newspapers in the British Provinces of North-America. The events presented here are what the Inhabitants of the Cities, Towns and Villages were reading concerning the French and Indian War; and, they inform the reader of the anxieties and deep concern during that trying period of American History.

The reader will find descriptions of the same events seen by different eyes, and the events presented differently by each publisher. Also printed were facts, hearsay and proparganda doled out by the different provincial governments to inflame the passion of the British subjects as a means to unite all Colonies into one defensive union to wage war on the encroaching French and Indians.

There is no attempt to correct punctuation, spelling, and presentation, yet a few minor changes have been made for the sake of readibility and clarity.

CONTRIBUTORS

Boston Gazette. Boston Massachusetts.
The Boston Evening Post. Boston Massachusetts.
Connecticut Gazette. New-Haven Connecticut.
Maryland Gazette. Annapolis Maryland.
New-Hampshire Gazette. Portsmouth New-Hampshire.
New-London Summery. New-London Connecticut.
New-York Mercury. New-York New York.
New-York Gazette [Weyman's] New-York New-York.
Pennsylvania Gazette. Philadelphia Pennsylvania
Providence Gazette. Providence Rhode Island.
Virginia Gazette. Williamsburg Virginia.

Armand Francis Lucier

FEBRUARY 1754

PHILADELPHIA Feb. 5. Extract of a Letter from a Gentleman in Virginia, to his Friend in the City of Annapolis, dated Jan. 16, 1754.

"Mr. Washington, the Ambassador sent to the Indian Country, is returned, which affords us now Conversation. It is undoubtedly affirm'd for Truth, that the French have settled and had fix'd several Forts near the Ohio Tract, especially one upon the French River, which Mr. Washington was at, and that proper Officers, and Five Hundred Men, are in each Fort, chiefly French, and that they have twelve Cannon mounted on each of them, and great Numbers of French and Indians are close at Hand to assist at a small Warning. Mr. Washington was received in a polite genteel Manner by the Commandant of the Fort, who read and answer'd our Governor's Letter, and at the same Time told Mr. Washington, that it was his instructions from the King his Master, to keep Possession, and to advance further and fight those who should oppose them &c. And added, that he had expected an Army to be sent for twelve Months past by the English, and that they were prepar'd for them, for he suppos'd they must knock it out, and he did not care how soon. Mr. Washington is now gone to Williamsburg, and 'tis suppos'd the Assembly will meet immediately, and that Men will be raised &c.

WILLIAMSBURG Feb. 14. The Speech of the Honourable Robert Dinwiddie, Esq; Lieutenant Governor, and Commander in Chief, of the Colony and Dominion of Virginia, in General Assembly of the said Province, on Thursday the 14th Day of February 1754.

Gentlemen of the Council, Mr. Speaker, and Gentlemen of the House of Burgesses,

Nothing less than a very important Concern, could have induced me to call you all together again, after so short a Recess; but the Dignity of the Crown of Great-Britain, the Welfare of all the Colonies on this Continent, and more especially of this Dominion, engaged me to have your Advice and Assistance, in an Affair of the greatest Consequence.

Major Washington, who was sent by me to the Commandant of the French Forces on the River Ohio, being returned, informs me he has found that Officer at a Fort they had erected on a Creek running into the Ohio, and that they were then preparing all necessaries for building another Fort on that River; that they had Two Hundred and Twenty Canoes made, and many more rough hewed to be made, in order to transport, early this Spring, a great Number of regular Forces, no less than Fifteen Hundred Men, with their Indians in Friendship with them, down the River Ohio, in order to build many more Fortresses on it; and that they propose Loggs-Town to be the chief Place of their Rendezvous.

Major Washington further reports, That he asked why they had seized the Goods of our traders, and sent their Persons Prisoners to Canada; to which the Commandant answered, 'That his orders from their General, the Governor of Canada, were, Not to permit any English Subjects to Trade on the Waters of the Ohio, but to seize their Goods and send them Prisoner to Quebec.' He also asked the reason of taking Mr. Frazier's House from him, which he had built and lived in upwards of Twelve Years? He said, 'That man was lucky that he had made his Escape, or he would have sent him Prisoner to Canada.'

These Transactions are entirely inconsistent with the Treaties subsisting between the two Crowns, and contrary to any Instructions from his Majesty, whereby I directed to prevent any Foreign Power, settling or building any Fortresses on his Majesty's Lands.

Add to the aforementioned injustifiable Insults of the French, the cruel barbarous Murder in cool Blood, of a whole Family in the Dominion, Man, Wife, and five Children, no longer ago than last Month; and very lately a poor Man on the South Branch of Potowmack, robbed of his Son. These Depredations were said to be done by the French Indians, but if I be rightly informed, some of the French Subjects always go with the Indians, on these Incursions, and are both privy in, and Instigators of, their Robberies and Murder.

How compassionate must then be the distressful Situation of that poor unhappy Family! surrounded bu a Crowd of Miscreants, dreadfully rushing on to perpetrate the most savage Barbarities, insensible to the Cries of the tender Infant, basely determined to destroy, without Provocation, those who could not resist their Violence.

Think you see the Infant torn from the unavailing Struggle of the distracted Mother, the Daughters ravished before the Eyes of their wretched Parents; and then, with Cruelty and insult, butchered and Scalped. Suppose the horrid Scene compleated, and the whole Family, Man, Wife and Children (as they were) murdered and scalped by these relentless Savages, and then torn to Pieces, and in Part devoured by wild Beast, for whom they were left Prey by their more brutal Enemies.

But how much your Indignation rise when you extend your View to the Abettors of these Villanies! Such are the People whose Neighbourhood you must now prevent, or with the most probable Expectation think to see, in the Bobin of your Country, these Evils, that you as yet have only the melancholy tidings of from your Frontiers.

Consider the bloody Villains, thievishly lurking about a Man's Plantation, and where they dare not attack like Men, basely like Vermin, stealing and carrying away the helpless Infant, that happened to wander, tho' but a little Distance, from his Father's Threshold.

I Assure you, Gentlemen,, these Insults of our Sovereign's Protection, and Barbarities of our Fellow Subjects, make deep Impressions on my Heart, and I doubt not, as you must hear them with Horror and Resentment, but you will enable me, by a full and sufficient Supply, to exert

the most vigorous Efforts, to secure the Rights
and effects the Honour and Dignity of our Sovereign; to drive away these cruel and treacherous Invaders of our Properties, and Destroyers
of our Families, and thereby to gratify my warmest Whishes in establishing the Security and
Prosperity of Virginia, on the most solid and
permanent Foundation.
   Gentlemen of the House of Burgesses,
   I must earnestly recommend to you His Majesty's Commands, for a proper Supply, the immediate Necessity whereof, at this Time, I desire
you will seriously consider, and by a ready and
effectual Compliance, recommend yourselves and
the Country his Royal Favour.
   This is your Part, Gentlemen. ——— What I
could, before your Meeting, I have done, for the
Public; and by the Advice of the Council I have
array'd some Part of the Militia, which I have
order'd up to the Ohio with all possible Expedition, to build a Fort there, at the Forks of
Monongalea. And as his Majesty's gracious present of Thirty Pieces of Cannon, Eighty Barrels
of Powder, and other Ordinance Stores suitable,
are arriv'd, I have sent Ten of the Cannon, and
a proportion of Ammunition to Alexandria, to
from thence transported as soon as possible to
the Ohio.
   I have wrote the neighbouring Colonies for
their Aid and Assistance, which I have good reason to expect; but I must observe to you, that
their Eyes are fix'd on your proceedings, and I
hope you will engage them, by a laudable Example, to contribute sufficiently for the common
Cause.
   The late Occasion having suggested to me some
Defect in the act for making Provisions against
Invasions and Insurrections, I think proper to
observe to you, that the Pay is very unequally
proportioned, being too high for the Soldiers,
and too low for the Officers,; and there is no
Provisions made for a Doctor, a Commissary of
Stores, and several other Requisites. ————— I
think it would be better to pay the Militia in
Money than Tobacco, by which there may be a
Saving to the Country, and the Men much better

satisfied.

Gentlemen of the Council, and Gentlemen of the House of Burgesses,

I look upon the Safety and Welfare of Virginia to depend on your Councils and Determinations, in this critical juncture, which therefore ought to be uninterrupted by any Avocations from Prejudice, or unseasonable Divisions, at all Times the Bane of public Consultations, but which, at present, would be particularly fatal; and I doubt not, when you seriously consider the Importance of what is laid before you, you will find Duty, Honour, and your own Preservation, all united, to engage you to exert your efforts equal to the Occasion.

The Season for entering upon Action being so near at Hand, your Session can be but short, and I design to conclude with an earnest Exortation to Concord and Expedition, lest if we be divided or flow in Deliberation, our Enemies may seize the Time we lose, and render any future Efforts ineffectual.

And in all Measures for His Majesty's Service, and the Good of this Colony, you will have my ready and Zealous Concurrence.

WILLIAMSBURG Feb. 16. The Humble Address of the Council,

Sir,
We his Majesty's faithful and loyal Subjects, Colony of Virginia, now met in General Assembly beg Leave to return your Honour our every thanks for your kind Speech at the Opening of the Session.

We cannot forbear to express our just Indignation at the unwarrantable Encroachments, and hostile Proceedings of the French, and at the same Time to testify our Approbation of the prudent steps already taken by your Honour, for the Defence and Security of the Colony.

The ardent Zeal for the support of His Majesty's Crown and Dignity, and our tender Regard for the Welfare and Prosperity of our Country, will incline us, by a chearful Concurrence with the House of Burgesses to exert our most vigorous Efforts to support and effectually your Honour's Proceedings, in what we agree to be the common Cause of all the British Colonies upon the Continent, and more especially of this Dominion: And we assure your Honour, That in all our Consultations we will proceed with that Harmony and Dispatch, that the Importance of the Subject, and advanced Season requires.

We cannot conclude without our earnest Prayers, that your Honour's constant Labour may be crowned with their deserved Success; and our warmest Wishes, that our Country may long continue to flourish under your Honour's Administration; from whence we may with reason hope to see her Security and Prosperity established, on the most solid and permanent Foundation.

PHILADELPHIA Feb. 16. Extract of a Letter from Charlestown South Carolina, Feb. 2. 1754.

"We hear from Ohio that a Party of French are come down from the upper Parts of the River to Logg-Town, near which they have built a large Oven, and are making other Preparation, for the Reception of the Troops which they give are to follow them in the Spring. That a considerable Body of French are likewise come up the Ohio from Missisippi, and are now near the Fall; it is said are to build a Fort at the Mouth of the Miamis River, which runs into the Ohio, and then proceed up to meet the other French who are to come down the River: That they have engaged the Chipaways, Outaways, and Adirondacs, to take up the Hatchet against the English: that a Party of French Indians who last Fall made an Incursion in Virginia, as they return'd thro' Kuskuskies, near the Ohio, was observ'd to have an English Boy with them a Prisoner, suppos'd to be Mr. Cooper's Child of Potowmack, that some of our friendly Indians at Kuskuskies would have recover'd the Boy from the Enemy, but they got him over the River, and carried him off: that a Party of the Six Nations Warriors, which had Pass'd by Logg-Town intending to go against the Southern Indians, calling in their Way at an English House on the Frontier of Virginia, found all the Family, viz. three Mem, two Women, and two Children, all lying in their Beds murder'd and scalp'd, suppose to be done by the French Indians above mentioned; and the six Nation

Indians immediately return'd to Logg-Town to give Notice of this, lest they should be Suspected.

WILLIAMSBURG Feb. 18. To the Honourable Robert Dinwiddie, Esq; His Majesty's Lieutenant Governor, and Commander in Chief, of the Colony of Dominion of Virginia;

The Humble Address of the House of Burgesses,
Sir,

We His Majesty's dutiful and loyal Subjects, the Burgesses of this his most ancient Colony and Dominion of Virginia, now met in General Assembly, humbly beg Leave to return your Honour our Thanks for your kind Speech to the Council and this House.

With Hearts full of Zeal for his Majesty's Service and the Interest of this Country, and fired with Resentment and Indignation at the unjustifiable Proceedings and Encroachments of the French, and French Indians; we do, in the strongest Terms express our utmost Abhorrence of their barbarous Cruelties and Depredations, committed on the Frontiers, and his Majesty's Subjects inhabiting there.

We are truly sensible of the great Importance of the several Matters recommended to us by your Honour, and we do assure you, that we will take the same into serious Consideration, and act therein agreeable to the Duty we owe to our King and Country.

WILLIAMSBURG Feb. 19. By the Honourable Robert Dinwiddie, Esq; His Majesty's Lieutenant Gov. ernor, and Commander in Chief of the Dominion.

A PROCLAMATION

For Encouraging Men to enlist in his Majesty's Service for the Defence and Security of the Colony.

Whereas it is determined that a Fort be immediately built on the River Ohio, at the Fork of Monongahelia, to Oppose any further Encroachments, or hostile Attempts of the French and the Indians in their Interest, and for the Security and Protection of his Majesty's Subjects in this Colony; and as it is absolutely necessary that a sufficient Force should be raised to erect and support the same: For an Encouragement to all who should voluntarily enter into the said Service, I do hereby notify and promise, by and with the Advice and Consent of his Majesty's Council of the Colony, that over and above their Pay. Two Hundred Thousand Acres of his Majesty the King of Great-Britain Lands, on the East side of the River Ohio within this Dominion (one Hundred Thousand Acres whereof to be continguous to the said Fort, and the other Hundred Thousand Acres to be on, or near the River Ohio) shall be laid off and granted to such Persons, who by their Voluntary Engagement, and good Behaviour in the said Service, shall deserve the same And I further promise, that the same Lands be divided amongst them immediately after Performance of the said Service, in a Proportion due to their respective Merit, as shall be represented to me by their Officers, and held and enjoyed by them without paying any rights, and also free from the Payment of Quit-rents for the Term of Fifteen Years. And I do appoint this Proclamation to be read and published at the Court-Houses, Churches and Chapels in each County within the Colony, and the Sheriffs take Care the same be done accordingly.

   Given at the Council-Chamber in Williamsburg, on the 19th Day of February in the 27th Year of his Majesty's Reign, Annoque Domini 1774.

                                  Robert Dinwiddie

   WILLIAMSBURG Feb. 24. Our General Assembly met the 14th Inst, and were last Night prorogued. They have given to Commissioners 10,000 Pounds for the Defence of the Frontier. Three hundred Men are order'd to be immediately rais'd and sent to Ohio: And 'tis expected, that at the Meeting of the Commissioners more will be order'd, in order to reimburse the Treasury the Money expected on this Occasion, they have laid on additional Duty of Five per Cent, on all Slaves imported; Two Shillings Sterling on every Writ and Subpaena issued from the General-Court; One Shilling Sterling from a County Court, Twenty Shillings on every Coach and Chariot; and Ten Shillings on every Chair, per Annum to continue three Years; which will be more than sufficient.

MARCH 1754

ANNAPOLIS March 14. Letters from Messieurs Trent and Gist, to Major Washington of Virginia, giving some Accounts of the Situation near the Ohio. The first letter is dated Feb. 19, at Yaughyaughgany big Bottom. The 17th Mr. Trent arrived at the Forks of Monongahelia (from the Mouth of Red Stone Creek, where he had built a Strong Store House) and met Mr. Gist, and several Others: In two or three Days they expected down all the People, and was soon as they came were to lay the Foundation of the Fort, expecting to make out for that Purpose about 70 or 80 Men. The Indians were to join them, and make them strong, They requested him (Major Washington) to march out to them with all possible Expedition. They acquainted him, that Monsieur La Force had made a Speech to some of our Indians and told them, that neither they nor the English there, would see Sun above 20 Days longer; 13 of the Days being then to come: By what Mr. Croghan could learn from an Indian in the French Interest, they might expect 400 French down in that Time: A Messenger sent from the French Fort had Letters for the Commander of the other Forts to march immediately and join them, in order to cut off our Indians and Whites, and some French Indians were likewise expected to join them: When La Force had made his Speech to the Indians, they sent a String of Wampum to Mr. Croghan, to desire him to hurry the English to come, for that they expected soon to be attack'd and press hard to come and join them; for they wanted Necessaries and Assistance, and then would strike: They further write, that 600 French and Indians were gone against the lower Shawanese-Town, to cut off the Shawanese; 200 Ottoways and Chipawas came to Mushingum and damaged the White People there, and showed them the

French Hatchet; the Wayondotts, tho' not above 30 Men, refused to let them kill them in their Town; but they expected every Day to hear they had cut off the Whites, and likewise the Wayondotts.

The other Letter is Dated at Monongahela, Feb. 23. Mr. Gist writes, "An Indian who was taken Prisoner from the Chickasaws, by the Six Nations some Years ago, has been this Year to see his Friends there; in his Passage up the Ohio, fell in with a Body of near 400 French coming up the River; he parted with them below the Falls, and then came Company with 10 of them that were sent up to treat with the Shawanese at the Lower Town; on their arrival there, the English Traders had agreed to make Prisoners of them, but the French getting a Hint from some Indians, they fled away in the Night without discovering their Business: We have also News 600 French and Indians, gone down to fall on the Shawanese, if they will not admit the lower Army to pass up the River or to join that above; it would therefore be prudent, to let the Governor know this, perhaps he might send a Number of Cherokees to join the Shawanese at the lower Town, and defeat them, or prevent their joining those above. Pray. send a Line by Mr. Stewart, and let us know the exact Time you will be here, that we may speak truth in all we say to our Friends."

We hear from Virginia that they go on very briskly in raising Men, and that 500, under Officers, will be soon ready then to March to Alexandria.

WILLIAMSBURG March 15. We have Advice from the back Part of the Country. That a Party of French, under the Command of one Chivalrie, are come down from the Log-Town, where they have held a Treaty and made Presents to the Indians, built a large Oven and are making other Preporations for the Reception of the Troops, who they gave out are to follow them in the Spring; That a large Body of French are likewise come up to the Fall of Ohio from the Missisippi, intending to build a Fort at the Mouth of the Miami's River; and then proceed to join those of their

Nation, expected to come down the Ohio, from Canada: That the Ohio Company have almost compleated their Fort, amd Captain Trent, at the Charge of this Government has begun another. We have likewise a Report, but not well Confirmed, That Captain Trent, with a Party of Indians, is gone to Loggs-Town intending to drive off the French that are there.

ANNAPOLIS March 21. We have just now received Intelligence from the Westward, of 400 French come down from the Lakes, 100 which, stay'd about Mushingum, and the other 300 went down to the lower Shanoah-Town; they have demanded the English Traders that are there (about 20 in Number) to be delivered up to them, which the Shanoahs have refused to do, and have sent up for the Catawas, to come to their Assistance. These 400 French expects to be join'd by 400 more, as soon as they can come down from the Lakes. There ar 22 French at Loggs-Town, who about 5 Weeks ago, held a Council with the Indians; in which they told them, That as they Determined not to make their Fire with them, but had done it with their Brothers the English, they might expect to be struck, and that their Brothers the English, should see the Sun but 20 Days, and then they would destroy all the Indians: Upon which Monocatoocha took his Tommahawk out of his Bosom, and said "You have often deceived us, but now you tell us, You will strike our Brothers the English, we believe you speak the Truth, come on, we are ready for you, and will stand by, and join our Brothers against you." A few Days before the above Council was held, The French had taken one Joseph Patten Prisoner, which the Half King hearing went to them, said to this Effect: "We have suffered you to take our Brothers often, and have taken no Notice of it; but since you have the Impudence to take our Brother before our Faces, we see your Design;" upon which he went up to the French Captain and knock'd him down, and then turning to Patten, he said "My Brother, you are a Freeman, I discharge you, go about your own Business.

ANNAPOLIS March 21. The Storm arissing in the

West, being the present Topic of Conversation, we think we cannot oblige our Readers, at this Juncture, with anything more entertaining than Major Washington's Journal to Ohio, who was sent last Fall, by the Governor of Virginia, to the Commandant of the French Forces there.

Major Washington's Journal to the River Ohio.
Wednesday October 31st 1753.

I was commissioned and appointed by the Honourable Robert Dinwiddie, Esq; Governour, &c. of Virginia, to visit and deliver a Letter to the Commandant of the French Forces on the Ohio, and set out the intended Journey the same Day; the next I arrived at Fredericksburg, and engaged Mr. Jacob Van Braam, to be my French interpreter; and proceeded with him to Alexandria where we provided Necessaries: from thence we went to Winchester, and got Baggage, Horses, &c. and from thence we persued the new Road to Wills Creek, where we arrived the 14th of November.

Here I engaged Mr. Gist to pilot us out, and also hired four other as Servitors, Baneby Currin, and John Macquire, Indian Traders, Henry Steward and William Jenkins, and in Company with those Persons, left the Inhabitants the Day following.

The excessive Rain and vast Quantity of Snow that had fallen, prevented our reaching Mr. Frazier's an Indian Trader, at the Mouth of Turtle Creek, on Monongahela till Thursday the 22d. We were informed here, that Expresses were sent a few Days ago to the Traders down the River, to acquaint them with the French General's Death, and the return of the major Part of the French Army into Winter Quarters.

The Waters were quite impassable, without swimming the Horses; which obliged us to get the Loan of a Canoe from Frazier, and send Barneby Currin, and Henry Steward, down Monongahela, with our Baggage, to meet us at the Forks of Ohio, about 10 Miles, to cross Aligany.

As I got down before the Canoe, I spent some time in viewing the Rivers, and the Land in the Fork, which I think extremely well situated for a Fort, as it has the absolute Command of both Rivers. The Land at that Point is 20 or 25 Feet above Common Surface of the Water, and a considerable Bottom of flat, well timbered Land all around it, very convenient for Building: The Rivers are each a Quarter Mile, or more across, and run here very near at right Angle: Aligany bearing N. E. and Monongahela S. E. the former of these two is very rapid and swift running Water, the other deep and still, without any perceptible Falls.

About two Miles from this, on the South East Side of the River, at the Place where the Ohio Company intended to erect a fort lives Shingiss, King of the Delawares' we called upon him, to invite him to Council at the Logg's Town.

As I had taken a good deal Notice Yesterday of the Situation at the Forks, my Curiosity led me to examine the more particularity, and I think it greatly inferior, either for Defence or Advantages; especially the latter, for a Fort at the Forks would be equally well situated on Ohio, and have the entire Command of Monongahela, which runs into out Settlements and is extremely well design'd for Water Carriage, and it is of a deep still Mature: and besides, a Fort at the Fork might be built at a much less Expence, than at the other Place. ——

Nature has well contrived the lower Place, for Water Defence; but the Hill whereon it must stand being about a Quarter of a Mile in Length, and the descending gradually on the Land side, still render it difficult and very expensive making a sufficient Fortification there. —— The whole Flat upon the Hill must be taken in; or the Side next the Decent made extremely high; or also the Hill cut away: Otherwise, the Enemy may raise Batteries within the Distance without being expos'd to a single Shot from the Fort.

Shingiss attended us to Logg's Town, where we arrived between Sun setting and Dark the 25th Day after I left Williamsburg: We travelled over some extreme good, amd bad Land, to get to this Place. ——

As soon as I came into Town, I went to Monacatoocha (as the Half King was out at his Hunting Cabbin on little Beaver Creek, and about 15 Miles off) and inform'd him by John Davison my

Indian Interpreter, that I was sent a Messenger
to the French General; and was ordered to call
upon the Sachems of the Six Nations, to acquaint
them with it —— gave him a String of Wampum,
and a twist of Tobacco, and desired him to send
for the Half King; which he promised to do by a
Runner in the Morning, and for other Sachems.
I invited him and the other great Men present
to my Tent, where they stay'd about an Hour and
return'd.

According to the best Observations I could
make, Mr. Gist's new Settlement (which we pass'd
by) bears about W. N. W. 70 Miles from Wills
Creek; Siranappins, or the Forks N. by W. or N.
N. W. about 50 Miles from that; and from thence
to Loggs Town, the Course is nearly West about
10 or 20 Miles; so that the whole Distance, as
we went and computed it, is at least 135 or 140
miles from the back of the Inhabitants.

25th. Came to Town four of ten Frenchmen that
deserted from a Company at the Cuscuscas, which
lies at the Mouth of this River: I got the following Account from them. They were sent from
New-Orleans with 100 Men, and 8 Canoe Loads of
Provisions to this Place; where they expected
to have meet the same Number of Men, from the
Fort this Side of Lake Erie, to convoy them and
the Stores up, who were not arrived when they
ran off.

I Enquired into the Situation of the French,
on the Missisippi, their Number, and what Forts
they had built: They inform'd me, That there
were four small Forts between New-Orleans and
the Black Islands, garrison'd with 30 or 40 Men,
and a few small Pieces in each: That at New-
Orleans, which is near the Mouth of the Missisippi, they are 35 Companies of 40 Men each,
with a pretty strong Fort mounting 8 Carriage
Guns, and at Black Islands there are several
Companies, and a Fort with 6 Guns. The Black
Islands are about 130 Leagues about the Mouth of
the Ohio, which is about 350 above New Orleans:
They also acquainted me, that there was a small
pallisado'd Fort on the Ohio, at the Mouth of
the Obaish heads near the West End of Lake Erie,
and affords the Communication between the French

on the Missisippi and those on the Lakes. These Deserters came up from the lower Shanoak-Town with one Brown, an Indian Trader, and were going to Philadelphia.

About 3 o'Clock this Evening the Half King came to Town; I went up and invited him and Davison, privately to my Tent, and desired him to relate some of the Particulars of his Journey to the French Commandant, and the Reception there; and to give me an Account of the Ways and Distance. He told me, that the nearest and levellest Way was now impassible, by reason of many large Miry Savannas; that we must be obliged to go by Venango, and should not get to the near Fort under 5 or 6 Night's Sleep, Good Travelling. When he went to the Fort, he said he was received in a very stern Manner by the late Commandant; Who ask'd him very abruptly, what he had come about, and to declare his Business, which he said he did in the following Speech;

Fathers, I am come to tell you your own Speeches; what your Mouths have declared. Fathers, you, in former Days, set a Silver Bason before us, wherein there was the Leg of a Beaver, and desir'd of all Nations to come and eat of it: to eat in Peace and Plenty, and not to be churlish to one another; and that if any such Person should be found to be a Disturber, I here lay down by the Edge of the Dish a Rod, which you must scourge them with; and if I your Father, should get foolish in my old Days, I desire you may use it upon me as well as others.

Now Fathers, it is you that are Disturbers in this Land, by coming and building your Towns, and taking it away unknown to us, and by Force.

Fathers, We kindled a Fire a long Time ago, at a Place called Montreal, where we desired you to stay, and not to come and intrude upon our Land. I now desire you may dispatch to that Place; for be it known to you, Fathers, that this is our Land, and not yours.

Fathers, I desire you may hear me in Civilness; if not, we must handle that Rod which was laid down for the use of the Obstreperous. If you have come in a peaceable Manner, like our Brothers the English, we should not have been against your trading with us, as they do; but to come, Fathers, and build great Houses upon our Land, and to take it by Force is what we cannot submit to.

FATHERS, Both you and the English are White, we live in a Country between; therefore the Land belongs to neither one nor t!other: But the Great Being above allow'd it to be the place of Residence for us; so Fathers, I desire you to withdraw, as I have done our Brothers the English; for I will keep you at Arms length: I lay this down as a trial for both, to see which have the greatest Regard to it, and that Side we will stand by, and make equal Sharers with us. Our Brothers the English have heard this, and I come now to tell it to you, for I am not afraid to discharge you off this Land!

This he said was the Substance of what he said to the General who made this Reply.

Now my Child, I have heard your Speech, you spoke first, but it is my Time to speak now. Where is my Wampum that you took away, with the Marks of Towns in it? This Wampum I do not know, which you have discharged me off the Land with; but you need not put yourself to the Trouble of speaking, for I will not hear you: I am not afraid of Flies or Musquitos, for Indians are such as these; I tell you, down this River I will build upon it, according to my Command: If the River was block'd up, I have Forces sufficient to burst it open, and thread under my Feet all that stands in Opposition, together with their Alliances; for my Force is like Sand upon the sea Shore: Therefore, here is your Wampum, I fling it at you. Child you talk foolish; you say this Land belongs to you, but there is not the Black of my Nail yours: I saw that Land sooner than you did, before the Shanrahs and you were at War: Lead was the Man that went down, and took possession of the River: It is my Land, and I will have it, let who will stand up for, or say against it. I'll buy and sell with the English, (mockingly). If People will be rul'd by me, they may expect Kindness but not else.

The Half King told me he enquired of the General after two Englishmen that were made

Prisoners, and received this Answer,

Child, You think it is a very great Hardship that I made Prisoners of these two Venango, don't you concern yourself with it, we took and carried them to Canada, to get Intelligence of what the English were doing in Virginia.

He informed me that they had built two Forts, one on Lake Erie, and another at French-Creek, near a small Lake about 15 Miles asunder, and a large Waggon Road between; they are both built after the same Model, but different in Size; that on the Lake the largest; he gave me a plan of them, in his own drawing.

The Indians enquired very particularly after their Brothers in Carolina Goal.

They also asked what sort of a Boy it was that was taken from the South-Branch; for they had, by some Indians, heard, that a Party of French Indians had carried a white Boy by the Cuscusea Town, towards the Lakes.

26th. We met in Council at the Long-House, about 9 o'Clock, where I spoke to them as follows,

Brothers, I have called you together in Council, by Orders of your Brother the Governor of Virginia, to acquaint you that I am sent, with all possible Dispatch, to visit, and deliver a Letter to the French Commandant, of very great Importance to your Brothers the English; and I dare say, to their Friends and Allies.

I was desired Brothers, by your Brother the Governor, to call upon you, the Sachems of the Nations, to inform you of it, and to ask your Advice and Assistance to proceed the nearest and best Road to the French. You see, Brother, I have got this far on my Journey.

His Honour likewise desires me to apply to you for some of your young Men, to conduct and provide Provisions for us on our Way, and be a safeguard against those French Indians who have taken up the Hatchet against us. I have spoke this particularly to you, Brothers, because his Honour our Governor treats you as good Friends and Allies, and hold you in great Esteem, to confirm what I have said, give you this String of Wampum.

After they had considered some time on the above, the Half King got up and spoke.

Now, my Brothers in Regard to what my Brother the Governor has desired of me, I return this Answer.

I rely upon you as a Brother ought to do, as you say we are Brothers and one People: We shall put Heart in Hand, and speak to our Fathers the French concerning the Speech they made to me, and you may depend that we will endeavour to be your Guard.

Brother, as you have asked my Advice, I hope you will be ruled by it, and stay till I can provide a Company to go with you: The French Speech-Belt is not here, I have it to go for to my hunting Cabbin; likewise the People which I have ordered in, are not yet come, nor cannot till the third Night from this, till which Time, Brother, I must beg you to stay.

I intend to send a Guard, to Mingos, Shannoaks, and Delawares, that our Brothers see the Love and Loyalty we bear them.

As I had Orders to make all possible Dispatch and waiting here was very contrary to my Inclination, I thanked him in the most suitable Manner I could, and told him that my business required the greatest Expedition, and would not admit to that Delay: He was not well pleased that I should offer to go before the Time he had appointed, and told me that he could not consent to our going without a Guard, for fear some Accident should befal us, and draw a reflection upon him; besides, says he, this is a Matter of no small Moment, and must not be entered into without due Consideration; for now I intend to deliver up the French Speech-Belt, and make the Shannoaks and Delawares do the same: And accordingly he gave Orders to King Shingiss, who was present, to attend on Wednesday Night with the Wampum, and two Men of their Nation to be in Readiness to set out with us next Morning. As I found it was impossible to get off without affronting them in the most egregious Manner, I consented to stay.

I gave them back a String of Wampum that I met with at Mr. Frazier's, which they had sent with a Speech to his Honour the Governor, to inform him, that three Nations of French Indians, viz. Chippoways, Ottoways and the Orundacks, had taken up the Hatchet against the English and desired them to repeat it over again, which they postponed doing till they met in full council with the Shannoaks and the Delaware Chiefs.

27th Runners were dispatched very early for the Shannoak Chiefs, the Half King set out himself to fetch the French Speech-Belt from the Hunting Cabbin.

28th. He returned this Evening and came with Monocatoocha, and two other Sachems to my Tent; and begged (as they had complied with his Honour the Governor's request, in providing Men, &c.) to know on what Business we were going to the French? this was a Question I all along expected, and had provided a satisfactory Answer to, as I could, and which allayed their Curiosity.

Monocatoocha informed me, that an Indian from Venango brought News, a few Days ago that the French had called all the Mingos, Delawares, &c. together at that Place, and told them that they intended to have been down the River this Fall, but the Waters were growing Cold, and the Winter advancing, which obliged them to go into Quarters: But they might assuredly expect them in the Spring, with a far greater Number; and desired that they might be quite passive, and not to intermeddle, unless they had a Mind to draw all their Forces upon them, for that they expected to fight the English three Years, (as they supposed there would be some Attempts made to stop them) in which Time they would conquer, but if they should prove equally strong, that they and the English would join to cut them all off, and divide the Land between them; that tho' they had lost their General, and some few of their Soldiers. yet they were Men enough to reinforce them, and make them Masters of the Ohio.

The Speech, he said, was delivered to them by one Captain Joncaire their Interpreter in Chief, living in Venango, and a Man of note in the Army.

29th. The Half King and Monocatoocha, came very early, and begged me to stay one Day more, for notwithstanding they had used all the Diligence in their Power, the Shannoak Chiefs had not brought Wampum they ordered, but would certainly be in To-night; if not, they would delay me no longer, but would send it after us as soon as they arrived: When I found them so pressing in this Request, and knew that returning of Wampum was the abolishing of Agreement; and giving this up, was shaking off all Dependence upon the French, I consented to stay, as I believed an Offence offered at this Crisis, might be attended with greater ill Consequence, than another Day's Delay; They also informed me that Shingiss could not get in his Men, and was prevented from coming himself by his Wife's sickness, (I believe, by fear of the French) but that the Wampum of that Nation was lodged with Custaloga one of their Chiefs at Venango.

In the Evening late they came again and acquainted me that the Shannoaks were not yet come, but it should not retard the Prosecution of our Journey. He delivered in my Hearing the Speeches that were to be made to the French, by Jeskakake, one of their old Chiefs, which was giving up the Belt the late Commandant had asked for, and repeating near the same Speech he himself had done before.

He also delivered a String of Wampum the this Chief which was sent by King Shingiss, to be given to Custaloga, with Orders to repair to the French, and deliver up the Wampum.

He likewise gave a very large String of black and white Wampum, which was to be sent up Immediately to the Six Nations, if the French refused to quit the Land at this Warning; which was the third and last Time, as was the Right of Jeskakake to deliver.

30th. Last Night the great Men assembled to their Council-House, to consult further about this Journey, and who were to go; the Result of which was, that only three of their Chiefs, with one of their best Hunters, should be our Convoy: The Reason which they gave for not sending more, after what had been proposed at Council the 26th, was, that a greater Number might give the French Suspicions of some bad Design, and cause them to be treated rudely: But I rather think they could not get their Hunters in.

We set out about 9 o'Clock with the Half King, Jeskakake, White Thunder, and the Hunter, and travelled on the Road to Venango, where we arrived the 4th of December, without any Thing remarkable happening but a continued Series of bad Weather.

This is an old Indian Town, situated at the Mouth of French Creek on Ohio, and lies near N. about 60 Miles from Logg-Town, but more than 70 the Way we were obliged to go.

We found the French Colours hoisted at a House which they drove Mr. Frazier, an English Subject, from; I immediately repaired to it, to know where the Commander resided: There were three Officers, one of whom, Capt. Joncaire, inform'd me, that he had the Command of the Ohio, but that there was a General Officer at the next Fort, which he advised me for an Answer. He invited us to sup with them, and treated us with the greatest Complaisance.

The Wine, as they dosed themselves pretty plentifully with it, soon banished the restraint which at first appear'd in their Conversation, and gave a Licence to their Tongues to reveal their Sentiments more freely.

They told me, That it was their absolute Design to take Possession of the Ohio and by G-- they would do it; for they were sensible the English could raise two Men for their one: Yet they knew, their Motions were too slow and dilatory to prevent any Understanding of theirs. They pretend to have an undoubted Right to the River, from a Discovery made by one La Sol 60 Years ago; and the Rise of this Expedition is, to prevent our Settling the River or Waters of it, as they have heard of some Families moving out in Order thereto. From the best Intelligence I could get, there have been 1500 Men on this side Ontario Lake, but upon the Death of the General all were recalled to about 6 or 700, who were left to garrison four Forts, 150 or thereabouts in each, the first of which is on

French Creek, near a small Lake, about 60 Miles from Venango, near N. N. W. the next lies on Lake Erie, where the greatest Part of their Stores are kept, about 15 Miles from the other; from that it is 120 Miles to the Carying Place, at the Falls of Lake Erie, where there is a small Fort which they lodge their Goods at, in bringing them from Montreal. the Place that all their Stores come from: The next Fort lies about 20 Miles from this, on Ontario Lake; between this Fort and Montreal there are three others, the first of which is near opposite to the English Fort Oswego. From the Fort on Lake Erie to Montreal is about 600 Miles, which they say requires no more, (if good Weather,) than four Weeks Voyage, if they go in Barks or large Vessels, that they can cross the Lake; but if they come in Canoes it will require 5 or 6 Weeks, for they are oblig'd to keep under Shore.

5.th. Rain'd excessively all Day, which prevented our Travelling. Capt. Joncaire sent for the Half King, as he had but just heard that he came with me: He affected to be much concern'd that I did not make free to bring them before; I excused it in the best Manner I was capable, and told him I did not think their Company agreeable as I had heard him say a good deal in Dispraise of Indians in general: But another Motive presented me from bringing them into Company; I knew he was Interpreter, and a Person of very great Influence among the Indians and had lately used all possible Means to draw them over to their Interest; therefore I was desirous of giving no Opportunity that could be avoided.

When they came in, there was a great Pleasure express'd at seeing them; he wonder'd how they could be so near without coming to visit him, made several trifling Presents, and applied Liquor so fast, that they were soon render'd incapable of the Business they came about, notwithstanding the caution that was given.

6th. The Half King came to my Tent, quite sober, and insisted very much that I should stay and hear what he had to say to the French; I fain would have prevented his speaking any Thing, 'till he came to the Commandant; but could not prevail: He told me that at this Place a Council Fire was kindled, where all their business with the People was to be transmitted, and that the Management of the Indian Affairs were left solely to Monsr. Joncaire. As I was desirous of knowing the Issue of this, I agreed to stay, but sent our Horses a little Way up French Creek, to raft over and encamp; which I knew would make it near Night.

About 10 o'Clock they met in Council; the King spoke much the same as he had before done to the General, and offer'd the French Speech-Belt which had before been demanded with the Marks of four Towns on it, which Monsieur Joncaire refused to receive; but desired him to carry it to the Fort Commander.

7th. Monsieur La Force, Commissary of the French Stores, and three other Soldiers came over to accompany us up. We found it extremely difficult getting the Indians off To-Day, as every Stratagem had been used to prevent their going up with me: I had last Night left Davison (the Indian Interpreter that I brought from Loggs-Town with me, strictly charg'd not to be out of their Company, as I could not get them over to my Tent they having some business with Custaloga, to know the Reason why he did not deliverup the French-Belt which he had in keeping) but was obliged to send Mr. Gist, over to-Day to fetch them, which he did with great Persuasion.

At 11 o'Clock we set out for the Fort, and were prevented from arriving there 'till the 11th by excessive Rains, Snow, and bad Travelling, through many Mires and Swamps, which we were obliged to pass, to avail crossing the Creek, which was impossible, either by fording or rafting, the Water was so high and rapid.

We passed over much good Land since we left Venango, and through several extensive and very rich Meadows; one of which I believe was near four Miles in Length, and considerably wide in some Places.

12th. I prepar'd early to wait upon the Commander, &c. was received and conducted to him by the Officer in Command: I acquainted him

with my Business, and offer'd my Commission and
Letter, both of which he desired me to keep
'till the Arrival of Monsieur Riparit, Captain
at the next Fort, who was sent for and expected
every Hour.

   This Commander is a Knight of the Military
Order of St. Louis, and named Legardeur de St.
Piere. He is an elderly Gentleman, and has much
the air of a Soldier; he was sent over to take
Command, immediately upon the Death of the late
General, and arrived here about seven Days be-
fore me.

   At 2 o'Clock the Gentleman that was sent for
arrived, when I offer'd the Letter &c. again;
which they received adjourn'd into a private
Apartment for the Captain to translate, who understood a little English; after he had done it,
the Commander desired I would walk in, and bring
my Interpreter to peruse and correct it, which
I did.

   13th. The Chief Officer retired, to hold a
Council of War, which gave me an Opportunity of
taking the Dimensions of the Fort, and making
what Observations I could.

   It is situated on the South, or West Fork of
French Creek, near the Water, and is almost
surrounded by the Creek, and a small Branch of
it which forms a Kind of Island; 4 Houses com-
pose the Sides; and Bastions are made of Piles
driven into the Ground, and about 12 above, and
sharp at the Top, with Port-Holes cut for Cannon
and Loop Holes for the small Arms to fire
through; there are eight 6 lb. Pieces mounted,
two in each Bastion, and one Piece of four Pounds
before the Gate; in the Bastions are a Guard
House, Chapel, Doctor's Lodging, and the Commander's private Stores, round which are laid
Plat-Forms for the Cannon and Men to stand on:
There are several Barracks without the Fort,
for the Soldiers Dwelling, and covered, some
with Bark, and some with Boards, and made chiefly of Logs: There are also several other Houses
such as Stables, Smith's Shop, &c. I could get
no certain Account of the Number of Men Here;
but according to the best Judgement I could
form, there are an Hundred exclusive of Officers,

of which there are many. I also gave Orders to the People that were with me, to take an exact Account of the Canoes that were hauled up to convey their Forces down in the Spring, which they did, and told 50 of Birch Bark, and 170 Pine, besides many others that were block'd out, in readiness to make.

14th. As the Snow increased very fast, and our Horses daily became weaker, I sent them off unloaded, under the care of Barnaby Currin and two others, to make all convenient Dispatch to Venango, and there wait our Arrival if there was a Prospect of the Rivers freezing, if not, then to continue down to Shannapin's Town, at the Fork of the Ohio, and there wait till we came to cross Aligany, intending myself to go down by Water, as I had the Offer of a Canoe or two.

As I Found many Plots concerted to retard the Indian Business, and prevent their returning with me; I endeavour'd all that lay in my Power to frustrate their Scene, and hurry them on to execute their intended Design; they accordingly pressed for Admittance this Evening, which at Length was granted them privately, with the Commander and one or two other Officers: The Half King told me, that he offer'd the Wampum to the Commander, who evaded taking it, and made many fair Promises of Love and Friendship; said he wanted to live in Peace, and Trade amicably with them, as a Proof of which he would send some Goods immediately down to Loggs Town for them; but I rather think the Design of that is, to bring away all stragling Traders they met with as I privately understood they intended to carry an Officer, &c. with them; and what rather confirms this Opinion, I was enquiring of the Commander, by what authority he had made Prisoners of several of our English Subjects; he told me that the Country belong'd to them, that no Englishman had the Right to trade upon those Waters and that he had Orders to make every Person Prisoner that attempted it on the Ohio, or the Waters of it.

I enquir'd of Capt. Riparti about the Boy that was carried by, as it was done while the command devolved on him, between the Death of the late

General, and the Arrival of the present; he acknowledged, that a Boy had been carried past, and that the Indians had two or three white Mens Scalps, (I was told by some of the Indians at Venango Eight) but pretended to have forgot the Names of the Place that the Boy came from, and all the Particulars, though he question'd him for some Hours as they were carrying him past: I likewise enquired what they had done with John Trotter and James Clocklan, two Pennsylvania Traders, whom they had taken, with all their Goods: They told me, that they had been sent to Canada, but were now returned Home:

This Evening I received an Answer to his Honour the Governor's Letter from the Commandant.

15th. The Commandant ordered a Plentiful Store of Liquor, Provisions, &c. to be put on board a Canoe, and appeared to be entirely complaisant, though he was exerting every Artifice that he could invent to set our Indians at Variance with us to prevent their going 'till after our departure: Presents, Rewards, and every Thing that could be suggested by him or his Officers —— I can't say that ever in my Life I suffer'd so much Anxiety as I did in this Affair; I saw that every Stratagem that the fruitful Brain could invent, was practiced, to win the Half King to their Interest, and that leaving Him here was giving them the Opportunity they aimed at. I went to the Half King, and press'd him in the strongest Terms to go: He told me the Commandant would not discharge him 'till the Morning. I then went to the Commandant, and desired him to do their business, and complain'd of ill Treatment; for keeping them, as they were Part of my Company, and was detaining me: which he promised not to do, but to forward my journey as much as he could: He protested he did not keep them, but was ignorant of the cause of their Stay; though I soon found out: —— He had promised them a Present of Guns, &c. if they would wait 'till Morning.

As I was very much press'd by the Indians, to wait this Day for them. I consented, on a Promise, That nothing should hinder them in the Morning.

16th. The French were not slack in their Intentions to keep the Indians this Day also; but as they were obligated according to Promise, to give the Present, they then endeavoured to try the Power of Liquor, which I doubt not would have prevailed at any other Time than this, but I urged and insisted with the King to closely upon his Word, that he refrained, and set off with us as he had engaged.

We have a tedious and very fatiguing Passage down the Creek, several Times we had like to have staved against Rocks, and many Times were obliged all Hands to get out and remain in the Water Half an Hour or more, getting over the Shoals; at one Place the Ice had lodged and made it impassable by Water; therefore we were obliged to carry our Canoe across a Neck of Land, a Quarter of a Mile over. We did not reach Venango, till the 22d. where we met with our Horses.

This creek is extremely crooked, I dare say the Distance between the Fort and Venango, can't be less than 130 Miles, to follow the Meanders.

23d When I got Things ready to set off, I sent for the Half King to know whether he intended to go with us, or by Water, he told me that White-Tunder had hurt himself much, and was sick and unable to walk, therefore he was obliged to carry him down in a Canoe: As I found he intended to stay here a Day or two, and knew that Monsieur Joncaire would employ every Scheme to set him against the English as he had before done; I Told him I hope he would guard against his Flattery, and let no fine Speech influence him in their Favour: He desired I might not be concerned, for he knew the French too well, for any Thing to engage him in their Behalf; and though he could not go down with us, he would endeavour to meet at the Forks with Joseph Campbell, to deliver a Speech for me to carry to his Honour the Governor. He told me he would order the young Hunter to attend us, and get Provisions, &c. if wanted.

Our Horses were now so weak and feeble, and the Baggage heavy, as we were obliged to provide all the Necessities that the Journey would required; that we doubted much their performing it; therefore myself and others (except Drivers which were obliged to ride) gave up our Horses for Packs, to assist along with the Baggage; I put myself in an Indian Dress, and continued with them three Days till I found there was no Probability of their getting in, in any reasonable Time: the Horses grew less able to travel every Day; the Cold increased very fast, and the Roads were becoming much worse by a deep Snow continually freezing; and I was uneasy to get back, to make Report of my Proceedings to his Honour the Governor, I determined to prosecute my Journey the nearest way through the Woods, on Foot.

Accordingly I left Mr. Bramm in charge of our Baggage, with Money and Directions, to provide Necessaries from Place to Place for themselves and Horses, and to make the most convenient Dispatch in.

I took my necessary Papers, pulled off my Cloaths, tied myself up in a Match Coat, and with my Pack at my Back with my Papers and Provisions in it, and a Gun, set out with Mr. Gist, fitted in the same Manner, on Wednesday the 26th. The Day following, just after we had passed a Place called Murdering Town, where we intended to quit the Path, and steer across the Country for Shannapin's Town, we fell in with a Party of French Indians, who had lain wait for us; some of them fired at Mr. Gist or me, not 15 Steps but fortunately missed. We took this Fellow into custody and kept him till 9 o'Clock at Night, and then let him go, and walked all the remaining Part of the Night without making a Stop, that we might get start so far, as to be out of the Reach of their Pursuit the next Day, as we were well assured they would follow our Track as soon as it was light: The Next Day we continued travelling till quite dark, and got to the River about 2 Miles above Shannapins: we expected to have found the River frozen, but it was not, only about 50 Yards from each Shore; the Ice I suppose had broke up above for it was driving in vast Quantities.

There was no Way of getting over but on a Raft,

which we set about, with a poor Hatchet, and got finished just after Sun Setting, after a whole Day's Work; we got it launched, and on board of it, and set off; but before we were half Way over, we were jammed in the Ice in such a Manner that we expected every Moment our Raft to sink and ourselves to perish; I put out my setting Pole to try and stop the Raft, that the Ice might pass by, when the Rapidity of the Stream threw it with so much Violence agaist the Pole, that it jerked me out into 10 Feet water, but I fortunately saved myself by catching hold of one of the Raft Logs; notwithstanding all our Efforts we could not get the Raft to either Shore, but were obliged, as we were near an Island, to quit our Raft and make to it.

The Cold was so extremely severe, that Mr. Gist had all his Fingers, and some of his Toes frozen, and the Water was shot up so hard, that we found it Difficult in getting off the Island on the Ice in the Morning, and went to Mr. Frazier's. We met here with 20 Warriors, who were going to the Southward to War, but coming to a Place upon the Head of the great Cunnaway, where they found 7 People killed and scalped, all but one Woman with very light Hair, they, turned about and ran back, for fear the Inhabitants should rise and take them as the Authors of the Murder: They report that the People were lying about the House, and some of them much torn and eaten by Hogs: By the Marks that were left, they say that they were French Indians of Ottaway Nation, &c.

As we intended to take Horses here, and it required some time to find them, I went up about 3 Miles to the Mouth of Youghyauhgane to visit Queen Alliquippa, who had expressed great concern that we passed her in going to the Fort. I made her a present of a Match Coat and a Bottle of Rum, which latter was thought much the best Present of the two.

Tuesday the 1st Day of January, we left Mr. Frazier's House and arrived at Mr. Gist's at Monongahela the 2d, where I bought Horse, Saddle, &c. The 6th we meet 17 Horses loaded with Materials and Stores for a Fort at the Fork of the Ohio, and the Day after some Families going out to Settle: This Day we arrived at Wills Creek, after as fatiguing a Journey as it is possible to conceive, rendered so by excessive bad Weather: From the first Day of December to the 15th, there was but one Day but it rained or snowed incessantly, and throughout the whole Journey we met with nothing but one continued Series of cold wet Weather, which occasioned very uncomfortable Lodging, especially after we had left our Tent, which was some Screen from the inclemency of it.

On the 15th I got to Belvoir where I stopped one Day to take necessary Rest, and then set out, and arrived in Williamsburg the 16th, and waited upon his Honour the Governor with the Letter I brought from the French Commandant, and to give an Account of the Proceedings of my Journey, which I beg Leave to do by offering the foregoing, as it contains the most Remarkable Occurrences that happened to me.

I hope it will be sufficient to satisfy your Honour with my proceedings; for that was my Aim in undertaking the Journey, and chief study Throughout the Prosecution of it.

With the hope of doing it, I with infinite Pleasure, subscribe my Self, Your Honour's most Obedient and very Humble Servant.

G. Washington.

BOSTON March 28. The Speech of his Excellency William Shirley, Esq; To the Great and General Court or Assembly of the Province of Massachusetts-Bay, in New-England, March 28th 1754.

Gentlemen of the Council and House of Representatives,

Having received in the recess of the Court some Dispatches, which nearly concerns the Welfare of the Province; I thought id necessary to require a general Attendance of the Members of both Houses at this Meeting of the Assembly, that the Matters contain'd in them may have a full and speedy a Consideration, as the Importance of them seems to Demand.

By Accounts sent from Richmond Fort, and Declarations made before me and His Majesty's Council, by two of the Settlers at Frankfort upon the River Kennebeck, I am inform'd, that in the Summer before last, a considerable Number of French settled themselves on a noted Carrying-Place made use of by the several Indian Tribes inhabiting that Part of the Country in their Passage to and from Canada, which separates the Head of the aforesaid River from that of the River Chaudiere, which last fall into the great River St. Lawrence at four Miles and a half above the City of Quebeck.

And I have received further Intelligence, that the French are settled very thich for 12 Miles on each side of the said River Chaudiere, at about 30 Miles Distance above the Mouth of it, in the Mid-way between the River St. Lawrence and before mentioned Carrying-Place; and the Captain of Richmond Fort in his Letter dated 23d last January informs me, That the Norridgewalk Indians have declared to him, "that they have given the new French Settlers upon the Carrying-Place, Liberty to Hunt any where in the Country, as a Recompence for the great service they will be to them, in a Time of War with the English, by supplying them with Provisions and Military Stores."

The same Officer further acquaints me in another Letter dated February 11th, That several Indians of the Arressinguntocock and some of the Penobscot Tribe, amounting, together with the Norridgewalk Indians, to Sixty effective Men, besides Boys, capable of bearing Arms, were then lately arrived in the Neighbourhood of the Fort under his Command: And that tho' they assembled there in pretence of Writing a joint Letter to me, as they have done, yet he had reason to expect from their haughty insolent Behaviour, the repeated open threats of some of them, and the private Warnings from others, that as soon as the Rivers should be free from Ice, they would commit Hostilities against the English, upon that and Neighbouring Rivers; in which they intemate, they are to be assisted by a Number of French from Canada, disguis'd like Indians: And in another Letter dated the 10th of March he acquaints me, that the French Priest, Missionary of the Indians of the River Kennebeck, appeared to him to be continually using Artifices to excite the Indians to prevent our Settlements from being extended higher up it; to set them at Variance with the English; and dispose them to a War with them this Spring.

Most of these Accounts are confirm'd by the Declaration of the before mentioned Settlers at Frankfort, with the Additional Circumstances that the French Priest had been very inquisitive after Roman Catholick Families in the Settlement: and used Endeavours to draw off some of the Inhabitants into the Service of the French; particularly for building a Chapel and a Dwelling House for himself upon the River, about three or four Miles above Cushana, and at the Distance of 24 from Frankfort; and been very industrious to Perswade them that it was within the French Territories: And the Indians have further declared, that they have been instigated by the Governor of Canada to hinder the English from settling upon any Part of the River; which is strongly confirm'd by a Deposition of Capt. Lithgow, made in August last.

Upon this Occasion, Gentlemen, I sent as soon as might be, with the Advice of His Majesty's Council, the necessary Reinforcements of Men and Stores to all the Eastern Forts; issu'd Commissions for raising Six Independent Companies in the Townships and Districts next adjacent to them in Order for the Officers and Soldiers to hold themselves in constant readiness to march upon any Alarm, to the Succour of any neighbouring Fort or Settlement which may be attack'd; to cut off the Enemy in their retreat; and in case that they shall find that the Norridgewalk Indians have committed Hostilities, to break up their Villages and Settlements upon Kennebeck and to kill or captivate all they can meet with their Tribe: I likewise ordered an Officer commissioned by me for the purpose, to proceed by the first Opportunity to the suppos'd Place of the New French Settlement, in order to discover the Certainty and Circumstances of it; and to require the French Commandant to retire and withdraw the People under his Command from that spot, as being under His

Majesty's Dominion, and within the Limits of this Government.

And I doubt not Gentlemen, from your distinguish'd Zeal for the Defence of his Majesty's Territories, and the Protection of his Subjects within this Government upon all Occasions, but that upon a refusal of the French to comply with that Requisition, you will make sufficient Provisions for enabling me to compel them with Arm'd Forces of the Province to free it from Incroachments.

The concern, Gentlemen, which you express'd in your Message to me at your Meeting in December last, upon your Apprehensions of the iminate Danger which the Province was in, from the Fench's having fortify'd themselves upon the River St. Johns, close to our Border, leave me no Room to doubt of your being sensible of the fatal Consequence in the general that must Attend Incroachment, which it seems plain they are now pushing into the Heart of the Province, (as the General Court in a Vote pass'd the 16th of January 1749, justly called the River Kennebeck) unless they are timely remov'd.

But it may not be improper for me to observe to you in particular that it appears from an Extract which I have lately caus'd to be made of some original Letters taken among Father Ralle's Papers at the breaking up of the Indian Settlement at Norridgewalk in 1724, and which pass'd between him, Father Lanverait Priest of the Penobscot Tribe, and Father La Chasse Superior of the Jesuits at Quebec, during the Indian War in the year 1723 and 1724; That the head of the Kennebeck River, near which the Indians have declared the French had made a New Settlement was the center of most of the Tribes then at War with us, and the general Rendezvous of all that came to the Eastern Parts: The Hurons, the Iroquois of the Fall of St. Lewis, the Tribe of St. francis, (or Aressigunticooks) and the Indians of Seignoris (as the French call them) of Becancour on one Hand, u'sd to assemble with the Norridgewalks here, from their several Settlements, and the Penobscots from their River, on the other: Here is where they held all their

Counsultations, and from hence issu'd out in parties united or seperated, as best suited them against the English; hither they retired after Action, and brought their Wounded for Relief; and here, if they met with Privisions, they far'd well, if not, the suffer'd greatly for want of them.

It appears further from the Letters, that the several French Missionaries chiefly conducted and managed this War; that they had the Care of supplying the Indians with the necessary Provisions and Stores for carrying it on; were employed to make them preserve in it, and to push them on to their boldest Enterprizes; that they transmitted Accounts of their Proceedings to the Government of Canada, thro' the Hands of the Superior of the Jesuits at Quebec, thro, whom likewise they received their Directions from thence; as the Governour of Canada seems to have done his upon the Occasion, from the Court of France.

And I would further observe, that this Route affords the French a shorter Passage for making Decents from Quebec upon this Province, and destroying the whole Province of Main, with the King's Woods there, and in the Government of New-Hampshire, than any other whatever from Canada.

The Advantages, which the Possession of this River would give the French over this Province, make it easy to account for their constant Endeavours ever since the Treaty of Breda, at which it was determined in the most solemn Manner, between the two Crowns, that the River Pentegotc or Penobscot, was the Boundry between New-England and Arcadia or Nova Scotia, to extend the Limits of the Claim upon all Occasions (as in Fact they have done) to the Eastern Side of the River Kennebeck; tho' they never attempted, until within these few Years, to pass over the River St. Lawrence, within extent of this Province.

I am satisfied it is needless for me, Gentlemen, to urge any Thing more to shew how necessary for the Safety of this Government it is, that we should secure to ourselves Possessions of this important River against the incroachments of the French without Delay: And I think the present Situation of Affairs in that Country must convince you, how vain a Scene it would now be to have your sole Dependence for gaining this Point upon making annual Presents to the Indians, who appear to have enter'd into an offensive Alliance with the French against you; and have shown evident Marks of a Disposition to put the River into their Power.

How different are such Proceedings from those of the French? Whilt we have been suing in vain to a few Indians for their Permission to settle Lands within the undoubted Limits of this Province, and which themselves can't deny to have been purchased of their Ancestors; and have in Effect promis'd them a Yearly Tribute to restrain them committing Acts of Hostilities against us; the French have marched Armies into distant Countries of numerous and powerful Tribes, which without any Colour of Right they have invaded; They have forbid them to make further Grants of any of their Lands to the English, and have built and are still building strong Forts with an avow'd Intent to drive them off from the Lands already granted to them, and to exclude them from all Commerce with those Indians whom they have treatened with Destruction, if they shall presume to interfere in their Favour.

It is Time, Gentlemen, for you desist from having your chief Dependance upon temporary Expedients, which seem rather to have expos'd the Government to the Contempt of these Indians, than to have conciliated their Friendship to it; and to take Council in Part from the Policy of our Neighbours.

Vigorous Measures against the French, in case they shall refuse to quit his Majesty's Territories within this Government, without being compel'd to it by Force; building a Strong Fort bear the Head of the River Kennebeck, above the Settlements of the Norridgewalk Indians, and pushing on our own Settlements upon it, in a defensible Manner, would effectually rid the Province of the Incroachments of the former, and eithr hold the Latter in a due Dependence upon us, or oblige them to abandon the River.

And further by making ourselves, through this Means, Masters of the Pass, which was the general Place of Rendezvous during the Indian War in 1723 and 1724, of all Tribes engaged in it, both in their Incursions and Retreats, we should have it in our Power to curb all those Indians for the future; and in a great Measure prevent them from attempying to make Depredations in our expoesd Settlements.

I must further observe to you this Occasion Gentlemen, how dangerous Delays to make suitable Preperations for removing the French would be.

How practicable was it at first, to have put a stop to their Proceedings in building their Fort at Crown-Point? And you can't but remenber what mischievous Effects of the neglect to do that in the Beginning, were felt by this and the Province of New-York, in the Ravages which they suffer'd from thence during the last War.

A short Delay to dislodge them from their Incroachments near the River Kennebeck, might give them an Opportunity of making themselves Masters of that River likewise in the End; and in the Case we may expect soon to see another Fort built by them near the Mouth of it, and the French in Possession of all the Sea Coast, between that and the River St. Johns.

I hope you will proceed in the Consideration of these Matters with the Unanimity and Dispatch which his Majesty's Service and the Safety of the Province requires; and that you Gentlemen of the House of Representatives, will make the necessary Supplies.

Council Chamber, March 28th 1754.

W. Shirley.

APRIL 1754

BOSTON April 1. We have very good Intelligence that Eight Thousand Troops, with their Wives and Children were sent out from France to North America in the Year 1752. viz. two Thousand five Hundred to Canada, three Thousand five Hundred to Missisippi, and two Thousand to St. Domingo, and that those Troops are arrived at the several Places in their Destination ——— From this Intelligence, and the certain accounts that we have of the Encroachments of the French both from Canada and Missisippi, upon His Majesty's Territories, back of the present Settlements of the Southern Colonies, the Forts they are building, their having engaged three large Tribes of Indians living upon the Lakes, to take up the Hatchet against the English, added to the Encroachment upon Nova Scotia, and the New Fort they are building near Kennebeck River, within this Province, contrary to the most Solemn Treaties, and all done since the last Peace; it is very easy to penetrate the Design of the French, and without any Spirit of Prophecy to foretell, that if there is not vigorous and united Opposition effectually to prevent it, they will in Five Years lay a solid and lasting Foundation, for making themselves in Time Masters of North America.

Boston April 1. We hear from Porthsmouth in New-Hampshire that last Wednesday night, a Number of armed Men supposed 2 or 300 come to the Prison there, broke the Door to pieces and carried off two Men who had been confined about three weeks, on a strong Suspicion of their having killed two of the Eastern Indians several months ago.

We hear from Halifax dated March 16. Capt. Cooke, Mr. Randall, and some other Gentlemen in this Town are going to erect a very considerable saw Mill upon a fine Run of Water somewhere in Mahony-Bay; A Block house to cover the Work is actually building here for that purpose, and will be finish in a few Days. We also hear that a Ship of 200 Tons is to be sent up here this Spring.

BOSTON April 2. On the 2d Instant His Excellency the Governor was pleased to make the following Speech to the Great and General Court or Assembly of the Province of Massachusetts-Bay, then sitting here, viz.

Gentlemen of the Council and House of Representatives,

The Occasion of my speaking to you now is to acquaint you, That I received a Letter from the Right Honourable the Lord Commissioners of trade and Plantations, signifying to me, that his Majesty had been pleased to order a Sum of Money to be issued for presents to the Six Nations of Indians and to direct the Governor of New-York, to hold an Interview with them for delivering those presents at such Place and Time as he shall appoint. And I am directed to lay this Matter before you, and to recommend to you to make proper Provisions for Appointing Commissioners from this Government to meet Commissioners of Virginia, Maryland, Pennsylvania, New-Jersey, and New-Hampshire, (to the respective Governors of which Colonies their Lordships have wrote to the same Effect): as also for making such presents as hath been usual upon like Occasions.

I have likewise to acquaint you; That I find by a Paragraph of their Lordships Letter upon this Occasion to the Governor of New-York, which His Honour Lieutenant Governor De Lancey, Commander in Chief of that Province, hath communicated to me, that he is therein directed to take Care that all Provinces be (if practicable) comprized in a general treaty to be made in His Majesty's Name: And that Mr. De Lancey hath given me Notice, That he hath appointed the said Interview to be held at the City of Albany on the Fourteenth of June next.

I am persuaded, Gentlemen, I need not use

Arguments to convince you, that it is of very great Consequence to the Interest of His Majesty's Colonies upon this Continent at all Times, that as many of the Tribes of Indians inhabiting it, as may be (those of the Six Nations more especially) should be kept in Friendship with the English, and a Dependence upon the Crown of Great-Britain; and that as free a Commerce and Intercourse should be maintained with them as is possible: But I think it my Duty at this Time to enter into a particular Detail of these Matters.

"At the Treaty of Utrecht, which is confirm'd by that of Aix-la-Chapelle, these were look'd upon to be Points of that Importance to the British Interest in North-America, that Care was taken in that Treaty to have the Indians of the Six Nations acknowledged by France to be subject to the Dominion of Great-Britain: and it is therein expressly stipulated, that the French shall give no Hindrance or Molestation either to them, or other Natives of America, who were Friends of the English; it is also stipulated that the Subjects of both Crowns should enjoy full Liberty of going or coming [upon the Continent] on account of Trade, and that the Natives of the Countries (upon it) should, with the same Liberty, resort as they please, to the British and French Colonies, for promoting Trade on the one Side and on the other, without any Molestation or Hindrance, either on the Part of the British Subjects or the French."

With regard to the Indians of the Six Nations in particular, I would observe to you, that according to an Account given by them in an open Council at Turpebawkie, at the return from the Indian Treaty at Philadelphia, in 1742, of the several of the Indian Nations which had been conquer'd by them, and are now in their Alliance, and trade with the English, and which seem to be depended upon, the Warriors belonging to those Tribes may be computed to amount to 16000 or 17000 at least; and one who must be a good Judge of Strength of the Five Nations Themselves, upon being interrogated by me concerning the Number of their fighting Men, made

Answer, "That he did not know their Number, but well knew that they are a numerous People, a terrible Body of Men, and able to burn all the Indians in Canada."

You must be sensible, Gentlemen, what frequent Attempts, the French have made from Time to Time to draw off the Six Nations from the English Interest into their own; and from the repeated Advances, we have received from His Majesty's Southern Colonies on this Continent, what efforts they have lately exerted to win their allies, together with the other numerous Tribes inhabiting the vast Country lying along the great Lakes and Rivers, and to the Westward of the Apolachian-Mountains, (all which may be reckon'd to exceed double the Numbers of the Indians of the Six Nations and those in their Alliance), as also what Measures the French are taking to exclude the English from all Trade and Commerce with those Indians.

To Compass this, they have in manifest Violations of the afore said Treaties, enter'd the Country of these Indians upon the Back of His Majesty's Southern Colonies, and within the limits of his Territories, with large Bodies of Troops, seiz'd the Effects, and captivated the Persons of the English who they have found trading there, absolutely deny'd their Rights to Traffick with those Nations, and erected a Line of Forts upon the Lakes and the Rivers from Canada to Missisippi to cut off all Commerce and Intercourse between them; they have committed Hostilities against some of the Tribes in Friendship with the English, engag'd others to take up the Hatchet against them, and threatened those with destruction who shall interfere in their avowed Design to drive the English out of that Country.

Should the Indians of the Six Nations at this Conjuncture desert our Alliance,, and go over to the French how fatal an Influence must such an event have upon the English Interest; On the other Hand, should proper measures be taken to attach them firmly on it; how greatly would it disappoint and check the present Scheme and Enterprize of our dangerous Neighbours?

It is well known how wavering the Disposition of these Indians hath of late been; and how visibly they have abated their former Enemies to the French; and we can't be at a Loss to discover the real Cause of it. Nothing could at this Time so effectually reclaim them to their old Alliance with us, the Measures directed to their Lordships of the Board of Trade, One general League of Friendship, comprizing all His Majesty's Colonies, to be made with them in His Majesty's Name; with stipulations to build such Forts in their Country as they shall choose, and may be judg'd necessary for their Shelter and Protection against the French.

Such Coalition of the Colonies for their Defence would be a convincing Proof to them, that they might safely depend upon His Majesty for Protection, and confirm them in their antient Alliance with the English; and how necessary such a Confederacy of the Colonies for their Safeguard is, may appear to you from the following Account given by an Indian Trader, who, for more than 20 Years had carried on a Trade among the different Nations of Indians some hundred Miles West of Philadelphia, the Truth of which I've great Reason to depend on, viz. "That at the Commencement of the late War he, with sundry other Traders of the English, was taken Prisoners by some Frenchmen belonging to a Fort upon the River Ohio, and from thence was transported from the Fort to Quebeck, by Means of which Forts and the Lakes the French he says, have a Communication open from Quebeck to Missisippi; that they have Forts there within 20 or 30 Miles distance of each other, with a Command of from 10 to 20 Men in each; in which, he says they put the Squa's and Papooses of the Indians in Alliance with them for Protection, whilst the Men go out to War, and there keep them until the Men return; and, he observed, that by means of these Forts they did fair in a little Time to seduce the Indians in Alliance with the English, as the English do not afford the same Protection to the Women and Children whilst the Men are gone to War, as the French do."

I would therefore earnestly recommend to you, Gentlemen of the House of Representatives, to make a suitable Provision for the sending Commissioners on the Part of this Government to join in the approaching Interview at Albany, duly authorized to concert such Measures in Conjunction with the Goverment of New-York, and Commissioners of the before mentioned Governments, as shall be judg'd proper to be enter'd into for cementing a firm League of Friendship with the Indians of the Six Nations, and returning them to the British Interest; and to give those Commissioners full Powers to agree with the other Governments upon the Quota of Money and Men to be furnish'd by the Province for this Service.

I have taken the Liberty to propose the same Thing to be done by the other Governments concerned in this Interview, in my Letters to His Majesty's Governors; and have reason to hope they will promote so salutary a Measure.

Such an Union of Councils, besides the Happy Effects it will probably have upon the Indians of the Six Nations, may lay a Foundation for a general One among all His Majesty's Colonies, for the mutual Support and Defence against the present dangerous Enterprizes of the French on every side of them.

I have already let you know, Gentlemen, His Majesty's Orders to me and His other Governours upon this Point, signified to us in the Earl of Holdernesse's Letter of the 28th of last August: and how necessary it is that such a Union should be immediately form'd in the Common Cause, whoever takes a Survey of the whole Extent of the Invasions and Incroachments which the French are surrounding His Majesty's Territories upon this Continent with, from their most Eastern to their most Western Limits, must soon be confin'd.

Close on the Back of the Settlements of His Majesty's Southern Colonies they are joining Canada to the Missisippi by a Line of Forts and Settlements along the great Lakes and Rivers, and cutting off all Commerce & Intercourse between the English & the numerous powerfull

Tribes of Indians inhabiting the Country, whom they are attempting to engage in their Interest by all Manner of Hostilities and Artifices: And at the same Time they are pushing on their Incroachments with equal Vigour quite round His Majesty's Eastern Colonies, where they have secur'd all the Indians in those Parts to join them against the English.

Should the French prevail in the former Part of their Scheme, and gain a general Influence and Dominion over the Indians behind the Apelacian Mountains, which they must in the ordinary Course of Human Events do in a short Time, if they are not timely prevented by an Union of His Majesty's Colonies, they will have in a very few Years a most formidable Army of those Indians at their Command, maintained without any Expence to themselves; but on the other Hand, with great Profit arising from an immense Fur-Trade carried on with them: And what fatal Consequences such an Army of Warriors (a few of which have been found sufficient to keep a large Frontier in continual Alarm) must have upon all His Majesty's Southern Colonies, by continually harassing them at the Direction of the French, and supported by them from Canada on one side, and Missisippi on the other, and cover's in their retreat behind the Mountains by a strong Line of Forts commanding the Navigation of all the Lakes and Rivers, is easy to conceive; especially if the Indians of the Six Nations should desert our Alliance, and join the French, which must in such Case be a decisive Blow to the British Interest on that Part of the Continent.

At the same Time if they are not prevented by a Coalition of the Colonies from furnishing the Scheme, which it is most manifest they are forming against the Eastern Provinces and already far advanc'd in, they must soon have it in their Power equally to distress them likewise: And all the English Colonies will be involv'd together in one general Flame.

It is true, those Colonies are far Superior to the French in their Numbers and Strength; but if that Strength, Gentlemen, is not properly exerted by a Union among themselves, how little will it avail?

It is difficult to imagine that such a Body of Troops as the French may soon collect, together with the Assistance of all the Indians scatter'd throughout this Continent, on the Back of the English Colonies (as the French Settlements likewise are) under the Command of the Governour General of New-France, who upon all Emergencies can direct their Forces as he pleases, may reduce a Number of disunited Provinces, many of them very remote from each other, tho' much superior to them in Point of the Number of Inhabitants.

For forming this general Union, Gentlemen, there is no Time to be lost: The French seem to have advanc'd further towards making themselves Masters of this Continent within these last five or six Years, than they have done over since the beginning of their Settlements upon it: And how determin'd they are to accomplish their Scheme as soon as possible, appears from their breaking thro' the most recent solemn Treaties and Agreements made between the two Crowns in order to effect it.

Gentlemen,
His Majesty hath given the strongest Proof of His parental Care of his Colonies and constant Attention to their Safety, in the directing his Honours to promote this Union within their Respective Governments, and I hope you will not be wanting on your Part, to contribute all in your Power towards effecting it, by improving the Opportunity with the approaching Interview with the Indians of the Six Nations at Albany happily presents for that Purpose: And I doubt not but that you may depend on all reasonable Support and Protection on the Part of His Majesty against all present and future Enterprizes and Attempts of the French against you.

Council-Chamber April 2 1754.

W. Shirley.

WILLIAMSBURG April 5. Last Sunday an Express returned here from Charlestown, South Carolina, which Place he left the 14th ult. by whom we learn, that the Assembly of the Province was sitting, that both Houses seemed very sanguince in raising a Supply for the Ohio Expedition and that the Sum agreed on was One Hundred Thousand Pounds.

Philadelphia April 18. Extract from Williamsburg, dated March 25.

"I am sorry Pennsylvania has as yet contributed nothing to the Ohio Expedition, but hope at their next Meeting something will be done. The Province of North-Carolina has given 12000 Proc. [equal to 9000 Pounds Sterling] and ordered 750 Men to be immediately march'd into Virginia, under the Command of Colonel Innis. There is no doubt but Men will be rais'd, for several of the Officers will be able to complete their Companies in five or six Days. This advice we have from an Officer just come in from Carolina."

BOSTON April 19. By His Excellency William Shirley, Esq; Captain-General and Governour in Chief in and over His Majesty's Province of the Massachusetts-Bay in New-England.

A PROCLAMATION.

Wereas it is apprehended necessary for His Majesty's Service, that a Number of Soldiers should be raised for the Security of His Subjects inhabiting the Eastern Frontiers of this Province from the Attempts that may be made by the Indians; And whereas the Great and General Court of this Province have pass'd a Vote encouraging the enlistment of Voluntiers for that Service, and have made Provisions for a Premium of Forty Shillings for every able bodied effected Man that shall so enlist; and Twenty six Shillings some Pence fer Month, for the Term of three Months;

I have therefore thought fit to issue this Proclamation, to signify to all Persons concerned, That I shall commissionate proper Officers to enlist Soldiers into His Majesty's Service, under such Officers, upon the Encouragement before Mentioned; Hereby promising that the Persons so enlisting shall be discharged at the Expiration of three Months after their Imbarkation for the Eastern Parts, or entering upon actual Duty.

Given under my Hand at Boston the Nineteenth Day of April, 1754. in the twenty seventh Year of the Reign of our Sovereign Lord George the Second, by the Grace of God, of Great Britain, France and Ireland, King, defender of the Faith, &c. By his Excellency's Command.

L. Willard, Secr.   W. Shirley.

ELIZABETH-Town Aptil 25, 1754. The Speech of His Excellency Jonathan Belcher, Esq; Captain General and Commander in Chief, in and over His Majesty's Province of Nova Caesarea, or New-Jersey, and Territories depending thereon in America, Chancellor and Vice Admiral of the same &c. to the Council and General Assembly of the said Province.

Gentlemen of the Council and the General Assenbly,

Although I am sensible it is a busy Season yet, His Majesty's Royal Orders have made it Absolutely necessary to call you together at this Time; and I have directed the Secretary, to lay before you the following Letters: One from the Right Hon. the Earl of Holderness, one of His Majesty's principal Secretaries of State, dated Whitehall, August 28, 1753: And another from the Right Hon. the Lord Commissioners for Trade and Plantations, dated Whitehall, September 18 1753. The first Letter you will see, relates to any hostile Attempts or Incroachments that should be made on the Limits of the King's Dominions. And the other respects an Interview that is to be held in the Middle of June next, with the Chiefs of the Six Nations at Albany.

I have also ordered to be Communicated to you, three Letters from the Hon. Mr. Dinwiddie, Lieutenant Governor and Commander and Chief of his Majesty's Territories and Dominion of Virginia; which gave you the Particulars of the Invasion and Depredations made by a Body of French and Indians, on the King's Lands; and of the cruel Barbarities and Murders committed by them, on His good Subjects; and all done in Infraction of the Treaties of Peace; made between His British Majesty and the French King.

I also send, with the other Letters mentioned, one from his Excellency Mr. Shirley, Governor of His Majesty's Province of the Massachusetts-Bay in New-England: Another from the Hon. Mr. De Lancey, Lieutenant Governor and Commander and Chief, of His Majesty's Colony of New-York.

By these two Letters you will find the unjust Attempts the French are making upon the King's Territories in New-England; and they seem to be Laying Schemes for a general Destruction and Ruin of the English Provinces on this Continent: As also, the great necessity of our joining with the other Colonies, in sending Commissioners to Albany in June next, there to consult the most prudent Measures for holding and confirming the Six Nations in English Interest. Yet if, upon the whole, there becomes a strict Union among all His Majesty's Colonies, we may reasonably hope (with the Help of God) the Designs of the French will soon be rendered vain and abortive; which at present so nearly affects the Honour and Interest of the Crown of Great-Britain, as well as the future Peace and Welfare of this, and the Neighbouring Provinces: I therefore earnestly, recommend to you most deliberate and mature Consideration, these extraordinary Proceedings; and then I shall not doubt your doing every Thing in your Power in Aid and Assistance with the rest of the English Colonies: I say, I hope you will chearfully unite with them to ward off from yourselves and your Posterity, the fATAL Consequence that must attend the present unjustifiable Violences and Insults of the French (in conjunction with the Indians); and on this Occasion it is, with Pleasure, Gentlemen, that I mention to you the Zeal and Alacrity with which many of our Neighbours have already exerted themselves, for the King's Honour and Interest, and in Compassion to their Fellow Subjects, on this uncommon Exigency. And your answering the King's Expectations in these important Affairs. You may depend will greatly recommend you to the Royal Grace and Favour.

Gentlemen,

You will, according to your wonted Care, make Inquiry into any temporary Laws that are expired, and ought to be reviewed.

Gentlemen of the Council, and the General Assembly,

As the Provision made in your last Session, for the Support of the Government, expires the next Month; I shall not doubt your now doing what may be necessary for maintaining the Honour and Justice of the Province..

Gentlemen of the Council, and the General Assembly.

I desire you will consider of any Thing you may think further needful to be done at this Session, for His Majesty's Service, and for the Welfare of His good People; and on your laying it before me, you may be assured, I shall heartily concur with you therein.

J. Belcher.

NEW-YORK April 29. By a Vessel just come from North Carolina, we are well assured of 1000 Men being on their March from thence to Virginia.

MAY 1754

PHILADELPHIA May 2. To the Printer of the Gazette.

As the following Extract of a Letter from a Gentleman residing in one of the Colonies to the Northward, contains a more full and exact Account of the Armament sent last Summer from Canada, and the ferocious Consequence that may attend the French setting on the Ohio, than any I have yet seen published, your inserting this in your next Week's Paper, may perhaps be agreeable to more of your Readers than, Gentlemen, yours &c. April 8, 1754.

"I am extremely sorry to hear that the Governments of Pennsylvania and Maryland, have not view'd the Encroachment of the French in their proper Light; or, if they have, that they won't exert themselves at this Time of emminent Danger. Should the French once gain a Settlement on Ohio, they will then have great Advantage over the Southern Colonies as must be obvious to every Person the least Acquainted with their Situation. In time of Peace between the two Crowns, they will continually be spiriting on the Indians in their Alliance, to Murder and to Scalp the Inhabitants of your back Countries in order to prevent the Extension of your Settlements; and, in time of War, how easy will it be for a Number of Troops, collected from their several Forts, or perhaps sent from Old France for the purpose, to make a Descent upon some one or other of the Colonies. What then must be the Consequence! --- Unarm'd, and disunited as you are, will you be able to repel the Invaders, or prevent their ravaging & laying waste your country, or hinder them from committing their too well known Barbarities on such of your Inhabitants as may fall within their Power? The Evil

Day may a while be put off, but sooner or later it will surely come, unless you rouse from the Lethargy you seem at present in, and make Use of those Means to protect yourselves when the Almighty has put in your Power; the most proper way of doing which is, to obstruct those Incendiaries, the French and their Indians, from Settling in your Frontiers. By a hearty Union of the Colonies and proper Management, We might, with little Assistance from the Mother Country, not only dislodge the French from Ohio, but from Quebeck itself. But to send three or four Hundred Men against five times their Number, can answer no other End than to expose us to the Contempt of our Indian Allies, who will think themselves obliged to quit the Interest of those that seem unable to protect them..

----- "You desire me to acquaint you with what I hear that may be depended on, concerning the Designs of the French, in sending so large a Number of Troops from Canada as they did the last Summer. In Answer to which I can inform you, that I have lately seen Mr. B_____r, who was at Oswego at the Time their Forces passed by that Fort; who says, he learnt by sundry deserters, and others, that Monsiers Duquesne, the new Govenor General of Canada, a young Gentleman formerly Captain of a Man of War, declares he will have a French Fort on each of the Waters that empty themselves into St. Lawrence or Missisippi; that he believes the late Governors of Canada have been all asleep, but that he will make every Officer under him know his Duty, and do it. ——— That four or five Detachments were, during the last Summer, sent from Canada to the Ohio, making in the whole about 2000 besides Indians, under the Command of Mesier Morin (or Morany, as some call him) whose Knowledge of the Indians recommended him to the new Governor for that Office.

The Detachment that accompanied Morin, consisted of about 40 or 50 large Battoes, and Canoes many of them suppose to carry more than 30 Men; they sailed within Musket Shot of Oswego, without ever striking their Colours, and had their Trunpets blowing, Drums beating, &c. This was in sight of many of the Six Nations, and foreign Indians, who could not sufficiently express their Surprize at such an Armament, and askes whether the English and French were not at Peace. —— Some of the Troops returned to Canada to Quarters during the Winter, but great Part of them were left, as is supposed, at the Forts on or near the Lakes, to be ready to go down the Ohio early in the Spring: These that returned had with them the Pennsylvania Indian Traders so often mentioned to be taken by the French on the Ohio; these poor Wretches were in Irons, and lodged a Night within a few Miles of Oswego. One of the famous Chiefs of the Cahuga Nation, proposed to some of the Traders to attack the French and recover the Prisoners, but they could not muster a sufficient Party to do this. —— Monsieur Morin built two or three Forts, but many disputes arising between him and his Officers, together with a severe Fit of the Gout, made him desired to quite his Command; for which Purpose, and Express was last September sent to Canada, and I suppose the Gentleman who writes to Governor Dinwiddie was made his Successor, who if he exceed Morin, as much in Humanity as he does in Politeness, a good sense, may be of Service to those who have the Misfortune of being taken Prisoners in that Country.

—— I saw Morin and his Son, some Years ago in Canada; they have all the vain Airs of the French, joined with the Savageness of the Indians, without the least of the Politeness of the former, or native Simplicity and Grandeur of the latter. The Father commanded when brave Donahew, Capt. of one of the Boston Sloops, was decoyed ashore and killed; the Son was one of his Party; As Trophies of the Victory, the old Man show'd me a Tobacco Pouch, which he, and a young Brute, let me know was made of the Skin of poor Donahew's Arm: The Father had also Donahew's Ring, which the Son acquainted me he cut the Finger off to get, as it would not come easily.

After this, I saw of Donahew's Men who were Prisoners, they not only confirmed the above, but assured me the brutish Father did himself cut off several Pieces of their dead Captain's

Flesh, and threw them into the Fire, encouraged the Indians to do the like; and when they were roasted, the Canibal Son and sundry Indians, tore them with their Teeth. ——— This may serve as a specimen of Neighbours you are now like to have,"

PHILADELPHIA May 9. Thursday last an Express arrived here from Major Washington with Advice, that Mr. Ward, Ensign of Capt. Trent's Company, was compelled to surrender his small Fort in the Forks of Monongahila to the French on the 17th past; who fell down from Venango with a fleet of 360 Battoes and Canoes, upward of 1000 Men, and 18 Pieces of Artillery, which they planted against the Fort, and Mr. Ward having but 44 Men, and no Cannon to make a proper Defence, was obliged to surrender on Summons, capitulating to march out with their Arms, &c., and they had accordingly joined Major Washington what was advanced with three companies of the Virginia Forces, as far as the new Store near the Allegheny Mountains, where the Men were employed in clearing a Road for the Cannon, which were every Day expected with Col. Fry, and the remainder of the Regiment. ----- We hear further, that some few of the English Traders on the Ohio escaped, but 'tis supposed the greatest Part are taken, with all their Goods, and skins, to the amount of near 20,000 Pounds. The Indian Chiefs, however have dispatched Messages to Pennsylvania, and Virginia, desiring that the English would not be discouraged, but send their Warriors to join them, and drive the French out of the Country before they fortify; otherwise the Trade will be lost, and, to their great grief an eternal Separation made between the Indians and their Brothers the English. 'Tis further said, that besides the French that come down from Vanango, another Body of near 400 in Coming upon the Ohio, and that 600 French Indians, of Chippaways and Ottaways, are coming down Siota River, from the Lake, to join them; and many more French are expected from Canada; the Design being to establish themselves, settle their Indians, and build Forts on the Back of our Settlements in all our Colonies; from which

Forts, as they did at Crown-Point, they may send out their Parties to kill and scalp the Inhabitants, and ruin our Frontier Counties. Accordingly we hear, that the Back Settlers in Virginia, are so terrify'd by the Murdering and Scalping of the Family last Winter, and of the taking of this Fort, that they begin already to abandon their Plantations, and remove to Places of more Safety. ----- The Confidence of the French in their undertaking seems well grounded on the present disunited State of the British Colonies, and the extreme Difficulty of bringing so differen Governments and Assemblies to agree in any speedy and effectual Measure for one common Defence and Security; while our Enemies have the very great Advantage of being under one Direction, with one Council, and one Purse. Hence, and from the great Distance of Britain, they presume that they may with Impunity violate the most Solemn Treaties subsisting between the two Crowns, kill seize and Imprison our Traders, and confiscate their Effects at Pleasure (as they have done for several Years past) murder and scalp our Farmers, with their Wives and Children, and take an easy Possession of such Parts of the British Territory as they find most convenient for them; which if they are permitted to do, must end in the Destruction of the British Interest, Trade and Plantations in America.

WILLIAMSBURG May 9. When all the Forces now ordered for the Ohio, from this and neighbouring Governments, are arrived, they will make up about 1100 Men besides the Assistance we expect from Pennsylvania, Maryland and South Carolina, &c. and a great Number of Indians that are ready to join us.

The Speech brought by the Indian Messenger from the Half King, is full of the warmest Expressions of Friendship and Attachment to the English Interest. His Honour the Governor dispatched him on Tuesday, with firm Assurance of a vigorous Assistance.

NEW-YORK May 13. The making an Establishment on the River Ohio, is no new or partial Scheme of the French, merely for the Sake of Trade, or a Settlement on the Lands, but a Thing long ago concerted, and but Part of a grand Plan for rendering themselves Masters of North America. That this Plan has been concerted, laid before the Court of France, and met with the highest Approbation, in the Year 1680; and has engaged the constant Attention of the Court ever since, it openly avow'd in the printed Works, 'Tis felt too in their Actions, and disguis'd no where but in their most solemn Treaties, and the sacred Engagements of their Faith. ----- The whole Plan may be seen in the 12th Book of Fathers, Charlevoix's History of New-France. The first step to be taken is (Garde, les pricipaux Poste due Payé) to fortify and Garrison all the principal Passes of the Country. This Part of the plan they have effected, in the Year 1754. The part of this Scheme which they are now executing, was first laid down in the Year 1721, Nov. 8. "There is not, says Father Charlevoix, in all Louisania, a Spot more proper for a Settlement than this on the Ohio, nowhere it is a greater Importance to the French to have one. The whole Country that is washed by the River Quabash and Ohio, is most fertile; there are vast Pastures finely water'd, where the wild Cattle graze by Thousands: Besides the-Communication with Canada is, this Way, much easier, better, and infinitely shorter, than thro' the Rivers of the Ilinois: A Fort with a good Garrison here, wou'd be compleat and Sufficient Curb on the Indians in general; but above all, on the Cherokees, at present the most numerous Nation on the Continent." The next Step is to become Master of Albany, the River Hudson, and New-York. There is no other way (says Chevalieres, in the Memorial and Plan which he presented to the Court of France) for the Preservation of Canada, but to render the King Master of New-York: "The absolute Necessity of doing this, renders it lawful and justifiable. And it was proposed at the Court of France, as the only Measure to conpleat and secure the Settlement of Canada; to conquer and secure the conquest of the Indians, and make them sue for Peace on any Condition the French shall please to impose on them."

The three several Plans that they are proposed for this Enterprize: The means and Manner in which they are to be executed: The ease & small Expence with which the French are sensible they can effect them: And the deplorable State which the Country, and the ruin'd Conditions which the poor Inhabitants are to be reduced to upon the Conquest, may be all read in fair Black and white; together with the Measures which the French are to pursue in the mean While, 'till all be ripe for the Execution. When they cajole the English, or have Reason to know that they will sit still, then to attack the Five Nations: when then can persuade the Indians to keep their Arms under their Blankets, then to Attack the English. ——— Sous pretexte d' allo faire la guierra oux irequois, et losque je serai arrive dans leur payé, je leur declrerai que je veux bein vivre avec aux, et que je ne veux qu aux Anglois. ---- Surtout de garde un Grand Secret et decovair, --- Sous les pretextes, quil jugrro it les plus convenable et les plus Plausible. And this while to use any Disguise or Pretexts, that will be received as probable or plausible.

 Last Wednesday his Majesty's Ship Centeaur, Archibald Kennedy, Esq; Commander, fell Down to Watering Place, with two of the Independent Companies that were posted in this Province, on board, bound for Virginia.

 BOSTON May 14. The Answer of both Houses of the General Assembly to His Excellency's Speech to them, on the 28th of March, and the 2d of April.

 May it please your Excellency,
The Council and House of Representatives of this his Majesty's Province having been given great Attention to the two Speeches which you have been pleased to make from the Chair on the 28th of March, and the 2d of April. We are sensible they contain Matters of the last Importance not only to the Inhabitants of this Government but to every other of his Majesty's Subjects in America, to the British Interest in general, and to the Interest of all Europe.

 It now evidently appears that the French are

far advanced in the execution of a plan projected more than fifty Years since for the extending their Possessions from the Mouth of the Missisippi on the South, to Hudson's Bay on the North, for securing the vast Body of Indians in that Inland Country, and for subjecting this whole Continent to the Crown of France. This Plan, agreeable to the Genius and Policy of the French Nation, was laid for a future Age, the operation of it has been gradual and almost unsensible, whilst the British Government in the Plantations, have been consulting temporary Expedients & they are in Danger of continuing to do so until it be too late to defeat it. And however improbable it may seem that this Scheme should succeed, since the French Inhabitants on the Continent, at present, bear but a small Proportion to the English, yet there are many other circumstances which gives them a great Advantage over us, and which, if not attended to will soon over-balance our superiority in Numbers.

The French pay no Regard to the most Solemn Engagements, but immediately after a Peace take & keep Possession of a Country which by Treaty had just before expresly ceded, whilst the English in the Plantations, afraid of incurring Displeasure, and of being Instrumental of bringing on a War in Europe, suffer these Encroachments to be made and continued. The French in Time of Peace were continually exciting the Indians settled down among them to come upon the Frontiers to kill and captivate our People, and to carry their Scalps, & Prisoners to Canada, where, as we have full Evidence, a Reward is given for them, and by this Means we are prevented from extending our Settlements in our own Country, whilst the English from the Principle just mentioned, scruple to avenge themselves by carrying the War into the Indian Settlements, lest they should annoy his Majesty's Allies, with whom our most barbarous Enemies are intermix'd, and by whom they are cherished and encouraged, The French have under their Influence by far the greatest Part of the Indians on this Continent, whilst the English, by the different measures of the several Governments, are in Danger of losing the small Proportion which at present are attached to them. The French has but one Interest, and keep one Point in View, the English Governments have different Interest, are disunited, some of them have their Frontiers covered by their Neighbouring Governments, and not being immediately affected seem unconcerned. The French are supported by the Crown and the Treasury of France, which seems now more than ever to have made the Plantations the Object of its Attention, the English Governments are obliged to carry on any Scheme at their own Expence, and are not able long to support any great Undertaking.

These are some of the Disadvantages which the English at present labour under, and they are not likely to be removed without his Majesty's gracious Interposition.

We therefore desire your Excellency to represent to his Majesty, the exposed Hazardous State of these his Governments, and humbly to pray, that he would be pleased to cause the most effectual Measures to be taken for the removal of any French Forts or Settlements that are or may be made in any Part of his Territories on this Continent; and in particular that the Subjects of the French King may be compelled to quit the Province of Nova Scotia, where a direct Violation of the most express Agreement to the contrary, they are daily Increasing and fortifying themselves; that his Majesty would and order that whatsoever the Indians who are settled among the French or are under their Direction and Controul shall captivate and destroy his English Subjects, his respective Governments shall suffer and encourage the Indians who are in the English Interest, to make Reprizals upon the French, there being no other Way of putting a Stop to the Incursion of the French Indians, or of the forwarding the Settlement of our Frontiers; That Affair which relates to the Indians of the Six Nations, and their Allies under some general Direction as his Majesty shall think proper may be constantly regarded, and that the Interest or Measures of particular

Governments or Persons, may not be suffered to interfere with such Directions, That the several Governments may be obliged to bear their Proportion of the Charge of defending his Majesty's Territories against the Encroachments of the French, and the Ravages and incursions of the Indians; and that in Case of any great and heavy charge, his Majesty would be graciously pleased to afford Relief.

In the mean Time, we assure your Excellency, that we are ready to do every thing that can be expected from us on the present Emergency. We think ourselves happy that we have a Gentleman at the Head of the Province, who is so perfectly acquainted with his Majesty's just Title to the Countries encroached upon by the French, who have given such distinguished Proof of his Zeal for his Majesty's service, whose endeavours to defend his Territories, and enlarge his Dominions in Time of War, have been attended with such happy Success, and whose Abhorrence of such perfidious Invasions in Time of Peace we are so well acquainted with. We take great Pleasure and Satisfaction in the Measures taken by your Excellency, with the Advice of his Majesty's Council, in the Recess of the Court, and will chearfully Support the Execution of them.

We look upon it to be of absolute Necessity that the French should at all Events be prevented from making any Settlements whatsoever on the River Kennebeck, or the Carrying-Place at the Head of it.

As Richmond Fort on the River it is in a decayed State, we desire your Excellency to order a new Fort to be erected of about One Hundred and twenty Feet square, as far up the river above Richmond Fort as your Excellency shall think fit, and to cause the Garrison, Artillery and Stores at Richmond, to be removed to the new Fort, and the old One to be Demolished.

We pray your Excellency likewise to order a sufficient Force up to the Carrying-Place to remove any French that may be settled there: But as we apprehend that our Success, under Providence will depend very much on your taking this Affair into your immediate Care and

Direction; We therefore pray your Excellency to submit to the Inconveniencies of a Voyage to the Eastern Parts of the Province; and there to give such Orders for the Purpose aforesaid, as you shall find necessary. And that your Excellency's Person may be secure against any Attempts of the French and Indians, and that you may be enable to affect the building the Fort aforesaid, and to destroy any French Settlements that may be carrying on; we will make provisions for the Pay and Subsistence of Five Hundred Men; which Number, including the Six Independent Companies already ordered, we desire you to cause to be inlisted as soon as you shall think proper, We will also make ample Provisions for your Excellency's Voyage, and for an Interview with the Indians, if you shall find it expedient.

We hope, by your Excelly's prudent Management these Indians will be convinced that it is their interest to continue at Peace with us; and we are sincerely desirous that every thing may be done which may tend to perpetuate the same.

We will readily defray the Charge of supporting a considerable Number of the Principal Indian Children, if your Excellency can prevail on their Friends to agree to it.

We are situated remote from the Six Nations, and have never had the benefit of a Trade with them, yet we have frequently joined in their Treaties with them, and have contributed largely towards Presents and the other Expences attending such Treaties, and are still ready to do all that can be reasonably desired from us for securing their Attachment to his Majesty's Interest.

Your Excellency must be sensible that an Union of the several Governments for their mutual Defence, and for the Annoyance of the Enemy, has long been desired by this Province, and Proposals made for this Purpose; We are still in the same Sentiments, and shall use all our Endeavours to affect it.

ANNAPOLIS May 16. Yesterday a Vote passed the lower House of Assembly, for granting 5000 Pounds towards the present Expedition; and 500 Pounds for a Present to be made to the Indians, at the Treaty to be held at Albany next Month.

PHILADELPHIA May 23. We hear from the Western Frontier on Ohio, that most of our Traders by the friendly Assistance of the Half King and other Indians, escaped with their Skins and Goods, and did not fall into the Hands of the French, as had been apprehended.

PERTH AMBOY May 27. The following Orders in an Extract from the Votes of the General Assembly of the Province of New-Jersey in answer to the Speech of his Excellency Jonathan Belcher Esq; Governor of the Province.

Ordered, That Mr. Lawrence and Mr. Hancock, do wait on his Excellency, and Acquaint him that the House had his Speech under Consideration on a Committee of the whole House, and by the Papers he was pleased to order to be laid before them, it does not appear what Scheme are concerted by the several Governors of the Colonies for preventing the Incroachments of the French upon his Majesty's Dominions; nor does it appear that the Colonies of Maryland or Pennsylvania have yet done any Thing in that Affair, tho' they are situated much nearer to the French Forts; That this House is of Opinion with your Excellency, that there should be strict Union among all his Majesty's colonies, on this important Affair: But as this Colony never have seen Parties with the Five Nations and their Allies, nor Partakers of the benefits of the Indian Trade, and consequently quite unacquainted with the Interest and Trade of those Nations; they therefore hope it will not be taken a Neglect of common Cause at this Time, to leave the Management of the Treaty to those Colonies that are accustomed to carry on these Negotiations: They are of Opinion from Lieutenant Governor Dinwiddie's Letter to your Excellency, That nothing appears in them, more than a Design to build a Fortification in the Forks of the Ohio, in order to check the Incroachment of the French, and to protect the Indians in Alliance with Great-Britain, in that Part of the Country. And from the Time these Things have been in Agitation, in the Colony of Virginia, they are in Hopes they are, before this time happily compleated.

However the Duty and Loyalty of the good People of this Colony sufficiently appears by their Conduct on former Expeditions. The Colony, tho' lying under a great Load of Debts, by assisting his Majesty in the late Wars against Spain and France are, however, willing chearfully to contribute to the Assistance of the other Colonies in what is necessary towards preventing the Incroachments of the French on his Majesty's Dominions; but at present are not of Ability to do it, having no Money in the Treasury, nor any Funds upon which it can be raised, which this House hopes the Colony will soon be relieved in, by his Majesty's giving Leave to your Excellency, to pass a Bill for emitting a Sum of Money on Loan, whereby they may be enabled, not only to discharge their old Debts, but to have a constant Fund to assist his Majesty upon Cases of the like Emergency: And that this House returns his Excellency Thanks, for his Care in calling them together on this emergent Affair; and should have been well pleased had his Excellency'd Health permitted him to have met at Perth Amboy. As it is impracticable at this time to do any Thing in Assistance of the Neighbouring Colonies, they beg your Excellency would be pleased to dismiss them till your Health will permit you to meet them at Amboy, where they will take the other Matters of your excellency's Speech into Consideration.

By Order of the General Assembly.

                         Abraham Clark, Jun. Clerk.

BURLINGTON. Governor Belcher's Reply.

Gentlemen of the General Assembly,

In Answer to your Message of the 27th Day of this Instant, by Mr. Lawrence and Hancock, I must observe, that the Method you have taken of answering my Speech by a Message, is unusual, if not without Precedent, and treating his Majesty's Representative with less Respect than is due to the Commission he has the Honour to bear, or to his own kind and benevolent intentions, for the promoting the Welfare of the good People of this Province whom you represent. Nor can I think you should have looked into the Conduct of such of his Majesty's Colonies who have least extended themselves, in order to put a stop to the Incroachment of the French, for and Example to follow in the critical and dangerous Time.

There is no Room to doubt, but that Pennsylvania and Maryland have appointed Commissioners to represent them at the Treaty to be held at Albany, in June next; and it is probable their Commissioners may be instructed to concert Measures for their Mutual Defence in Conjunction with the Commissioners of the other Colonies, who shall be present there.

At the House of Assembly declare it to be their Opinion, That they should be a strict Union among all his Majesty's Colonies, on this important Affair, I cannot think their having hitherto escaped the Expence of treating, or their not being Partakers in the Trade with the Indians, can be a sufficient Excuse for their declining to be Parties to an Interview, so strongly recommended by the Right Honourable the Lord of Trade.

As the Alliance and Friendship of the Six Nations, and their Dependence on the Crown of Great-Britain, must by every thinking Man, be looked upon as the Security the Settlers on the Northern Boundaries of this Province can have, to prevent the Incursion of those Nations of Indians, who, unprovoked have taken up the Hatchet against us, together with the horrid Murders and Confusions consequent thereupon.

If nothing more should be intended by the Government of Virginia than building a Fortification in the Fork of Ohio, as by your Message you suggest, the very Reason you assign for doing it, is a very cogent and powerful one, to wit, to check the Incroachment of the French, and to protect the Indians in Alliance with Great-Britain and supposing it should be by that Time compleated, (which is not to be expected) yet the whole Expence would be useless, unless it should have a Garrison sufficient to answer the good Purposes in its Erection; the Charge of which ought to be defrayed by all the Colonies on the Continent, in Proportion to the Advantage they receive from the Friendship and

Protection of the Six Nations.

I would not derogate in the least, from the Loyalty the good People of this Province have shewn, by the Aid they have afforded his Majesty in some Expeditions; and it will doubtless have some due Weight, when the Petition to his Majesty, for Leave to emit a Sum of Money on Loan, shall be under Consideration of his Ministers: But I am sorry so frequently to hear the Want of that Bill given as an Excuse against raising such sums of Money, as the Government, and Honour of the Province necessarily require, when it is well known that the private Circumstances of the landed Men, and other Inhabitants in it, take in general, equal those of any Gorvernments; and I am afraid your entirely declining assisting in the Common Cause at this perilous Conjecture, may be an Obstacle to your obtaining his Majesty's Favour to that Particular.

It gives me a sensible Satisfaction to find you express your Gratitude on my calling you together at this Time, in Obedience to the Royal Orders; and am sorry you esteem it impracticable to yield any Assistance to the other Colonies at this Time.

There are very few Colonies under his Majesty's immediate Government who have any other Method of Supplying Money for necessary and Immergent Service, but by Tax; and the Method of raising it here, is chiefly your Province.

I understand at the last Session at Burlington, from many of the Members of your House, that the Middle of May was a season at which you could as well spare a few Weeks from your private Affairs, as at any Time of the Year, and I should not have called you sooner, but in Observance to the Command I had received, and which I have communicated to you. That Season of the Year is a Time of Plenty, the Weather agreeable to most Conditions, and the Day long. The last Happy Session, is an evident Proof that more business may be done in a few Weeks at that Season, than has commonly been dispatched in as many Months of the Winter Sessions, whereby your Constituents are eased of a great Expence.

As to your desire of being dismissed till my Health will permit my attending at Amboy, I am very willing to gratify you; but I can give you but little Expectation of my attending there, for a long Time to come, unless it should please the infinite Disposer of all things, to strengthen me beyond my utmost Expectation.

The Dispatch I have always gave to the business before me, the Ease which the Province have enjoyed under my Administration, and the great Weakness of my Body, of which you are Eye Witness, gave me Reason to think the House could not have been so void of Humanity and Tenderness to me, as to complain of my calling them here on this Occasion; as I always have paid a punctual Obedience to the general Instructions, when my Health permitted me so to do. I doubt whether any impartial or dispassionate Inhabitant of this Province, would advise their Representatives, to make my not coming to Amboy, when prevented by the Act of God a Pretence for deferring the necessary Business of the Government; and the Recess which you shall have, till the First Day of June next, then to meet at Amboy, without further Notice will give you an Opportunity, and I hope you will consult with them in the Matter recommended in my Speech, and then by your Conduct at our next Meeting, I shall be able to judge whether the good People of this Province have that Regard to a Governor, who has entered his public and private Interest for the good of them and their Posterity that such a Conduct deserves.

JUNE 1754

New-York June 3. The Centaur, the Honourable Dudley Diggs, Esq; Commander, weigh'd Anchor on Tuesday last, and set sail from the Watering-Place near the Narrows, on her Voyage to Virginia, having on Board two of the Independent Companies from this Garrison, designed for the Ohio Expedition. We are told that after having landed the Soldiers she is immediately to return to Great-Britain, having been on this Station two Years and seven Months.

The 27th last Month, Capt. Jackson spoke with a Sloop from this Port, bound to Virginia, having on board a great Number of Women, Wives to some of the Soldiers on board the Centaur Man of War; Who are determined to follow their Husbands to Ohio, and will assist in, the better peopleing of Virginia.

NEW-YORK June 10. On Friday last embark'd for Albany, the Honourable James De Lancey, Esq; Governor of this Province, in order to hold the Treaty with the Indians on Friday next in that City.

On Wednesday last came in Town, from Pennsylvania, the Honourable John Penn Esq; Richard Peters, Isaac Norris, and Benjamin Franklin Esq; Commissioners appointed by the Governor of that Province, to assist at the approaching Treaty at Albany. And did likewise the next Day, the Honourable Benjamin Tasker, Esq; and Major Abraham Barnet, Commissioners from the Government of Maryland. And, Yesterday they embark'd on board Sloops provided for that Purpose, and sail'd with a favorable Wind for Albany, each with their respective Government's Presents for the Indians.

PHILADELPHIA June 13. Extract from Fredericksburg, in Virginia, May 29, 1754.

"Our Governor is gone to Winchester with design to confirm and renew all Treaties with the Indians in our interest; they appointed to meet him the 20th Instant; but he had no News of them after his continuance there for three Days, he sent two Men Express to invite them down to receive a considerable Present sent them by the Government, &c. which now lies at Winchester, where he intends to stay a Fortnight longer to wait their coming. --- When the French took our Fort at Ohio, it was said they had 1000 Men, but an Express arrived since, advising us from our Camp, that one of the Indian Half Kings had been among them, who numbered of them in their Fort, and could not make their Number exceed 600, so that we shall soon be stronger than they are ---- It is said one of the Kings of the Six Nations is gone over to the French Interest, but the Half King seems determined to adhere to ours."

By a Gentleman from Lancaster we have Advice, that three Persons had arrived there from North Carolina, who brought the following Intelligence, viz. That as they came through Winchester, in Virginia, they saw Twenty-one French Prisoners, that had just been brought in by a Party of the Virginia Forces; and on their asking how they happened to meet with them, were told, That the French at Ohio were then, and had been for some Time past, in great Want of Provisions, and hearing of a Convoy, with Stores of different Kinds going to the English, proposed to intercept it, and send out three Parties for that Purpose. But a Deserter from the French went to the Virginians, and told them what was intended; upon which Forty of their Men, with some Indians , were ordered our to meet them, the Indians being lie an Ambush in the Woods till the Enemy should pass by, and then having them between two Fires, (as it were) to close in and attack them, which was accordingly done, when fourteen Frenchmen were kill'd on the spot, and Twenty-one made Prisoners. Of the Virginians their was one Man killed, and another wounded. And we are further informed by the same Gentleman, that he heard another Person had come to

Lancaster, from the South Branch of Patowmack, who relates the Affair in the same Manner, but he did not see the man himself.

PERTH AMBOY June 12. Last two Paragraphs of Governor J. Belcher's Speech to the General Assembly of New Jersey, June 12, 1754.

Your Conduct has rendered it absolutely my Duty, for the Honour of His Majesty's and for the future Well being of this Colony, disolved this present Assembly, thereby putting it in the Power of the good People of this Province, to show how they stand affected in the Choice of future Representatives, for the good of the great and common Cause, recommended you this Session.

I do therefore, by Virtue of the Power and Authority to me given, disolves this present Assembly, and you are accordingly disolved.

J. Belcher.

ANNAPOLIS June 13. We have certain Accounts from the Westward of the Engagement between a Party of English and French, on the 27th of May past, beyond the Allegany Mountains, in a Place called the Flats, about 80 Miles our back Settlements, about 240 Miles near N. W. of this Place, and some Miles to the Eastward of the new Fort on the Ohio, which was lately surrendered to the French by Capt. Trent. Some of the particulars are as follow: Major Washington had Intelligence from our Friend the Half King, that a Party of the French were encamped on this side the Fork, on which he immediately marched at the Head of a Company of about 40 Men, but during their March the Rain fell so heavy that they could scarce keep their Ammunition dry; the French observed them before they came on, and speedily put themselves in Order of Battle, being under the Command of Monsieur Le Force: When the two Parties approached nigh, the French (who were about 36 in Number) gave the first Fire, by which one of Major Washington's Men was killed, and another knock'd down: Then English return'd the Fire, and killed 7 or 8 of the French, on which the Rest took to their Heels; but the Half King, and his Indians, who lay in Ambush to cut them off in their retreat, fell upon them, and soon killed and scalped five of them. Monsieur Le Force finding that they were all likely to lose their Lives under the Hands of the Savages, Called to his Men, and advised them to surrender to the English: they immediately, with a great Precipitation, ran towards the English, flung down their Arms, and begg'd for Quarters. Major Washington interposed between them and the Half King, and it was with great Difficulty that he prevented the Indians from doing them further Mischief, the half King insisting on Scalping them all, as it was their Way of Fighting, and he alleged that those People had killed, boiled, and eat his Father, and that the Indians would not be satisfied without all their Scalps; however, Major Washington at length persuaded him to be content with what scalps he had already got. One of those Five which were killed and Scalped by the Indians, was Jumonville an Ensign, who the Half King himself dispatched with his Tomahawk, Monsieur Le force. and 20 more Frenchmen, who were taken Prisoners, are carried down to Williamsburg. One or Two it is said, got away before the Rest surrendered, and it is not known what is become of them. Le Force has the Character of an expert Officer, and Half King reckoned that the English had gained a great Advantage in taking him, telling Major Washington, that That Man (Le Force) was a Thousand.

Col. Joshua Fry, who had lately the Misfortune of falling from his Horse, whereby he was much bruised, and died soon after at Will's Creek.

CHARLESTOWN SOUTH CAROLINA June 13. At the Motion of the French on the Ohio River, and the Measures they are pursuing there, threaten to disturb the Tranquility of the British Provinces; it is greatly to be wish'd that the British Provinces would unite in some System of Scheme for the Publick Peace and Safety; Such an Union would render us respected by the French, for they are not Strangers to out Power, tho' may perhaps suspect our Prudence; let us show them this Proof of our Wisdom, and they will hardly make any experiment of our Strength.

WILLIAMSBURG June 13. Copy of a Letter from a

Gentleman attending his Honour the Governor to Winchester.

We were most agreeably entertained last Night by Mr. Christopher Gist, from Colonel Washington's Camp, at a Place called the Great Meadows, with the welcome News of the total Defeat of a Party of French, that came to our People in the Night of the 28th of last past. Some friendly Indians informed the Colonel of their Design, and he, with the Vigilance and bravery of a good Officer, met them with a Party of about 40 Men, and gave them a proper Reception, that ten of them fell in the Action, one was wounded, and the remaining 21 were made Prisoners, whom his Honour the Governor has ordered to Williamsburg under escot. There are several Persons of Note among the Prisoners, particularly Monsieur La Force, who was considered by the French as one of the most enterprizing and useful Men they had, as he is a Person of great influence among the Indians, whose Language he speaks perfectly and extremely acquainted with the Country. This well timed Success has riveted the Indians to our Interest, who scalped those they had killed, and have sent the Scalps, and a black Belt, to all their Allies, to oblige them to take up the Hatchet (as they express it) and strike the French, whose Numbers we are assured, from good Intelligence, do not in the whole amount to 600.

And on Tuesday Evening last, the above mentioned 21 Prisoners arrived in the City, under a strong Guard, amongst whom are 4 Officers, who acquaint us, that the Commander, Captain Dejonville was killed in the Action.

Colonel Fry's illness has greatly retarted the March of the Division under his Command, which would otherwise long ago have been at the Camp, where we hourly expect to hear of the Arrival, and that of the Company from South Carolina. We hear they are all in good Health, and high in Spirits, and express the most ardent whishes to deliver their Country from these violators of Peace, and the Intruders of our Sovereign's Property on the North-American Continent.

BOSTON June 21. By His Excellency William

Shirley, Esq; Captain-General and Governor in and over His Majesty's Province of the Massachusetts-Bay in New-England.

A PROCLAMATION

Whereas it is a great Importance to this Province, that it should always be in a Posture of Defence against any invading Enemy, which is more especially Necessary in the present Conjuncture of Affairs:

I have thought fit to issue this Proclamation, hereby strictly commanding the several Colonels or other Officers of the respective Regiments of Militia whithin this Province. to cause their whole Regiments to be assembled, and put under Arms, at once and the same Day for each particular Regiment, either in a Body, or in two or three several Divisions, as the Situation and other circumstances of the several Companies do, in the Judgement of the Field-Officers, require. And that the Field-Officers, either together or apart, do carefully review the said Companies, and strictly inspect and survey the Arms of every single Man, and see that every one be compleatly furnished with Arms according to Law; and that the same (their Fire Arms more especially) be in good Order, and sufficient for actual Service: And that after such review, and on or before the Twenty-first Day of September next, they make a careful and exact Return to Me on the Condition which they find the Arms of their respective Regiments, and several Companies belonging to them, are in; and take effectual Care that such Officers or Soldiers as are deficient in any respect of what the Law requires but oblige to have such Defects forthwith supplies. And the Captains of the several Companies of Militia in the Province are hereby required, without Delay, to make Inquiry into the Town-Stock of Powder and Arms of the respective Town to which they belong; and where the Law has not been duly observed, that they make Report thereof to the several Colonels of the Regiment to which they belong; and the said Colonels are commanded Immediately to issue their Warrants for levying the Penalties ordered by law for such Delinquency; and that the said

Colonels are hereby directed to make Return to Me of their Doing therein, on or before the aforesaid Twenty-first Day of September.

Given in Boston the Twenty-first of June, 1754 in the Twenty-sevent Year of the Reign of our Sovereign Lord George the Second, by the Grace of God, of Great Britain, France and Ireland, King, Defender of the Faith &c,

By His Excellency's Command   W. Shirley.
J. Willard, Secr'y

NEW-YORK June 24. A Gentleman from Albany, who came to Town since our last, informs us, That his Honour our Governor arrived in that City on Thursday last was 2 Weeks, and was received with the greatest Demonstrations of Joy and Satisfaction, by the Inhabitants of the City and County; their Militia being very regularly drawn up and their Fort, and several Block-Houses Artillery firing upon his Arrival. The Commissioners from the several neighbouring Provinces, arrived two Days after; all in good Health as the Fatigue of their Passages by Water could admit. ——— The Indians of the several different Tribes designed to form the Congress the 14th Instant, were not come down to Albany the Day appointed, owing, 'tis said to one of their Sachems having died on or about that Day twelve Months, and their then being busy with the Ceremonies customary among them, so long a Time after the Death of such Personages: They however, were to be in Albany the Monday following, being the 7th instant.

Williamsburg June 27. On Monday last arrived in this City, Col. Innes, who left the remainder of the Carolina Troops, on their March to Hampton, where it was expected they would arrive last Night. Col. Innes left this Place on Tuesday to take upon him the Command of all the Troops assembled upon this Expedition.

This Morning one Hundred Stand of Arms and Ammunition, &c. were sent from this Place to Hampton, there to be shipped for Alexandria, for the use of the North Carolina Forces, who, we are told, will amount upwards of our Hundred Men.

ANNAPOLIS June 27. We have conformation, that

nine of the French Soldiers, from the Fort which was delivered up by Ensign Ward, has deserted, and come over to Major Washington. Upwards of 300 who are to march in a few Days, to join and reinforce Major Washington, so that it is hoped his Army will soon be able to withstand & repel any Attacks that may be offered him by the French.

JULY 1754

PHILADELPHIA July 4. We are inform'd by a Gentleman, who has lately been at the English Camp, about forty Miles from that of the French, that the latter having sent out a small party, in order to get Information of the Situation of our Forces, and they getting Intelligence thereof, Captain Montaur, with some Men, went in Search of them; with whom he accordingly fell in and engaged, some of which were killed, and the rest Prisoners.

NEW-YORK July 8. By the last Advice from Albany we are informed, That none of the Indians came down 'till the 20th of June past: That the Mohawks did not arrive 'till the 27th in the Evening; Hendrick, their Sachem, the next Day: That the Governor deliver'd his Speech to the Indians, in behalf of this and all the Provinces, on the 29th: That several of the Indian Sachems spoke to the Governor before his Speech to them: That they were to give their set Answers on Monday the first Instant: And, That the Indians seem to be in very good Temper with the English, notwithstanding the Articles of the French to induce them to the Contrary.

BOSTON July 9. We have Advice by Letters from Falmouth in Casco-Bay of the 2d and 4th Instant, That the Transports were all got in well, and the Soldiers all in Health: —— That they were met with forty-two Indians, 27 of which were Males chiefly of the Norridgewock Tribe. ——
That on Friday the 28th ult. His Excellency our Governor was pleas'd to open the Treaty with them: And the Day following let them known his Design and Resolution of Building a Fort on Teutonic-Falls; which the Indians on the Monday following objected to; but after further Conference, they took the Matter again under

Consideration, and the next Day declared, That they were willing the Governour should build a Fort according to his Desire; and that he might do it where he pleas'd on Kennebeck-River; and that the English might settle their Lands which they had fairly purchased without any Molestation from them. —— That the Indians discover a very peaceable Temper; and seem very desirous of continuing of Friendship: That on the 3d Instant the said Indians had a great Dance, and the next Morning departed Home well satisfied. —— That on the Friday before the Governour sent an Express to St. George's to invite the Penobscot's; and that they have since had certain News that they were coming, and were daily expected.

PHILADELPHIA July 11. A Gentleman arrived here from Alexandria, in Virginia, and informed us, that before he set out, he saw a Letter from Colonel Washington to his Friend there, advising that he designed to march immediately and attack the French with the Force he had then under him, being above 500 white Men, besides Indians, and not wait the Arrival of the other Troops designed for his Camp. That all with him, white Men and Indians, were in high Spirits, and eager for Action, having plenty of every Thing and that on the contrary, he had good Intelligence the Enemy were in great Want of Provisions, their Numbers vastly inferior to that it had been represented, and that in general they were dissatisfied, which occasioned a daily Desertion among them; so that he was in great Hopes of getting the better of them without much Bloodshed.

The Gentleman further added, that 170 of the North Carolina Men, who came by Water, and the New-York Companies, were at Alexandria when he left it; and that 300 more had marched fron North Carolina by Land, but where they were he had not learnt. He likewise said, that above a Hundred stout Men, from South Carolina had gone from Alexandria for the Camp, but whether or not they had got to it he could not tell.

BOSTON July 16. Wednesday last arrived here from Falmouth in Casco-Bay the Ship Bureyau,

Capt. Joseph Inches, with several Gentlemen of His Majesty's Council, the Speaker and divers Members of the Honourable House of Representatives, who attended his Excellency our Governor at the late Conference with the Indians at the Eastward. —— By them we have the agreeable News, That the Norridgewalks and Penobscotts readily came into Ratification of the former Peace; behaved very well, and as Proof of their Sincerity several of the young Men desired to come and reside with the English: Five of whom are already in Town & several of their Children may be expected in the Fall of the Year, in order to receive a suitable Education: Also that Forces under the Command of Major-General Winslow, were gone to Kennebeck River, in order to build several Forts thereon to which the Norridgewalks, inhabiting the same, informed his Excellency the Governor that they had no objection: And that his Excellency intended to tarry at Falmouth some Time longer, in order to expedite this Affair, and then to return to Boston; and that Capt. Inches will sail for Falmouth in a few Days for that purpose.

WILLIAMSBURG July 19. On Wednesday last arrived in Town Colonel Washington, and Captain Maccay, who gave the following Account to his Honour the Governor, of the Action between them and the French, at the Great Meadows in the Western Part of the Dominion.

The third of this Instant July, about nine a Clock, we received Intelligence that the French having been reinforced with 700 Recruits, had left Monongahela, and were in full March with 900 Men to attack us. Upon this, our Numbers were so unequal (our Force not exceeding 300) we prepared for our Defence in the best Manner we could by throwing up a small Intrenchment, which we had no Time to perfect, before our Centinel gave Notice, about 11 a Clock of their Approach by firing his Piece, which he did at the Enemy, and as we learned afterwards, killed three of the Men, on which they began to fire upon us, at about 600 Yards Distance, but without any Effect: We immediately called all our Men to their Arms, and drew up in Order before our Trenches; but as we looked upon this distant Fire of the Enemy only as an Artifice to intimidate, or draw our Fire from us, we waited their nearer approach before we returned their Salute.

The were advanced in a very irregular Manner to another Point of Woods, about 60 Yards off, and from thence made a second Discharge; upon which, finding they had no intention of Attacking us in the open Field, we returned into our Trenches, and still reserved our Fire, as we expected from their great Superiority of Numbers, that they would endeavour to force our Trenches; but finding they did nor seem to intend this neither, the Colonel gave Orders to Fire, which was done with great Alacrity and Undauntedness.

We continued the unequal Fight, with an Enemy sheltered behind the Trees, ourselves without Shelter in Trenches full of Water, in a settled Rain, and the Enemy galling us on all Sides incessantly from the Woods, till 8 a Clock at Night, when the French called to parley: From the great Improbability that such a vastly superior Force, and possessed of such an Advantage would offer a Parley first, we suspected a Deceit, and therefore refused to consent that they should come among us; on which, they desired us to send an Officer to them, and engaged their Parole for his Safety; we then sent Capt. Van Braam, and Mr. Peyronee to receive this Proposal, which they Did, and about Midnignt we agreed that each Side should retire without Molestation, they back to their Fort, at Monongahela, and we to Will's Creek: That we should march away with all Honours of War, and with all the Stores, Effects and Baggage. Accordingly the next Morning, with our Drums beating, and our Colours flying, we began our March in good Order with our Stores, &c. in Convoy; but we were interrupted by the Arrival of a Reinforcement of One Hundred Indians, among the French, who were hardly restrained from Attacking us, and did us considerable Damage, by the pilfering of our Baggage.

We then proceeded, but soon found it necessary

to leave our Baggage and Stores; the great scarcity of our Provisions obliged us to use the utmost Expedition, and having neither Waggons nor Horses to transport them, The Enemy had deprived us of all our Creatures, by killing, in the Beginning of the Engagement, our Horses, Cattle, and every living Thing they could; even to the very Dogs. The Number of the killed on our Side was 30, and 70 wounded; among the former was Lieutenant Mercier, of Capt. Maccay's Independent Company; a Gentleman of true Military Worth, and whose Bravery would not permit him to retire, tho' dangerously wounded, 'till a second Shot disabled him, and a third put an End to his Life, as he was carrying to the Surgeon.

Our Men behaved with singular Intrepedity, and we determined not to ask for Quarters, but with our Bayonets screw's, to sell our Lives as deadly as possible we could. From the Number of the Enemy, and our Station we could not hope for Victory; and from the Character of those we had to encounter, we expected no Mercy, but on Terms that we positively resolved not to submit to. The Number killed and wounded of the Enemy is uncertain, but by the Information given by some of the Dutch in their Service to their Countrymen in ours, we learnt that it amounts to above 300; and we are induced to believe it must be very considerable, by their being busy all Night in burying their Dead, and yet many remained the next Day; and their wounded we know was considerable, by one of our Men, who had been made Prisoner by them after signing the Articles, an who, on his Return, told us, that he saw great Numbers much wounded and carried off upon Litters.

We were also told by some of the Indians after the Action, that the French had an Officer of distinguishable Rank killed, Some considerable blow they must have received, to induce them to call first Parley, knowing as they perfectly did the Circumstances we were in. Col. Washington, and Capt. Maccay, left Capt. Clarke at Winchester, on the 11th last, and his Men were not then arrived there. Thus have a few brave

Men been exposed, to be butchered, by the Negligence of those, who in Obedience to their Sovereign's Command, ought to have been with them many Months before; and it is evident certain, that had the Companies from New-York been in expedition as Capt. Maccay's from South Carolina, our Camp would have been secure fron the Insults of the French and our brave Men still alive to serve their King and Country. Surely this will remove the Infatuation that seem to have prevailed too much among our Neighbours, and inforce a late ingenerous Emblem well worthy of their Attention and Consideration.

NEW-YORK July 22. Copy of a Letter from Paxton, about 90 Miles back of Philadelphia.

Sir,

I here met with Mr. Robert Callender, who was just arrived from Winchester, and brings the conformation of the Disagreeable News of Major Washington's Defeat, at his Camp at Big Meadows 64 Miles above Cocsaps, on the 3d Instant. At Winchester he met Col. Innes, who now commands the whole Troops, who had the following Intelligence from Major Washington, Viz.

"That two Days before the Attack, he had advice of the March of the French from their Fort, by Monagatootha, and made the necessary Preparations for their Reception. The French and Indians marched up within a small Distance of the Camp, & beat their Drums as usual, and immediately fired: which the English returned very warmly for above three Hours: The French then beat a Parley, and sent the English a Summons, of which inclos'd is a copy, to which they agreed, But no sooner had they delivered up the Camp, that the Indians got in, and pillag'd them and all their Baggage and Provisions, shot down all their Cows and Horses, and, in short took every Thing from them but their Powder, which they themselves destroyed, by throwing it in the Ditch that surrounds the Camp; they also killed two of the wounded, and scalp'd them, and three of the Soldiers, unhappy Mortals, who happen to get Drunk, and were asleep. Upon this, Major Washington complain'd of the ill Treatment they receiv'd, so contrary to the Conditions agreed on, and the French Commander pretending to put a stop to it, run in among the Indians, with his Sword drawn, but instead or persuading them from it (according to their well know Custom) he commended them by their Courage, and the Treatment they gave the English, which some of our People, who understood the Language he spoke in, heard him tell them. The Number of the French was 900 and 200 Indians; and what is most severe upon us, is, That they were all our own Indians, Shawnese, Delaware, and Mingos, (or Six Nations) for many of the English knew them, and called them by their Names, to spare their Goods; but all the Answers they returned, was in calling them the worst Names their Language could admit of. The English had 30 killed and 50 wounded 7 of whom are already dead; and no Officers killed, except one of the Lieutenants of the Carolina Company. The French it is thought, left 200 Men. The English had not one Indian to fight for them; the Half King, when he heard of the French being on the March, set off with about 20 Indians, to convey their Women into the Inhabitants; and Andrew Monteur, with the Indians he had with him, to watch the Motions of the french, did not come up to them till after the Engagement. --- By Major Washington's Account, there is only about 60 Indians declared in our Favour.

While Mr. Callender was in Winchester, a Gentleman arrived from North-Carolina, and inform'd Col. Innes, that the two Companies who was on the March from Virginia, were countermanded, the Governor having Advice that a Body of French and Indians, were erecting Forts near the back Inhabitants of that Province, ---- Another Gentleman arrived a little after him, from South Branch of Patowmack, and informed Col. Innes, that most of the Inhabitants were coming down to Winchester, with their Effects, for fear of being cut off by the Indians.

The Terms of the Capitulation granted by Momsieur De Villier, Captain and Commander of the Infantry of his Most Christian Majesty, to the English Troops actually in Fort Necessity, which is built on the Land that's of the King's

Dominions.

As our Intention have never been to trouble the Peace and Harmony with reigns between the two Princes in amuty, but only to revenge the Assassination which has been done on one of our Officers Bearer of a Station, as appears by his Writing; as also to hinder any Establishment on the Land in the Dominions of the King my Master: Upon there Consideration we are willing to grant Protection and Favour to all the English that are in the said Fort, upon the conditions hereafter mentioned.

Article 1. We grant the English Commander to retire with all his Garrison, and to return peaceably into his own Country; and promise to hinder his receiving any Insults from us French, and to restrain as much as shall be in our Power, the Savages that are with us.

Article 11. That the English be permitted to March out, and carry every Thing with them, except the Artillery, which we keep.

Article 111. That we will allow the English all the Honours of War; and that they March out with Drums beating, & with a swivel Gun; that we are willing to shew that we treat them as Friends.

Article IV. That as soon as the Articles are signed by both Parties they strike the English Colours.

Article V. That to-morrow at Break of Day a Detachment of the French shall make the Garrison file off, and take Possession of the Fort; and as the English have a few Horses or Oxen, they are free to hide their Effects, and come and search for them when they have met their Horses: and that they may for this End have Guardians in what Number they please, upon Condition, that they will give Word of Honour, not to work upon any Buildings in this Place, or any other Part this side of the Mountains, during a Year, to be accounted from this Day. And as the English have now in their Power an Officer, two Cadets, and most of the Prisoners made in the Assassination of Defamonville, that they promise to send them back, with a safe Guard to the Fort Du Guerre, situated on the Fine River; and for Security of Robert Stobe, both Captains, shall be put as Hostages, till the Arrival of the Canadians and French above mentioned. We oblige ourselves on our Side, to give an Escort to return in Safety these two Officers, a Duplicate being made upon, or of the Post of our Blockade   July 3, 1754.

PHILADELPHIA July 25. Last Friday came to Town an Express from the back Part of this Province, by whom we have the Conformation of Col. Washington's Defeat at the Great Meadow, near the Ohio. The following is a Letter from Col. Innes, who now commands all the forces on the Ohio Expedition, to his Honour the Governor of the Province.

Honourable Sir,
Having Notice of a Person going to your Province immediately, I thought proper, on this Occasion to give you a short Detail of what has lately Happened.

After having regulated the March, and the Transportation of the North-Carolina Regiment, I immediately proceeded to Williamsburg, and by my Commission from Governor Dinwiddie, as Commander and Chief of the Expedition, I set out for Winchester, where I arriv'd the 30th June, in order to take Command upon me, and to bring up the New-York two Independent Companies, with those of the North Carolina Regiments, then upon their March from Alexandria for this Town.

Colonel Washington with the Virginia Regiment ad Captain M'Kay with the South Carolina independent Company, together did consist but of Four Hundred Men, of which a good many were sick, and out of order.

On the third of July the French, with about Nine Hundred Men, and a considerable Body of Indians, came down upon our Incampment, and continued to fire, from all Quarters, from Eleven in the Morning till Night, when the French called out to our People, they would give them good Conditions, if they would capitulate, a Copy of which I have inclosed to you.

After the Capitulation the French demolished the Works, and in some Time after retired to the Ohio, taking two Captains as Hostages along with them. We all know the French are a People that never pay any Regard to Treaties longer than they find them consistent with their Interest: And this Treaty they broke immediately, by letting the Indians Demolish and destroy every Thing our People had, especially the Doctor's Box, that our Wounded should meet with no Relief. In this Action it is said we had about 100 Men kill'd and Wounded, a Third whereof supposed to be kill'd; and it is reported we kill'd double the Number of the French. If this does not alarm the neighbouring Governments, nothing can; and I make no Doubt but the French will soon claim this fine Body of Land as their Right by Conquest, if we do not immediately raise a sufficient Force to convince them of the contrary. What I can learn of their Forces, is, that they had 700 Men in their first Division, 800 in the next, and 500 in the last, not as yet join'd; with their Indians, made a considerable Body.

Colonel Washington and Captain M'Kay told me, there were many of our Friend Indians along with the French, sundry of which came up and spoke to them, told them they were their Brothers, and ask'd them how they did, particularly Sasquehanna Jack, and others, who distinguished themselves by their Names; and it is also said, that some of the Delawares were there. We had not an Indian to assist when the Engagement commenced or ended.

It is my real Opinion that nothing, will continue to us the Indians now in our Friendship, if we allow ourselves to be bassted by the French; as it is very natural and common for a more polite People than the Indians to side with the strongest: So that there is a Necessity either to go into the Affair in dispute heartily at once, or to give up entirely.

      I am, Sir,
    Your most obedient humble servant,
Westchester, July 12.   James Innes.

AUGUST 1754

BOSTON Aug. 1. This Day fortnight came to Town the Hon. Thomas Hutchinson, Esq; Judge of Probate for the County, and one of the Commissioners of the late Convention at Albany: ---- That the Commissioners from the several Governments were unanimously of Opinion, that an Union of Colonies was absolutely necessary in order to defeat the Schemes of the French. ---- That Representation of the State of the British Interest on the Continent, as it stands related to the French and Indians, have been drawn up and approved of: And that a Plan or Union has likewise been projected, and will, by the Commissioners, be laid before their respective Constituents. ---- All the Commissioners left Albany the 12th Instant.

ANNAPOLIS Aug. 1. We are assured that his Excellency our Governor had ordered two Companies of Men to be raised in this Province who are to receive eight Pence a Day, each private Soldier, from the Time of enlisting and Cloaths, Arms, Accroutrements, upon their marching to join the Troops under the Command of Col. Innes: After which Time they will be supplied with Provisions at free Cost.

We are also informed, that his Excellency commissioned John Ross, Esq; of this City to enlist any Men that shall offer themselves as Voluntiers for his Majesty's Service.

ANNAPOLIS Aug. 1. On the 27th Instant his Excellency the Governour put an End to the Session of the General Assembly, after passing An Act for his Majesty's Service, & some continuing Acts.

By the forementioned Acts, the Assembly have granted Six Thousand Pounds towards the Assistance of the Virginians, and for the Relief and support of the Wives and Children of our Indian Allies, who shall be put themselves under the Protection of this Government; the whole to be disposed of as his Excellency our Governour shall think proper. —— The Act directs, that all Ordinaries Licenses taken out the August Court this present Year, shall Pay 20 Shillings each over and above what was formerly paid.

BOSTON Aug. 1. By letter from Custenors, on Kennebeck River, dated the 18th Instant, we are informed, that General Winslow has erected several Block-Houses and Watch-Boxes there: —— That they were busy building a Number of Battoes, which would be finished in two or three Days, and then upon the Arrival of Col. Fry, who was hourly expected with a Reinforcement of Men, and a good Quantity of Stores, the General intended to set out for Treconic with 500 Men, there: That the Men were in good Health (notwithstanding their hard Service) not having so much as one sick among them.

NEW-YORK Aug. 5. Last Week it was currently reported in Town, that the French and Indians from Canada, came down on our Frontier, as far as Saraghtogo, and cut away all the Bridges between that Place and Albany; that they Carried off some Prisoners and Scalpes from the Eastward, and that our Indians told the Inhabitants residing in the back Part of the Province, that now was their Time to withdraw, as they daily expected an Army of French and Indians to come against them: But as we have no Advice of any Act of Hostility being committed at the Eastward, and the Accounts received here very imperfect, we would hope the Reports are groundless, 'tis imagined the whole to be only the Surmise of some, who no doubt think, and not without Reason, that that, if not something worse, will be the Consequence, unless some speedy Remedy is tho't of and put in Execution in order to stop the Engroachments of all our Enemies, who are now surrounding us from all Quarters.

Boston Aug. 6. By the last Advices from Falmouth in Casco-Bay we learn, That His Excellency and the Gentlemen with him, were in good

Health; and that they had Intelligence by an Expert, That the Cannon which were transported were arriv'd and mounted at Treconick; and the Ground marked out for a Fort ——— That 550 Men were arrived in good Health, and expected to be joined in two or three Days by the remainder except what were left to cover the Fort at Cushnock. That the Norridgewalk Indians have behav'd very friendly; and have given information to General Winslow of two Deserters going off from our Forces to Canada, and afterwards bro't them in on a Reward propos'd. One of them an Irish Man, the other a New-England Man; and, they have promis'd, to do the same by other Deserters.

WILLIAMSBURG Aug. 15. Tuesday last passed thro' this City, on their way home, six officers belonging to the Regiment from North Carolina, whose Company are all Disbanded, and gone to their respective Habitations; by them we have advice that General Innes, was preparing to march immediately with the remaining Troops, to build a large Fort at Will's Creek.

Yesterday at Four o'Clock in the Evening Monsieur Druillon, Monsieur La Force, two Cadets and 17 Private Men who were Prisoners here, set out under escort, for the French Fort at the Ohio.

WILLIAMSBURG Aug. 15. Yesterday the General Assembly of this Colony met at the Capital, in this City, when his Honour the Governour opened the Session with the following Speech,

Gentlemen of the Council, Mr. Speaker, and Gentlemen of the House of Burgesses.

I am very sensible the great expence the country is at, in frequent Meetings of the Assembly, but I am persuaded when you seriously consider the present dangerous Situation on our Affairs, you will agree with me in the absolute necessity of calling you together at this Time.

The ambitious Views of the French, for universal Monarchy, have been particularly observed in Europe, for many Years. They have for these last Seven Years been oppressing the British Subjects in the East and West Indies, His Majesty's Colonies on this Continent have been greatly disturbed with repeated Incroachments:

They began with the Northern Settlements, and are now carrying their unjust Designs, to the Southern Colonies of the British Subjects.

What more immediately effected us, is that in Open Contempt and Violation of the Treaties now subsisting between the Crowns of Great-Britain and France, they have, unjustly, invaded his Majesty's Lands on the River Ohio, and with an armed Force taken a Fort, that by His Majesty's Orders, I had directed to be built at that River; after which, they have, committed the most violent hostile Act, by attacking our Forces, which were sent, by His Majesty's Command, to build some Forts on his Lands, near the River Ohio, and killed many of our People.

These affairs, I hope you will seriously consider; and I fear, this is only a Prelude to their further Design of invading, and taking from us the Lands we are now, and have been long possessed of.

I could expatiate very largely on these Affairs, but my Heart burns with resentment at their Insolence on the Dignity of the Crown, and disturbing the Quiet of this Dominion.

Gentlemen of the House of Burgesses,
I think there is no Room for many Arguments to induce you to raise a considerable Supply, to enable me to defeat the Design of these troublesome People, and Enemies of Mankind. I earnestly desire all Animosities may subside, that your deliberations and Councils, at this perilous Time, be distinguished by Loyalty, Duty to the best of Kings and true Patriotism for the Defence of your Country; which is now so much exposed to the Insults of a merciless Enemy.

The Expences to this Time, your Committee can inform you, and I believe the Money is wholly expended.

The conducting of the Expedition, for the future, will require great Supplies, but surely the Necessity of our Affairs call for it; and no Doubt, it will be thought reasonable, to advance Part of what we are possessed of, to save the rest.

Gentlemen of the Council, Mr. Speaker, and Gentlemen of the House of Burgesses.

Never was a Time which more strongly called for your Unanimity & Dispatch; and, as every Individual becomes now concerned in your consultations, that you will exert yourselves on this Emergency, by granting Supplies equal to the pressing Occasion.

I pray, God may direct your Councils for his Honour, and the Protection of your Country, by granting such Assistance in this Time, as to qualify me to repel the Force of the Enemy.

Gentlemen,
I have nothing in View, but the Prosperity, Happiness, and Safety of this Dominion; I therefore desire to assure you, that I will, with Chearfullness, join in every Thing you may propose for these salutary Ends, consistent with my Instructions.

ANNAPOLIS Aug. 15. We are now every Day raising Recruits to go against the French in Ohio.

We hear from Virginia, that they are about raising 1500 Men in that Colony, immediately to join Col. Innes.

PHILADELPHIA Aug. 15. In January, 1753, four of our Indian Traders, viz. Alexander M'Gerty, Jabez Evans, Daniel Hendrick, and William Powell, were taken trading on the Kantutqui River, near the Ohio, by a Party of French Indians called the Cagnawaga's who plundered them of Goods to the Value of several Hundred Pounds, and carried them to Canada; where they were made Slaves. But acquainting the Mayor of Albany with that miserable Situation, by a Letter which he communicated to this Government, Measures were taken to procure their Release. The Indians at first Demanded a Negro Boy for each of them, or as much Money as would buy one; but at length were prevailed on by the Commissioners of Indian Affairs at Albany, to take less; tho' the whole paid them, with the Charges, amounted to Seventy two Pounds, Five Shillings and Three Half Pence, for the four Prisoners, which Sum has been repaid by this Province. However, the Indians it seems pretend not to be satisfied; and Colonel Myndert Schuyler, one of the Albany Commissioners for Indian Affairs, who translated this Matter with them, received lately the following

Letter from the Chief of that Nation on the Subject, viz.

     Falls of St. Louis June 14, 1754.

 I pray thee, my Brother Anagarondon,** to acquaint the Gentlemen, That I have not been satisfied for the Prisoners that were delivered to you at Albany last Year. My young Men tell me every Day that they do not like your Management, and that for the future they will bring no living Prisoners, since they do not receive as much for one of them as will buy a little Slave. You know, my Brother, that I had only ninety Livre of our Money. I charge Montandre with this Commission, who will explain my sentiments to you, when he delivers you this Letter. The least that ought to be paid for a Prisoner is 400 Livres.* Let those that have the Management of these Sort of Affairs, give due Attendance to this: otherwise I will not answer, for what may happen hereafter, when my young Men make Prisoners.

 **Anagarondon, is Colonel Schuyler's Indian Name.

 *About Twenty Pounds Sterling.

 By this Insulting Letter from a People whom this Province has not had the least Difference, to whom we have never given the least Occasion of Offence, we may see the Contempt in which we are held by the Savages; who not content with plundering our Pepole of their Goods with Impunity, propose to make Slaves of all they can catch, or to have a Sum for each sufficient to purchase a Slave, otherwise threatning they will not be at the trouble of saving our Lives. If they are suffered to go on in this Manner, and to make a Trade of catching our People, and selling them to us, again for 400 Livres per Head, it may in Time cost us more to satisfy the Demands of that Handful of Barbarians, that would serve to defend the Province against all its Enemies.

 PHILADELPHIA Aug. 22. Extract of a Letter from Cumberland County, to a Gentleman here, dated August 15, 1754.

 "I am informed, that some of the French were a few Days ago, within 30 Miles of my House, who kill'd some steers, and carried off others, belonging to one Robert Backer.

Alexander Cook, a young Man who kept a Store in this Neighbourhood, went to the South Branch of Potomack, about two Months ago, in order to collect some Debts, intending not to stay above two Weeks, since which there is a Report that he is killed; and his Staying from his Harvest, and so long beyond the Time he designed to return in, makes his Friends believe to be true."

NEW-YORK Aug. 26. We hear that the General Assembly of this Province, have (at the present Sitting) voted the Sum of Five Hundred Pounds Currency to be immediately sent to the Virginians, in order to enable them to extirpate our well known Friends the French, from the Frontier of that and neighbouring Provinces.

We hear from Albany, that about a fortnight ago, five Canoes with Utawawa Indians arrived there: They give out that they had been at Canada, when the French Commandant had offered them the Axe, and desired them to go against Saraghtoga; but that they refused him, and told him they had already shed too much English Blood, and would continue at Peace with the English, unless they should offer to Attack Crown Point, which if they did, they would then take up the Axe against them.

BOSTON Aug. 27. We have certain Intelligence from Baker's Town (the most northerly Settlement on the Merrimack-River, and the Province of New-Hampshire) That on Thursday sennight as Mr. Philip Call and his Son were at work in his Field, they saw a Number of Indians (suppose to be of the St. Francis Tribe) enter'd his House, where his Wife was (a Woman about 70 Years of Age) whom they haul'd out, kill'd and scalp'd before the Door, the Husband being hid in the Bushes was a sorrowful Spectator of the Tragedy; the Son having made his Escape to Comoccook the next English Settlement, and returning with eight Men who had join'd him, were way lay'd and assaulted by the Indians as they were stand-under some Trees as a shelter from a plentiful rain which fell all that Time; one of the Number was kill'd and scalp'd, and another is missing: It is also greatly feared that two other

Men who were at work at a Meadow about two Miles distant from Mr. Call's House have fallen into the Hands of the Indians.

WILLIAMSBURG Aug. 29. We have Advice from Fort Duquesne, the Fort the French took from us on the Ohio, on the 29th of July, that there were about 200 Men there at the Time, 200 mor expected in a few Days, that the Rest went off in several Detachments, to the Amount of 1000 besides Indians.

We have also certain Intelligence of several of our Men having been taken Prisoners since the Treaty, and offered by the Indians for sale at 40 Pistoles per Head, and for want of Purchasers since sent to Canada.

PHILADELPHIA Aug. 29. Last Week an Express arrived here from Auchwick, with Advice, that 300 Indians, Men, Women, and Children, were areived there from the Ohio, being drove of by the French, and had demanded Protection and Provisions from this Government; and we hear orders are accordingly sent for their Support. It is said 200 more were soon expected at Auchwick, on this Side the Mountain.

SEPTEMBER 1754

BOSTON Sept. 2. On Saturday John Shirley, Esq; Son of His Excellency our Governour, arrived here from Falmouth in Casco-Bay, by whom we have the following Account, viz. That the Forces under General Winslow set out from Teconnet with some thing more than 500 Men, and 15 Battoes, on the 8th of August past but after proceeding two Days up the River the General, was taken so ill, that he was oblig'd to return, leaving the Command, with the Instructions to him, with Col. Prebble, who on the 10th, at 9 in the Morning, proceeded with 13 Batoes, one half the Men on the one Side, and the other half on the other Side the River, and on Tuesday the 13th arrived at Norridgewalk, which is 31 Miles and a half above Tecconet, beautifully situated, near 400 Acres of clear Land, and which the Grass is generally five and six Feet High; here they found 6 Indian Men, 3 Squaws, and several Children, who appear'd at first surpriz'd to see such a Number of Men and Battoes, so far advanc'd into their Country; but after they were told by Col. Prebble, that they had nothing to fear from him, and that none of his Men should hurt the least Thing they had, nor go into their Houses, and that Governour Shirley had order'd, they should be treated with civility and Kindness; They appear'd well satisfi'd, and were kind and friendly; and Passequcant, one of their Chiefs, presented him with two fine Salmon, and Squashes of their own Produce, and were all very free in drinking King George & Governour Shirley's Healths, and told him he was welcome there.

The Camp'd that Night half a Mile above the Town: and the next Day leaving the Battoes there, with a Detachment sufficient to guard them, they proceeded on their March to the Great Carrying

Place between Kennebeck and the River Chaudiere where the French were said to be building a Fort, and arrived there the 18th, which is 38 Miles & 3 Quarters above Norridgewalk, a few Miles below which the met with three Birch Canoes with eight Indians in them, who had lately come over the Carrying Place, and as they suppos'd from Canada: the Indians were much surpriz'd on discovery of the Party, and Endeavour'd to return up the River with their Canoes, buy the Rapidity of the Stream prevented their Speedy Flight, on which they run their Canoes ashore on the opposite side of the River, catch'd one of them up and run off into the Woods, leaving the other two on the Spot, and made their escape to the Carrying Place and to return to Canada, to carry Intelligence, as Col. Prebble suppos'd for he track'd them in his March across the said Carrying Place; the Coarse of which from the Head of Kennebeck-River, is due West, and the Distance three Miles 3 Quarters and 22 Rods to a Pond about two Miles long and 1 & half Miles wide, beyond that there is another Carrying Place about one Mile of which leads to another Pond thar runs into the River Chaudiere.

The return'd from the first mention'd Pond the same Day, and came to Norridgewalk the 21st od Aug. early in the Day, when they found Capt. Wright, and a Detachment under his Command, all well, and 35 Indians, Old and Young, who upon the Knowledge of Col. Prebble's Return, dress'd themselves up, in their Way, very fine, by putting on clean Shirts, painting & decorating themselves with Wampum, they saluted him with a Number of Guns, and three Cheers, and then a Number of them waited on him at the Camp, welcom'd him back, and seem'd to express a good deal of Satisfaction at his Return. After Drinking Kink George's and Governour Shirley's Health, they invited him to their Houses, and ten or twelve of the Chiefs, desired a short Conference with him; and having clear'd the House of Young Men, who diverted themselves in the meanwhile, playing Ball,&c. told, "That he had passed and repassed thro' their Country, they were glad to see him come back & he was heartily Welcome: And that they had told him before he went, there was no French Settlements at the Carrying Place and since he had been there, and found it so, hop'd he would now look upon them as true Men: And that we were now all Brothers; and if their young Men should get in Liquor & affront any of the English, hop'd we would take no Notice of it; That they were determined to live in Friendship with us; and if the Canada Indians had any Design to do any Mischief on our Frontier, they would certainly let us know it; and if any disputes arose bewixt the French and us, they they were determined for the future to set still and smoke the Pipe."

The Colonel told them, the Resolution they had taken, would be very pleasing to Governour Shirley, and as long as they kept their Faith with us, they might depend on being treated as Friends and Brethren, and be supplied with all Necessities at Teconnet; which would be much more convenient for them than Richmond. All which they told him, they liked very well; and were sorry they had no Liquor to treat him with, but desir'd he would see their young Men dance, and they ours, which they said was a Token of Friendship, & was accordingly perform'd.

Next Morning, on the Colonel's taking Leave of them, they wish'd him safe to Teconnet, saluted him with 30 or 40 small Arms, as fast as they could load and discharged.

The Army arriv'd at Teconnet on Friday the 23d of August, at five o'Clock in the Afternoon, having been 16 Days on the March.

As to the Course of the River into the Country, it must be defer'd till a Plan of the same, which has been taken by a skilled Surveyor, shall appear. The Soil for the most Part in extremely good, and appears to be fertile: There are many Beautiful Islands in the River, some of which contain near a Thousand Acres of Intervals; but the land is not plentiful stored with Timber. The Navigation from Teconnet to Noridgewalk is considerably difficult, by Reason of the Rapidity of the Stream and rissing Falls, but 'tis like will be much easier when the water is higher. There is but one Falls above Toconnet Falls, that it is necessary to carry the Battoes round, before we come to Norridgewalk, betwext which and the Carrying Place the Navigation is vastly better than below, there being only two Fall to carry round, one which, notwithstanding a Mile in Length, there is a plain beated Path; the other is not above thirty or forty Rods.

His Excellency was in good Health when Mr. Shirley left him, and proposed to be in Town, with the Gentlemen who attended him, in about ten Days time.

On tuesday last Died here the 31st Year of her Age, after a long Indisposition, and on Saturday was decently and honourably interred, Mrs. Judith Shirley, Daughter to his Excellency our Governor.

NEW-YORK Sept. 2. Extract of a Letter from a Gentleman at Albany, to his Friend at New-York, dated August 28th 1754, brought by Express which arrived here last Saturday Night.

"Last Sunday Morning came down an Express from the Carrying-Place a Cousin of D.V.D.H. who lies there to track. Some Indians who had been here, sent by that Young Man (I think) four Strings of Wampum to give Notice that some of the Orandax Indians were gone to destroy Hosack: Upon this Alarm, most if not all the Inhabitants of Saratogue, Half-Moon, Schaachkook, Tamhermick and Hosack, left their Habitations; many of them came into Albany, others staid above (a) Barent Bratt's, Van Der Heyden's Van Arnem's and the Neighbourhood, for two or three Days; some were gone back to their Habitations, others making ready to return. This Evening came here Peter Hogg, an Inhabitant of Hosack, who went from hence this Morning; and as he was near home, met one of the Neighbour's by the Way, who had escaped, and told him to return with all Speed, for Hosack was all on Fire, and some People killed, and others taken Prisoners; I have not yet heard the Particulars, the Man at the Time of my Writing, being with the Commissioners.

After Writing the above, I went to Lotterige's and was informed, that the Commissioners had taken Hogg's Affidavit, which I suppose will be sent to the Governor. I am told, he swore, That the young Man who met him on the Road, told him that he had seen the Army, and computed them to be near 300, or more, and many Frenchmen among them. I wish the Assembly might do something towards fortifying our Frontiers; I reckon that Tomorrow every Soul to the Northward of the (b) Patroon's will be in Town; if they think themselves safe, which I must doubt of: For if such a Number of Indians would, in several Parties, fall on the Town in different Places, as we are all open. I think they could destroy us all.

The French Indians who came here more than two Weeks ago, to make Peace and open the Path, have always told the Commissioners, that their was no (c) Danger; That the Path was now open and clear, and this Peace was not made for a short Time, or during their Lives, but for ever. As I heard an Express was going to New-York, I had just Time to write this. I am, &c.

(a) About six Miles from Albany.
(b) A mile from Albany.
(c) As much faith is to be put in the Promises of the Indians, as in that of a Frenchman.

Since the above, we hear, that the French Army are come down as far as Kinderbrook, (20 Miles below Albany) where they have taken a Prisoner. "Tis said another Express is hourly expected.

By a Gentleman directly from Virginia, in seven Days, we are credibly informed, That two very eminent Persons in that Province, had offered to raise 1500 Men, in a few Days Time, in order to send in Ohio, if the Legislature would agree to the Proposal made: And the Governour Dinwiddie, had call'd both the Council and Assembly together upon the Occasion, but had come to no Determination when he left Virginia.

WILLIAMSBURG Sept. 4. Our Assembly met the 22d of last Month, and have voted 20,000 Pounds for the Ohio Expedition, to be raised by Poll-Tax of Five Shillings per Head. In Consequence of the late Capitulation, Monsier Le Force and the French Prisoners were sent off, and has got

beyond Winchester, on their way to the Ohio, but by an Express from Governor Dinwiddie, they were stopp'd and ordered back to Winchester, where they are to remain till further Orders. ———
This Morning Mr. Gist was here, who left Will's Creek on Saturday, and says, the New-York Independents were within six Miles of that Place and that an Indian came in the Day before from the French Fort, and informed, that when he came away, there were only 200 Men in it, the rest being drafted and sent off, in order to erect a Fort higher up, at or near the Falls of Niagara, having no Apprehension from the English till the Spring.

PHILADELPHIA Sept. 5. 1754. From the Pennsylvania Gazette To the Inhabitants of Pennsylvania.

Gentlemen,
I have hitherto contented myself with being a peaceable Member of Civil Society, without giving you or myself any considerable Trouble about political Affairs; I shall therefore hope for your Indulgence, while, alarm'd with our Danger, and oppressed with the most gloomy Apprehensions from the present State of the publick Affairs, I take the Liberty of laying before you such Considerations as tend to rouze you up from the Lethargy which seems every where to prevail amongst us, that we may have ourselves, and our Children, from the Ruin and Destruction which has already begun to lay waste our Borders, and which, if not speedily prevented will spread Horror, Distress, and Desolation, throughout the Land. ———

I intend, in what I have to say, carefully to avoid giving just Cause of Offence to any and I hope none will take Offence when none is Design'd. ———— In order to put things in such a Light as will awaken us to a Sense of our Duty, it will be necessary to consider what Aspect to the present State of Publick Affairs bears, both on our political and our religious Interest. With Regard to the former, we should do well to remember that the French have long meditated our Ruin: ———— That what they are now doing on our Frontiers, in in Consequence of a Scheme laid out above fifty Years ago for universal Empire of North America: ---- That tho they are not at present so numerous in this Part of the World as the English, yet, in Europe their Power, makes the Nations around them tremble: That it would be a small matter for the King of France to send Fifteen thousand Men to America, in order to accomplish so grand a Design, and adding an Empire to his Kingdom, which is ten Times as large as all he possesses in Europe; now can we suppose they are ignorant that the present is the Time to strike a Blow, when our Indians are wavering, and afraid to assist us, and theirs are more firmly Attach'd to them, bu their late Victory over the Virginians, and while our Colonies are in a disunited State, and will neither exert their Power separately by themselves or in Conjunction wit one another. ---- Let us, my Friends, (at least for once) when our all is at Stake, divert ourselves of Prejudice and Party Views, and with that Seriousness and Attention which the Importance of the Case requires, consider the Particulars above mentioned, and then let us say, what will be the Consequence of these Things, if timely Care is not taken to prevent the impending Stroke.

It is not natural and reasonable to suppose, that the French will establish themselves all along the Back Parts of our Colonies, quite from Canada to the Mouth of the Missisippi. The Forts they have built, and still are building, will afford a Shelter to their Settlers on any sudden Attack. In a little Time they will raise Provisions enough for their Support; their Marrying and living among the Indians, and using all imaginable Means to gain them to their Interest, will soon unite the numerous Indian Nations to them; this will be such an Addition to their Force, as will enable them not only to withstand any Attack from the English, but also put it in their Power to Attack us in such a Manner as will greatly distress us. The Inhabitants of our Frontiers must abandon their Settlements, which will soon will be possessed by the French and their Indians. ---- Our Indians must for their own Safety join the strongest Party and then they are prepared to accomplish our Destruction. ---- In this dreadful Situation, what can we do? We must choose either to submit to the French, and become Vassals of their Grand Monarch or die a barbarous and cruel Death, by the Hands of their Savage Allies, ---- But if we consider the Affairs in a religious View, it increases the Horrors of Scene beyond Expression. Can we whose Ancestors left their, native their beloved Lands, and fled to the American Desarts, to seek a Shelter from ecclesiastick Tyranny, and enjoy unmolested the invaluable Privilege of worshiping God according to the Dictates of thier Consciences; can we, I say, endure the Thought of having our Children enslaved by the Church of Rome, and forced, contrary to the Light of their Minds, either to comply with all its idolatrous Superstitions, or fall a Sacrifice to the cruel and Bloody Zeal of bigotted Priest, & their blinded Followers, who think they do God good Service by cutting off such as they call Hereticks, from the Face of the Earth; and such is their Esteem are all those who are not of their Community. ----

Nor will it afford us a more agreeable Prospects, to view the tender Offering of our dear Children whom preistly Rage has murder'd sitting at the Feet of those inhuman Butchers, and meckly ----eiving for divine Truths, all the monstrous Tenets of that anchristian Church; and how cutting the Consideration, that we ourselves should be accessary to all those intolerable Evils: ---- even we, whom God has entrusted with the Guardianship of our Posterity, and who are bound, by all the Ties of Duty, and parental Tenderness, to preserve them inviolate. ---- The Temperal, and spiritual Liberty and Happiness of our Children, are a sacred Trust, which the supreme Ruler of the Universe hath committed to our Charge; and if we betray the Trust we not only act a Part more unnatural and cruel then even the Brute Creation, but bring an aggravated Guilt upon ourselves. ---- Do not imagine, my Friends, that I am endeavouring to amuse the Ignorant with frightful Representations of Things which are never likely to happen;

I Speak what I verily believe will be the Case, unless some effectual Measures are seasonably taken to prevent it. ---- The present cruel Persecution, and Murder of our Protestant Brethren in France, may shew us what we are to expect even from the mild and gentle Reign of Lewis their Beloved, if he once brings us into his Subjection. How many of the greatest and worthiest Men of that Kingdom, who were Members of their own Church, have of late fallen a Sacrifice to the Rage and Ambition of their Clergy; Nor must we expect to fare better, if we suffer ourselves to fall into their Hands. These, my Friends and Brethren are serious Truths, and ought seriously to be consider'd; and let us remember, that it is the Duty not only of a few, but of every one of us, to do what we can to prevent those dreadful Calamities from coming on us & our Children. Even the tender Sex may here be of Service; Arise then ye Debarahs, ye Mothers in Isreal, and save your People from Ruin; the silent, but perswasive, Oratory of your Tears, may do more to awake a thoughtless Husband to a sense of his Danger, and his Duty, than all the gravest Arguments of Reason and Religion. ---- It will not do for us to sit still, and expect God to deliver us by a Miracle; we are not so holy a People, as to deserve Miracles to be wroth for us; nor is it God's ordinary Method to work Miracles to save his People, when common Methods will do; let us not then deceive ourselves with vain Hopes and Expectations till our Ruin is unavoidable, but let us humble ourselves before the Lord for our Iniquities; let us arise from our Lethargy; let us use the means which God hath put in our Power; and while on going into the Lord's Way, we may with humble Confidence rely on him for Protection, and he will not fail those who thus put their Trust in him: ——— But if you will persist in your present Insensibility, remember you have been warn'd of your Danger; ---- The Sword is coming, the Alarm is sounded; and if you will not hear, you must answer for the Blood of all those who shall hereafter be slain through your Neglect; you will have to answer both for the temporal and spiritual Ruin of your Posterity; and you will (at least in Part) be answerable for the Idolatries of the Heathen round about us, who ought to have been brought by our Means to the Knowledge of the only true God, and the Way of Salvation by Jesus-Christ. ---- These my Friends, are solemn Considerations, which ought deeply to impress our Spirits, and it is Truly amazing, that we have hitherto been so little affected by them. Were any other People, in the like Circumstances, to act exactly as we have done, and the surprizing story should be told us, could we possibly believe it true, without the most incontestable Evidence; but if once convinced of it, should we not conclude, that some strange Infatuation had possessed them; and could we help dropping a Tear over such unhappy Creatures? Why then shall we continue to act so strange a part ourselves? It is high Time for us to awake out of our Sleep; and happy will it be too late, like Solomon's prudent Men, sense the Evil, and hide ourselves; and not like his simple Ones, pass on, and be punished.   Philanthropos.

 NEW-YORK Sept. 9. We are credibly informed, that the Report of an Army of French and Indians having surrounded Stockbridge in Time of divine Service, last Sunday se'nnight is entirely false; and what gave the rise to the said Report, was, That two Indians, (supposed to be of the sort called Friend Indians) went into a House in Stockbridge the same Day, and, tis said to revenge the Death of one of their Tribe, killed and scalp'd one Man and two Children, and the Servant Maid, the Woman of the House escaping in the Fray, as did also a Man who was up Stairs, by jumping our of a Window, and not far from the House perceived a Body of Indians coming from Meeting, imagin'd they were an Army of French, design'd to destroy the Town: In the Interim, the other two Indians made their Escape, and carried off a little Girl with them; but being pursued the next Day by 1000 Men, they scalp'd the Child, and left her in the woods, where she was found by two Persons, with some Symptoms of Life remaining, but soon after expired.

Last Saturday a Detachment of 40 Men, with proper Officers, from his Honor's Company Posted in this City embarked on board a Sloop for Albany, the Better to defend that Place in case any hostile Attempts should be made upon either by the French, or the Indians that are in their Interest.

BOSTON Sept. 10. By a Person who came to Town from the Westward, we are informed, that on the Lord's Day the forst Instant, two Indians got into a House , at Stockbridge, in the County of Hampshire, and kill'd and scalp'd a Woman and two Children, and afterwards shot a Man dead as he was riding to the Meeting, One Informer met with two of the three companies of Armed Men on their March from Connecticut to assist the Inhabitants on the Frontier.

We hear that a Road of Communication is order'd by his Excellency, to be made between Cusenock & Teconnet, for the Transportation of Stores, and marching Soldiers and will be Finished in a few Days: And General Winslow hath receiv'd a Message from the Norridgewalks, by two Delegates, affirming him their Satisfaction at the building the Fort at Teconnet, and that they shall shortly send a Number of their chiefs there to declare the same to him in form.

PHILADELPHIA Sept. 12. We hear that the French have lately been at the Plantation of one Vendall Brown, living in the back Part of Virginia, and kill'd his Stock of Cattle and Horses, and likewise destroyed all his Grain and other Effects.

NEW-YORK Sept. 16. By one of the Inhabitants of Hosak, near Albany, arrived here directly from thence, we are told, that on his return home to his Farm, after his Escape from the Indians in their Attack of the Place in August last, he found his own together with sundry of his Neighbours Plantations entirely destroy'd, all the Horses and Barns in the Neighbourhood, except two, burnt to ashes, himself without House or Home; and a great smell thro' out the Country by means of the Cattle that was kill'd.

BOSTON Sept. 17. We have Advice by an Express

from the Westward, That the Dutch Buildings at and about Housack were much of them burnt by the Indians, and also their Wheat, of which there was some Thousands of Bushels, their Horses, Cattle, Sheep, Hogs, &c. killed, the latter in some Places thrown into Heaps: The Damage is computed at Fifty Thousand Pounds York Currency: one Man killed and another captivated. That on Sabbath Day the first Instant, one Man was killed at Pontoosok, and a Man and two Children at Stockbridge the same Day, Several Scouts are ordered from one place to another, in order to discover the Approach of any large Number of the Enemy —— That one of the Scouts saw a Man come out of the City of Albany the 2d Instant, who inform'd that some Gentlemen of the City were desirous he would go to Fort Massachusetts, and acquaint them, that on the 25th or 26th of Aug. Forty-two or Forty-four Canoes of Indians, with five, six or seven in a Canoe, cross'd the Lake, with a Design to make a decent on our Frontier; which Account they had from the French indians then in the City —— That the People in the new Plantations were under great Surprize, and were generally withdrawn, except some few that have shut themselves up in poor Forts and pickted Houses —— A Number of Men rais'd in several Towns in the County of Hampshire, being on their March for the Relief & Defence of Stockbridge and other Places expos'd to the Enemy, were met by a large Number which some gather'd from many Parts of Connecticut.

WILLIAMSBURG Sept. 19. On Monday last arrived here, from Winchester, Capt. Waddil, of the North-Carolina Regiment, who brought with him, under and Escort Monsieur Le Force, who is now confined in the publick Goal in this City.

BOSTON Sept. 23. By a Vessel from Fort Halifax, at Teconnet Falls on Kennebeck River, we have Advice, that by this Time it is expected the Works at that Fortress and Fort Western at Cushnoc, are finished, and also the Road of Communication between those two Forts; and that the Remainder of the Soldiers rais'd for the late Expedition upon Kennebeck River (except such a Number as shall be left in Garrison for the

Defence of the Forts there) are dismissed together with General Winslow, and the other Officers, will soon return to Boston.

A few Days ago came to Town by Land, five Frenchmen, who on Friday last were examined before his Excellency and the Council, and we hear they gave the following Account of themselves, viz. That they belonged to the French Army near the River Ohio, which being in want of Provisions, and their Service very hard, they with 27 others, deserted to Col. Washington, who sent them all away a litthe before the fatal Action on the third of July. ——— That the French Soldiers in general were so dissatisfied with their Service, that if the English had a Force in those Parts sufficient to protect them, they would all Desert, except the Officers. ———
That the other 25 Deserters had disposed of themselves some in one Place and some in another among the English, but that those five being desirous to get to England, came hither for that purpose, with Letters of Credence from Colonel Washington, &c.

BOSTON Sept. 24. We have the following Article from the New-York Papers.

Paris (in France) July 1. The Earl of Albemarle has made Representation to the King's Ministers about the present Sitiation of Affairs in North America. It seems, as our Court sets forth, that the Commandant of the French Troops in Canada, being desirous to secure that Province from being insulted by the Indian Allies of the English, have advanced toward a River called Ohio, in order to cover their Territories on that Side, & maintain themselves in the Enjoyment of the Lands that make Part of their Ancient Possession. However we hope that the Hostilities committed in those Parts will not be attended with very bad Consequences, and that all Things will be made easy, as soon as the two Crowns come to a right Understanding about the Limits of their respective Possessions.

BOSTON Sept. 24. We are inform's His Excellency at his late Visit to Taconnet and Cushnoc, nam'd the Fort lately erected at the former of those Places, Fort Halifax, and that of the

Latter, Fort Western: and that the Ceremony of naming the former was perform'd by his Excellency's laying the Corner-Stone, the Garrison being drawn up under Arms; after which he drank Success to Fort Halifax; which was seconded by a general Discharge of Cannon there.

ANNAPOLIS Sept. 26. Last Monday a party of Soldiers raised in this Province to go against the French on the Ohio, marched out of Town, for Fredrick County, under the Command of Lieut. John Forty; & we hear the Remainder will march the beginning of next Week.

BOSTON Sept. 30. Friday last, in the Afternoon, Capt. Saunders, in the Province Sloop, arrived here from Kennebeck-River, in the Eastern Part of the Province, and brought with him Major-General Winslow, with several other Officers; and in the Evening three other Sloops arrived with between three and four hundred Soldiers: These had all served in the late Expedition, which being over, they are now discharged.

We are told, that the Road between Fort Western at Cushnoc, and Fort Halifax at Taconnet is finished, and about 130 Men are left in Garrison at the two Forts above-mentioned.

OCTOBER 1754

BOSTON Oct. 1. Last Friday arrived here from the Eastward the Sloop Massachusetts, Capt. Saunders, with Major-General Winslow Commander of the Land Forces rais'd by the Government, for the late Expedition to those Parts; and also several Transport Vessels with most of the Officers and Soldiers employ'd in the said Expedition, generally in very good Health; By whom we learn, That Fort Hallifax at Taconnet, and Fort Western at Cushnoc were almost Completed, the Cannon & Mortars mounted, and a sufficient Number of Men left to garrison each of them: And also, that a Road of Communication had been open'd by Land, from one Fort to the other, which is 18 Miles in Length.

WILLIAMSBURG Oct. 3. Last Monday Captain Dogworthy's Company of Soldiers march'd out of Town under the Command of Lieutenant John Bacon, and are to join the others in Frederick County.

WILLIAMSBURG Oct. 3. By Lieut. Lyon, who arrived here last Tuesday from Fort Duquesne, upon the Ohio, (whether he was sent by Col. Innes with a Flag of Truce, and which he left the 22th of last Month) we are Advised, that at that Time, the whole force of the French at that Fort, did not exceed 100 Men, and those very indifferently supplied with Provisions, &c. His chief business there was to propose to the French Commander, an Exchange of Monsieur Druillon, and two Cadets, for Mossieurs Stobo and Van Braan, which would not be accepted of on which Account Mr. Stobo was ordered away for Montreal, the Day Lieutenant Lyon left the Fort.

CHARLESTOWN South Carolina Oct. 3. Monday last came an Account that Twenty-five of the Settlers on Broad-River, (a Branch of the Santee) were lately so Murder'd and scalp'd in and about their Houses; and that more were missing: And on Tuesday, we hear, an Express came to Town on this Occasion. We cannot yet inform our Readers by what Indians these Murders were committed, but we may reasonably suppose them to be French. The first Person that discovered this Scene, was a young Man who had been at some Distance to be married, and on his Return found his Father and Mother, then others, murdered as aforesaid.

BOSTON Oct. 8. His Excellency's Speech to the Great and General Court or Assembly of the Province on Friday Oct. 8th 1754.

Gentlemen of the Council and House of Representatives,

In Compliance with the Request of the late Assembly contain'd in the Message of both Houses to me on the 9th of April last, and your own Vote pass'd in the May Session following, I caus'ed Eight Hundred Men to be rais'd for the Service therein mention'd and soon after the Rising of this Court embark'd, in Company with them, for Falmouth in Casco-Bay, where I had separate Interviews and Conferences with the Norridgewalk and Penobscot Indians: After the former of these was finish'd, I caus'd the Forces and Workmen to proceed to the River Kennebeck, for building a new Fort there above that at Richmond, with Orders for a Detachment of five Hundred of the former to march to the Head of the River, and the great Carrying-Place between that and the River Chaudiere; and to remove any French Settlements which might be found; and I took measures as much as was possible, the Execution of these several Matters under my immediate Care and Direction, according to the particular Desire of the Assembly expir'd in the before-mention'd Message to me.

You are already Gentlemen, fully acquainted from the printed Copies of the Journal of my Proceedings at Falmouth, before and at the time of the two Conferences, (which for saving your Time at this Session, I order'd to be printed and distributed among you for your Perusal during the Recess of the Court) with the Intelligence, I receiv'd after my arrival there, of the

Practice of the French Jesuit of the Penebscot Indians for preventing the Tribe, and the Norridgewalks from meeting me, and the Influence his Artifices had upon the Penobscots; As also of the Sign'd Letter writen by him in the Name of the Tribe to the Governor of Canada, with a View of exciting him to send Forces to oppose the March of our troops, on Pretence of their being sent to dispossess the Indians of their Lands; and likewise with the Particulars and Result of the two Conferences I had with the Norridgewalk and Penobscots, and the Reason why I chose to speak with those Tribes separately: I shall therefore refer you for an Account of these Matters to that Journal.

The Place which I pitch'd upon for erecting the New Fort, and for my better Information caus'd to be survey'd, together with the Navigation of the River between that and Richmond, as also the Lands adjacent, and to have a Plan taken of it, before I left Boston, is a Fork or Point of the Land form'd by the meeting of the Rivers Kennebeck and Sabastoocook, the latter of which empties itself into the former at the Distance of about three Quarters of a Mile from the Falls of Taconnet.

The Spot, which is thirty-seven Miles higher up the River Kennebeck than the old Fort Richmond, and the utmost extent, to which it was advisable or safe to carry a Fort up the River at first, is computed to be not quite fifty Miles distant from Penobscot, and, as measur'd by the Chain and Compass, is not more than thirty-one fron Norridgewalk by Water, and twenty-two by Land; and is on many accounts the most advantageous one for the Situation of a Fort, between that and Richmond.

The only known Communication, which the Penobscots have with the River Kennebeck and Norridgewalk Indians inhabiting it, is thro' the River Sabastoocook, by means of a Carrying-Place which they cross within ten Rods Distance from Taconnet Falls; and their most commodious Passage from Penobscot to Quebeck lies thro' Kennebeck to the River Chaudiere.

But as the River Kennebeck is not navigable

for Sloops beyond Cushenock, and the Navigation between that and Taconnet, being eighteen Miles, is for much the greatest Part of it, so incumber'd with Shoals and Rocks, and strong Currents occasioned by frequent Falls, that the Transportation of bulkey and heavy Stores in impracticable, unless perhaps in the Time of the Freshets; not only the carrying up a Fort as high as Taconnet, but the supporting of it, when built, appear'd to be attended with inseparable Difficulties, unless a large defensible Storehouse should be built at Cushenock, to lodge the Province Stores at their Passage to Taconnet.

To remedy this, the Proprietors of some Lands upon Kennebeck River, commonly call'd The Plymouth Company, made me an offer, that if I would cause the intended Fort to be erected at Taconnet, they would at their Expence build at or near Cushenock, as I should order, a House of hewn Timber no less than ten Inches thick, one hundred feet long, thirty two wide, and sixteen high, for the Reception of the Province's Stores, with conveniencies for lodging of the Soldiers, who may be placed there by the Government; and would picket it in at thirty Feet distance from every Part of the House, and build a Block-House of 24 Feet Square at two of the opposite Angles, to be mounted with four Cannon, agreeable to a Plan ready to be exibited when it should be call'd for; the Government to protect the People while employ'd in building the said House; which Vote and Plan shall be communicated to you.

This offer I readily accepted for the Province, and that the Company hath built a fortify'd Storehouse at Cushenock according to the said Plans, which will not only serve to lodge the public Stores in, but add to the Defence and Protection of the River, and greatly encourage Settlements upon it: And to make it still more beneficial, I have caus'd a Road of Communications between Cushenock and Taconnet and to be clear'd for Wheel-Carriages, whereby the Trasportation of Stores by Land from Fort Western at the former to Fort Halifax at the latter, in the space of one day, will be render'd practicable, and the want of a convenient Carriage by Water supply'd.

A Plan of Fort Halifax, Gentlemen, shall be lay'd before you: It is capable of entertaining four Hundred Men, and when garrison'd with a Hundred is sufficient Strength to withstand any Assault, which may be reasonably expected to be made upon it, either by Indians or French with small-Arms. And transport Cannon and Mortars by Land to attack it, there is but little Danger of their attempting to do that soon; and I doubt not but it will effectually answer the Service for which it is design'd in every Respect.

The March from Tacconet was perform'd by 500 Men on both Sides of the River Kennebeck up the the great Carrying Place at the Head of it, and as far as the first Pond upon that; which is computed by the Indians to be half Way over it; to which Bounds I thought it most advisable to limit the March: It was seventy five Miles in length, and ingoing from Taconnet took up ten Days and a half, but the Return from the Head of the Pond to Taconnet was perform'd in four Days and a half: In this March the County and River was measur'd and survey'd by Chain and Compass, and a Plan taken of it, which I shall order the Secretary to lay before you.

No Sign of any French Settlements were found; However, I can't but think, Gentlemen, for several Reasons, that the information given us by the Indians concerning that Matter, was founded upon what they had heard the French declare they had a Design upon their Hands in the Ohio.

As many unforeseen Events might happen in the Course of this Expedition which would require further immediate Support, and fresh Orders to be sent, it seem'd to me requisite that I should remain as near as it was impracticable, to prevent Intelligence from being carry'd the the Governour of Canada, of all our Motions, and the Strength of our Forces; and a Report of War's having been lately declar'd in England against France prevail'd at that Time: I therefore propos'd this for the Consideration of his Majesty's Council then with me at Falmouth; who unanimously advised, "that I should remain at Falmouth until the Troops should judge, his Majesty's Service requir'd my stay, upon the Advices I should receive from Major-General Winslow."

This, Gentlemen, was agreeable to the late Assembly's special Request to me, that I would make a Voyage to the Eastern Parts, and there take the immediate Care and Direction of those affairs upon me: Wherefore I determin'd to stay at Falmouth, and retain a Quorum of his Majesty's Council to assist me with their Advice in all Cases which might require it: And for maintaining as constant an expedition as corresponds with the General and Officers of the Forts upon the River Kennebeck as was possible, I settled a Route for Expresses by Whaleboats to be continually passing and repassing between Falmouth and Taconnet upon all needful Occasions; by which Means I might receive Dispatches from Fort Halifax in about Nineteen Hours, and return my Orders thither in Twenty four: How necessary this was to be done, the frequent Dispatches, which pass'd between me and the General, and his Absence between me and Major Fry, shew'd us more and more: The Service of the Expedition must have been at least much retarded and attended with more considerable Expence, if not insuperable Difficulties, in some material Parts, without it, and after all this, and the Opportunity I had of conferring with the General at Falmouth soon after his Return from his March, I found it necessary for me in order to secure in the most effectual manner the Execution of some principal Parts of the Service, to make a Visit to Fort Western and Fort Halifax, which I did; and I think every Thing which could be propos'd to be done within the Time for which the Troops were rais'd is executed in the best Manner it can be expected.

The General's Journal Gentlemen, of the proceedings from the Day the Troops Sailing from Casco-Bay being the 4th of July, to the time of their landing at Cushenoc, and his accounts of their Proceedings afterward to the End of them, and on the State in which he left Fort Halifax, contain'd in his Letter to me dated the 21st of September (copies of both which the Secretary shall lay before you) Will I am perswaded, satisfy you how well the Troops comply'd their Time: And I should not do Justice to the Officers in general, if I did not express to you my Approbation of their Behaviour in the whole Course of the Service: But the Extraordinary Vigilance, activity, and good Conduct of the Chief Commander in every Part of his Command and of his principal Officers, in Performing the several Parts of their Duty under him; Particularly in the Transportation of the Cannon and Military Stores from Cushenock to Taconnet, and the March from thence to the Middle of the Carrying-Place, and back to Fort Halifax, merit an especial Regard.

As to the nine Days the Troops remain'd incamp'd on Rang's-Island from the Time of their Arrival at Casco-Bay, to the Day of their Imbarkation for Kennebeck; I did not think it proper that they should proceed to execute any Part of the intended Service, before I had finish'd the Conference with the Norridgewalk Indians: —— Tho' I had determined to have the March made to the Head of Kennebeck River, and half way over the Carrying-Place, and have a Forts erected at Cushenock and Taconnet, whether they gave their Consent or not; yet that might have given them, or the French, too much Colour to have tax'd us with stealing an Opportunity to march thro' the Country of the Norridgewalks, and build Forts upon the Kennebeck, whilst we had drawn them to Falmouth, and engag'd them in Treaty with us there: such a Reproach would have ill suited the Honour of this Government; where as now we have obtain'd their declar'd Consent in a formal Treaty, not only to our doing this, but to the making of new Settlements upon the River; to all which they were ever before, and even at the beginning of the late Conference, greatly averse; And besides, I am perswaded that this Appearance of the Troops at Casco contributed not a little to our gaining this Consent from them.

In effecting these Services, Gentlemen, I have

been as good an Husband for the Province as I could within hazading the success of them by an ill tim'd Parsimony. I dismis'd the Ship which was taken up to carry me, and such of the Genthemen of both Houses as thought fit to accompany me. to Falmouth, and attend the Conferences there with the Indians, as soon as it had carry'd those Gentlemen back to Boston, and brought others of his Majesty's council to Falmouth; and equal Care was taken in dismissing the Transports after the Soldiers were landed at Cushenock, no more of which were retailed, that what it was judg'd necessary to remain there for the Troops and Materials for building Fort Halifax; the Troops were likewise discharg'd from Time to Time as soon as ever the Service would admit it; and although the Expence of this Expedition will exceed the sum which was at first rais'd for the Service of it, yet I hope the good Fruits of it will make the Province a considerable Gainer by it in the End.

Though the Troops. Gentlemen, found no French Settlements to be remov'd; yet by their late March on both Sides of the River Kennebeck to the Head of it, and the first Pond on the Carrying-Place; you have probably prevented them from Attempts to make one there; and gain'd the Knowledge of a River and Country, which it behov'd you as nearly to be acquainted with, and perhaps any other River in the Province, and of which you knew very little before, higher up than Richmond Fort.

You are now in Possession of the Part of the River Kennebeck, near which was the Place of general Rendezvous for the Eastern Indians inhabiting as far as the River St. Francois and the Village of Becancour, in Time of War, and from whence the Province felt continual Devastation in its Eastern Parts by their Incursions in 1723, and 1724.

And tho' the good Effects of this Expedition should ever reach no further than the present Time (which I am perswaded will not be the Case) yet I might venture to say that it has sav'd the Province more than the whole Charge of it will amount to: For if it is consider'd what was the

Spirit of the Eastern Indians in the Spring of the Year, excited by our Neighbours of Canada, and the French Jesuits sent from thence among them, it must be acknowledg'd that in the situation of our Affairs there was not the least Probability that any other Expedients could have prevented the Miseries, and much greater Expence of a general War with the Eastern Indians from the beginning of the Summer, than that which we have put in Practice.

I have one more Advantage still to mention, will arise to the Province from the Expedition; I have the Pleasure to let you know from a Letter which I have had the Honour to receive very lately from the Right Honourable Sir Thomas Robinson, one of his Majesty's Principal Secretaries of State which shall be communicated to you have the utmost Reason to be assur'd that the Part which this Government hath acted in it, will meet with his Majesty's Royal Approbation; and recommend the Welfare of the Province greatly to his immediate Attention.

And now, Gentlemen of the House of Representatives, I hope you will chearfully and immediately make the Supplies necessary for Paying off the Soldiers employ'd in the Service, all which are now disbanded, except 120, which I have retain'd out of the impress'd Men, and old Garrison at Richmond Fort, as necessary at present for the Forts at Kennebeck viz. 100 to garrison Fort Halifax, and 20 for Fort Western; together with all other just debts which has attended this Service, as well as other Services for the Support of the Government, and the necessary Defence of the Inhabitants, particularly what has been unavoidable occasion'd by the Assaults made by the Canadian Indians on our Western Frontiers during my absence in the Eastern Parts; and which was needful, for Depredations of the Indians.

The Informations I have receiv'd of those Disasters, and the Orders I gave out thereupon, shall be laid before you: And in a special Manner I must recommend to you to provide for the Establishment of the Garrisons I have left on Kennebeck for the Defence of the two Forts there, and to secure to us the Possession of that River, as also for maintaining the Scouts proposed by Col. Israel Williams, in his Letter of the 12th of September last (which shall be lay'd before you) to be kept up between Fall-Town and Hudson River, for the Protection of the Western Frontier: And some particular Person in those Parts have been at great Expence in fortifying their Houses, and thereby actually made a Stand against the Enemy, which is of public Service, I would recommend it to you Gentlemen, to make them some Allowance for this extraordinary Expence, that they may not be ruin'd by it.

I shall order the Treasurer and Commissary General to prepare the Accounts of what has already been expended, and what still remains due to defrey the whole Debt contracted by the Government.

Gentlemen of the Council and House of Representatives,

I shall now lay before you a Journal of the Proceedings of the Commissioners of several Provinces and Colonies in the late Convention at Albany, wherein (besides their renewal of the League with the Indians of the Six Nations) is contain'd a Representation of the dangerous State of his Majesty's Dominions in North America are in, by reason of the Encroachments and Power of the French, and their growing influence over the Indians; with a Scheme by the said Commissioners projected and agreed upon for such Union between all English Governments in North America, as was by them judg'd necessary for their Mutual Defence: This is an Affair of such Moment; as will require your most deliberate Attention, and the speediest Dispatch to ripen it for the seasonable Consideration of the Parliament of Great-Britain, whose Authority is judg'd requisite for effecting and consolidating so desirable an Union.

I think it material to lay before you an Extract from a private Letter which hath been Communicated to me, dated at Onoh'quanghe the 14th of September, last, in which among other Things there is a Paragraph, "Our Indians inform us, that the French spare no Pains to disengage the Six Nations from the English, and attach them to their Interest. —— That the Governor of Canada has sent six Battoes into their Country with Goods, two of the Oneida's Castle, two to the Cayougas's, and two to the Onandaga's; and that a French Priest lately sent a Belt of Wampum to Oneody, to prepare the way for his Reception among them. The Priest tells them that he compssionates their Ignorance, and is desirous, with their Leave, to come and instruct them in the Christian Religion."

If the last Circumstance, Gentlemen is true, we must look upon it as done with the Privity, at least, if not by the Direction of the Government of Canada; and if the French are suffered to put in Practice this Artifice among the Indians of the Six Nations, we may give them up entirely lost to the English.

I therefore think it my Duty to observe, that it is a most unwarrantable Practice in the French, under the Pretence of gospelizing the Indians, to send their Missionary Priests into his Majesty's Territories, and the Countries subject by the Treaties to his Dominion, in order to debauch the Indians there in Alliance and Friendship with the English, from their Fidelity and Attachment to him; and engage them in Acts of Rapine and Slaughter against his Subjects: It is the suffering of this, that we chiefly owe the Mischiefs and Depredations we have for so many Years felt from our Eastern Indians: And I think it high Time that some public Notice should be taken of this Practice to the Government of Canada, expressing a proper Resentment at this injurious Treatment; and I should be glad of your Advice upon this Matter.

Gentlemen of the House of Representatives, I hope you will proceed in raising the necessary Supplies with the same Spirit of Unanimity and Dispatch which was exerted in providing for the Service of the late Expedition; it would be extremely happy at the Conjuncture if you could agree upon such Ways and Means of gathering in the Taxes as would be the least exceptionable, to the People in general, as well as what would secure the Sums which the Funds ought to Produce.

Gentlemen,
I am sensible it is still a busy Season for Husbandry Affairs, and therefore I would not detain you at this Session longer than the business to be done in it shall require your attention.

Council-Chamber, October 8th 1754

W. Shirley.

NEW-YORK Oct. 14. We hear the General Assembly of New-Jersey, has resolved on assisting the Virginians in the Ohio Affair.

On Thursday last his Majesty's Ship Shoreham, the Hon. Julian Legg, Esq; Commander sailed from Sandy-Hook, bound for Virginia with 5000 Pounds in Cash on board, granted by the Province in order to aid the Virginians, in repelling the French and their Indians, from the Frontiers of that Province.

CHARLESTOWN SOUTH CAROLINA Oct. 17. We hear that there were 16 of the Settlers om Broad-River murdered, but they were 14 carried away Captive; that a young Man (one of the 14) had made his Escape from the Indians, the Day after being taken, while they were rejoicing at having met with another large Body of their Nation; that the young Man avoided a Pursuit by taking a River, and swimming near 5 Miles, and saw the Indians come down to the Place where he took the Water; and that he said they were all French Indians.

WILLIAMSBURG Oct. 18. Yesterday the General Assembly of this Colony met at the Capital in this City, when His Honor the Governor opened the Session with the following Speech,

Gentlemen of the Council, Mr. Speaker, and Gentlemen of the House of Burgesses.

I once more call you together, to consult on the unjustifiable Invasion and Encroachment of the French; and I am in Hopes, that during your short Recess, you have seriously considered the miserable Circumstaces of your Affairs, and, in Course, the absolute Necessity of granting immediate, considerable, and adequate Supplies; to unable me to put a Stop to their injurious Designs, and to drive them from His Majesty's Lands upon the Ohio.

I have the Pleasure to acquaint you, that His Majesty, considering the pernicious Measures taken by the French, and the great Regard he bears for his Subjects in these Colonies, has been graciously pleased to send me Ten Thousand Pounds Sterling in Specie, and also to order from his Royal Stores, Two Thousand Stands of Arms, with their proper Accoutrements, which I daily expect the Arrival of, for your Aid and use.

Gentlemen of the House of Burgesses,
The distinguished Marks of His Majesty's paternal Care for His Subjects in these Colonies; His Solicitude for the safety; and His earnest Desires to defeat the Designs of the French; I hope will raise in you a just Dense of Duty and Gratitude to the best of Kings, and engage you more effectual Attention to His Majesty's repeated Commands for granting Supplies.

The voice of Nature, Gentlemen, and what you are sensible is among the most prevailing Motives of human Actions, your own interest, loudly call on you with the most urging Emphasis, to rouse from your Inactivity and assert their Rights.

And can you continue deaf to such Interest? Shall your Posterity, groaning under the galling Yoke of civil and religious Slavery, dispoiled of every Thing that renders Life desirable, amidst their Despondence, find their Misery still aggravated by reflecting on the Cause? That their own Progenitors, who might have transmitted to them Inviolated, the Liberties, the Properties, and the pure Religion that they enjoyed; by a Supineness and Neglect, as unaccountable, as it was unnatural, suffered all to be taken from them!

Gentlemen, The Eyes of His Majesty, nay, of all your Fellow Subjects, are fixed on your present Determination. I wish I had Words strong enough to convey to you the absolute Necessity there is at this Time for a generous Supply; but Words cannot be so strong as Facts. Consider what the Enemy have done, and what they further threaten to do; and I am convinced that is sufficient to raise the Spirit of every

British Subject to an immediate Resentment, and thorough Resolution, with their Lives and Fortunes, to repel the impending Ruin.

Let me prevail with you then, Gentlemen, to prevent Evil, that, but in Prospect, must affect ever serious Considered with Honor; and be persuaded to exert the true Spirit of Patriotism, and convince the World that no Motive can impede, or any Consideration whether, Obstruct, the great and important Business now recommended to your Consideration.

It is at this Time, that, by an Exertion of your Strength, you may answer the Expectation of His Majesty promote the Interest of Great Britain, secure the Peace and Happiness of your Country, and by a brave, vigorous and united Effort entirely defeat the Machinations of France, the ancient Enemy of Great Britain, and the Disturber of Mankind.

Gentlemen of the Council, Mr. Speaker, and Gentlemen of the House of Burgesses,

At this critical Juncture, I sincerely recommend you, Harmony and Unanimity, ever propitious to public Councels, never more indispensably necessary than on this Occasion. Let all Cavils and Disputes Subside, and cordially unite in concerning the most suitable Measures to be persuaded in the present evident Emergency. For my Part I do assure you that I will, with the greatest Pleasure, join with you in every Step you take for these just and salutary Purposes, agreeable to my Instructions.

WILLIAMSBURG Oct. 18. Last Saturday Evening arrived here his Excellency Horatio Sharpe Esq; Governor of Maryland, who we hear, has a Commission from his Majesty as Commander in Chief of the Forces that are or may be raised to defend the Frontiers of this and the neighbouring Colonies, and to repel the unjustifiable Invasion and Incroachments of the French, on the River Ohio; and that his Excellency intends to set out very shortly, to take the Command on him.

NEW-JERSEY Oct. 22. To his Excellency Jonathan Belcher, Esq; Captain General, Governour and Commander in Chief in and over His Majesty's

Province of New-Jersey, and Territories thereon depending in America, Chancellor and Vice-Admiral in the same &c.

The Humble Address of the Representatives of said Province in General Assembly met.

May it please your Excellency,

We his Majesty's most dutiful and loyal Subjects, the Representatives of the Colony of New-Jersey, in the General Assembly met, beg Leave to acquaint your Excellency, that we have taken the Incroachments of the French (with their Indians) upon His Majesty's Territories, into our most serious Consideration.

We can truly say, we want not Arguements to convince us of the absolute Necessity of the strictest Union among all his Majesty's Provinces and Colonies for the Preservation of the whole; and on our Part have endeavoured to cultivate a Union, by contributing our Endeavours in the best Manner the Circumstances of this Colony will admit. Your Excellency must be sensible that the Scarcity of a Currency in this Colony at this Time, makes it very difficult for the Inhabitants to exert themselves as fully as the Exigency of the Times seem to require: And therefore, we cannot doubt, but the measures we have fallen upon, not only to give a handsome Sum to the King's Use at present, but to provide a fund to do it hereafter, in Case of a like Necessity, will prove agreeable to your Excellency, and all concerned.

We have duly considered the Militia Act now in Force, and are of Opinion it will sufficiently answer the Proposes intended by it.

We have also taken into Consideration the Plan for the Union of the British Colonies on the Continent of America, as agreed on in the late Congress at Albany; and are sorry to say, that we find Things in it, which, if carried into Practice, would affect our Constitution in its very Vitals; and for that Reason we hope and believe they will never be countenanced by a British Legislature.

We thank your Excellency, for the Care and Concern you have shewn in the several Matters recommended to us; and we hope Unanimity and

Dispatch with which they have severally been treated in this House, will recommend our Determination, and be agreeable to your Excellency.
By order of the General Assembly.
                    Robert Lawrence, Speaker.
BOSTON Oct. 30. To His Excellency William Shirley, Esq; Captain-General and Governor in Chief, in and over His Majesty's Province of Massachusetts-Bay.

The humble Address of the Council, and House of Representatives of said Province.

We His Majesty's loyal and dutiful Subjects, the Council, and House of Representatives of the Province of Massachusetts-Bay, return your Excellency our sincere and hearty Thanks for the Particulars Account, which your Speech you have given us of the late Expedition to the Head of the River Kennebeck, and of your proceedings in the Eastern Parts of the Province.

We thank your Excellency for undertaking so troublesome and fatiguing a Voyage.

His Majesty's Service and general Interest of his Governments on this Continent, we are well assured, were the Motive which prevailes with you to be absent from your Family, and the Seat of Government so much longer than was expected.

We are convinc'd of your Excellency's great Prudence in holding a Conference with the Indians of the Penobscot and Norridgewalk Tribes at so seasonable a Juncture; A Conference so judiciously manag'd that we with it may serve as a Precedent in all Treaties with those Indians for the future.

We have a grateful Sense of your Excellemcy's constant Attention to the Affairs of the Expedition which was at first propos'd by your Excellency, and readily agreed to by the Assembly.

You have given the necessary Orders from Time to Time in the several Steps of it; and these Orders , thro' the Favour of Divine Providence have been executed with desired Success.

The Indians, by your Excellency's Influence, have agreed to Measures which under the Instigation of the French, they have heretofore express'd a great Aversion to.

A new Fort hath been erected for His Majesty's

Service in a valuable Country, possess'd & improv'd by the Crown of Great-Britain, above an Hundred Years ago: And we have obtain'd an exact knowledge of a Part of the Province which we were but too little Acquainted: May this be an happy Prelude to a farther Extention of his Majesty's actual Possessions, even to the utmost Bounds of his just Claim: And may the Steps, which have been taken, lead in proper Time to such further Measures, as shall effectually prevent our restless and perfidious Neighbours from all attempts to invade his Majesty's Territories on any Part of the Continent.

It gives us Pleasure to find, that the Officers & Soldiers have perform'd their several Parts so much to your Excellency's Acceptance, and the Honour of their Country: We hope the same Spirit will remain in them, if there should be further Occasion for their Service.

We very well knew before we engag'd in this Expedition, that an heavy Charge must be the necessary Consequence of it: And here we would humbly beg leave to represent to your Excellency, that although we have and shall at all Times chearfully exert out utmost Strength, in the Defence and Security of his Majesty's American Dominions, yet we apprehend it impossible in the present distress'd Circumstances of the Province, to maintain a Force necessary for the Defence of so extensive a Frontier, and therefore we must humbly rely upon his Majesty's paternal Goodness, through the Interposition of your Excellency's good Offices, for Assistance as to the Charge we have been, and may be at; and rest assur'd, that we shall never be expos'd to Ruin by our Seal for his Majesty's Service; especially as what we have done is for the Safety not only of this, but all his Majesty's Governments.

Your Excellency could not have communicated to us any Advices more acceptable, than those which you have receiv'd from the Right Honourable Sir Thomas Robinson, one of his Majesty's principal Secretaries of State; His Majesty's great Condescension in this signifying his Royal Approbation of our Conduct had made a very sensible Impression upon us which cannot easily be effac'd: We hope we shall never render ourselves unworthy of his Royal Favour.

Your Excellency has recommended to our Consideration the transactions of the Commissioners from several of his Majesty's Governments at Albany in the Summer past: We are expecting the Report of the Commissioners on the Part of this Province, and when the same is laid before us, we imagine that we shall be better able to judge what is proper for us to do on this Occasion.

October 30, 1754. In the Name and by the Order of the Council.   J. Willard, Secry.

In the Name and Order of the House of Representatives   T. Hubbard Spr.

To which Address His Excellency was pleased to make the following Answer.

Gentlemen of the Council and House of Representatives,

I thank you for your Address delivered to me by your Committee: The sense, you therein Express of my Attention to his Majesty's Service and the general Interests of this Governments on this Continent, as well as to that of the Province in particular, in the Course of the late Expedition, as also of the Success which hath hitherto attend it, give me very great Satisfaction.

I shall with great Pleasure exert my best offices to procure for you all needful Assistance, as to the charge you have been or may be at in Consequence of this Expedition or any other Future Instance of your Zeal for his Majesty's Service.

I am persuaded what you have now done in for the Safety not only of this, but, all His Majesty's Governments in North-America.

         October 31st, 1754.   W. Shirley.

NOVEMBER 1754

BOSTON Nov. 5. By Express from Fort Halifax in Taconnet at the Eastward, Advice is brought, that about a Week ago, Men belonging to the Fort went out a small Distance from the same to procure a Piece of Timber, when they were fir'd upon and pursu'd by some Indians who kill'd one, carried away four into captivity, and one made his Escape into the Fort.

WILLIAMSBURG Nov. 7. On Saturday last the General Assembly was prorogued, when his Honour the Governour was pleased to make the following Speech.

Gentlemen of the Council, Mr. Speaker, and Gentlemen of the House of Burgesses,

I Sincerely thank you for your Vote of Supply, for conducting the necessary Expedition. I shall take proper Care of representing to his Majesty our Loyalty, & the Aid you have granted.

Be assured, Gentlemen, the Money now given shall be, with great frugality, and due Occonomy, applied for the Use it's intended.

And you have unanimously granted this Supply, I am to desire your Interest in the different Counties you Represent, to encourage the Subjects, by your Arguments, and Reasons, freely to enlist for the Protection of our Lives, and Fortunes; and to give your Countenance to such Officers that may be commissioned to raise the Levies.

And I heartily desire Love and Friendship may subsist among the different Ranks of our People. Your Example, Gentlemen will be great Encouragement to others; and I hope, for the future, generous Benevolence will incite every Member of the Community, to a due and just Regard, for the Happiness, and peace of the whole.

I therefore prorogue you to the second Thursday

in March next, and you are accordingly prorogued to that Time.

BOSTON Nov. 11. About a Week ago, we had Advice by an Express from Fort Halifax, on Kennebeck River, that a few Days before, as six Men belonging to the Fort, were out upon Business at some distance from it, they were fired upon by Indians, who kill'd one (whose name was Newell, of Lynn) took four Prisoners, and wounded the other, who notwithstanding some of 'em pursued him and threw their Hatchets after him, made his Escape to the Fort.

NEW-YORK Nov. 11. Last week arrived in this City, a young Woman aged about 19 Years. The Account she gives of herself is that when she was about seven Years old she was taken prisoner in Company with two other young Girls, by some French Indians, at her Aunt's, whose first Name she remembers to have been Lydia, where she, with the other Children were taught to Read, &c. The Indians carried her to their Village, where after being kept about a Year, she was sold to the French, at a Place called the Three Rivers, below Quebeck.

ANNAPOLIS Nov. 13. Last Tuesday Morning at Five o'Clock, his Excellency our Governor attended by some Officers of the Virginia Regiment, and others, set out from hence to Will's Creek.

CHARLESTOWN SOUTH CAROLINA Nov. 13. The following Speech was made by Governor Glen, of South-Carolina to the new-chosen Assembly of the Province.

I know no Province is a more happy and flourishing Condition than this; no Enemies interrupt the Peace we enjoy, no Parties discomposed the Tranquility that reigns among us; and to crown all, we have the Smiles of Heaven upon our Labour, in constant and plentiful Crops. But. American Affairs are subject to sudden Changes, this Sunshine may be soon obscured; and for some Time past Clouds have been gathering to the Northward that threaten to ruffle the Serenity of our Southern Skies, happy were it for us they had they been timely dispersed! but Matters seem to have now gone too far for an Eclaircissement, if you shall find this to be the Case, I doubt not that you will be of Opinion, that it is necessary to have Recourse to Force, for we cannot be idle unconcerned Spectators, if the Subjects of a Foreign Prince have presumed to make Encroachments on any Part of his Majesty's Dominions on this Continent, tho' not within the Limits of this Province: I hope therefore, we shall lose no Time, in concerting such Measures, with other Provinces, as the Common Safety of all the Provinces call for.

In such a Situation of Affairs, it is a great Comfort to me that I can promise myself the Assistance of the Council; I am Sensible of the happy Effects of it upon every Occasion; And it gives me particular Pleasure to see so many Gentlemen of Prudence and Consideration elected by their Country to represent it in the New General Assembly; the experience that I have had of former Assemblies forbids me to doubt of the Advice and Assistance of this; but yet, whoever happens to have the Helm in his Hand in such a Conjuncture will find it a critical one. A watchful Eye must be kept upon the French who as this present Moment are endeavouring to draw our Indians from our Interest. The greatest Attention must be given to these Indians for, tho' they be all in Treaty with us, yet they may not always prove so faithful as we have found them for some Years past; and, it must be considered, that they consist of many Thousands, all Accustomed to the use of Arms, and all acquainted with every Corner of the Country, But, Gentlemen, let us consider that the Eyes of all our own Indians; and the other Indian Nations, are at present open to the Behaviour of the British Provinces: If we permit the French to gain ground, we shall certainly lose the Indians; on the contrary, if we exert ourselves properly, we shall for ever fix their Friendship, and I am persuaded the French will never after choose to measure their Strength with ours on this Continent.

I know how unnecessary it is for me to say any Thing to animate you upon this great Occasion. If the Subjects of an absolute Prince can shew such Keeness to enlarge their Master's Territories; What Spirit and Zeal should inspire the Sons of Liberty in the Defence of theirs? for, not only our Country, but our Constitution is worth contending for; We enjoy the happiness and most perfect Government in the World; it is the Envy of all Nations; the Language off all Nations is, Who would not be a Briton? By this Constitution, this Colony, from small Beginning has in a short Space of Time, become very considerable, and highly beneficial to Great-Brittain: When our Fathers came from thence to settle here, they brought with them the Laws of the Mother Country as their Birth right; and a glorious Inheritance they are: They brought with them that inestimable jewel, the Privilege of enacting Laws for their good Government, without which they could have made no Progress; this Privilege I hope we shall ever possess, in the same pure Manner, we do at present, by three distinct Branches of the Legislature. The sure Way to do so is, to continue to use the greatest Care and Circumspection in passing our Laws; to be cautious not to intrench upon His Majesties Prerogative and just Rights, who during the Course of His glorious Reign has never invaded the Privilege of the meanest of his Subjects, to pass no Act by which the Inhabitants of this Province may be put upon a more Advantageous Footing than His Majesty's Subjects in Great-Britain, And in general, to pass no Laws of an unusual or extraordinary Nature, without inserting a Clause suspending the Execution thereof 'till His Majesty's Pleasure be known concerning the Same.   J. Glen.

  (The Assemblies Answer to this Speech is only expressive of their Duty and Loyalty to his Majesty; Affection of the Governor; a just resentment against the Encroachment of the French on the British Territories; and a becoming Resolution to unite against every Invader, in the Defence of every Part of His Majesty's American Dominions: After presenting their Address the 15th of November, the Day following they Adjourn'd themselves to the 6th of January.)

  WILLIAMSBURG Nov. 15. This Day marched from

this City 27 Recruits, in order to be embark'd at York for Alexandria, to serve against the French on the Ohio.

BOSTON Nov. 25. Whereas I am empowered by an Act of this Province made and passed at the present Session, to borrow a Sum not exceeding Six Thousand Pounds, to be applied for the Payment of the Officers and Soldiers concern'd in the late Expedition at Kennebeck, for which Monies so borrowed, I am directed to give my receipt of Obligation in behalf of the Province to repay by the first Day of December 1756, with lawful Interest for the same annually Paid:

This therefore to give Notice to all Gentlemen possessed of Cash. and dispos'd to lend the same, that I shall be ready to receive it on Friday next at my Office, where constant Attendance will be given.   H. Gray Treasurer.

BOSTON Nov. 26. By an Express from the Westward, we hear, That a number of Indians having lately come across the Lake, 'twas fear'd that an Assault was intended by them upon Stockbridge, or some other Settlements on our Western Frontier.

PHILADELPHIA Nov. 28. Extract of a Letter from a Gentleman in New-York, to his Friend here, dated November 13, 1754.

"The following Particulars I have just received from Albany, viz. The French Government at Canada, and his Clergy, are doing what they can to draw off the two Castles of Mokawks from us, which if not soon prevented, they will effect, promising them very largely, The Governor has sent by the last Cachnawaga's, a very hearty invitation to them to come to Canada, and that he will receive them with open Arms. The Onondaga's, Cayouga's and Tuscararoes, went to Canada last Month, to the Number of 140. The Indians at Oswego have behaved very insolently to our People, and more particularly so since Washington's Defeat.

Many French and Indians marched to the Ohio in September. Last Month twelve of the Cachnawaga's and Schaweidadda's were sent from Canada to the Shawana's and the River Indians, living at and about the Ohio; their Orders are to treat

with these Nations, and demand an Answer to the
Message sent them last Years by the Governor of
Canada; and they are to do what they can to
alienate them from us, or at least to make them
neuter in the Ohio Affair."

DECEMBER 1754

NEW-YORK Dec. 2. The Assembly of the Counties of New Castle, Kent, and Sussex upon Delaware, and Pennsylvania, at a Session held at New Castle the 22d of October past, after receiving several Messages from Governour Morris, in which he earnestly intreated them to contribute their best Endeavours for the Defence of this country; voted the Sum of One Thousand Pounds for his Majesty's Use, to better to enable Mr. Morris to act in Concert with the Governors of his Majesty's other Colonies, to repel the present unjust Invasion of his Majesty's Dominions.

By a private Letter from Philadelphia, we learn, that a Gentleman was just arrived from Will's Creek, who reported, that the French were 900 strong in Garrison at the Fort at the mouth of Monongehela; and that they are able to muster a Thousand more from the neighbouring Forts. By the same Letter we learn that the Regements are expected at Virginia from England, this Winter.

BOSTON Dec. 2. Extract of a Letter from Virginia.

"By what fatal Conduct our Scheme of driving the French from the Ohio was blown up. I don't doubt but before now is publickly talked of on London. The treating the French Troops with a contempt they never deserve, is the Reason given here for our Miscarriage; and we must wait till the Troops arrive from all the other Colonies before Misfortune can be repaired. I am afraid it will be but a little Advantage to us for the Government in England to send us great Guns for our Forts without sending People capable of managing them. The trifling Advantage gain'd over a Handful of French, who came to surprize our Convoy, by almost double their

Number, is, no doubt, the Occasion of our present unhappy Affair. It is a new Scheme of fighting, for 3 or 400 Men to go to seek the Enemy tripple their Number, when by only delaying and restraining the Impetuosity of their Courage for a few Days, they would have been able to have fought the Enemy even handed. I hope the Loss we have met with will be of no very bad Consequence, and only confirm us all in the Opinion of uniting with the other Colonies for the general Good, and for the future, instead of being so many single Twigs, which are easily broken, making one bundle that will be quite irresistible.

PHILADELPHIA Dec. 5. Extract of a Letter from an Officer at the Camp at Will's Creek, dated November 21, 1754.

"We have now got a Fort completed, with Barracks for our Men at the back of it, well built, and comfortable for the Winter —— We had the Pleasure of being joined three Days ago by his Excellency Col. Sharpe, with one Company from Maryland. —— Mr. Sharpe appears to be a stirring active Gentleman, and by his Method of proceeding, I believe a very good Soldier, chearful and free, a Man of good Conduct, and one who won't be trifled with. —— In the Spring if we have a good Body of Men, I make no doubt but we shall be able to do something to Purpose. By the present Situation of the French, they are not to be drove out of their Forts, without our Numbers are greatly increased."

ANNAPOLIS Dec. 5. Extract of a Letter from a Merchant in Philadelphia, to his Corespondent in Maryland November 22, 1754.

"Our Assembly are to meet the second of the Month: They will I believe, vote largely for the Ohio Affair; but I am afraid, the Governor's and the Governor's and their Obstinacy in Regard to the Sinking Fund, will prevent any Thing being done to Effect. Instead I am pretty well convinc'd that nothing considerable in the Military Way can ever be done by the Colonies in their present disunited State. —— The Plan of Union, as concerted by the Commissioners at Albany, if carried into Execution would soon make us a formidable People. Disinterested, Public Spirited, Men of Sense, who are vers'd in the Nature of Government, do declare that no objection can be made to it, but what likewise makes against all Kinds of Government, the English more especially: The Prerogative, the Rights of the People, are therein both preserved, without the least Infringement of one upon the other."

This Day his Excellency our Governor returned Home, from Will's Creek.

ANNAPOLIS Dec. 12. The Speech of his Excellency Horatio Sharpe, Esq; Governor and Commander in Chief in and over the Province of Maryland to both Houses of Assembly, an the 12th of December 1754.

Gentlemen of the Upper and Lower House of Assembly,

As the late Transactions of the French on the Continent, and the fatal Consequences, that must inevitably attend their Execution of the Scheme they have projected against us, have been so often descanted on, in the most public Manner, since the same unhappy Cause that calls us together at this disagreeable Season, first obliged me after my Arrival to desire an Extraordinary Meeting of the several Branches of this Legislature; I presume there is little Occasion for me, at this Time, to repeat the several Arguments as which the present Posture of Affairs must suggest to you, as sufficient Motives to prompt you to exert yourselves, at this important Juncture. You are not, I conceive, now to learn, that in Pursuance of a Plan to secure a Communication between their Northern and Southern Settlements, and, in Time, render themselves Masters of all the Continent, from Cape Breton to the Gulph of Mexico, that Restless and ambitious People have, proceeded to build several Forts on his Majesty's Lands; one especially at a small Distance from the Frontiers of this Province, and have it with a large Body of Regular Troops; that they already extend their Claim to Lands far within the Limits of this Province, and are making great Preperations for enlarging their Conquest; that not Satisfied with cutting us off from all Intercourse with the Indian Natives, with whom we have hitherto, it seems, presumed to carry on a Contraband Trade, they have employed Numbers of those Natives to depopulate and distress these Colonies; and have also themselves committed every Kind of Hostility on our Fellow Subjects, who have been unfortunate enough to be exposed to their Cruelty and the likes.

These, Gentlemen, are Circumstances they present to our View, no very agreeable Prospect, and I doubt not but the Reputation of them makes every one of us burn with Resentment, and urges us to take the most speedy and effectual Measures to prevent the dreadful Calamities that our Posterities must otherwise feel, from the vicinity of such People.

What Resolutions the Virginian have hereupon taken, I apprehend you are no Stranger to; and I am encouraged to hope, that the other neighbouring Governments, whom I have solicited will shew an equal Zeal, and emulate their Conduct. That your Resolutions will confirm the Opinion his Majesty has been pleased to entertain of you, and merit the Confidence that he has thought us to repose in the Affection and Loyalty of his Maryland Subjects, by distinguishing their Governor with the Honour of Commanding the combined Forces that shall be assembled to oppose the Enemy's hostile Attempts. I entertain the most sanguine Hopes, and that you will generously concur with the neighbouring Provinces, to unable me to answer his Majesty's Expectations, and Royal Intentions, in honouring me with such a Commission. A Commission also, from his Lordship the Lord Proprietary, whereby his Lordship, from an earnest Desire and Solicitude to contribute to the Restoration of Peace and Tranquility to this, and the other British Colonies, had been please to disperse with my temporary Absence from the Government, that I may pay the most ready and punctual Obedience to his Majesty's Commands, shall, with the Royal Commission, be laid before you: And I will assure you, that the View of being thereby enable to contribute in a more particular Manner, Then

I could have otherwise done, to the Security and future Quiet of this Province, makes me receive these testimonies of his Majesty's and Lord's Favour with infinite Pleasure, and enter on the Service with the greatest Alacrity. And Gentlemen, as my future Reputation will, in great Measure, depend on the Issue of the Meeting, I cannot help again repeating my Hopes, that your Resolves will be such, as must demand my Acknowledgements, and make it my future constant study to express my Gratitude, by my Endeavours to promote, to the utmost of my ability, the welfare and Prosperity of the People you are here to represent.

ANNAPOLIS Dec. 13. To his Excellency Horatio Sharpe, Esq; Governor and Commander in Chief in and over the Province of Maryland.

The humble Address of the upper House of Assembly.

May it please your Excellency,

We return your Excellency our sincere Thanks for your Speech at the Opening of this Session, and for calling us together, at this Time, when the common Safety so much requires the most effectual Measures to be taken, to repel the hostile Invasions of the French, who have now advances almost to our Door.

We would think ourselves unworthy the Blessings we enjoy, if, on this Occasion, and at this juncture, when so many Motives concur to induce us, we do not every Thing in our Power, to convince your Excellency the Hopes you have Placed in us are not vain.

We congratulate your Excellency upon the Honour his Majesty has done you, in promoting you to the Command of the combined Forces upon the Ohio, and ourselves in being so honoured in our Governor; but, we are sensible, which ever of his Majesty's Colonies had had the Happiness to be governed by your Excellency, would have been distinguish'd, and you would have been the Object of his Majesty's Choice.

His Lordship the Lord Proprietary's Regard to you, and inclination to promote your welfare, and his Goodness in Contributing his Endeavours for the Restoration of the Peace and Tranquility of this and the neighbouring Colonies, demand your most grateful Acknowledgement. Your Excellency's Abilities, are sure Presages to us to Success; we earnesttly wish it; and that your Absence may be as short as possible: ant that you may return to us, after every Campaign, in Safety, with Honours.

       B. Tasker, President.

    The Governor's Answer

 I am extremely obliged, by the satisfaction you are pleased to shew at the Honour which his Majesty has been pleased to conference; by your Assurance of enabling me, to the utmost of my Power, to answer his Majesty's Expectations from me and by the earnest Whishes you express for my Success in important Undertaking.

        Horatio Sharpe.

 BOSTON Dec. 16. Extract of a private Letter from Paris dated October 19.

 "Some people here, who pretend to be already informed of the Instructions given to the Duke de Mirepoix, who is on his return to London, confident affirms, that his Excellency is charged to assure the British Court upon his Honour, that if it can be proved that the French have encroached upon English Territories in North America, they shall be immediately ordered to withdraw and evacuate the same, without any need of sending troops from England to Virginia; and that if the English will not rely upon such assurance, but persist in their resolution to embark succours for that Colony, a declaration of War must be the Consequence. —— The imperious Stile of this Intelligence naturally induces us to doubt its authenticity; however, a little Time will discover whether it is well grounded in the whole part."

 Orders were given on Thursday se'nnight last, that all military stores preparing for America, with tents, &c. for about 8000 men should be got ready for embarkation in seven days from that time.

 PHILADELPHIA Dec. 19. Monday the second of this Instant, the General Assembly of this Province met here, and the next Day his Honour the Governor made the following Speech.

Mr. Speaker, and Gentlemen of the Assembly,

As you are now met for the Dispatch of Business, I think it my Duty to remind you of what I said at the Opening of the last sitting, and to lay before you a letter I have since received from Sir Thomas Robinson, one of his Majesty's Principal Secretaries of State, signifying to me, "His Majesty's Express Commands, That I should not only act vigorously in Defence of the Government under my Care; but that I should likewise be aiding and assisting His Majesty's other Colonies, to repel any hostile Attempts made against them."

At the Time of writing that Letter, on the fifth of July last, His Majesty, and His Ministers, were only informed, That the French had drove some of the Virginia Troops from a Place on the Ohio, at the Mouth Monongahela, and erecting a Fort there; and you will observe, they think those Advantages, gained by the French, "might have been in a great Measure, if not totally, prevented, if everyone of His Majesty's Governments had exerted themselves according to the Directions in the Earl of Holdernesse's Letter of the 28th of August."

You are sensible that many Things have happened since the retreat from the Forks of Monongahela, that have put our Affairs on the Frontier in a very bad Situation much worse than His Majesty and the Ministers have any knowledge of, or than they can possibly imagine, and they are well informed of the flourishing case of these Colonies, of the Number of Men they are capable of raising; and had great Reason to expect, that in a Matter, in which the Interest & Safety of the Colonies was so nearly concerned, they would have excerted themselves with uncommon Vigour.

From the Letters of Intelligence I have ordered to be laid before you, it will appear that the French have now at their Fort at Monongahela, above a Thousand regular Troops besides Indians: That they are well supply'd with Provisions, and that they have lately received an additional Number of Cannon; that their Upper Forts are also well garrisoned and provided, and that they are making a Settlement of Three

Hundred Families in the Country of the Ficka-willanee, at the south-west-End of Lake Erie.

From those Papers you will likewise be informed of the Use they have made of their last Year's Success among the Indians of the Six Nations, having prevailed with many of them remove from Canada, who will either be neuter in the present Dispute, or take up Arms against us, while such few of the Indians as still retain their Attachment to the English, dare not be active for us, till they see a Force in the field superior to that of the French; and if that be not soon, they will certainly give up our Cause and embrace the tempting Offers made them by the French.

Gentlemen, It is now several Years since the French undertook the Expedition & we have long had full Intelligence of their Design, and of the Steps they have taken to carry them into Execution; their Progress indeed has been very surprizing, owing chiefly to the inactivity of the English Colonies, who, I am sorry to say, have looked with too much Indifference upon an Affair that must end in the Ruin, If not timely prevented.

When you have maturely considered the Conduct of the French upon the present Occasion, and observed the Steadiness with which they have pursued a well-laid Plan, you cannot doubt but very considerable Men have been concerned in the Formation of this Scheme, and that proper Persons are employed in the Execution of it; and as the Circumstances of the Colonies are by no Means unknown to the French, they are doubtless prepared to make a vigorous Defence, and will not easily give up what they have taken so much Pains, and been at such Expence, to gain; but rather will be induced to attack us, knowing our weak and defenceless State, as that we are, as it were, an open Door for the Conquest of the rest of the Provinces. We must therefore resolve to act with Vigour, or not at all; for in my Opinion, we had better not attempt than be defeated.

These Encroachments of the French upon the Territories of the Crown of Britain in America, have turned the Eyes of Europe to this Quarter of the World, and it is uncertain what Effect they may produce; the Conduct therefore of the Colonies will be more than ever the Object of their Attention, and ours in particular, who are most immediately concerned; for whether the French Forts are within the particular Limits of the Province or not, I look upon to be very immaterial in the Present Case, tho' in my opinion they are clearly so; but be as it may, our Situation at present is certainly very alarming ----- The French on our Borders are numerous, strongly fortified, well provided & daily increasing ----- The small Body of English Troops on the Frontiers, weaken by the Desertions from the Independent Companies, and the want of Discipline Levies ---- The Six Nations of Indians, formerly our firm Friends, devided among themselves, many of them gone over to the French, and others wavering and in Doubt whether to follow their Brethren, or continue with us ---- The neighbouring Provinces (except Virginia) though not rely interested in the issue of the present Affairs, either contributing nothing towards the common Cause, or sparingly; and thereby Virginia has indeed given Thirty Thousand Pounds, yet it will equal but little, unless a considerable Body of the Troops be sent from another Province and kept up till the Worh is done.

 Permit therefore, Gentlemen, to press this matter upon you, exert yourselves upon the present Occasion; dissipate the Cloud that hangs over your Country, and save her from the threatened Destruction. His Majesty, ever anxious for the Welfare of all his Subjects, excite and commands us ---- The Eyes of a British Parliament of the People of our Mother Country, the Happiness or misery of your Posterity, very much depend on your Resolution.

 I cannot therefore admit myself to doubt but you will enter seriously upon the Consideration of this Important Affair; and by enabling me to carry the King's Command into full Execution, convince his Majesty of our readiness to pay Obedience to his Royal Orders, for a seasonable and noble Example to the other Colonies, and shew your Constituents, that you have nothing more at Heart then to secure to them and their Posterity, the Continuance of the many unvaluable Blessings they enjoy.   December 3, 1754.

Extract of a Message from the Assembly of Philadelphia to their Governor, on his Speech to them on the 3d of December last.

The Governor has been pleased repeatedly to inform us, "That the French have already posses'd themselves of great Part of the Province and that we are the very Province invaded." And yet we find the French Forts, and their Acquisitions, on the Ohio, are constantly considered and called in Great Britain, an invasion upon his Majesty's Territory of Virginia. And we have now before us a Map, which we have good reason to believe was made from Intelligence and some Drafts, supplied by the Board of Trade, and by our Proprietaries, by which now it Appears that every fort built by the French, either on the Buffalo River, or on the Ohio, are beyond the Western Boundaries of Pennsylvania; and we presume the King may have granted lately Tracts of Land to the Eastward of the Fort the French have built at the Fork of Monongahela: But whether this Map prove true or otherwise, or whether our Western Boundaries are rightly adjusted by it, cannot immediately concern us, till they are undoubtedly ascertained and agreed to; for till then the Earl of Holdernesse, by the Letter of the 28th of August, 1753, to which Sir Thomas Ratiasen's two Letters expressly refer, has so minutely set down, and so carefully guarded the Terms upon which each Colony is to Act in Regard to the French Encroachments, that we cannot think it would be prudent, or answer any good purpose, to contravene them, whilst the Crowns of Great Britain & France continue in Amity with each other, and especially as our King has now graciously interposed, and is certainly the most proper Judge of the Limits of his own Dominions in America. And therefore we think the Governor and ourselves may safely leave it under that Direction, without engaging ourselves in any Dispute, which can or may arise

Concerning the Rights of the Crown, or the Property or Proprietaries may clain in those Lands.

The Intelligence of the Governor has lately received and laid before us, upon the Hearsay of One, and on the Deposition of another French Deserter, is unexpected, and indeed Wonderful.

It really appears so to us, that nigh Six Thousand of the best Troops of France should arrive, in Six Men of War, in the River St. Lawrence, and after ascending that River and the Lakes, should be now actually at the Lower Fort upon the Ohio; that they should be able to carry with them a sufficient Quantity of Provisions and other Necessities, for so large a body of Force, to sustain and accommodate them thro' the Winter in that uncultivated Country, and all this without the least Account of their Embarkation in Europe; and without the least Intelligence of this Passage or arrival at the Place of their Destination, from any other Colonies, or from our own Back Settlements, from whence the Governor has been pleased to lay before us very late Letters and Accounts. It is true, those Depositions are made in a very critical Juncture, but they cannot have the same Force as they ought to carry with them, had the same Accounts been transmitted to us from Oswago near which they must necessarily have passed, and from whence we receiv'd very minute accounts of the Passage of the French Forces, who first laid the Foundations of their Strength upon the Ohio. Nevertheless, as we have no Inclination nor any Interest in discrediting the Report, or diminishing the Number of the French there, which was acknowledged is abundantly too great, and has justly alarmed the British Nation, we shall leave the Arrival of these Forces, as well as Quality of them, upon their own Evidence.

WILLIAMSBURG Dec. 19, By a Vessel just arrived from Plymouth we are credibly informed, that Merchants, &c. trading with Virginia, have raised by Subscription the Sum of 20,000 Pounds, for our Protection, and to defend us from the Insults & Encroachments of the French.

ANNAPOLIS Dec. 26. Tuesday last his Excellency our Governor prorogu'd the General Assembly (after passing an Act for taking and detaining able bodied Men for his Majesty's Service) with the following Speech.

Gentlemen of the Upper and Lower Houses of Assembly,

As I want words to express, I must leave it to you to imagine, how great must be my Surprize & Concern, at being requested to put an End to this Session, before you have the least Degree, satisfied the Expeditions that your several addresses, presented soon after the Opening thereof, had raised in me, and I presume in every one, who might have had an Opportunity of seeing them: However as I am unwilling to detain you a Moment against your Inclinations, I have thought fit, with the Advice of his Lordship's Council of State, to prorogue you to the Fifteenth Day of January next, hoping, that in that Time you will endeavour to convince your Constituents of the Necessity of their permitting you to contribute, without any further Hesitation, to prevent the Success of the Fatal Scheme which our common Enemy is now preparing, and proceeding to put in Execution; wherefore you are to take Notice you are prorogued to the said Fifteenth Day of January next accordingly.

PHILADELPHIA Dec. 30. The two following Paragraphs are in Governor Morris's Message to the General Assembly of the Province of Pennsylvania, on Monday Dec. 30, 1754. Viz.

An Invasion of the Civil and Religious Liberties of a People, which are in their Nature sacred & ought to be so esteemed by all Governments, is among the worst of Crimes, & is greatly aggravated when done by One who is bound by Duty & Oath to preserve those Blessings, & protect the People in the Enjoyment of them. His sacred Majesty, who thro' the Course of a long and happy Reign has studied to preserve the Rights and Liberties of all his Subjects, and has always made the Laws & Constitutions of his Kingdom the Rule and Measure of his Government. I am sure disdains a thought of doing or approving any Thing that may be injurious to them; and I am satisfied, a British Parliament will never esteem a Royal Instruction, issued at their own Request, and intended to enforce a good & wholesome Law, in the least destructive of the Civil or Religious Liberties of any Part of his Majesty's Subjects, what ever you the Representatives of Pennsylvania may do. And Give me particular Concern, that you should purposely enter into a Dispute about that instruction, & cause to express & publish such Sentiments of his Majesty's Government, at a Time like this, when a French Army are fortifying themselves in your Country.*

I have lately received Intelligence, that a Body of nigh 6000 of the best Trained Troops of France, selected, and sent over upon this Particular Service, are arrived at the Lower Fort upon the Ohio, and are employed in fortifying that Country. This must convince us, that the Court of France has formed some grand Design with Regard to this Continent; and as they have made their first Attack upon this Province, without Doubt upon Account of its being the most plentiful and only defenceless Part of his Majesty's Dominions, it behoves us in a partucular Manner, to exert ourselves, upon the present Occasion. I must therefore, Gentlemen, once more intreat you to lay aside every Thing that may admit of Dispute between us, till a more favourable Season, and enter seriously into the Consideration of the Danger to which your Country is exposed; and not only grant the Supplies recommended by the Crown, but unable me to raise a considerable Body of Men, to be employed in Conjunction with the Troops of his Majesty has determined for this Service; and by establishing a regular Militia, and providing the Necessary Stores of War, for lack of Discipline, an easy Prey to a much weaker Body of Men than are now encamped within a few Days March of this City.

*He relates to the Governor's refusing his Assent to a Bill for stricking off 20,000 Pounds Paper, Currency without a suspending Clause.

PHILADELPHIA Dec. 31. Friday last came to Town several French in the Northern Colonies, who affirms, that in the Month of July last there arrived at Quebeck in Canada, Six Men of War with seven Thousand Land Forces; many of whom are now at the Ohio, where the French were using the utmost Diligence in Strengthening themselves.

JANUARY 1755

PHILADELPHIA Jan. 6. The assembly of this Province have resolved to give Five Thousand Pounds, for purchasing of Provisions for the King's Troops that may arrive hereafter in this Province; and have appointed Commissioners for laying out said Money.

BOSTON Jan. 13. To The Printer.
I take the Liberty to send you a few thoughts upon an Affair of the utmost Consequence to this Nation; which as they are well intended, and highly seasonable. I flatter myself they cannot fail of a few favorouble Reception.

We are told, the Administration intended to send two Regiments only to drive the French from the Posts which they have seized upon the River Ohio. The End proposed is certainly national and noble, if the means were as well proportioned. But it is to be apprehended, this will only serve to alarm the French. We have a remarkable Instance of the like Nature which happened in 1730, when Commodore Brown was sent with a Squardron of seven Ships of War, to cruize before the Havannah, without any Land Forces on board, as if it had been to apprize the Spaniards, and put them on their Guard, who had not at that time thirty Pieces of Cannon well mounted, in all the Fortifications of that important Place. Whereas, if with this Squadeon three Thousand regular Troops, under proper Officers, and a competent train of Artillery, had been sent, the Havannah had fallen in our Hands, and, as it is the Key to the West Indies, the Spaniards must have made Peace with us upon our Terms which had saved, not only the War with them, but with France, the necessary Expence of which forced us to add thirty Million to our National Debt.

What is the present Case I would propose without any Aim or Motive, but that of the public Good, is that these two Regiments shall be compleated to a thousand Men each and double Officer'd, and that, besides a Number of Half pay Officers, of distinguished Characters, should be likewise sent over, with one hundred Experienced Serjeants at least to discipline the Troops that may be raised in North America, which would enable our Countrymen there to take the Field next Summer under proper General Officers, with an Army adequate to the Design of protecting our Colonies, and maintaining the Rights of the Crown.

Other Methods, I am afraid, will, in the Consequence, be found to be only starving the Cause, and yet instead of Economy, will lead us into an immediate Expence, by making it necessary to send supplies every Year; and at last may be forced to yield disgracefully to the French, not only all the fine Country upon the Banks of the Ohio, but also the largest and best Part of Nova Scotia; by which the French will obtain Ports of their own upon the Western Ocean, at which they have been grasping these threescore Years; and which they once obtain to, they will very soon worm us out of all North America.

We are assured from good Authority, that there will be a Coalition of all the English Governments on the Continent of America; that each Colony will send in its respective Quota of Troops; and that they will be effectually supported by the Mother Country. We hear likewise, that several Independent companies will be raised, which, with Halket's and Dinbar's Regiments, preparing to embark, and Sir William Pepperell's, and Governor Shirley's Regiments ordered to be raised in New-England, when joined with the Forces already there, will make a Body of near 10,000 regular Troops. Several fine Pieces of Artillery, with a sufficient Number of Mattrosses, &c. are ordered to be in readiness; and it is not doubted that we shall not only dispossess the French from the Ohio, but compel them to keep such Limits as were presented to them by the Treaty of Utrecht.

PHILADELPHIA JAN. 14. On Wednesday last several Chiefs of the Mohawk Indians and some of their Warriors, arrived here, but upon what Business we have not heard.

And Yesterday Ten of the Cherokee Indians came to Town, who, we hear, were taken Prisoners by some French Indians about 2 Years ago, and carried to Canada, from whence they later made their Escape, and got to Albany, and from thence travelled to this Place, in there way to South-Carolina.

ANNAPOLIS Jan. 16. Monday last his Excellency our Governor set out for the Camp on Will's Creek.

NEW-YORK Jan. 20. The late unwarrantable Encroachments of the French King, upon his Majesty's British Territories in America, are not more evincive of his utter Disregard of public Faith, than of our Danger of falling a Prey to an Enemy, who tramples upon the most solemn Engagements. As the Strength of Treaties consist solely in the Honour of Princes, nothing being a greater Security to national Compacts, than a Power sufficient to compel their Observances. The bare Possibility of a War, should, methinks, strongly induced a People to prepare for waging it successfully: Nor is that State well regulated or conducted, whose Borders are not strengthened against so destructive an Occurrence.

The French Nation are convinced by their own repeated Practice, how easily the firmest Ties are dissolved, to gratify the Pride of an ambitious Monarch: They therefore wisely improve their Retreat from the Fatigues of War, in an constant Preparartion for some ensuing Conflict. Nay, so far have they probably stretched their Policy, as to make Use of the present Peace, as a Means to renew their Hostilities, with redoubled Vigour. Our nation, on the contrary, tho' brave in Action, are strangely improvident in Danger. No sooner in the Temple of Janus shot, than we sink into an absolute Forgetfulness of our Toils, from which nothing but the acutest Feelings can rouse us. If we seriously consider the Benefit arising from the one, and the innumerable Evils following from the other, part of this Contract, at the same Time, that we shall be enable to account for the Advantages which our Enemies often gain over us, a Conviction that we are the Authors of our own Misfortunes, may perhaps, wound us deep with the Salutiferous Sting of Remorse, shameful it is indeed, that our Negligence should inable the inglorious Sons of despotic Tyranny, to take the Field with British Sons of Heaven born Freedom! Shameful to the last Degree, that they who have nothing to lose, but their gilded Chains, should be more solicitous concerning the Event of uncertain Wars, than those from whom the substantial Enjoyment of Liberty, Prosperity and Religion, may by an hostile Invasion, unexpectedly be ravished.

The opposite Character I have given of the two Nations, were never so strongly exemplified, as they now are, in the English and French Settlements in North America. The former are a numerous People, possessing a wide extended Coast, rich in Trade and seated in a Country, where luxuriant Nature pours forth her Blessings with unlimited Profusion: The latter, till of late, an inconsiderate Handful, shut upon in barren wiles, Strangers to the Sweet of Traffic, almost excluded from the World and dependent on their Enemies for their daily Bread. Who cannot see that our Situation must necessarily give us such Advantages over the Enemies, as would enable us with a little Prudence, not only to baffle their utmost Efforts, but even to blot out their Names from the Face of the Earth? And yet, such has been our Indolence, such our Unconcern, at their repeated Attacks, as to afford them an Opportunity in spite of those Advantages, to rival us in War harass our Borders, and defuse Terror over the Face of our Country. Ought we not to blush, that by our own Negligence, we thus give Courage to our Foes, and that their Strength should consist of our Weakness? Are we not covered with the utmost Shame and Confusion, while we are thus sacrificing our Interest, to those whose Attempts are founded not in a confidence of their own Abilities, but in a Presumption, that we will tamely suffer their outrageous Insults? Up, then My Countrymen, let the British Lyon, be rouzed into our Breasts: let us advert to out Danger, consider in what our Weakness consents; and apply industriously in Search of a paper Remedy.

Amidst all the Advantages that Nature and Art has bestowed on us, we labour under our Inconveniences, the means to remove which, are clearly evident on the last Attention. Such is our Situation, that we have an extensive Frontier, and a great Variety of Ports to defend, which nothing but good Fortifications can secure. For, were we entirely open to Invasions both by Sea and Land, in spite of our Numbers, we should at length be given up a Prey to our designing Enemies. Hence the Necessary of compleating fortifying ourselves, and that the more especially, as the French are daily increasing by Thousands, building Forts on the most important Passes from the river St. Lawrence to Missisippi, and by that means securing a Line of Communication from one to the other. Thus that politic Nation improves the Blessings Peace, while on the other Hand, we, with a perfect Indifference, see them increasing in Strength, raising a Wall around themselves, and against us, and erecting Fortresses on our Land, to strengthen their own Borders, and among us. Do we turn our Eyes to the Sea Ports, we behold them almost naked and unfortified; and as the Prospect of Danger naturally increasing our Fears, we are apt to consider them as so many rich Sacrifices to gratify the Ambition of an imperious Tyrant, whose Aims are nothing short of universal Dominion: In this imperfect State of Defence, what will our rich Fleets, laden with the Harvest of the whole World, avail us? What our stately Buildings, adorn'd with the most costly Furniture? What our Markets, growing under the weight of Plenty, and stored with the whole Produce of a Nature? May they not become the Instruments of our ruin, by inviting our Enemies to Spoil the Plunder?

This indeed id the Case of the Provinces in general, but it is more particularly our

Unhappiness to be ignorant of Danger. We have given repeated Proofs, of a tame Submission, to the Abuse of our Adversaries, and suffered them in the late War to lay waste our Frontiers, with the utmost Rage and Barbarity. They have built Forts at our very Doors, without the least Opposition, and seized on our most important Passes, with Impunity. A flagrant Instance of this, is the Citadel at Crown-Point, which, tho' indisputably within our Province, we have suffered them peaceably to rear, and as peaceably enjoy, for a Number of Years. A People thus patient of Insults, must necessarily become the Scorn of the Enemies. How are our out Garrisons provided? Are they prepared to stand the shock of Armies, and to prevent the French from marching into the Heart of the Province? our imposing them to be well furnished and defended (a matter which ought duly to be considered) in their Number sufficient to exclude the hostile Band? Let us survey this fair Metropolis; famous for riches, and therefore perhaps doomed, tho' not very easy of Conquest to the fall of the first Victim to our relentless Foes! Here is a Scene exiting Pity, exciting Wonder! We have Fortifications indeed, with which, at the Expence of many Lives, we might probably repel the fiercest Attacks, were they properly improved, would enable us to do equal Justice to out Cause at a much smaller Expence of Blood, we are thus regardless of improving our Fortresses, those necessary Instruments for preventing so melancholy an Effusion.

If we view the Inhabitants of this City, shall we find them fully instructed in the Art of War, and able to defend to the utmost what they have purchased with infinite Labour and unwearied Industry? Here also, whether may be our Capacity, we shall doubtless fall short of that Perfection which the Rules of good Discipline strictly requires. And yet, unprepared as we are against the dreadful Day, we are loitering away our Time, regardless of those means that are necessary to put us in a Posture of Defence. Perhaps we confide in out Numbers. Vain Confidence indeed! An unerring Omen of impending Destruction! 'Tis true, we are numerous; but unless, we are also well accustomed to martial Exercise, we shall prove an unweildy Multitude, and consequently unfit to meet our Enemies in Battle, who 'tis well known, are experience Soldiers, thoroughly disciplined, and bred to the Field; and therefore, the comparatively few may possibly rival us, in spite of our Nunbers. Our Courage I will not dispute. It will soon perhaps be tried in Battle. This Virtue will undoubtedly, be excited in us, when we see our Wives, our Children, our Liberty, our Lives, and our Religion, suspended in the doubtful Balance of uncertain Victory, for Blessing so countless and invaluable, the greatest Coward must fight. But the Misfortune is, that possessed of this Virtue without sufficient Skill to exercise it, many of us will become a readier Prey, to an artful Enemy, and much out the more willingly to inevitable Slaughter, even tho' the Scale should preponderate to our Favour.

What then would be our Situation, should the French Army march into our Province, spread Desolation through the Country, and lay waste our Plantations? And to all other Misfortunes, should an hostile Fleet, wasted by auspicious Gales, ascend our Port, and in a formidable Line draw up before this City; should we be able vigourously to return the dreadful Salutation of their Thundering Cannon? Would our Fortifications cover us from the Fire of our Enemies? No: And who but Madmen can think of withstanding a naval Armament, without a proper shelter, while they have it in their Power, by improving their Fortifications, to command all the Security that the Fate of War will permit. In such a Case, Thousands would be doomed to Death; and tho' by a continual Supply of fresh Forces, we might be able to prevent the Enemy Landing, what would secure us against the dreadful Explosion of Flaming Bombs, which, with swift Destruction, would reduce the Houses to Ashes? Such are the Evils, which may still easily be averted, by a timely and wise Interposition.

But in the midst of my Concern for the Publick Weal a well grounded Prospect, that our Assembly will speedily compleat all of our

Fortifications, gives me hope, that when our Enemies shall think proper to pay us so unwelcomed a Visit, we shall have the Strength to frustrate their Attempts, and hasten their return, to receive the Instructions of their imperious Masters, Upon an Errand in which he may promise himself more Success.

Let therefore our Militia be reformed, and experience Officers appointed, the Companies repeatedly exercised, and the Regiments frequently reviewed. Let every Man among us, be compelled, under the severest Penalties, to keep himself well provided with Arms and Ammunition; and let neither Rank nor Office excuse anyone from the Military Service. Let us submit chearfully to a Tax, or voluntarily contribute, to fortify our Port, and garrison our Frontiers. Let every man be thought to know his proper post, upon the most sudden Alarm. In short, let us prepare as tho' we had the most certain Intelligence of an Invasion; that when the Evil Day cometh, we may not be ashamed to meet the Enemy in the Gate.

PHILADELPHIA Jan. 21. Extract of a Letter, from an Officer at Will's Creek, to a Gentleman here.

Camp-Mount-Pleasant Jan. 3, 1755.

"The Treaty with the Indians ended the last Day of the Year. They insisted strongly, that they came from seven Nations near the Lakes with seven Belts and Strings of Wampum to make a Peace with their Brethren the English; and for that purpose they accordingly made a very long Speech, and received our answer to the same, with a very handsome Present, which they accepted, with great Joy and Thanks, declaring, that they would represent to their Nations the Civility they had received from their Brethren the English. If we can get but the Indians, we shall easily find a Method to manage the French, and I believe it is what the Indians in general much desire."

BOSTON Jan. 27. Extract of a Letter from a Gentleman at New-York dated Jan. 6, 1755.

"You will find by a Paragraph in the Mercury, taken from Governor Morris's Message given to the Assembly, he mentions the French having received a Reinforcement of nigh 6000 Troops at the Lower Fort on the Ohio. —— I have seen two Examinations of French Deserters, taken before Judge Allen at Philadelphia who made affidavit. —— That about three Months ago six Men of War arrived from old France at Quebec, each having 1000 Soldiers; but that many of them died on the Passage. —— That the 6000 Men were all Grenadiers, picked as the ablest Men out of the best Regiments of France —— That one of the Examinants embarked with these Soldiers in 600 Battoes. —— That they all arrived (except some who were sick, perhaps 200, left at the upper Fort) at the Fort commanded by Monsieur Contrecour on the Ohio. —— That about 8 Weeks ago the Examinant deserted from that Fort, and 200 deserted before him. —— That the Soldiers, after their Arrival, were employed in digging Mines, in order to blow up the English on the Approaches to Attack them, and that they talk'd of making Mines all about the Fort at a great Distance —— That the French had heard the English were making great Preperations against them. —— That there were a great Number of French Indians in the Camp, who speak French and are extremely attached to them. —— That the French say, they will by Force compel the English Indians to join with them. —— This I fear may be the Case, unless we take, and that speedily, proper Measures to secure our Indians in our Interest. It must give no small Pleasure to every Will-wisher to his Majesty's Provinces in North America to find, that his Majesty and Ministry take Heart our present melancholy Situation; but 'tis fear'd without something is speedily done to reclaim such of the Six Nations as have deserted us, these two or three Years past, and attach the wavering ones, you left, more stedfastly to his Majesty's Interest, it will prove abortive. —— If we lose the Six Nations, you may depend on it, we lose every other Indian on the Continent. —— maybe so flush'd with the additional Strength of Men and Money we are like to have from Home, that many will laugh at any one who may make mention of the Consequence the Indians may be of to us, or offer to mention, that our Scheme will prove abortive without them; But I think, I may venture to say, if the Indians are neglected, and nothing more done to secure them in our Interest than has been, Time will shew the great Disparity between us (be we ever so regular) and Indians in the Woods, for we are an unequal Match to them in the Wilderness. —— Two Indians from the Southward, one of them Successor to Half-King, who was killed by the French last Summer, have passed through here in their Way to the Six Nations: They are gone to invite the Six Nations to join the Indians, to the Southward, to cut off the French on the Ohio."

FEBRUARY 1755

BOSTON Feb. 3. Whereas some of the Soldiers that inlisted in the Expedition at Kennebeck, have not as yet applied for their Pay, altho' the Money is, and has been ready for them some Time; This is to desire all such Soldiers to come immediately to my Office, and receive what is respectively due to them.
H. Gray Treasurer.

PHILADELPHIA Feb. 4. On Tuesday last Mr, Pitcher, Commassary of the Musters, arrived here from New-York, and on Friday proceeded on his Journey for Will's Creek.

CHARLESTOWN SOUTH-CAROLINA Feb. 6. A Message from the Governor to the Assembly.

Mr. Speaker, and Gentlemen,
I send for your Perusal and Consideration, the Copy of a Letter from the Right Honourable Sir Thomas Robinson one of his Majesty's principal Secretaries of State.

It were Presumption in me, to recommend what comes from such authority: The high Station of the Persom who writes it, the clear and perwasive Manner in which it is written, the Importance and Interestingness of the Subject, all bespeak your serious Attention. How great an Instance of the Tenderness and Affection, hath our royal Master, and great Father of his People, here given to us, in resolving with his known couragious Constancy and Steadiness to assert our Rights! Such a Conduct in the best of Kings, must make the most deep and lasting Impression on the grateful Hearts of dutiful Subjects, and will not suffer you to hesitate, in raising, forthwith, as large a common Fund, to be employed provisionally in the general Service of America.

Let us vie with the Zealous Provinces, in

shewing a Regard for the general Cause of securing his Majesty's American Dominions against all Encroachments, by giving a Portion out of that Plenty which Providence hath bestowed upon us for the Series of Years.

Every one who owns a Duty, and possesses Loyalty to his Majesty, a Love to his Country, or a Regard for himself, will give chearfully and liberally: And if any would be so mistaken, as to prefer their Riches to these Considerations, they will find it their Interest to give liberally also, as the most proper Means to secure their All. In short, Preparations for War, is the most ready and effectual Way of preserving Peace.

In the Council Chamber the 11th Day of January 1755.   James Glen.

A Message from the Assembly to the Governor in Answer to the foregoing.

May it please your Excellency,
This House having considered your Excellency's Message, brought down with a Copy of a Letter from Rt. Honourable Sir Thomas Robinson, one of his Majesty's principal Secretaries of State, on the 14th Instant: And being very ready and willing to contribute, to the utmost of our Ability, towards defraying the Expence of the Service mentioned in your said Message, have ordered a Bill to be brought in, for stamping and signing public Orders, to the Amount of Forty Thousand Pounds current Money (being equal to Five Thousand seven Hundred and fourteen Pounds five Shillings & eight Pence half Penny, Sterling) to be sunk in seven Years, by a General Tax; and for granting the said Sum of Forty Thousand Pounds to his Majesty, for the Defence of his Majesty's Dominions in North America.

In the Common House of Assembly, the 21st Day of January 1755, by Order of the House (in obedience to his Majesty's Orders, signified to the Governor by one of the principal Secretaries of State) have endeavoured, to the utmost of their Power, to raise and grant to his Majesty, an Aid toward defraying the Expence of defending all of his Majesty's Dominions in

North-America, as considerable as the present Circumstances of the Inhabitants of this Province (who have other large Sums to provide for their own immediate Security and Defence) would admit..

Resolve, That the Governor's Message, which was brought down to the House on the 14th of last Month, with the Message in Answer thereto, and the said Bill, with the above Resolves, by printed in the Gazette, By order of the House.

Childerman Croft, C.D.C.

ANNAPOLIS Feb. 6. Extract of a Letter from a Gentleman at Wells Creek, to his Friend here, dated Jan. 27, 1755.

"Yesterday arrived here Sir John St. Clair, Bart. Colonel and Quarter-Master General to his Majesty's Troops intended for this Service, and sets off To-morrow Morning with Governor Sharpe. ---- Your worthy Governor has been here about a Week, on his second Visit to the Camp within two Months, and we shall be sorry, very sorry, if he should not cross the Allegany Mountains with us, in a Station agreeable to himself, and equal to his great Merit. ---- Three Deserters came here Yesterday in 13 Days from Fort de Quesne; their Information not public; one of them told me the 15 Savages who were here some Time ago, arrived 8 or 9 Days at Fort de Quesne before they deserted, and all acknowledge the good usage at Will's Creek. ---- Two of our Indians were lately sent with a Letter from one of the Prisoners at Winchester, when they return we may have some news. ---- We daily expect to hear of the Arrival of General Braddock, with the Troops. ---- His Majesty's three Independent Companies here, have built a Fort, with several large Store Houses, &c. and Barracks for all the Men, by way of a Fortified Camp, sinking and flanked, by the Fort with Ten Four Pounders, besides Swivels; all this since the 11th of September last, without any Assistance (either from Virginia or Maryland) of Workmen of any kind, and were a long while without a sufficient Number of good Tools, beginning only with a Spade and two or three Axes. ---- A very good Company from Maryland came here about two

Months ago, and are in Hutts which they built for themselves near us. ---- We have heard of the Virginia Levies marching about 4 Months ago, but none of them have appear'd yet."

We are assured that at Chester-Town, in Kent County several Men inlisted immediately on the arrival of the Officer in that Town, before the Drum was beat, and that Officer, wanting but 30 Men, got his Compliment, and marched with them, within a very little while: such is the Commendable Spirit of that Place! They are gone to Will's Creek, and some young Maryland Gentlemen (true Patriots) are gone from thence as Voluntiers: The Mother of one of them, at parting took leave of him with Saying, My dear Son, I shall with much greater Pleasure to learn of your Death than of your Cowardice, or Ill Conduct.

His Excellency our Governor, and Sir St. Clair are returned from Will's Creek and gone to Williamsburg; and we hear they came down Potowmack 200 Miles in Canoe.

Monday Evening last, James Pitcher, Esq; Commissary to the Forces expected in, came to Town, from the Northward, and is gone to Virginia expecting to meet them there.

WILLIAMSBURG Feb. 8. From Hampton we are advised, that two French Men of War have been off our Coast; and it is said that the Garland, Capt. Abuthnot and the Gibraltar, Capt, Spry, are ordered out in search of them.

BOSTON Feb. 12. By a Vessel in 12 Days from Virginia, we have Advice, that Capt. Spry, in a 20 Gun Ship, was arrived there from England, and brought with him several Officers of the Troops expected there from Ireland. We also hear, that Capt. Spry having delivered the Dispatches brought by him for the several Governors on the Continent, sail'd directly back for England.

Several of the said Officers we hear, are come to Town by land from Virginia.

By Letters from Halifax in Nova Scotia, we have Advice, That they are building two new batteries upon the Beach, one near the South Gate and another at the Place call'd the Point, near the King's Wharf; that the three Gun Battery at the South End is to be greatly enlarg'd, and more Cannon added to it; that each of these Batteries are to have Barracks, &c. to them, as is the new Batteries on the other Side of the Harbour, capable of containing some Hundreds of Men.

We have Advice, that Six Men of War are arrived at Gaspee, on the South Side of the Gulph of St. Lawrence, in Nova-Scotia, where they are to Winter, and where great Stores of Provisions &c. are laid up for them.

We likewise hear, that some French Men of War and Transports landed a great Number of Soldiers in the River Missisippi a few Months ago. These great Preparations of the French, bode no good to our Northern Colonies.

PHILADELPHIA Feb. 11. By a Gentleman, who left Winchester, in Virginia, the third Instant, and from some private Letters, we have the following Intelligence viz. That Sir John Sinclair & Governor Sharpe, has been at Will's Creek and were returned; and that they had view'd the Great Falls at Potowmack, and were in hopes of blowing them up for as to make the River navigable there for flat bottom'd Vessels, which, if effected, will be of the greatest Service, in transporting Necessaries for our Forces. --- That one of our Indians was lately arrived at Will's Creek from the Ohio who said that he could not form a Judgement of the particular Number of Troops the French had then in that Country: but that in general they seem'd to be very Numerous. Parties daily arriving, and marching from Fort to Fort; that they had begun to build another Fort; and that they were not well supplied with Bread, but had enough of other Provisions. ---- That a Party of French and Indians were, not long since, seen a few Miles from Camp, in order as it were thought to get Intelligence of our Strength, &c. ---- The Lieutenant Colonel Stephens, with the last Detachment of the Virginia Forces, arrived the first Instant at Winchester, on their Way to Will's Creek, having marched upward of Ninety Miles in four Days, notwithstanding the Deepness of the Roads at this advanced Season, (a good presage of what may be expected from Troops, animated by the influence and Example of Officers of Such Spirit and Activity.) That our Forces, when all join'd at the Camp, will amount to about 1000 Men. --- That it was reported the Train of Artillery, from England arrived on the 27th ult. in Virginia, with 150 Matrosses, Clothes and military Stores, of all sorts, for several Thousand Men, that a Camp was mark'd out for them at a Place called Watkin's Ferry; and that they sailed in company with the Transports bound to Cork, to take on board the two Regiments there for America, which, with General Braddock, may be Daily expected. ---- And that there was a Number of Men at Work at Potowmack building Battoes, for transporting the Cannon, &c.

NEW-YORK Feb. 17. His Majesty has been graciously pleased to give One Thousand Flintlocks, & Accoutrements to the Province of North-Carolina; and Governor Dobbs tell the Assembly, that he has "a well grounded Expectation, that proper Artillery, with military Stores will be granted for the several Forts that may erect in the Province."

PHILADELPHIA Feb. 18. Since our last two Gentlemen came to Town from Annapolis, who informs us, that on the Eight Instant an Express arriv'd there from Williamsburg, which they heard, had brought Advice of the Arrival of the Forces from England.

ANNAPOLIS Feb. 20. By an Express of Yesterday from Virginia, we are informed, That a vessel is arrived there from Ireland, which sail'd some Days after their forces. And by a Gentleman from Worcester County, we hear, that a few Days ago a Number of Ships were sent off, standing in from the Bay; so that it is probable they are, by this time arrived in Virginia.

WILLIAMSBURG Feb. 21. By Express just arrived from Hampton, we are advised that three Men of War arrived there, on board of which are General Braddock, and several other Officers of Distinction.

ANNAPOLIS Feb. 22. The speech of his Excellency Horatio Sharpe, Esq; Governor and Commander in Chief in and over the Province of Maryland, to the General Assembly of the said Province on Saturday the 22d of February, 1755.

Gentlemen of the upper and Lower House of Assembly,

As you have already expressed yourselves sufficiently sensible of the fatal Consequences that must attend the Enemy's remaining Masters of that Part of his Majesty's Dominions to the Westward, on which they have lately presumed to raise Forts, and make Settlements; and have lately promised that nothing shall be wanting on your Part to avert the imminent Danger with which their Vicinity threatens us; it only remains with me now to hope, that you will fall on the prudent and unexceptionable Measures, to raise as large a Sum as circumstances of this Province will allow, and generously and gratefully express your Duty to the best of Kings, and your Care and Regard for the Lives and Fortunes of yourselves and fellow Subjects. The Advice and Instructions I have received from home, since our last Meeting, might give me Occasion to enlarge on the tender and paternal Care that his Majesty has been most graciously pleased to shew, for the Security and Welfare of his Subjects in these Parts of his Dominions; but as I am persuaded that I need not attempt to add to the Weight of a Letter, that I have received from one of his Majesty's principal Secretaries of State, which sets, in the strongest Light, that and the several other Motives, which should prompt us to exert ourselves on this Occasion, I will satisfy myself with laying it before you; and with exhorting you to consider how far the Season is already advanced, and to finish the Business for which you are assembled, with the greatest Dispatch.

Gentlemen, I take this Occasion of recommending to you, to regulate the Hire of Wagons and Horses, in Case of Service should require us, at any Time, to impress either in this Government; which I do not doubt but you will think highly proper and reasonable, when I acquaint you, that a short Expence has shewn, that many of the Inhabitants have raised the Price of

Carriage since the beginning of these unhappy Disturbances, in Proportion as they found we stood in the Need of their Assistance.

I must also observe to you, that the few Men we have from hitherto obliged, to quarter in, or march through, this Peovince, have occasioned a very extravagant Expence, by reason the Ordinary-Keepers refused to receive any into their Houses, or afford them Entertainment, but at the Rates that have been settled by the Magistrate of the respective Counties for private Travellers and Passengers: These Prices doubt not, you will think to great to be paid by private Soldiers; and you will, I hope, regulate them by a Bill, in a moderate and reasonable Manner, which will remove all Occasions of Dispute between the Soldiers and the Inhabitants.

Gentlemen of the Lower House,

I shall acquaint you, by a message, how Part of the 6000 Pounds which you granted some Time since, has been disposed of for the Service; and, shall be much pleased, in my Manner of expending it, receives your Approbation.

BOSTON Feb. 24. Extract of a Letter from Paris, dated November 1, 1754.

"To give the English their Due, it must be acknowledged, that they excel in every Art and Science, except Politicks; otherwise they would not have appeared so much surprized as they have been at what has happened on the River Ohio. There is much more Land in North-America than both Nations could occupy and people these 500 Years to come. where they to continue in Peace together all that Time; but our Nation is in Haste to grow rich, to supplant our Rivals, in Trade, and to raise a powerful Navy; and our natural Vivacity will not allow us to wait patiently for the slow return of painful Industry, which would gradually enable us to carry those Points, without venturing any Thing upon the Fortune of war.

We are sensible it is not the Interest of the English to quarrel with us, considering their Circumstances; and we are likewise sensible, that, bad as those Circumstances are, we can thrive better by Peace, than by War with them: But considering the general State of Europe, our Ministers, it seems, think they may be provoked with Impunity. It is of no great Importance, to the general System of Affairs where a War Begins. Broils may e'er long arise in Poland, about the Election of a Sovereign or other Matters; another sovereign may die at or about the same Time, either in the East or the West, according to the Course of Nature; The Election of a King of the Romans may occasion some Disturbances or Heart-burning in Germany; some Mischief may happen in Italy, in consequence of certain Articles of the Treaty of Aix la Chapelle. In any Cases, all the Powers of Europe; pursuant to their connections and Engagements with each other, will Matter standing thus, would our Ministry pass for shallow Politicians if they had not taken Opportunity by the Firelock by invading the Lands on the Ohio, before the English Colonies were provided for a Vigorous Opposition. We have now Carried the Point, and our People there will fortify themselves while the Commissaries canvass the Affair here, examine their respective Claims to the Territories in Dispute, and pore upon Maps. To have postponed such an Expedition, till a War in Europe were unavoidable upon other Accounts, would have been a great Weakness as Politicians could be guilty of. We have done what is right, at least in our own Eyes; and now let England do her best, by War or Negotiation to prove us in the Wrong."

———— A pert conclusion indeed! But if Britain will but act honestly, it will soon appear that the French are the worst Politicians in Europe.

NEW-York Feb. 24. Wednesday last his Honor our Lieutenant Governor was pleased in Council, to give his assent to the Three following Acts.

An Act for raising a Supply of Forty Five Thousand Pounds, by a Tax on Estates real and personal, for putting this Colony into proper Posture of Defence, for furthering his Majesty's Design against his Enemies in North America, and other Purposes therein mentioned; for emitting Bills of Credit for the like Sum and for sinking and concelling the said Bills in short Periods.

An Act for regulating the Militia of the Colony of New-York. and,

An Act to refrain the sending of Provisions to Cape Breton, or any other French Port or Settlement on this Continent of Nort America, or Islands nigh or adjacent thereto.

PHILADELPHIA Feb. 25. An Extract from a Letter from the Camp at Will's Creek, dated February 10, 1755.

Two Indians which was sent to Fort Du Quesne, with a Letter from one of the French Prisoners in Virginia, arrived in this Camp, who informs us, that the English Indians which were some Time since with us and who pretended in our Council to be Friends with the English, were at the French Fort and delivered to the Commandant the Speech we made to them, and the presents they received from us; they further say, that the French would not admit them into their council with the French Indians; that the French Officers told them that he intended in a very few Days to march a large Body of French and Indians and drive us out of our present Situation for that we had no Business to build Forts at Will's Creek: we had put ourselves in a Proper posture of Defence to receive them, and made no doubt if they do come that they will meet with a warmer Reception than they imagined. We have cleared all the Land within Cannon shot of us, both this Side of the River and likewise the other Side beyond the New Store which is upon a higher Ground then our Fort stands upon, but the knol is very narrow, and not fitting to erect any Fortifications upon, and under the Command of our Guns about 320 Yards distance from the Fort.

We expect the first Division of the Virginia Forces to join us this Evening, when we intend a strong guard to be mounted at the New Store.

Sunday last arrived an Express from Virginia, who advises, that no Stores or Artillery was arrived as mentioned lately; but Troops daily expected.

MARCH 1755

BOSTON March 1. A Barrack of 200 Feet long 36 Feet wide, and 14 Foot Studd, to have 16 Rooms on each Floor, 4 main Enteries, 4 Stacks of Stairs and Cabbins sufficient to lodge 700 Men; the outside to be rough boarded, with feathered edge Boards, and clapboarded; the inside to be lined with Boards plained and feathered edged or groved; also to have 4 double and 4 single Stacks of Chimneys, and the whole Building to be well underpinned is proposed to be built forthwith at Castle William.

Any Person or Persons who are willing to undertake the same, either by sending stuff and doing all the Work, or by doing the Work only, are desired to send in their Proposal in writing, and sealed up, on or before the 7th of this Instant March, to John Osborne, Esq; Chairman of a Committee appointed for that Purpose, who will attend at the Council Chamber in Boston, on Wednesday next, in the Forenoon, and all the Friday following, to receive any such Proposals, or to treat with any Persons about the said Building. By order of the Committee.

Boston 1st March 1755.   J. Osborne.

BOSTON March 3. From the Gazette and London Daily Advertiser, Nov. 2, 1754.

Part of a Letter to the Right Hon. Lord ******.

My Lord,

King William the Third formed a Design of adding to his Dominions the Missisippi River, with the Countries about it; which being delayed, Louis the Fourteenth sent Forces there, and took Possession. The French have built many Forts on the River, always designing to settle and fortify the Country on the West of the Appalachian Mountains, and joining their Settlements on Canada to those of the Missisippi. Behind these

Mountains, which are nine Hundred Miles in Length between Canada and the Missisippi, there is an Extent of Country larger than all France, Germany and Poland, and well provided with Rivers; The Air very wholesome, and the soil rich: It greatly concerns the Interest of his Majesty and his Subjects, to drive out the French, and erect a new Government in this inestimable region, and send a competent Number of Soldiers to secure and protect the People that will settle there, which would be in great Numbers, because the Situation adjoins to, or is near the Carolina's, Virginia, Maryland and Pennsylvania; the three last are very fill with People faster than any Province ever did in America, and effectually prevent the French from a Communication between Canada and Missisippi.

The French have acted with great Prudence in the Management of the Colonies; their Governors and Intendants have Power to Act as they think most conductive for their King's Service, and Advantage of the People.

The British Governors in America are often loaded with and fettered with numerous Instructions frequently impracticable, and such as the General Assemblies will not submit to.

The French Governors and Officers are commonly brave Men, skilled in Military Affairs.

There is not one Governor, nor Commander in Chief, in all the King's Provinces on the Continent of North America (Nova Scotia excenpted) who was bred in the Army ('Tis suppos'd the Author has forgot Mr. Sharpe, Governour of Maryland) His Majesty would be much better served, if the Governors were Officers of Experience, capable of commanding such numerous Forces as can be raised in the British Colonies. Were the Inhabitants of Pennsylvania regimented as the other Provinces, the Militia in all the Governments would amount to Four Hundred Thousand Men sufficient and capable of performing great Service, is well commanded, and had some regular Forces to serve with them.

It must be judged a marvellous Compliance or Negligence, to resign or suffer the French to possess such immense Regions to which they have no Right, and would in Time prove very prejudicial, if not destructive to the British Empire in America; for then this Nation would be under the Necessity of Fortifying a Frontier of Two Thousand Miles in Length.

The Parts of North America which may be claimed by Great Britain or France are of as worth as either Kingdom: If acquired by the Nation, in two Centuries, probably they will contain more People than Great-Britain.

In a War on the Continent of North America against the French, England will have great Advantages, having Twenty Times as much Shipping; Possession of all the Ports and the Sea Coasts, from Nova Scotia to Florida; with a Communication by Land that cannot be interrupted; most of the Ports in the British Governments are always open: arm'd Vessels to carry Soldiers, Artillery, Ammunition and Provisions down the Streams, may be built on all the considerable Rivers where the French inhabit; The Colonies have Provisions sufficient to supply great Armies at moderate Charges; to these may be added, the Number and Bravery of the Men, always ready to take Arms for the Service of their King and Country.

If the French are vigorously attacked on Canada, their profitable Traffick in Skins and Furs will soon be lost; the Inhabitants and Garrisons reduced to the want of Ammunition, and almost every Necessary of Life: The Navigation on the Canada River is so much impended by Currents, Fogs and Ice, is not to be safe above half the Year. If the Inhabitants are obliged to be one Summer on Militia Service, the Women, Children and Cattle will be in Danger of perishing for want of Food the next Winter.

The Finances in France at this Time are very low; the annual Expences of the Crown exceed the Revenues, cause Anticipations, and oblige the general Farmers to pay before the Money is due. France will not recede from any Pretensions of Value, however defective the Title, if by Art, Fraud or Force, Possession may be obtained. It is in vain to imagine or expect the French will retire from Nova-Scotia, or desist from their Claim of the vast Countries between The Missisippi and the Canada River, before they are beat out of them, which may be compleated in three Years, and all the Nation it possessed of the Continent of North America, if the Force of Great Britain be rightly exerted:

My Lord, in Obedience to your Command, I have given your Lordship my Thoughts on the Circumstances and Differences between Great Britain and France on the Continent of North America, in a plain and concise Manner. If I have erred misrepresented Facts, it is to be hoped, That some ingenious Gentlemen annimated with Zeal for the good of their Country, may be induced to write in the Publick Papers, and rectify the Mistake of, Your Lordships most Humble, and most obedient Servant, Geo. Burrington.

NEW-YORK March 3. A Report is prevalent in Town, that a Frenchman, who fled from Canada, and arrived at Albany a few Days ago, brings Advice, that last Summer three French Men-of-War, two of 80 Guns, and the other 50, arrived at Quebeck, with 1000 Soldiers on board; That soon after their arrival, one of the Ships was lost at Quebeck, and another of them was afterwards lost in going down the River St. Lawrence.

BOSTON March 3. We have sundry late Accounts from the Eastward, that upward of 300 Indians, with French Officers among them, have been hovering about the Settlements for several Days; and it was generally expected they would soon make an Attack upon some of them.

BOSTON March 4. By a Letter from Quebec in Canada, dated December 15th 1754.

We are informed, that Michael Divinall, Richard Gulford, David Delage, and Sallen Witmarsh, four of our Soldiers taken by the Indians near Fort Halifax, sometime in September last, were alive and well in the City of Quebec, at the Time when the said Letter was dated.

PHILADELPHIA March 4. Extract of a Letter from a Gentleman in Annapolis dated Feb. 26.

The Post rider informs me, that Major Carlisle told him at Alexandria, that 1500 Arrived at Hampton last Wednesday.

It is Certain Major General Braddock is now

arrived. We every Minute expect an Express from Virginia with a particular Account. Our Assembly this Day voted Ten thousand Pounds towards the Expedition, and it is to be hoped will be raised without differing as to Ways and Means.

BOSTON March 7. The following Act pass'd the General Court of this Province at the Session in February last.

An Act in Addition to an Act made in the twenty-seventh Years of his present Majesty's Reign, entitled, An Act for levying Soldiers, and to prevent Soldiers and Sea-Men in His Majesty's Service being arrested for Debt.

Whereas Doubts have arisen whether Soldiers that have or shall inlist into the Service of His Majesty are exempted from paying their Province Tax, and so liable to be taken and imprisoned by the several Constables or Collectors that have a Demand against them for the same:

Be it therefore enacted by the Governour, the Council and House of Representatives; That any Soldier that hath or shall inlist into his Majesty's Service (since the making of the Act aforesaid) shall not be liable to be taken, or have his Body distrained on, by any Constable or Collector, for his Province Tax, during the Continuance of said Act; and where no Estate of such Soldier can be found by any Constable or Collector to make Distress upon for such Tax, and the same be made to appear by the Oath of said Collector or Constable, that then and in every-such Case, the Loss of such Tax shall be born by the Province, and any Constable or Collector who shall make it appear to the Province treasurer, that he hath failed of collecting any Sums on any Soldier or Soldiers inlisted as aforesaid, by a Certificate from the Select-Men or Assessors, or the major Part of them that made the Tax, that such Person or Persons are inlisted and in his Majesty's Service at the Time of such Certificate's being made, that they and in every such Case, the Province Treasurer is hereby directed and impowered to abate such Sum or Sums to the said Constable or Collector, and charge the Province therewith.

This Act to continue in Force until the First Day of June, One Thousand seven Hundred and fifty nine.

HALIFAX March 8. By Captain Gay, who arrived here last Saturday from Louisbourg, we have Advice, that they were no Men of War in the Port when he left it; that they were carrying on their Fortifications, &c. only in the same Manner as they were last Fall, and that he did not hear any Talk of War.

NEW-york, March 10. By an Express that arrived here last Tuesday Night from Virginia, we learn that General Braddock was arrived there with three Men of War, viz. The Centurion, Commodore Keller, the Norwich, the Hon. Capt. Barrington, and the Syren, Capt. Proby. With General Braddock are come Capt. Orne, Aid de Camp, and Mr. Shirley, Secretary. The Transports with the Forces were not got in, the first Instant, but daily Expected.

BOSTON March 10. By His Excellency William Shirley, Esq; Captain-General and Governor in Chief in and over His Majesty's Province of the Massachusetts-Bay in New-England.

A PROCLAMATION

Whereas the Great and General Court or Assembly of this Province now stands prorogued until Tuesday the Twenty Fifth Day of March Instant, to which divers Matters of Importance will be laid before them for their speedy Consideration;

I have thought fit to issue this Proclamation, hereby requiring all and every the Members of the said Court to give their Attendance on the Day aforesaid.

Given under my Hand at Boston, the Eight Day of March, 1755, in the Twenty Eight Year of the Reign of our Sovereign Lord George the Second by the Grace of God, of Great Britain, France and Ireland, King, Defender of the Faith &c.

By his Excellency's Command   W. Shirley.
Thomas Clarke, Dep. Secretary.

Whereas there are a Number of Men Inlisted into his Majesty's Service, in a Regiment of Foot now raising under my Command, absent from their Duty or Furlough, and others that are inlisted have not yet repair'd to their Quarters in Boston: They are hereby Notified, that they have Leave to remain at their several Places of Residence, until they shall receive my further Order to repair to Boston,

Given under my Hand at Boston the 10th Day of March 1755.   W. Shirley.

BOSTON March 12. Province of Massachusetts-Bay. By His Excellency the Governour.

Whereas I have been inform'd, that the divers Militia Officers within this Province are now, under pretext of Authority from me, forming Troops of Horses, and enlisting Troopers, purely to have those Troopers exempted from Militia Duty;

I do therefore hereby command all Officers of the Militia within this Province, to forebear enlisting any Troopers, until further Orders from me; and the Colonels or other chief Officers of the Regiments of Foot within the same, forthwith to reduce all Troops, or pretended Troops of Horses in their Regiments, which have not been compleated for the Space of Two Months before the Date hereof, and been publickly muster'd, and to oblige them to military Duty in the Companies of Foot, as by the Law is directed.

Given under my Hand at Boston, the Twelft Day of March 1775.   W. Shirley.

BOSTON March 17, From the Westminster Journal September 21, 1754.

The Brave should fight, but for the Fobs of France, Tis theirs to cook to Talorize and dance.

It now begins to be pretty manifest that the grand monarch (as the French stile their sovereereign) notwithstanding his distinguished delicacy and politeness, has a month's mind to a Pipe of best Virginia.

The old scheme that was plan'd by Lewis Le Grand, viz. of extending the possessions of the French from the mouth of the Missisippi on the South, to Hudson's Bay on the North, seems now to be hastening into execution. It has been for many years to good policy of the French greatly to encourage and support their colonies and plantations, always considering them as vast seminaries of wealth and strength; and if we proportionably neglect those that belong to us, the consequence is too visible to be insisted on.

The last affair (of which however we have had but very imperfect, and blundering Accounts) demonstrates that the French have not the least regard to the most solemn engagements; the Indians are rewarded in proportion, as they assassinate and make inroads upon the English: War (though not proclaimed) is absolutely carried on, and our blood is spilt and property invaded on the sophistry of the most subtlety pretences; a remarkable specimen of which, I shall now lay before the reader.

When Governor of Virginia dispatched Major Washington to Mr. Legardeur de St. Pierre, a principal French officer, with complaints to the following amount, viz. "That though the lands on the river Ohio in the Western part of Virginia, were notoriously known to be the property of the crown of Great Britain, yet the French had erected fortresses and made settlements upon the very river. That he, the governor, received daily complaints of hostility and encroachment from the French, who had marched with an armed force from Canada, in open violation of the law of the nations, and the treaties now subsisting between the two crowns." To these allegations the French commandant sent the following shuffling, evasive, unsatisfactory answer: "I do not know (replied he) that in the progress of this campaign, any thing has passed that can be reputed an act of hostility, or that is contrary to the treaties subsisting between the two crowns. Had you been pleased, Sir, to have descended to particularize the facts, which occasioned your complaint, and (I am Persuaded) in the most satisfactory manner."

In the first place, I would fain be informed, what Monsieur can possibly mean by the progress of campaign, without an act of hostility?

In the next, did not Governor Dinwiddie descend to particulars enough, when he alleged that fortifications were actually erected on the river Ohio by the French, and an armed force actually marched from Canada? one would think

M Lagardeur de St. Pierre imagined the English have as little common sense, as they have conduct, by his endeavouring to impose such wretched stuff upon them by way of a satisfactory reply.

Such treatment as this call aloud for our warmest resentment. A good squadron properly accoutred, would soon bring these violaters of the law of nations to reason; and as the French have got custom of waging war, without declaring of it, I do not see why we should not take the hint.

BOSTON March 17. A Sloop from Philadelphia, with 70 or 80 new-raised Men for his Excellency's Regiment, meeting with a Storm near Cape-Cod, wisely put back, and got safe to Nantucket, from whence she arrived here last Wednesday.

WILLIAMSBURG March 21. The Transports with the Troops are all now safely arrived, and gone round to Alexandria, where, 'tis hoped, by this Time they are all disembarked. Tis remarkable, that notwithstanding a Winter Passage, not one Man died since they left Cock. and only two were sick on their Arrival.

His Honor the Governor, and his Excellency General Braddock, set off for the Northward To morrow, to meet his Excellency Governor Shirley, &c. at Annapolis in Order, as it is supposed, to concert the Plan of Operations for the ensuing Campaign.

NEW-YORK March 24. Saturday last his Majesty's Ship Syren, Capt. Proby, arrived here in 4 Days from Hampton in Virginia, and by several of the Officers we are informed, that about 3 Weeks ago 16 sail of Transports arrived there from Cock, with two Regiments of Foot on board, amounting in the whole, to about 1000 affective Men, exclusive of the Company of Matrosses; and that they were all marched for Alexandria, in their Way to Will's Creek; that a Ship sailed for Boston, in Company with the Syren, with some Officers, Money, Cloaths, &c. for Governor Shirley's Regiment, and that another Ship was to sail in a Day or two for this Place, with Officers, and the like Materials for Colonel Pepperell's Regiment.

BOSTON March 25. By His Excellency the Governour,

These are to Order all Soldiers in the Regiment of Foot, under the Command, that have been absent from the Regiment on Furlough, or otherwise, to repair to Boston, by the 15th of April next without Fail.

Given under my Hand at Boston March 24th 1755.
W. Shirley.

BOSTON March 31. Last Saturday Evening his Excellency was pleased to adjourn the General Assembly of this Province, till Tuesday the Twenty-second Day of April next; and Yesterday Morning his Excellency set out for Annapolis in Maryland, to hold a Conference with General Braddock, &c.

APRIL 1755

BOSTON April 7. The following Act pass'd the Great and General Court of this Province in the last Session.

An Act to Encourage and facilitate the Removal and Prevention of French Encroachments in His Majesty's North American Territories.

Whereas as it may be of very ill Consequence, if the several Measures taking by his Majesty's good Subjects of this and the Governments adjacent, to remove or prevent the Encroachment of the French, should be from Time to Time made known and exposed to the People in Louisbourg or other French Settlements in North America, before their Executions:

Be it therefore enacted by his Excellency the Governor, Council and House of Representatives, and hereby it is enacted and declared, That for the Space of four Months, to be computed from the last Day of March, one Thousand seven Hundred and fifty five, it shall be unlawful for any of his Majesty's Subjects of this Province; and they are strictly forbidden to hold any Correspondence or Communications with any Inhabitant of Louisbourg, or any other of the French Settlements in North America, either by Land or Water, and if any Person or Persons belonging to this Province, shall be so audacious as to go or send to Louisbourg, or any other French Settlement in North America during said four Months, the Ship, Sloop or other Vessel employed, with her Tackle and Appurtenances and her Cargo, shall be forfeited, one Half to his Majesty for the Use of this Province, and the other Half to him or them who shall inform and sue for the same in any of his Majesty's Courts within the Province proper to try the same, and be further liable, if a Ship or other vessel, the Master to have one Ear cut off, and be publickly whip'd thirty nine Lashes, and be Render'd for ever incapable of holding any Place of Honour or Profit under this Government; and the Owner or Owners, and Factor or Factors of the Owner or Owners of such Ship or other Vessel shall forfeit and pay each Five Hundred Pounds, to be recovered and disposed of as above and be also for ever disabled to hold any Place of Honour or Profit under this Government.

This Act was Published March 31, 1755.

BOSTON April 7. Whereas His Majesty's ship Mermaid, under my command, is intended for a convoy for the several vessel on this Expedition; and as it is generally imagined that she may be of great Service, if I can get seamen sufficient to man her:

These are to give notice to all those brave seamen that a willing to serve his Majesty King George, on board the said ship for the time of this expedition, that if they will repair on board her, or to my house in Hanover-Street, they will meet with the best of treatment, enter into immediate pay, receive all fitting encouragements, and, if they demand it, be Discharged at the end of the Expedition.

Given under my Hand at Boston on the 31st of March 1755.   Washington Shirley.

PHILADELPHIA April 10. On Tuesday Evening his Excellency William Shirley, Esq; Governor of Boston, and the Hon. James De Lancey, Esq; Governor of New-York, arrived in this City, accompanied by several Persons of Distinction, His Honour our Governor, and a great many of the principal Inhabitants of the Place, went some Miles out of Town to meet them. The next Morning Governor De Lancey proceeded on his Journey for Annapolis, and in the Afternoon the Governors Shirley and Morris set out for the same Place, attended by a Number of Gentlemen.

NEW-HAVEN April 12. From the Connecticut Gazette No. 1.

On Monday the 31st of last Month, His Honour the Governor of this Colony, issued a Proclamation, , by, the Advice of the other Branches of the Legislature, for encouraging Men to enlist in his Majesty's Service, By this Proclamation each able-bodied Man is to have a Premium of 30 Shillings lawful Money, or the equivalent in Bills of Credit: and whoever provides himself a good Firelock, Sword or Hatchet, Belt and Cartridge-Box, to receive 16 Shillings more, like Money, and a sufficient Blanket, 14 Shillings more: Those who can't thus provide themselves, to be provided by the Colony, but the Arms to be returned when the Service is over; and for such Arms as shall be inevitably lost, the Treasury is to pay; Each Man to have 26 Shilling 8 lawful Money per Month, rekoning 28 Days to each Month, and to have one Month's Wages advance paid before they march.

BOSTON April 14. Thursday last being the Day appointed for mustering on the Common in this Town, the New-England Regiment, commanded by his Excellency, near Two Thousand came in on that Day, and the two following Days, and 'tis said some hundreds more a daily expected.

NEW-YORK April 14. As his Majesty has been graciously pleased to send a Squadron of Ships of war under the Command of the Honourable Commodore Kepple, and two Regiments of Foot, which are already landed in Virginia, with two regiments more which are hourly expected from Ireland, for the Service and protection of the Lives, Religion and Properties of his faithful Subjects in North America, who are now threatened with a Formidable Invasion from France, the most dangerous Enemy to a free People; and as his Honour our Governor by his Proclamation issued the Twenty-ninth of March last, by and with the Advice of his Majesty's council, has heartily invited all good Subjects to distinguish themselves at this critical Juncture, by voluntarily enlisting themselves into His Majesty's Service, for the two Regiments that are now raising for the Defence and Security of the British Northern Colonies, under the Command of Col. Shirley and Sir William Pepperell, Bart. (both Natives of America) it is hoped, that the said two Regiments may be speedily compleated, and capable to take the Field in conjunction with the rest of his Majesty's Forces, who are distin'd for the present Expedition; especially as we shall thereby declare our Loyalty, and shew ourselves worthy of his Majesty's Grace and Favour.

N. B. The dread that many of the Inhabitants of this and neighbouring Colonies have been in which Regard to Press Warrants being issued to raise Land-Forces, and the extraordinary Encouragement given to inlist, has, we are told, afforded great Success in compleating the several Companies. It is hoped that the same Spirit distinguished itself in Places to the Eastward, will be no less conspicuous in this.

PHILADELPHIA April 17. Extract of a private Letter from London (via Virginia) dated Feb. 3.

"A War with the French is now generally expected, unless the vigorous Measures our Ministry are taking, in fitting out a large Number of Men of War, under the Famous Admirals Anson, Hawke and Boscawen, should strike a Damp on that Nation.

We hear that the New-Jersey Assembly have agreed to raise Five Companies for his Majesty's Service, and give Fifteen Thousand Pounds for the support of them.

NEW-YORK April 21. A Letter from Annapolis informs us, that his Excellency General Braddock the Hon. Governor Dinwiddie, and Commodore Kepple, arrived there the 3d Instant, and set off for Alexandria the 10th following; that the Hon. William Shirley, Esq; Governor of Boston, the Hon. James De Lancey, Esq; our Lieutenant Governor, and the Hon. Robert Hunter Morris, Esq; Governor of Pennsylvania, arrived at Annapolis the 11th; when they immediately set off, in Company with Governor Sharpe of Maryland, for Alexandria, in order to concert Measures with General Baraddock for his ensuing Campaign. And we hear that the Governors Shirley and De Lancey are expected in this City on Wednesday next.

NEW-YORK April 21. We are advised from the different Parts of Connecticut, That the Officers now recruiting there for the Service of that Province, meet with uncommon Success; that most of the Companies are compleat; and that on

Friday last, Lieutenant Waterburry, of Captain Stanford's Company, enlisted no less than 30 Superior Men of Stanford.

BOSTON April 28. To apprize the Inhabitants of this Province, or other Persons of this Consequence of harbouring or concealing Soldiers in his Majesty's Service, bringing or detaining their Cloaths, or other Furniture belonging to the King, the following Paragraph of the Act of Parliament against Mutiny and Desertion is here published.

That if any Person shall Harbour, conceal, or assist any Deserter form His Majesty's Service, Knowing him to be such; the Person so offending shall forfeit for every such Offence, the Sum of Five Pounds; or if any Person knowingly detain, buy, or exchange, or otherwise receiven any Arms, Clothes, Caps, or other Furniture belonging to the King, from any Soldier or Deserter, upon any Account or Pretence whatsoever, or cause the Colour of such Clothes to be changed; the Person so offending shall forfeit, for every such Offence, the Sum of Five Pounds; and upon Conviction by the Oath of one or more credible Witness or Witnesses, before any of His Majesty's Justices of the Place, the said respective Penalties of Five Pounds, and Five Pounds shall be leveled by warrant under the Hands of the said Justice of the Peace by distress and sale of Goods and Chattels of the offender; and one Moiety of the said first-mentioned Penalty of Five Pounds to be paid to the Informer, and the Residue of the said respective Penalties to be paid to the Officer, to whom any such Offender, who shall be convicted as aforesaid, of harbouring or assisting any such Deserters; or having knowingly received any Arms, Clothes, Caps, or other Furniture belonging to the King; or of having caused the Colour of such Clothes to be changed, contrary to the Interest of this Act, shall not have sufficient Goods and Chattels, whereupon Distress may be made, to the Value of the Penalties recovered against him for such Offence, or shall not pay the Penalties within Four Days after Conviction; then, and in such Case, such Justice of the Peace shall and may, by Warrant under his Hand and Seal, either commit such Offenders to the Common Goal, there to remain without Bail or Mainprize for the Space of three Months, or cause such Offenders to be publickly whipt, at the Direction of the such Justice.

BOSTON April 28. Whereas some of the Recruits rais'd for the Regiment of Foot under my Command, and for the Service and Defence of his Majesty's Provinces in North America, have not all of the kept to Order, by repairing to the Vessels taken up to convey them to New-York, the Place of Redezvous for the said Regiment's and as I should be loth to put the Act of Parliament in Execution relating to Deserters, hoping they had no Design to desert, but that some Accident prevented their attending their Duty in this Respect. These are to acquaint all Persons so enlisted, that if they will immediately hasten to the Regiment at New-York, or come and deliver themselves up to any of the proper Officers of it, what is past shall be forgiven, otherwise they must expect to be prosecuted as Deserters: And any Person inclin'd to enlist in said Regiment, shall have all due Encouragements.

Kittery, April 10, 1755.   William Pepperrell.

MAY 1755

Quebec May 1. "Two Spies were Hanged up here on the 25th past. The one was found to have made an Inventory of the Cannon cast here, also of those imported from Europe since the Year 1755; also a List of the Houses, Forts, Magazines, &c. at this Place, and on each side of the River as far as the Island of Montreal, was found on him concealed in his Stocking. The other was detected in tracing the Appearance of one of the Batteries Here: this Copy, however, to prevent Suspicion on the Approach of an Officer with File and Musqueteers, who had observed him, he put into his Mouth and swallowed it, The former is a Swiss and the latter a German. In return for the Favour done the English in dispatching these two of their Emissaries, we are apprehensive that one of our most ingenious Reconnoitres has met with a similar Fate, or has fallen into the Hands of the Indians. On the 20th past a Reinforcement of 80 Men, with four Pieces of Cannon were dispatched to our Fort at Crown-Point, and Information that the English were preparing to attack that Important pass."

BOSTON May 5. By the publick paper bro't by the Western Mail, we learn that his Excellency our Governor, accompanied with the Lieutenant Governor of Philadelphia, had returned there from the General Congress at Alexandria: That at there entering the City, they were complemented with a Peal of the new Sett of Eight Bells, in Christ-Church Steeple; and a Round of 21 Brass Guns: That our Governor was to set out from thence the 24th ult. in his Journey hither; and that he was expected at New-York on Monday last; so that it is not improbable he will be in Town this Week.

NEW-YORK May 5. Last Tuesday his Excellency Willial Shirley, Esq; Governor of Boston (and the whole Province too) and Robert Hunter Morris, Esq; Governor of Pennsylvania accompanied by several Gentlemen of Distinction arrived here from the Jerseys: At their landing there were saluted by the Cannon from Fort George, and received by the Hon. James De Lancey Esq; our Lieutenant Governor, the Members of his Majesty's Council, and the General Assembly of this Province, the Corporation, the Clergy of every Domination, and all the principal Gentlemen of this Place: The City Regiment of Militia, with five Independent Companies, and one Grenadiers, were under Arms, and lined the Street, and as they passed along, from the Whitehall to the Oswego Market, and many of them being dressed in their proper Uniforms, made a handsome Appearance; the whole was conducted with great Decency and Decorum. And on Saturday Governor Shirley set out for Boston.

We are assured that the Hon. William Johnson Esq; one of his Majesty's Council of this Province, is by Col. Shirley, appointed Major General and Commander in Chief of the American forces to be employed in an Expedition to the Northward, and also of such Indians as shall assist his Majesty in the same.

Major Johnson embarked Yesterday for Albany, and did likewise Two Hundred of the new raised Soldiers.

Yesterday a Number of Recruits, suppos'd to be between 150 and 200, arrived here from New-England. It was reported, and feared, a few Days ago, that they had been lost in the Passage.

BOSTON May 9. Tuesday last, about Noon, his Excellency returned in good Health from his Interview with General Braddock in Virginia, to the great Satisfaction of People of all Ranks among us: His Excellency the Night before arriv'd at the Seat of Henry Vassel, Esq; in Cambridge, where he lodged; from thence, attended by his Honour the Lieut. Governor and a great Number of our Gentlemen he was escourted by the Troop of Guards, and two other Troops, to the Province-House in this Town: Upon his arrival there, the Cannon of Castle Williams, and the Town Batteries were discharged: His Excellency alighted at the Province-House, where he was received by the Members of His Majesty's Council, and a great Number of civil and military Officers and other Gentlemen: and from thence, being proceeded by the Company of Cadets, march'd in Procession to the Town House, the Regiment of the Town being drawn up under Arms, and paying him the marching Salute as he pass'd along. At the Town House he received the Congratulation of the Officers and Gentlemen: During the Procession the Streets, Windows, Turrets, &c. were crowded with Spectators expressing the greatest joy on his Excellency's safe Return. The Militia being afterwards drawn up in King Street fired their Volleys. which were followed by three Huzzas; Afterwards his Excellency attended by the Company of Cadets, returned to the Province-House.

BOSTON May 12. Yesterday Captain Kirkwood arrived here in about nine Weeks from London, and has brought with him Arms and other Accoutrements for the Provincial Troops lately raised, who have impatiently waited here several Weeks for their Arrival. He has also bro't a large Quantity of Powder.

That Captain Cobb, in a Sloop in the Government's Service, has taken a French Schooner going from Louisbourg to St. John's with 1100 Barrels of Flour, a Number of Cannon and other warlike Stores on board, all which was condemned at Halifax. ——— Also, that Captain Cobb had taken a Vessel belonging to (our) Plimouth, laden with Provisions, which was going to trade with the French; but as both Vessel and Cargo have been condemned and sold, 'tis tho't the Owner will make but an indifferent Voyage on't. ——— May all such Traders meet with the same Fate.

PHILADELPHIA May 15. We hear from the Counties of Lancaster, York and Cumberland, that Notice being given there, that Waggons and Carriage Horses were wanting for the Use of the Army, great Numbers were immediately offered, and 150 Waggons, laden with Oats, Indian Corn, and other Forage, were dispatch'd to the Camp, in a few Days, and as many more might have been had as wanted, the People offering with great Readiness and chearfulness, from a Zeal for his Majesty's Service.

BOSTON May 19. Saturday last Capt. Treat arrived here from London but has bro't no late News than we have from Capt. Kirkwood. He has bro't several Barrels of Gun Powder, and a Gentheman is come Passenger with him, who is Paymaster General of the Forces now on Foot in America, who has bro't Fourteen Thousand Pounds Sterling in Cash for their Use.

The same Day the Master of a Vessel arrived in Town from Louisbourg, and gives the following Account viz. That having met with bad Weather at Sea, in which he lost his Mast, and also suffered much other Damage, he put into to Louisbourg to refit, and that while he was there, a 36 Gun Ship came in from France, and upon her arrival, 500 Men were immediately set to Work on their Fortifications, which were in ruinous Condition, except the Island Battery.

——— That there was not one English Vessel in the Harbour, nor had there been any for a Considerable Time, which the French much wondered at, and lamented the want of, they being greatly straightned for Provisions.

Upward of 20 Sail of Transport Vessels, with Troops and all Sorts of military Stores on board, now lie here ready to put to Sea, and will sail sometime this Day for Annapolis Royal in Nova-Scotia, under Convoy of three of his Majesty's Ship of War, of 20 Guns each.

We have Advice from the Eastward, that the Indians have burnt an House, and taken two Men Prisoners, on Kennebeck River.

We hear from New-Hopkington, in the Province of New-Hampshire, that a few Days ago, a Man and a Boy were taken Prisoner there by five Indians; but it happen'd that about two Hours after they were met with by nine Men who were out on Scout: One of the Indians discovering the English near them, held up two of his Fingers and whistled, which was a Signal to the rest; upon which they rose from their Ambush, and fired upon the

English but did no Execution. The English pursu'd them. and retook the Captives, and the Indians made off.

BOSTON May 19. By an Express from the Eastward, we learn that Yesterday was se'nnight a Number of Indians came and took two Men Prisoners, at a Place called Kennebeck, about 2 Miles above Richmond-Fort; and burnt one House, It is likewise reported, that Mischief has been done at Broad-Bay by the Indians.

We hear by a Person which left Fort Halifax the 4th Inst. that said Day two of the Norridgewalk tribe of Indians (who were concern'd in the Murther of some of our Men last Fall) came there and was very desirous of making Peace.

This Morning set sail, under the Convoy of Men of War, thirty-Five sail of Transport, having on board upward of 2000 Forces, which have been raised here, bound to the Eastward.

NEW-YORK May 19. We hear that 300 Connecticut Men, are taken into the Pay of this Province, to serve under their Officers, on the present Expedition; and that the Remainder of our Quota of Troops, (500 Men) will soon be ready.

We are informed by the Masters of several Albany Sloops arrived here last Week, that the Detachment from General Pepperrell's Regiment arrived there safe last Saturday se'nnight, and next Day set out for Schenectady, where they were provided with Battoes, &c. to expedite their March for Oswego.

Tuesday last his Majesty's Snow the Jamaican, Captain Hood, arrived here from Virginia, with several Officers for General Pepperrell's Regiment, and Arms, &c. for the New-Jersey Provincial Forces.

The Hon. Robert Dinwiddie Esq; Lieutenant Governor of the Colony and Dominion of Virginia, in his Speech in the General Assembly of that Colony, on the 2d Instant, says, "I have the Pleasure to acquaint you, that his Majesty, out of his great Regard for his Subjects on this Continent, and a proper Resentment of the unjustifiable Invasions and Incroachments of the French, on his American Dominions, has, of his gracious Goodness to us, ordered four Regiments consisting each of a thousand Men, with a large Train of Artillery, for our Aid and Assistance, besides the Regiments now at Nova-Scotia, all at the Expense of the Crown of Great-Britain.

His Excellency General Braddock, Commander in Chief of all his Majesty's Forces on this Continent; the Honourable Commerdore Keppel, Commander of his Majesty's Ships of War; the Governors of New-England, New-York, Pennsylvania, Maryland, and myself, met in council the 14th of last Month; where the Affairs of the Colonies were maturely considered, and a Plan of Operations for the Summer's Campaign adjusted, with so much Judgement, that, if properly supported, the Design of our Enemies will probably be defeated, and the Peace and Safety of our Country established on the most permanent Foundation.

PHILADELPHIA May 22. We hear from the Camp at Will's Creek, that his Excellency General Braddock, and all his Forces, were arrived there. That Capt. Dobbs, Son of Governor Dobbs, was also arrived from North-Carolina, with a fine Company of 100 Men; and Scarropady had likewise got to Camp, with a Number of Indians.

BOSTON May 26. From the Gentleman's Magazine for February 1755. An Account of Canada given to the Governor of New-York, 1751.

Quebeck, the metropolis, stands upon near as much ground as the City of New-York, but does not contain above half the number of houses. It is situated on the west side of the river St. Lawrence, where a small river to the westward, which is called by the French Le Petit Riviere, and empties itself into the river St. Lawrence, forms, a point on which the town is built, and is almost in form of a triangle: It is divided into two parts, one called the upper, and the other the lower town; the last lies on the river side, and has two batteries of eight pieces of cannon, tho' of little consequence in case of an attack.

In this part of the town the streets are regular and the houses well built, chiefly of stone. From that part the lower town next to the river St. Lawrence, there is but one way to ascend to the upper, which is cut shelving along the hill, or rather road, and is about 120 Feet in height, and overlooks all the lower town; It is certainly one of the strongest natural fortifications in America, being almost perpendicular, and entire rock.

On the top of this hill stands the part called the upper town, from whence there is a beautiful and extensive prospect of the river and country for several Leagues. Here are several good buildings of stone, the seminary and convent of friers of the order of St. Francis, two nunneries, part of one which is the King's hospital for the sick and wounded; seven churches beautifully adorned, and very rich; but the Jesuits College is yet more magnificent. On the back of the south part of the town they are building a strong stone wall, of a considerable height and tickness; which extends from the river St. Lawrence to the Petit Riviere; they having no occasion to carry it any further, as nature has fortified the other parts of the town much stronger than art could have done. On this hill, or upper town, are four batteries, the grand battery on that part which forms the point between the two rivers, and looks directly down the river St. Lawrence, has 43 pieces of cannon, four, six and nine pounders, and two mortar pieces of 14 inches diameter each; it has no parapets, or breast work to cover the Guns, nor do I think there is any occasion for them, as the hill is of such a prodigious height, and the access to it so difficult. At about 100 yards distance to the westward in another small battery of four pieces of cannon, two of nine, and two of 18 pounders. About 60 yards further west is another of the same sort, both intended to command the other side of the Petit Riviere, if any force should land below the town, and take that rout to get to the back part. It is plain they cannot command any part of the river where ships or vessels of any great bulk can pass, neither can they do much damage to the forces that should land and march that way, the opposite side of Petit Riviere being of fine land country, where the troops might pass far enough out of the reach of these cannon. The last of the four are to the southward of the grand battery about 250 or 300 yards, it has 26 pieces of cannon of four and six pounders, and a cover or breast work of stone about four feet height. The design of this battery seems to be to prevent ships passing the town to land forces above, to come down on the back part, as it only commands a-cross to the river St. Lawrence. These are all the batteries they have in Quebeck. I saw several other pieces of cannon in different parts of the town, but understood they were to be sent about three leagues down the river, to a place where they told me the channel was so narrow and difficult, that one ship could pass at a time, and that they were travelling carriages always ready to transport them to that place in case of fleets coming up the river. West from Quebeck, about three leagues, the Indian nation of Hurrons have a castle called by the French Lorrette, which contains about 74 houses. The country from Quebeck to this castle, and round about is very populous, the land hilly and broken, yet many places produce plenty of good wheat amd peas.

In my journey from Quebeck to Montreal, which I made on the west side of the river St. Lawrence, I found the land near the water side fertile and good, and full of inhabitants; but this is only to be understood of the land lying within half a league of the river; for thence backwards are no inhabitants, neither can there be, the land being so exceedingly barren, that it is impossible to improve it. Thirty good leagues south of Quebeck, on this side of the river, is a small inconsiderable town without fortifications, called Trois Rivieres, where resides a deputy governor. Three leagues to the westward of this is a fine iron mine, where they have a large Furnace and five forges, and there it is reported that they cast cannon; indeed I saw the moulds of several, and one cannon which they had attempted to cast, but had spoiled in the attempt. This Mine is the sole property of the king, and I was told that four hundred of his men are daily employed there.

The distance from Quebeck to Montreal is 60

leagues, and betwixt them are 58 parishes and churches, 29 on each side the river St. Lawrence.

The town of Montreal is situated on an island of the same name on the west side the river St. Lawrence, 10 leagues in length, but not of any considerable breadth.

The town is three fourths of a mile in length and one fourth in breadth, has a strong stone wall quite round: Near the center is a small hill, with a battery of 26 pieces of cannon, four, six, and nine pounders; it is called the Battery Royal, and commands the river and country round, besides this, there is no other battery, tho' they are some small pieces of cannon on the ramparts, but I cannot ascertain their number. The situation of the town of Montreal is beautiful, the streets are regular, and the houses neatly built of stone and wood. It is the of residence of a deputy governor.

A fine champaign country round about, a good soil, and well inhabited. Four leagues south from the town of Montreal, on the east side of the river St. Lawrence, is an Indian castle, called by us Cogna Wagah by the French Qsault St. Lewis; they compute that it contains in the whole 1000 souls, 400 of which are fighting men; It is picketted in has a church two Jesuits, and an Officer posted, as they have in every Indian castle.

Six leagues south of the castle is another, called Cana Sadagh; in this are the same number of souls as the other, but the inhabitants are two different nations, Orondocks and Cocknawagahs. These are all the Indian castles I was at in Canada.

On the east side the river St. Lawrence, two leagues distant from the town of Montreal, as a small village called Laprarie, not fortified, from whence there is a road to St. John's, about five leagues, and bears from Montreal S. E.

St. John's is a fort situated in the river Champlain, which leads to the lake of the same name, it is picketted in, has two blockhouses, but no cannon, being designed chiefly as a magazine for the provisions and other stores to supply the garrison at Crown Point by small brig.

About 32 leagues from St. John's on the lake Champlain, is fort Frederic, called by us Crown Point, where a bay and small river to the eastward form a point on which the fort stands. It is built of stone, the walls a considerable height and thickness, and has 21 pieces of cannon and swivels mounted on the ramparts and bastions, a few of the largest are six pounders. I observed the wall cracked from top to bottom in several places.

At the entrance of the fort is a dry ditch 18 or 20 foot square, and a draw-bridge to the lake, which I apprehend it to be made use of in time of need, to bring water to the garrison, as the well they have in it affords them but little. ——— In the N. W. corner of the fort stands the citadel, it is a stone building eight square, four story high, each turned with arches, mount 20 pieces of cannon and swivels, the largest six pounders, four of which are in the first story and are useless till the Walls of the fort are beaten down. At the entrance to the citadel is a draw-bridge and ditch, of the same dimensions as that to the entrance of the fort. The walls of the citadel are about ten feet thick, the roof is high, and very slightly covered with shingles.

To the S. S. E. and S. W. of the fort the ground is rising, and is very advantageous for erecting a battery in case of a siege, as it is not above 300 yards distant from the fort. Behind it the land is low, and some thousand of men may lie without receiving any damage from the cannon of the fort, as the ridge is a fine covert, and lies circular, so as to flank two of the bastions. They have a chapel and several other wooden houses within the fort, which are put to no other use than storing their Provisions. The land near the fort, and on each side of the lake, which they are settling, is level and good. Since the peace there are already 14 farms on it, and, a great encouragement is given by the king, I was informed, that by next fall, several more families would settle.

This fort is of very great importance to the French; for in time of war it supplies parties sent to our frontiers with necessaries, and serves for a place of retreat, as it lies north of Albany only 40 leagues.

I wish, it had been possible for me to have made any computation of the number of inhabitants in Canada, which by report is about 40,000.

Stodart.

NEW-YORK May 26. Tho' a proper deterrence is to be paid to the Determination of those who are at the Head of publick Affairs; yet as it is possible a private Gentleman may as just sentiments, with respect to what concerns the publick Welfare, as one of those at the Council-board; and therefore, I think, every Member of Society has a right, in a public Manner, not only to suggest any Thing which he thinks may be conclusive to the Good of his Country, but also to make proper Observations upon the Steps taken by his Superiors, provided it be done, not in a bold and arrogant, but humble and modest Manner.

A scheme, it seems, has been for some Time concerted, of having the different Armies, to Act in as many different Places this Summer; on to dispossess the French of the Ohio, &c. another to erect Fortresses near Crown-Point, and a third to drive off the neutral French and Indians from Nova Scotia; this was some time a secret in the Breasts of those who have the Direction of the publick Affairs in their hands, and perhaps it had been well had it continued so to this Day. What shou'd be the Motive that induces them to permit it to take air, I can't pretend to say; nor can I imagine, unless this Scheme be design'd only as a Feint, that the Enemy hearing of it beforehand might draw off their Forces to those Places, while the Expedition on Foot were really design'd against some others. In this View only does it appear any Time like good Policy: But I can't believe this to be the Case, for one Army is undoubtedly destin'd to the Ohio, Crown Point is a Place of no small Importance to the French, and we can't do better then to endeavour to find means to be even with them there, and the Expedition to Nova-Scotia, if succeeded, will conduce to our no small Advantage. In short the Sceme seems to be so well contrived, that I can't but think it real and is a Pity it shou'd be render'd abortive by an untimely Publication. Had we kept our Fingers upon out Mouth, till our Forces had reach'd the Scene of Action (as is said to be the Case on the famous Siege of Cape-Breton) thro' the auspicious Smiles of a kind of Providence, we might have been almost sure of Success; but now without a Doubt, the Enemy understands our Design, as thoro'ly almost as we do ourselves, long before our Forces are reasy to march.

Our Nation is naturally brave and valiant but we seem to trust too much to the Bravery; Tho' the French are superior in Number, yet we seem to be resolved to conquer by main Force, and take every Place by Storm; but why shou'd not we intermix a little Policy with the Force, expecially since we have such powerful and politick Enemy to deal with? The Poet, says, "Force void of Policy falls by its own Weight:" and another, "Its no Disgrace to be thought by a Foe." Everyone knows the French are very politick, and they are in reality more powerful than many imagine: They conduct their Enterprizes with all the possible Secrecy; not to mention their deceitful Pretences of a Willingness to accommodate Affairs. One Capt. Harrison, it seems, trading from New-Castle to Brest, where the French Armament is preparing, must not enter the Harbour, lest he shou'd discover the Greatness and Forwardness of the warlike Preparations; but must load and unload at Sea. And it's said some Frenchmen have been executed in France, for holding a secret Correspondence with the English Nation. Why can't we take such Precoutions, and be as careful to keep Counsel as they? Surely we had need be Politick, since they are superior to us in Numbers. And tho' the British Navy is larger than the French, yet as Things go on, we know not how much longer it will be so. Besides, notwithstanding the good Dispositions of Spain seem'd to show towards us some Time ago, we see there is a Treaty of Alliance and mutual Assistance upon the carpet, between France and Spain, and in Case of War, we may depend upon having them both upon our Backs, and then, how despicable soever the French, or even them in Conjunction with the Spaniards, may seem to some, who love their ease more than their Country, and affecting to be esteem'd bold, can bombastically brag of the British Lyon, &c. and despise our Enemies for their Folly in rousing him, (forgetting that, as strong as the Lyon is, if he be asleep or shut his Eyes, the Fox may gnaw his guts out) I say, how despicable soever our Enemies may seem to such, I fear they will be full, if not more than a Match for us. How much reason than have we to improve the united Forces of Arms and Policy, since either of 'em singly is sufficient! And oh what a Pity 'tis our Designs should be so soon made Publick (for a Bird of the Air will carry the Voice to our Enemies, and which hath Wings will tell the Matter) For my Part, as I Love my Country, when the Account of the Scheme of the ensuing Campaign come abroad, I was heartily both glad and sorry to hear it; glad that such a Thing was on Foot, but sorry to hear it so soon. Nevertheless I pray, the Almighty, on whom the Success, of every Enterprize depends, wou'd prosper our Understanding, and so succeed our Arms, that we may soon disposses our Foes, those Sons of Violence and Lies.

If I forgot thee, Oh, English America, let my Right Hand forget her Cunning; if I do not remember thee, let my Tongue cleave to the Roof of my Mouth; ---- Remember, O Lord, the children of France, who say of our Land, raze it, raze it, even to the Foundation thereof. O Daughter of Canada, who art to be destroy'd, happy shall he be that rewardeth thee as thou would'st serve us. Happy shall be that taketh and dasheth thy little ones against the Stones.

Philo-Americus.

PHILADELPHIA May 29. We hear from the Camp at Will's Creek, that his Excellency General Braddock was to march in a few Days for the Ohio: That Mr. Grogan, had arrived there with a number of Indians; and more were daily expected to come in.

Extract of a Letter from New-York dated May 26,
"A French Gentleman arrived here last Night, from Albany: He left Canada four Weeks ago, and says, that 950 Men were then about marching for the Ohio, where 250 kept Garrison all the Winter, and 400 more were soon to set out for Crown-Point."

Capt. Peter Spence, in the Sloop Jennet and Margaret, arrive here on Saturday last in four Days from Virginia; and informs us, That five Days before he sailed, an Express arrived at Williamsburg from General Braddock at Will's Creek, with Orders for sundry things useful to the Army to be directly sent up; upon arrival of which at the Camp, the Forces were immediately to march forward to the Great Meadows; And it's suppos'd they are moved by this Time, as the things sent for were in a few Hours after the Express arrived, dispatch'd. General Sinclare was returned to the Camp before the Express came off, from an Excursion he had made in Pursuit of a Number of French and Indians he had Intelligence of; but did not come a-cross them, altho' he was absent about Eleven Days.

JUNE 1755

BOSTON June 2. By a Letter from one of the Captives in Canada, we are informed, that a great Number of French Soldiers had lately marched from thence for the Ohio.

We have advice from the Eastward that about a Fortnight ago, as five Indians, wiz. 2 Sanops, 2 Squaws, and one Papoose, were passing a River in a Canoe, it overset and they were all drowned.

BOSTON June 2. We hear from the Back of North Yarmouth, that last Week a Man was taken Prisoner and one Snow, (who was in Company with him) kill'd there, by the Indians.

From Sheepscut, That one Mr. Ross, with his two Sons, and an Elderly Man and a Lad, were surpriz'd and fired upon by a Number of Indians as they were at work in a Field, by whom they were taken and carried off.

NEW-YORK June 2. Last Sunday Se'nnight a French Trader with a Woman (said to be his Wife) arrived here from Montreal, in Canada, which place he left about a Month since: We hear, he reports, That two Detachments of Men, amounting to 700, were, some Time before his Departure from Thence, sent to the Ohio; that another 250 were soon to follow, and that their whole Force on the Ohio this Summer would not (if we have Faith enough to believe a Frenchman) exceed 1200 Men, exclusive of Indians; that at Quebec they were very busy in building not less than 500 Battoes; and 'twas tho't some new Expedition was on foot, and would, without Hesitation or Delay, be speedily executed.

We hear that the New-Jersey Provincial Forces are to set out for Albany, the latter End of this Week, or the Beginning of the next, under the Command of Col. Peter Schuyler.

PHILADELPHIA June 5. We hear from Will's Creek,

that the Waggons and Horses lately contracted from the Counties of Lancaster, York and Comberland, were safely arriv'd at the Camp, and gave great Satisfaction to the General, and Officers, being, for the most Part, by far the best of any that have been engag'd in the Service of the Army since their Arrival. We likewise hear that there are fine Bottoms for several Miles round the Camp, in which there is a great Deal of good Grass and other Foods for the Horses: And that the Army in general are very healthy, inpatient to enter on Action, and wait chiefly for the Arrival of the Forage purchased in this Province.

In a Letter from Susquhanna dated, the 31st, ult. it is mentioned, that a Person was just return'd from the Camp, and brought Advice, that just before he left it, two Men came there, who were supposed to be Spies, one of them being known to have been among the Virginia Forces on the same Business before Washington's Defeat last Summer. They came from the French Fort, and pretended they were very numerous there. One of them attempted to make his Escape, he being a good Runner, but was overtaken only by one Man, who brought him back, when he was immediately put in Irons, and it was thought would soon be hanged.

WILLIAMSBURG June 6. Yesterday, Sen'night, Major Chapman, of Sir Peter Halkett's, with a Detachment from the British Regiments, Capt. Rutherford's independent Company, and the Virginian Companies of Captain Polson, Peyrouny and Waggoner, consisting in all 600 Men, marched out of Fort Cumberland, in order to pass the Alligany Mountains.

PHILADELPHIA June 6. We hear from Chester, that at the Court of the Quarter Session held there last Week, an Indictment was presented to the Grand Jury, and found by them, against one James Castelio, for speaking the following words, viz. "King George has no more Right to the Crown of Great-Britain than I, and if he had his Deserts, he would have his Neck cut off; I have a Sum of Money with me, and will give half a Crown a Day to each Man that will go with me, and join the French Forces that are backwards: Also for drinking a Health to the French King and the Pretender." To which he pleaded Guilty, and begg'd the Mercy of the Court. whereupon he receiv;d Sentence as follows. That he should stand one Hour in the Pillory on Thursday last, and the same on Friday, with these Words fixed on his Back; "I stand here for speaking seditious Words against the best King," which sentence was accordingly put in Execution.

BOSTON June 9. By a private Letter from Philadelphia, we are assured, that a Committee of their Assembly, a few Days ago, voluntarily made a Present of Twenty Horses, and Twenty Loads of Liquor, and necessary Refreshments, such as Wine, Spirits, Sugar, Fruit, Vinegar, Oil, Raisins, Rice, &c. to the Subaltern Officers belonging to the two Regiments of Peter Halket, and Col. Dunbar now at the Camp under the Command of General Braddock --- This Present as it was unexpected, was esteemed highly beneficial, and the Thanks of the two Colonels returned in a polite Manner to the Province in general, but more particularly to the Gentlemen who first moved it in Behalf of all the Officers concerned whose Pay was thought two scanty to furnish them with such Articles in a wilderness and a strange Land: But inasmuch as the Officers of the other Forces at that Place were excluded the Benefit, they thought something hard of it; When they were informed, that as they had been a great while in America, well acquainted with the Affairs thereof, and must doubtless have Friends and Acquaintances in those Governments where they resided, they could not be so destitute of Supply as those Strangers were. --- The Reflection frequently cast on Pennsylvania, for their Backwardness in War Affairs, must surely fall, when it is known, that that Government has given, exclusive of the Presents, 15,000 Pounds on the present Occasion, 5,000 Pound of which is entirely at General Braddock's Disposal; and furnishing the Army with upwards of two Hundred Waggons with four Horses each, and above 1500 Horses for Carriage, with their Provisions, besides cutting a Road through the Woods near

100 Miles extent. And yet this is not all the Service; for the King's Forces have been, and are recruiting in the Government with much greater Success than in any of the other Governments; which they could not so well do, if the province had raised any Men of their own.

NEW-YORK June 9. Tuesday last a Sloop arrived here from St. John's in Newfoundland, with an Officer and a Number of Matrosses on board, designed for the Expedition carrying on under the Command of General Braddock; and on Saturday they embarked for Amboy, to proceed to the Camp.

Last Saturday Sir William Pepperrell Baronet, who Commanded the Forces at the Reduction of Louisbourg, received a Commission as Major General in His Majesty's Army, and we doubt not will again distinguish himself in the intended Attack upon the French Encroachments on our Frontiers, his Regiment being almost 700 strong, all pickt Men, a great Part of them already on Duty.

BOSTON June 12. By His Excellency William Shirley Esq; Captain General and Governor in Chief, in and over his Majesty's Province of the Massachusetts-Bay in New-England, and Vice-Admiral of the same, and Major General in His Majesty's Army.

A PROCLAMATION

Whereas the Indians of Norridgewock, Arresaguntacook, Wewcenock and the St. Jonh's Tribes and the Indians of the other Tribes inhabiting in the Eastern and Northern Parts of His Majesty's Territories of New-England, the Penobscot Tribe only excepted, have, contrary to their solemn Submission unto His Majesty long since made and frequently renewed, being Guilty of the most perfidious, barbarous and inhumane Murders of the divers of his Majesty's English Subjects, and have abstained from all Commerce and Correspondence with His Majesty's said Subjects for many Months past: and the said Indians have fully discovered an inimical, tratorous and rebellious Intention and Disposition;

I have therefore thought fit to issue this Proclamation, and to declare the Indians of the Norridgwock, Arresaguntacook, Wewenock and St.

John's Tribes, and the Indians of the other Tribes now or late inhabitants in the Eastern and Northern Parts of His Majesty's Territories of New-England, and in Alliance and Confederacy with the above-recited Tribes, the Penobscots only excepted, to be Enemies, Rebels and Traitors to his Most Sacred Majesty: And I so hereby require His Majesty's Subjects of this Province to embrace all Opportunities of pursuing, capturing, killing and destroying all and any of the aforesaid Indians, the Penobscot excepted.

And whereas the General Court of this Province have voted, That a Bounty of Encouragement be granted and allowed to be paid out of the pubblick Treasury to the marching Army that shall be employed for the Defence of the Eastern and Western Frontiers from the Twenty fifth of this Month June, until the Twenty fifth of Movember next:

I have thought fit to publish the same: And I do hereby promise, That there shall be paid out of the Province Treasury to all and any of the said Forces, over and above their Bounty upon Enlistment,, their Wages and Subsistence, the Premiums or Bounties following, viz.

For every Male Indian Prisoner above the Age of Twelve Years, that shall be taken or brought to Boston, Fifty Pounds.

For every Male Indian Scalp, brought in as Evidence of their being killed, Forty Pounds.

For every Female Indian Prisoner, taken or brought in as aforesaid, and for every Male Indian Prisoner under the Age of Twelve Years, taken and brought in aforesaid Twenty-five Pounds.

For every Scalp of such Female Indians or Male Indian under Twelve Years, brought in as Evidence of their being killed, as aforesaid, Twenty Pounds.

Given under my Hand at Boston, in the Province aforesaid, this Twelfth Day of June, 1755, and in the Twenty-eight Year of the Reign of our Sovereign Lord George the Second, by the Grace of God, of Great Britain, France and Ireland, King, defender of the Faith &c.   W. Shirley.

By his Excellecy's Command, J. Willard Secr'y.

PHILADELPHIA June 12. We hear that near 60 Waggons laden with Forage for the Army, have been dispatched from this City, within a few Days, to Will's Creek; the Inhabitants of most of the Townships in this Country having chearfully given considerable Bounties to the Waggoners, to encourage them to undertake the journey.

We hear also that a Number of Waggons laden with Forage, are likewise gone from Lancaster, and Berks.

We have Advice that Yesterday Se'night, the 2d Division of Troops marched from the Camp at Will's Creek, on their way to the Ohio, and the rest had Orders to hold themselves ready for Marching.

BOSTON June 14. An Act for the more effectual Prevention of Supplies of Provisions, and Warlike Stores to the French, from any Part of this Province.

Whereas notwithstanding the Provision already made by the Laws of the Government, divers evil-minded Persons have found Means to Transport Provisions to Louisbourgh, either direct from this Province, or else from the Province of New-Foundland, and from thence to Louisbourgh; by Means wherof the present Measures now engaged in by his Majesty's Forces for the Secretary of his Subjects, and for removing the Encroachment made upon his Territories, may be prejudiced and defeated:

Be it therefore enacted by the Governor, the Council and House of Representatives. That no Provisions, except Cod-Fish, nor warlike Stores, except so much as shall be necessary for the ordinary Victualling and Defence of any Vessel during her proposed Voyage, shall be exported from any Port or Part of this Province, until Bond be first given by the Master of such Vessel with sufficient Sureties in the Penalty of One Thousand Pounds Sterling to the Officer or Commissioner, of Impost. That all such Provisions and War-like Stores so laden, shall be relanded in some Part of this Province, or landed in some one of his Majesty's Colonies to the Southward of Newfoundland or at Annapolis Royal, or Halifax in Nova Scotia; and that certificate shall be returned within twelve Months from the Officer of the Customs in the Places where shall be landed, and any Person shall presume to export Provisions or War like Stores from this Province in a clandestine Way, and without obtaining a Clearance from the Naval Officers, every Person so offending shall be subject and liable to all the Penalties provided by an Act of this Province made and pass'd this present Year, intitled, An Act to encourage and facilitate the Removal and Prevention of French encroachments on his Majesty's North-American Territories.

And be it further enacted. That the Naval Officer shall give no Clearance for any Vessel, until Certificate be produced from the Commissioner of Impost, that the Master of such Vessels has conformed to the Rules prescribe by this Act.

And be it further enacted, That Oath shall be made by the Master of every Vessel clearing out, before the Commissioner of Impost, as to the whole Quantity of Provisions, and War like Stores laden or intended to be laden on board such Vessel.

This Act to continue and be in Force until the twelfth Day of September next and no longer.

NEW-HAVEN June 14. This Week the Provincial Troops, raised in the Colony of Connecticut, for removing Incroachments at Crown-Point, began their March to Albany, being 1000 Men in two Regiments: each consisting of six Companies, under the Command of Phinehas Lyman, Esq; Major General of all the Forces raised for that Servicw, in this and the Neighbouring Governments; (under General Johnson, Commander in Chief.)

Field Officers

In the first Regiment	In the 2d Regiment
Col. Phinehas Lyman,	Col. Elihu Goodrich,
Lieut, Col. John Pitkin,	Lieut, Col. N. Withing
Major Robert Denison.	Major Isaac Foot.

Captains besides the aforesaid Field Officers.

Nathan Payson,	Samuel Sanford,
William Patterson,	Samuel Whiting,
Ezekiel Pierce.	Benjamin Henman.

About 1000 Men are raised in the Colony, some in His Majesty's immediate Pay, and some in the Pay of the Neighbouring Governments.

Last Saturday, Capt. White, one of the Transports in the Service of this Colony, sail'd from hence for Albany, with the Stores for the Troops destin'd to Crown Point, for this Government, and, On Wednesday last, march'd from this Town, for Albany, Col. Whiting's Company: It entirely consists of Healthy able-bodied Men, in the Vigour of Life; their Behavior was decent, regular, resolute and chearful: They drew up, the Morning of the Departure, before the House of the Rev. Mr. Noyes, Minister of the first Society of New-Haven, who pray'd with them for general and particular Blessings on his Majesty's Arms, and all those who venture their Lives for the Defence and Protection of their Country, it's just Rights, and Liberties, and the Protestant Religion; and concluded with a pious and affectionate Exhortation, to the Soldiers, to act up to the Character of Christians as well as Soldiers, and to place their chief Dependence for Success upon the Lord of Hosts assisting them in their honest Design and vigorous Endeavors, and not in their own Strength and Numbers.

BOSTON June 16. In the House of Representatives June 14, 1755.

Voted, That the same Bounty for the Indian Scalps and Captives be allowed to the Forces on Western Frontier, as is allowed to the Eastern Frontiers. Also, That the same Bounty be allowed to all persons who are Inhabitants of this Province, that shall Captivate or kill an Indian Enemy, and shall produce such Indian or Scalp in Evidence.

Sent up for Concurrence, T. Hubbard, Speaker. Read and Concur'd. Thomas Clarke, Dep. Secr'y. Consented to W. Shirley.

On Monday last the two first Companies of his Excellency's Regiment began to march from this Place to Providence and two more each Day 'till Friday for the same Place, where they are to take Shipping for New-York, &c. The above Regiment we hear consists of 960 Men, exclusive of

Officers.

We hear that a Serjeant of one of the Companies which marched on Wednesday, being very warm, drank so much cold Water, that it immediately put an End to his Life.

From St. George's in the Eastward, we are informed, that on the 5th Instant about 9 o'Clock two Scotch Lads, Brothers, named Brown, were kill'd or taken by the Indians, but 'tis tho't the former, as a Number of Guns were hear'd to be fir'd off.

By an Express last Saturday from the Westward, we learn, that on Wednesday last, a Place called Charlemont, two Men were kill'd; and Capt. Rice, his Son and Grandson, were taken Prisoners there by the Indians.

BOSTON June 18. By His Excellency William Shirley, Esq; Capt,-General and Governor in Chief, in and over His Majesty's Province of The Massachusetts-Bay, in New-England, Vice Admaral of the same, and Major-General in his Majesty's Army.

A PROCLAMATION

Whereas the Great and General Court or assembly of this Province here, in their present Session granted an Encouragement to such Persons as shall form themselves into Companies to penetrate into the Indian Country, in order to captivate and kill said Indians as have by this Government been declared Enemies, Rebels, and Traitors to his Majesty:

I have thought fit to give publick Notice thereto, and in the Name and Behalf of this Government, to engage and promise,

That to every Company rais'd as aforesaid, and consisting of not less than thirty Men, the Officers whereof shall by me be appointed and commissioned, thirty Days Provisions: And for every Indian Captive taken by any of the said Companies, or any Party or Detachment thereof, they shall be paid out of the publick Treasury to such Company, Party or Detachment, the Sum of Two Hundred and Twenty Pounds: and for every Scalp of such Indian Enemy, brought in and produced as aforesaid, the Sum of Two Hundred Pounds.

Provided that such Company shall have perform'd a March of at least thirty Days, or shall make it evident that their returning in shorter Time was caused by some special Reason for promoting the publick Service; Provided also, that the officers of such Company keep Journal, of their march, and present the same, being attested, to me for my Inspection.

And I do further promise to every Inhabitant of this Province, that whoever shall Captivate, or kill one of the Indian Enemies; and shall produce such Captive or Scalp of the Indian so killed, at Boston, in evidence thereof, to the Satisfaction of the Governor and Council, there shall be paid out of the publick Treasury, the Bounty or Reward following, viz.

For every Captive the Sum of One Hundred and ten Pounds, and for every Scalp, the Sum of One Hundred Pounds.

Given at the Council-Chamber in Boston, this Eighteenth Day of June, 1755, and in the Twenty eight Year of the Reign of our Sovereign Lord George the Second, by the Grace of God, of Great Britain, France and Ireland, King, Defender of the Faith.   W. Shirley.
By his Excellency's Command, J. Willard, Secr'y.
God Save The King

PHILADELPHIA June 20. Sunday last an Express arrived here from Will's Creek, who brought Advice, that General Braddock, with the last Division of the Forces, march'd on Tuesday the Tenth Instant, for the Little Meadow, where he will be join'd by the rest of the Army, and then proceed to the Ohio: And that he has left Col. Innes Governor of the Fort Cumberland, with a sufficient Garrison for the Defence of it, and the Magazine of Provisions, Forage and Stores; that are left there.

We hear that several Bodies of French Troops have lately been seen passing in Battoes on Lake Ontario, on their Way, as is supposed, to the Ohio.

HALIFAX June 21. Yesterday arrived Capt. Spry, in his Majesty's Ship Fougeux, who brought with him here, the Aleide, a French Ship of War of 64 Guns, taken by Admiral Boscawen's Squadron cruizing off Lewisbourg: The English Fleet have also taken the Lys a French 74 Gun Ship, with 8 Companies of French Troops on board, several Officers and Engineers, and Military Chest. It is hoped by this Time the Admiral has fallen in with the rest of that Squadron.

Capt. Spry also brought in with him a French Brigantine and a Schooner.

Besides the above Account we are informed, by Letters and Passengers, that the French were Designed for Lewisbourg, there to refit, and put themselves in a Condition to come and attack Halifax, and reduce all Nova-Scotia. —— That the Lys, was hourly expected at Halifax, Capt. Spry having left her but a few Hours before he came in. —— That the Lys had 1100 Men on board, and a General who was to command all the French Troops on the Ohio, and elsewhere in those Parts —— That the French Fleet had a very large Train of Artillery on board, and 30 Engineers, the chief by whom was kill'd by the first Broadside of our Ships. —— That Admiral Boscawen had wrote Governor Lawrence, that he should cruize between Cape Sable and the Gulph of St. Lawrence, and also keep 3 or 4 Ships close in with Lewisbourg. —— That Admiral Boscawen has Orders by Capt. Jones, for Expresses to be sent to the Commanders of all his Majesty's Ships in North America, to come forthwith and join him. —— That the Lys lost lost 70 Men in the Engagement, And that the Ship that took her, 30. —— And that Capt. Taggart was arrived at Halifax from England, with cannon and other military Stores, and that another Store Ship was daily expected.

Our Readers must be content with these short and confused Hints till we are able to procure a more particular Account, which probably will be by the next Vessel from Halifax.

BOSTON June 21. The following Address of the Honourable His Majesty's Council and House of Representatives of this Province to His Excellency the Governour, was presented Saturday the 21st of this Instant.

To His Excellency William Shirley Esq; Captain General and Governor in Chief, in and over his Majesty's Province of Massachusetts-Bay, in New-England, and Major-General of his Majesty's Army.

May it please your Excellency,

As His Majesty's Service calls for your Excellency's speedy Departure from the Province, in order to take upon you the Command of the Forces destined to Niagara: The Two Houses most heartily wish Your Excellency Health and Prosperity, while you are engaged in this important undertaking.

It is with great Concern that we part with Your Excellency at this critical Conjuncture, when we are alarm'd with an Account of a French Fleet in these Northern Parts of America, and with frequent Advices of the Invasion of our Frontiers by the Savage Indians. These Events call for the utmost Attention of the Government; and the Experience we have had of your prudent Conduct during the last War, makes us the more to regret Your proposed Absence now: And we could with that your personal Appearance at the Head of the Army had not been tho't necessary.

We pray the Almighty God would preserve Your Excellency, and carry You safely through the various Fatigues and Hazards to which you will be exposed, and return You very soon to your Government, crown'd with Victory and Success.

In the Name and by order of the Council.

J. Willard, Secr'y.

In the Name and order of the House of Representatives, T. Hubbard, Speak'r.

His Excellency's answer.

Gentlemen,

I thank you for your affectionate Address; I shall think myself happy if by engaging in the Service under my Command I shall be instrumental in the Recovery of his Majesty's just Rights and laying a Foundation for a solid Peace, and lasting Security of the British Colonies upon this Continent: I congratulate you upon the News of the happy Issue of the Expedition to Nova-Scotia hitherto: May equal Success crown every other Part of the General Plan of Operations now carrying on for his Majesty's Service in North-America: I hope the Divine Providence will protect the Province in my Absence, and restore me in due Time to my Government among you. W. Shirley.

NEW YORK June 23. We have Advice from Albany, that some of the Coghauwagae Indians, in Pursuance of their Treaty with, and Promise to, the Commissioners of Indian Affairs there, to give them Information of any intended Hostilities by the French or their Indians, did lately inform the said Commissioners, that two Parties of French Indians were about to attack some of our Frontiers, whereupon the People of Albany immediately dispatched an Express to New-England to carry the above Intelligence. From which it may be fairly collected, that the Neutrality observed by the said Commissioners and the French Indians, and the cultivating of Trade between Albany and Canada, is not of such pernicious Consequence as some People would insinuate. Nor is the remarkable Dispatch and Dexterity wherewith Albany and Schenectady forwarded Capt. Bradstreet's Progress to Oswego, by Means whereof, that expeditious Officer performed his March thither in a shorter Time than was scarce ever known, a less considerable Argument of their Zeal and Activity in his Majesty's Service.

BOSTON June 23. We hear that the Troops which have lately raised at Rhode-Island, for the Expedition to the Westward, sailed from thence the 10th Instant for Albany.

We also hear, that the Forces raised in the Province of New-Hampshire, marched from thence to the Westward, on saturday last, and not before.

By a Vessel arrived here last Tuesday From St. George's River, we have an Account, That on the 9th Instant, a Man was taken by the Indians at Broad-Bay and another endeavouring to make his Escape from them by getting off in a Canoe, was shot and kill'd. And, That on Thursday the 12th Inst. A Man and Boy were taken by the Indians, and carried off, at a Place called Pleasant Point, near the Mouth of St. George's River.

BOSTON June 26. In the House of Representatives, June 26 1755.

Resolved, That his Excellency the Captain General be desired to Commission proper Officers for raising by Enlistment not exceeding Five Hundred to march to Crown-Point to reinforce the Army destin'd there, if upon Advice from the Army had in the recess of this Court, it shall be adjudged by the Commander in Chief for the Time being with the Advice of the Council, that it be necessary the Army should be so reinforced.

That each Man be paid a Dollar upon his Enlistment, and in Case of there being actually ingaged in the Service, that they be allowed the same Bounty, including the Dollar mentioned, Pay and Subsistence, as the Forces already destin'd there have, they finding their own good and sufficient Fire Arms.

The Pay and Subsistence to commence from the Time of their Marching, and that they be discharged as soon as the Place is reduced, or the Nature of the Case will admit of not exceeding the Time the other Forces are enlisted for.

That the Enlisting Officer be allowed half a Dollar for each Man so enlisted and that his Excellency the Governor be desired to inform the other Governments of his Resolve.

    Sent up for Concurrence. T. Hubbard, Speak'r.
    In Council June 26, 1755   J. Willard, Secr'y.
    Consented to,   W. Shirley.
    Copy Attest, Thomas Clarke, Deputy Secretaty.

PHILADELPHIA June 26. From Fort Cumberland there is Advice, that on the 14th Instant, 150 Men marched from thence, to protect the Workmen that are cutting a Road from the back Parts of the Province towards the Ohio, from the French or there Indians: That an Indian Man and Woman had lately come there from Fort Du Quesne, and positively says, that there are not above 200 Men, French and Indians, in that Fort; and that a Party of the Indians, with some French, were to set out soon, in order to Harrass any Stragglers from our Army on their March.

HALIFAX June 28. To His Excellency Charles Lawrence Esq; Lieutenant Governor and Commander in Chief in and over his Majesty's Province of Nova Scotia, &c. &c.

    The Address of the Merchants, Traders, and

other Inhabitants of the Town of Halifax in Nova-Scotia.

May it please your Excellency,
We the Merchants, Traders, and other Inhabitants of the Town of Halifax, humbly beg Leave to offer our Compliments of Congratulations on the late happy Success of his Majesty's Arms in the Reduction of the French Fort at Chiegnecto, which (under God) is intirely owing to the wise and prudent Measures taken by your Excellency in the original planning of the Expedition; the Countenance and Assistance of his Excellency Governor Shirley; the Vigilence, activity, and Military Accomplishments of the Hon. Colonel Monckton, Commander in Chief; and the bravery and Spirit of the Troops, who generously engaged themselves in the Affair, from a just Resentment of the Encroachment made by the French on his Majesty's Territories in these Parts.

From this happy Beginning, we have the greatest Hopes of the success of any other enterprize you may have concerted for obtaining that Peace and Tranquility to us and the rest of his Majesty's loyal Subjects in this Province, which we have been long deprived of by the Machinations of our envious Neighbours, and their barbarous and blood-thirsty Emissaries, who by their cruel and unnatural Proceedings since the Commencement of this Settlement after the late general Peace, seem to have shaken off and trampled under Foot all Regard to Laws human and divine.

That all the wicked and vermicious Designs, plotted for depriving his Majesty of his just Rights, and his good Subjects of their Lives and Properties, may meet with Disappointment; and that your Excellency (who indefatigable Vigilance and Zeal for his Majesty's Service and the good of the Publick, has so greatly manifested itself upon all Occasions) may long remain at the Helm of the Government to over-awe our open as well as conceal'd Enemies, and to render this a happy flourishing Province, will, we doubt not, be the sincere Whishes of all who have the British Interest really at Heart, and who have the Honour to know your Excellency's Merit;

as they most unfeighedly are those of,

Your Excellency's most obedient Servants, &c.

HALIFAX June 28. We hear his Majesty's Ships now in this Harbour, will only tarry to Wood and Water and overhaul their Rigging, when they will immediately sail to join Admiral Boscawen, who is now cruising in the Gulph of St. Lawrence.

BOSTON June 30. On Tuesday last arrived in Town Major Bourn, who left the English Camp near Chenecto the 18th Instant, charged with Dispatches from the Hon. Col. Monckton to His Excellency Governor Shirley, and brings us the agreeable News, that on the fifth Day of this Instant in the Evening His Excellency Governor Shirley's two New-England Regiments of 2000 arrived at Chegnecto in the Bay of Fundy, and on the 2d landed and join'd His Majesty's Regular Forces there of 300 near Fort Lawrence; that the Troops march'd the 4th and invested the French Fort of Beausejour (now called Fort Cumberland) in the Evening, and in their Way took Possession of Pont de Buott, where the French had a battery of 4 small Pieces of Cannon and a Block House, and had posted 400 Men to oppose their Passage, who soon retired when closely attack'd and left their Block House, and sundry adjacent Houses in Flames: Our Forces began to bombard the French Fort from Batteries advanced within 500 Yards of it, on the 13th, which by a Constant Fire obliged the French to surrender befor our Gun-Batteries were finished, on the 16th Instant. The Fort is a regular-built Pentagon, with 26 Pieces of Cannon, mounted chiefly with 9, 12, and 6 Pounders, and one 10 Inch Mortar, was gerrison'd with 150 regular Troops and 400 Peasants, commanded by Monsieur Du Chambon, was plenty furnished with Provisions, as well as all other Kind of Stores. The regular Troops are to be transported to Louisbourg, and under a Prohibition of bearing Arms in North America for six Months: The Fort the French on the Bay Vert has accepted the same Terms of Capitulation, and Col. Winslow march'd with 500 Men, the same Morning Major Bourn came away in order to take Possession of it: And that the Forces were soon to sail for St. John's River, when it was not doubted they would have like Success.

Extract of a Letter from an Officer in the Army at Nova-Scotia. from the Camp before Beausejour, June 11, 1755.

"We had a very pleasant Passage of four Days from Boston to Annapolis Royal, where we were all arrived safe on Monday the 29th of May; we remained there 'till Sunday the 1st of June, when we all sailed and got up here the same Night; but did not land till Monday. We were not a little pleased to learn on our arrival, that the French had received no Reinforcement from Louisbourg (as we heard at Boston) nor were they apprized of our Design, 'till we got here. The Troops were quartered the Night we arrived, upon the Settlers, and Inhabitants; and Tuesday encamped near our Fort, which day was employed in preparing to March to the French Side on the next Day: Accordingly on the 4th of June, (being the Prince of Wale's Birth Day) at break of Day the Troops were under arms, and joined by all the Regulars of our Garrison, both Officers and Soldiers, except Capt. Hamilton who was left to Command Fort Lawrence, with whom was left Capt. Britnal, and about 80 of the New-England Troops. At 7 o'Clock the whole Army being about 2450 Men marched with four fine Field Pieces, six pounders, in the Front: As soon as they arrived at the Carrying Place, where was a Logg House, with some Swivel Guns, and a Detachment of French Troops; they fired upon us, which was soon returned, and they driven from their Post, and before Night, almost every House at Beausejour, together with their large new Mass House, the Priest's House, Hospital, Barns, &c. to the Number of about 60, were burnt down to the Ground. This Step they took that we might not be sheltered by them in our Approach or benefited thereby. In Case they were obliged to Surrender, as they undoubtedly expected they must. We had only one Man killed, (a Serjeant of our Garrison) and eleven wounded, one of which is since Dead; the French five or Six killed, and we suppose more, how many wounded, we can't tell. Our Troops traversed the Ground on their Side, and reconnoitred the Fort pretty near, without being fired at, their People were employed in Strnegthening their Fort, by a Glacis and Covert Way, as if they did not intend to Surrender without a Dispute, but turned their Defence chiefly against an Assault, Sword in Hand, expecting we should Storm the Garrison, as they did not apprehend we has any Artillery, except our Field Pieces, and some Cohorns. They have since taken off the Roofs from all their Houses, and pulled down the Chimneys, to prevent the ill Consequences of our Cannonading, as they are now satisfied we have Battering Cannon, and 13 Inch Shells.

We have landed our Cannon and Mortar, and the Troops have been employed in clearing a Road for Transporting them to the Place where we Design to open our Battery, (which we hope will be effective this Night,) within 300 Yards of their Ramparts. We had reconnoitering Parties frequently out within half a Musket Shot of the Fort, which they sometimes Fire at, but have not yet hurt us a Man. They have in the Fort about 150 Regulars, and as many of the Inhabitants, the remainder, with the Women and Children are gone off to Bay Verte, and other distant Places. We have not lost one of the Men we have brought from New-England, either by Enemy or Sickness; and have only three slightly Wounded. We have had a good deal of Rainy Weather, since our Encampment, which has been a considerable impediment to us. An Officer of our Garrison was Surprized by a Party of Indians, who were lurking in a Coops of Woods on our Side, and taken Prisoner, as he was returning (alone) from our Garrison to the Camp, early in the Morning a few Days ago. A Flagg of Truce was sent to Col. Monckton from the French Commandant, the same Day, with Letters from the Officer to acquaint the Colonel of his Misfortune, and that he was well dealt by. The same Day we took one of their Garrison Prisoner, by whom we learn that they expect a Reinforcement from St. John's, and Louisbourg; but I am in hopes they will arrive to late. Our Men are in Health, and high Spirits, and perform their Fatigues (which are not a few) with great Chearfullness. —— There was a large Ship seen cruizing off the Gut of Annapolis Royal for several Days, and stood over for St' John's, but the Friday before we arrived there; we suppose it was Mr. McCarty in a French 36 Gun Ship, I wish he had happen'd to sail in with us, as I dare say our Ships would have brought down his Colours.

Fort Cumberland, June 18, 1755.

"I have now the pleasure to congratulate you upon the Surrender of the French Fort, which we named as above. —— I have not Time to write you the Particulars. —— The Forts at Bay Verte and Gaspereau have surrendered upon Terms, and Col. Winslow is gone there this Morning to take Possession; we have lost but one of our New-England Troops killed in opening the Trenches, and about a dozen wounded, who are like to do well: We began to Fire some small Shells the 13th, some large on the 14th, the 15th with a few 13 Inch, and the 16th they desired to Capitulate; the Terms being agreed upon, Col. Scot who commanded in the trenches, marched in the same Evening, took Possession and struck the Colours Yesterday, (the memorable 17th of June) The English Flag was hoisted and saluted by all the Guns in the Fort. We found 24 Cannon, the largest 12 Pounders, one 10 Inch Mortar, plenty of Ammunition, and Provisions enough to have held out a long Seige. —— I heartily wish our Army at the Southward may meet with the same success as we have. I doubt not but our Acquisition will give them great Spirits, as well as give us all in Boston a sensible Pleasure; I believe there never was so considerable a Conquest with so little Loss. We have not a Man hurt by all their Cannon and Shells, and I suppose at a modarate Computation they fired 500 Shots, and 60 or 80 Shells, one of which fell and broke in the Trench, and cover'd near 40 of our People in Dirt. —— Nothing was to be heard but the roaring of Cannon and the Noise of Men. —— We did not expect, by their Preparations, they would have surrendered so soon, and it was chiefly occasion'd by a Shell, which broke thro' one of their Casinates whereby four

Officers were kill'd and several wounded: Among those kill'd was Mr. Hay an Ensign of ours, who had been taken a Week before by some Skulking Indians as he was passing from our Fort to Camp."

And we learn by other Letters that the New-England Troops behav'd to the Satisfaction of every Body. ——— That the only New-England kill'd was Joseph Pike, whose Friends belong to Newbury. ——— That Col. Pebble received a slight Wound in the Thigh. ——— That the French have lost in all 8 Officers and 51 private Men. ——— As also, That 3 indians were kill'd one of which was a Sachem of the Mickmac's a stout Fellow six Feet and half high about 40 Years old.

From Colrain we hear, That on Wednesday the 18th Instant, a Man being at a small Distance from the Fort there, espied an Indian sitting upon the Stump of a Tree with his Back towards him, shot at him, when he instantly fell: The Man in going to scalp him, saw several other Indians, upon which he made his Escape to the Garrison, and related what he had done: upon which some of the Garrison went in Pursuit of them, but did not discover any Thing, only that they had dragg'd the Indian that was shot a considerable Way: They found a long Track of Blood, some of which was cover'd with Dirt, to prevent it's being seen; and 'tis not doubted but he was kill'd.

We hear from York that on Friday the 20th Instant, as one How, a young Man 18 Years of Age was at Work a small Distance from the House there, he saw an Indian with his Gun presented towards him; whereupon he cried for Quarters, the Indian told him Very good Quarters if he would come up to him: As soon as the Indian had hold of him, he laid down his Gun against the Stump of a Tree, and put his Hands up to his Mouth (How imagining) to Whistle, and he supposing some other were near, gave him such a knock, with his fist, that he stun'd him and he fell to the Ground, when he made off, and got safe Home. Upon Intelligence thereof, a Scout went immediately in Pursuit of them, discover'd their Tracks, but could not come up with them.

Last Sunday Morning, his Excellency Major-General Shirley, set out from this Place, for Providence, (attended by his Troops of Life-Guard) in his way to Albany, in order to take upon him the command of the Forces destin'd to Niagara.

BOSTON June 30. We have the following News from Rhode-Island, dated the 17th Instant, viz.

About a Week ago a French Sloop with 20 Men, 14 Carriage Guns, 16 swivels, 40 Small Arms, and other War-like Stores proportionable, was taken in this Harbour, loaded with Molasses, and Bale Goods. There is a Gentleman on board who says he was a Resident for the French Court in London in 1752, during the French Ambassador's Absence, and affects the Nobleman, and has a great many Wash Balls, Combs, and other trinkets suitable for the Ladies, or Valet de Chambre, together with valuable Clothes; and gives out that he expected to be taken, and the Vessel and Cargo confiscated, otherways it would not answer his Designs. This Man and other Frenchmen are permitted to go about our Streets. and sail into our Harbours without Guard; ——— An Indulgence which if justifiable at a Time when our Armaments are just going upon Action, (and for any Thing we know, a War may be declared already between England and France,) Then our Armies and Expences are only Amusements.

Our ingenious, and humorous Rhode-Island Correspondent, further observes, That he thought proper to give us this Hint to communicate to the Publick that if the Conduct be right, it may be a precedent to other Governments to treat that polite Nation with the greatest Regard and Complaisance, not knowing how soon they may become our Masters and Conquerors, But this would be war shipping the Devil out of Fear Indeed.

NEW-YORK June 30. Monday last arrived here from Providence in New-England, twenty sail of Transport, and the next Day two others arrived, having on board Governor Shirley's Regiment, and the Rhode-Island Forces; and on Tuesday they weigh'd Anchor for Albany.

By the last Boat from Albany our Intelligence are, that on Wednesday the 18th Instant, a Man

Arrived from Canada, who had been taken Prisoner by the French about 4 Years ago, and gave out that the French were actually dispatching a Number of Forces from Canada for the Ohio: That after he made his Escape he got among a Tribe of Indians, in Friendship with the English, a party of whom coming down to Albany, offer'd to guard him thither. That they wanted to stop at Crown-Point but were beaten off by the French; and that near the Point they met 5 Indians that scalp'd one and carried off two young Men Prisoners from Hoseck, both of whom they had in Company with them, carrying them to Canada.

We hear General Johnson was to have a general Meeting of the Mohawks at Mount Johnson on Saturday the 21st Instant.

QUEBEC June 30. Since the arrival of the last Ships from Europe, an Estimate has been made of our Forces in these Parts, amounting on the whole to 23,000 effective Men, including the Garrisons of this City, Montreal, and the rest of the Forts in Canada. We are in Higher Spirits here than can easily be imagined, having within these three Days received Assurance that the English Colonies, which we thought were united to furnish an Invasion, are equally jealous and distrustful of each other, aa also the Commanders of their Troops: The former, lest they should bear a disproportionate Burthen of the War; and the Latter least they should not have an Equal Opportunity of Honour or Triumph.

JULY 1755

PHILADELPHIA July 3. Extract of a Letter from Oswego, on Lake Ontario Dated June 2.

"Within these three Weeks have passed by about 36 Battoes, with eight or ten French and Indians in each of them. We are busing getting a fine Row Galley ready, in order to stop the Passage for the future. They are obliged to pass in sight of our Fort, which lies on the Edge of the Lake, on the South Side, and cannot keep far from the Shore because of the frequent Squalls of Wind that happen, and would certainly overset them, if they could not quickly reach the Shore. Our People work on Sundays as well as other Days. Several large Vessels are going to be built. Some Carpenters arrived here Yesterday from Boston."

PHILADELPHIA July 3. Extract from a Letter from Winchester, dated June 26.

"This Morning arrived here from Patterson's Creek, on his Way to the Hon. Thomas Fairfax, Abraham Johnson, who informed that the Indians had killed and wounded several People on said Creek, and many were missing. It is said, Eleven are murdered, and that a Number of the Inhabitants are coming down here. The Number of the Indians is not known but they are still about the Creek."

Another Letter from Carlisle, dated June 29, mentions the Murder of one Willias, and his Wife, and a Grandson, a few Days before, on the North Branch of the Potomack, about 12 Miles above the Mouth of Will's Creek, by a Parcel of Indians; one of which being killed, proved to be an Indian who had lately been at our Camp, as a Friend, and was well treated there.

We hear that a Reinforcement of 150 Men, are come back to the Garrison at Fort-Cumberland, from the Army.

Major General Pepperrell, we hear, will set out in a few Days, for the Eastward, to take Command of 5,000 Men, provided with a fine train of Artillery, who are to rendezvous at Fort-Halifax, on the Kennebeck River, and thence to proceed immediately towards Quebeck in Canada.

HALIFAX July 5. On Saturday last, the first and second of His Majesty'd Regiment of Militia, for the Peninsula of Halifax and Parts Adjacent and the Town of Dartmouth, were received upon the Parade by his Excellency the Lieutenant Governour, when a Commission was read to them, appointing the Honourable Jonathan Belcher, Esq; Lieutenant Colonel of the regiment. The Military were numerous made a fine Appearance, and express'd the highest Satisfaction in having Mr. Belcher for their Commander.

BOSTON July 7. Thursday last a Sloop arrived in 4 Days from Annapolis Royal, and by her we have Advice, that on the 26th of June past, 3 of his Majesty's Ships of War, viz. The Success, Mermaid, and Syrene, with some of the Transports with Soldiers came down the Bay, and sail'd for St. John's River; and that the Vulture Sloop of War, with some other Vessels, having on Board the French Garrison of Fort Beausejour, had sailed four Louisbourg, to deliver them there, according to Capitulation.

Extract of a Letter from Ferryland in Newfoundland, dated June 17.

"I am credibly inform'd that 12 Sail of Men of War were off St. John's the 28th of May, and sent a Letter to the Governor acquainting him that they were bound Westward. ——— Last Saturday a 60 and a 20 Gun Ship were off the Harbour; the Purser of the 60 Gun Ship was ashore, and said they were under the Command of Admiral Holburn in the Terrible of 74 Guns, and that they were bound Westward, but to what particular Place he did not know. They were to make Cape Broyl, and wait 24 Hours for some othe Men of War as we hear."

We hear that two Families living about a Mile from Hinsdell's Fort in Northfield, were taken by the Indian Enemy on the 27th of June past, and two Men belonging to those Families, one of which was named Grout, the other Caleb How, were killed by them; also, that their Wives, and seven or eight Children were carried off: The Indians made but little Noise when they did this Mischief, so that they could not be heard at the Fort.

Since our last two of the Penobscot Tribe of Indians arrived here in a Sloop from the Eastward, with an Officer belonging to George's Fort, by whom we learn that 30 or 40 of those Indians had been at the Fort, where they had read to them the Proposals of this Government, respecting the Conduct during our War with the Tribes: which Proposal they seem willing to comply with, and have sent the two Fellows above mentioned to signify the same to the Government. These two Indians say. that just before they came from Fort George's some of their Tribe came from Canada, and informed that 2 Men of War were arrived at Quebeck, and that another was soon expected with a new Governor: ——— That there were 50 Transports below the River, with 4,000 Troops on board. ——— That there had been a fire at Quebec, which had Destroyed 70 Houses, and that the Small Pox was in the City, which carried off great Numbers of People. ——— That there had likewise been a Fire at Montreal which destroyed half the Town: and, that abundance of Soldiers had lately been sent from Quebeck towards the Ohio. [tho' some of these articles may possibly be true, yet we look on the Story in main, but as Indian News.]

NEW-YORK July 7. Wednesday Evening last arrived here, in the Providence Sloop of the Massachusetts-Bay, his Excellency General Shirley, from Boston, and on Friday Evening following he embarked on board the same Sloop for Albany.

The remaining Part of General Pepperrell's Regiment, that were encamp'd on Governor's Island mov'd thence on Friday last for Albany; and we are told the General himself proposes to follow in a few Days.

General Braddock with the Army under his Command, was at a Place called Bear Camp, near the Great Meadow, on the Twenty-first ult.

BOSTON July 7. As the Province of Nova-Scotia is become the seat of War, and as but few of our readers may have had Opportunity to acquaint themselves with its Importance to the British Nation, and especially to all our Northern Colonies, the following Extract from Mr. Little's Description of Nova-Scotia are now Published; and we hope they will prove an agreeable Entertainment to our Readers.

The general Advantage that will arise from fortifying and Settling Nova-Scotia, are to be considered as they regard the View of France, as well at Great Britain.

The French have artfully laboured to make the most of the Nova-Scotians, ever since the Subjection to the British Crown; they have not only secured to them the Enjoyment of their Religion and Estates, but take care to furnish them with Priests, who teach them to believe from their Infancy, that they are the Subjects of France, and they have always been equally useful to them; before the present War, they not only supplied the French at Louisbourg with Provisions, but with Wives, and were very serviceable to them in their Fishery, in piloting their Vessels, and assisting them in their Fortifications; and since its Reduction, have actually joined a Body of French and Indians, in order, if possible to get Possession of Annapolis Royal.

The Zeal and Attachment of the Nova-Scotians to the Romish Faith, will always prevent the Settlement of Protestants in the Country, unless it be done in compact Bodies, and under the Cover of Fortifications: but till this is accomplished, it can no more be said that the Province belongs to the Crown of Great-Britain, because it is possessed Annapolis Royal, than of the King of Spain, from our Possession of Gibralter.

It is therefore absolutely necessary for the Safety and Interest of the Northern Colonies, that some speedy and effectual Measures are taken, to put these Nova-Scotians on a different Footing, or to remove them; the last cannot well be done, and the first is nothing better than by encouraging a considerable Number of Foreign Protestants, and others, to settle among them.

This will not only be of immediate Service, but in a few Years will produce various good effects, as the Country abounds with Pine and Firs, it will be capable of supplying the Kingdom with the finest Deal Boards and Timber of all Kinds, in Vessels of our own, which are now imported from Norway, the Baltic, &c. in Foreign Bottoms, and drain the Nation of Immense Sums of Money; This is not only practicable on the first Settlement of the Country, but in the Course of a Few Years will become a steady and useful Branch of Business: But if none of these good Consequences ensue, yet settling the Province with Protestants is of the greatest Importance, as the French will otherwise continue to cherish the present Inhabitants, till they exceed the Number, and are of more Consequence than those in Canada, and it requires no long time to effect this, in a Country whose Inhabitants are not only very healthful, but very prolific; it must surely be deemed impolite then to suffer such a Colony of French Bigots to be reared up under the kindly Influence of a British Administration, to cut our People's Throats whenever the Priests shall consecrate the Knife; notwithstanding they hardly know the Name of a Tax or Duty, their Quit-Rent being but a Trifle, and those who are at a great Distance from Annapolis Royal, have seldom paid any; in the mean time they have on all Occasions manifested a Comptempt of the British Government when they could do it with Impunity, or were too remote from the Garrison to send their Resentment.

It therefore highly concerns this Kingdom, that some seasonable Step be taken to prevent their future Growth, and Defection; but it is very difficult to Attempt, and almost Impossible to effect their Removal without Bloodshed, and if they were dispossessed, they would be a very great additional Strength to Canada and Cape Breton, as we could not prevent their settling in those Places.

It seems then more eligible to continue them in the Country, to permit them to hold such Lands as are under actual Improvement, and to which they can make out a clear Title, for 'tis beyond Dispute, but they claim much larger Tracts than they have any Right to.

Their Estates are held by Patent from the French King, for which they pay a very small Acknowledgement, their Right was reserved to them by the Articles of Capitulation at the Reduction of Annapolis - Royal, and was finally ratified by the Treaty of Ultrecht; but as no civil Government has ever been established there, they have no more to do with their new Masters than to pay their Quit-Rent, which in the whole Province does not amount to forty Pounds a Year.

When the Form of Government was established, which is now exercised there, the Instructions to the Governor and Council were copied from those of Virginia, whereby the Power of granting Lands is vested in them, and restricted to such Conditions, as have hitherto proved a great Discouragement to his Majesty's Subjects; for the Patentee is not only to pay the Penny Sterling per Acre for the whole, but is subject to a Penny more whenever the Government shall demand it, and unless he has built a House, and brought Part of the Lands under Improvement within three Years from the Date of his Grant, he forfeits his Title: This attended with the constant Obstructions which both the French and Indians have made in Prejudice to any Protestant Settlements, when compared with the Easy Terms on which Lands are granted in other Parts of North-America, evidently accounts for the preent Situation of the Province.

Since it is apparently for the public Interest, that the growing State of these Nova-Scotians should be checked, that they should either be rendered useful, or prevented from becoming dangerous to the other Colonies, it cannot more effectually be done, that by erecting such Fortifications, as will keep their most populous Towns in Subjection, and at the same Time serve as a Protection to the proposed Settlements in the Province; a more particular Description of which seems necessary in order to carry so useful a design into Execution.

About seventeen Leagues North from Cape Sable, the Entrance of the Bay of Fundy commences, where it is about twenty Leagues wide, and extending near forty Leagues, divides itself into two Branches, one of which terminates in several Rivers, that discharges themselves into Minas Bay, and the other running more Northerly to Chinecto, form an Isthmus of that Name between this Branch and the Bay of Vert, which empties itself into the Gulf of St. Lawrence.

Twelve Leagues from the aforesaid Entrance on the South Side of the Bay, lies the Gut of Annapolis, which is about three Quarters of a Mile wide, and a Mile and a half long, on each Side of which the Land is very mountainous and Rocky; the Tides are so impetuous, as often to render this a Dangerous Passage for large Vessels, but when they are once in, a most delightful Harbour presents itself to View, Called the Bason of Annapolis, from the gradual Declivity of the Lands surrounding it, being three Leagues in Lenght from the North East to South West, and two in Width, with safe and commodious Anchorage in most Parts of it for all the Ships in England; on its South Side are two small Rivers of little Consequence, and the Land is Mountainous and rocky; on the North East Side a little Island forms the Entrance of Annapolis River, which continues navigable for large Vessels on that Course about ten Leagues.

North from the Entry of Annapolis lies a fine River of St. John, with a capacious Road for Ships at its Entrance; on the North Side of which is a small narrow Streight, not a Pistol Shot over, thro' which there is no passing but at the Top of the Tide, when the Water is upon a Level, at other Times the Fall is so considerable, especially at low Water, as to make a Descent of near thirty Feet, being lined on both Sides by a solid Rock, and having more than forty Fathom of Water in its Middle; this River spreads itself about half a Mile in Width, and with a gentle Current towards its Outlet admits of a delightful Navigation for large Ships fifty or sixty Miles into the Country, and much farther for small Vessels; from its several Branches the Indians traverse this Part of the Continent, by transporting their Canoes by land across some short Spaces, called by them Carrying-Places: Here are no more than three or four French Families, the Forces from New-England having destroyed all the Settlements in the last War, most of the Inhabitants removed to the other Side of the Bay; a few Leagues further Westward are several fine Harbours, amongst which the Harbour l'Etang, so called from its Resemblance of a Pond, as it is surrounded with Highlands, its Entry being deep, narrow, and free from Danger, and its Surface always unruffled; this is near the River St. Croix, the Western Boundry of the Province, from whence to New-Hampshire the Sea Coast is covered with Islands that almost form a continued Harbour for near two hundred Miles.

From the Entrance of the Bay of Fundy to Cape Sable, there are several fine Rivers and Harbours, and two small Villages; from Cape Sable so called from the Banks of its Shore, to Canso, the Islands and Harbours are so numerous as not to admit of either Description on Naming, the most considerable of which are Chebucto, Malegash, Port Rossignol, Port Mutton, Port le Have, Port Rozoir, Liscombe Harbour, &c. and Canson, which at present serve only as a retreat to fishing Vessels, and others in bad Weather, or to wood and water; a few stragling Savages, who shift their Habitations as the Seasons for Fishing and Hunting vary, are the only Inhabitants on this extensive Coast except a French Settlement at Malegash.

Canso and Chebucto on the Sea-Coast of this Province, naturally presents themselves first to Consideration; the former from its having once had a wooden Blockhouse, and a small detachment of Troops for its Protection, and the latter for its spacious and fine Harbour, and having been Rendezvous of Duke D'Avilles's Squadron.

Canso which is found very conveniently Situated

for the Cod Fishery, but claims the Preferance to the others on no account but its having been already improved, and probably sooner known: But this last greatly exceeds the former in several Respects viz. its Situation, its Harbour, and Aptness for Agriculture.

Its Situation is such, that it has a short and easy Communication by Land with all the Settlements on the Bay of Fundy, is equally commodious for the Fishery with Canso, and is more in the Way of all Ships passing to and from Europe to New-England that may occasionally, or by Stress of Weather seek a Port for Shelter or Relief.

Its Harbour gives place to none in the World, and by its natural Form, and an Island at its Entrance, is capable of being well defended by a regular Fortification.

BOSTON July 7. We have Advice from the Westward, that two Men have been lately kill'd by the Indians, near Bridgeman's Fort, and that two Women and ten Children were captivated by them. As the Indians were silent in doing the above Mischief, it is uncertain what Number this merciless Gang consisted of.

PHILADELPHIA July 10. Extract of a Letter from Admiral Bosawen, date on board the Tobary, off Cape-Breton, Junr 17, 1755.

"The French have sent into these Parts a strong Detachment of Troops, consisting of six Battalions of old Troops, under the Convoy of three large Men of War, and some Frigates. In Pursuance of His Majesty's Instructions to me, I have seized the Aleide, a Man of War of 64 Guns; and the Lys, pierced for 74 Guns, her lower Battery not mounted, having on board Eight Companies of Foot, several Engineers, and the Military Chest, or Part of it. Monsier De Belleger, who was to have Commanded the Troops in the second Post, was killed on board the Aleide."

CHARLESTOWN SOUTH-CAROLINA July 10. "The Governor is Returned as far as Ashley River, from an Interview with the Cherokee Indians, from whom he has purchased, for his Majesty, all their Country; of which they have made a formal Delivery, by a Bag of Earth, a Bag of Corn, the

Produce of that Earth, a Bow and four Arrows; the Bow and Arrows in Testimony that they will defend the Property (or in the European Stile, guarantee it.) To be Witnesses of this Delivery and Guarentee, they had all the Woman and Children, that they may hand the Act of the present Generation, down to Posterity."

ANNAPOLIS July 10. Saturday last Mr. Thomas Stoddard came to Town from Frederick County, and informed us, that many Families from the back Settlements, are come in as far as Col. Cresap's where they are fortifying themselves against the Indians: That among the many murders committed by the Indians, one was within three Miles of Fort Cumberland.

By Letter from Virginia, dated the fourth Intant, we lear, that two Parties of Indians and French amounting together to about 130 Men, have been seen in the Frontier Counties, where they have destroyed 9 Families, and plundered and burn their Habitations.

PHILADELPHIA July 10. We hear from Tulpehoken, that John Shickealami an Indian Chief, arrived there last Week, and informed, that the French Fort on the Ohio, had been strongly reinforced lately, with both French and Indians: That General Braddock would not allow his Indians to Scalp any Frenchmen that may fall into their Hands, which had occasioned a good many to leave him, and would not engage till they should hear from the English Governors: And that they wanted much to know whether it was War or Peace.

Since our last a Gentleman came to Town from the Camp, who informs us, that on the 26th ult. Sir John Sinclair, with the first Division of the Forces, marched from the Great Meadow for Fort Du Quesne; and that the General, with the whole Army, proposed to be there as on this Day. He likewise says, a Number of the Inhabitants, going to Fort Cumberland from the North Branch of Potowmack, for fear of being attacked by the French Indians, were fired at by a Party of them from the Woods, by which six were killed, and afterwards Scalp'd; and that a Boy was likewise knocked down and Scalped, but recovering, ran into the River, where he was some Time after found almost dead, and carried to Will's Creek; and proper Care being taken of him, it was thought he would recover.

QUEBEC July 10. At a late Council of War, held at Niagara Fort, by the principal commanding Officers, it was determined, that whatever should be the Success of any future Enterprize against the English, who were coming, Arm'd at all Points, to drive us out of Canada, the Troops on the Ohio, had at present nothing to do but maintain the Ground there already got, and by no Means to venture beyond the Allegany Mountains into the Province of Virginia, till repeated Success, or immediate Orders from Europe, should authorise them to vary their Conduct in this Point. At the same Time it was determined, that the Forces of Niagara had also nothing to do but Maintain that important Pass; and that those on the Erie, at Crown Point, and Northward Towards St. Lawrence Bay, being nearer the main Force at Quebec, and the neighbouring Places, and, in Consequence, more readily to be furnished with Supplies of every Kind, or favoured in Case of a necessitous Retreat, should push every material Advantage they might happen to gain, in order, if possible, to secure the chief Part of Arcadia, which, on Account of the Advantageous Situation of Cape-Breton, might lay such a Foundation for our own future Progress, as might not easily be in the Power of the English to root up.

HALIFAX July 12. On Monday last a Soldier in the New-Barracks, who belong'd to Major Warburton's Regiment, foolishly playing with a Flintlock, not minding it to be loaded; it went off and shot one John Bradbury, a Corporal in the same Regiment, through the Body, of which Wound he died about eight Hours afterwards.

NEW-HAVEN July 12. We hear from Hartford, that on Friday the 4th of this Instant, one Man was killed three Women and Eleven Children, carried off Captive, by a Number of Indians at Northfield.

BOSTON July 12. Province of Massachusetts-Bay, By the Honourable the Lieutenant Governor, and Commander in Chief.

Whereas I have by my Letter to the Indians of Penobscot Tribe, proposed to them, that for their Safety they would not come over to the Westward of St. George's River, lest they should be expos'd to out marching and scouting Parties of Men, that are employed for the Defence of our Frontiers, and Annoyance of the other Tribes of the Indians that have made War upon us:

I do therefore hereby strictly forbid all Officers and Soldiers scouting, and all Persons whatsoever acting offensively against the Indians within thirty Miles from St. George's Fort, except to the Westward of said Fort, or within twenty Miles of any Part of the River of Penobscot, on any pretence whatsoever.

Dated at Boston the twelfth Day of July 1755, in the 29th year of his Majesty's Reign.

S. Phips.

BOSTON July 14. To the Publisher of the Boston Gazette, &c.

Please to insert the following in your next, whereby you will oblige, Your humble Servant &c.

Whilst we are rejoicing in the "happy success of his Majesty's Arms in Reduction of the French Forts at Chiegnecto," it is a pity any Occasion should be given for contesting to whom the credit of this Success, under Providence, chiefly belongs. But there seem to be just Occasion given for this, in the Point will bear contesting, by the extraordinary Address of the Merchants, Trader, &c. of Halifax, to Lieut. Governor Lawrence, published there in the Gazette of June 28. A Person, not sufficiently Acquainted with this Affair, would naturally conclude from the Address, That these Forts were not reduced by Troops raised in New-England, under New-England Officers, but by his Majesty's regular Troops in Nove-Scotia; though not wholly without "Countenance and Assistance of his Excellency Governor Shirley." This is the Idea which the Language of the Address naturally conveys; in which Respect it must be confess'd, the Substance of it corresponds very well to the introductory Part, wherein they "humbly beg Leave to offer their Complements," &c. for there is really so little of Truth or Justice in this

Representation; that the Address can hardly be looked upon as any Thing more, or better than a Compliment. The Answer of both our Houses of Assembly to Governor Shirley's Speeches of the 28th of March and the 2d of April 1754, is alone sufficient to show how Much the Province of the Massachusetts-Bay has interested itself in the Welfare of Nova-Scotia. An Extract of the Answer is as follows ——— "We therefore desire your Excellency to represent to his Majesty the exposed hazedous State of these his Governments; and Humbly to pray, that he would be pleased to cause the most effectual Measures to be taken for the Removal of any French Forts, or Settlements that are or may be made in any Part of his Territories in this Continent; and Particular, that the Subjects of the French King may be compelled to quit the Province of Nove-Scotia, where, in direct Violation of the most express Agreement to the contrary, they are daily increasing and fortifying Themselves," &c. ——— It was, I humbly conceived, chiefly owing to Governor Shirley's representing and pressing this Matter at Home, agreeably to the Request of our General Assembly, that those vigorous Measures were entered upon for the Security of Nova-Scotia, which have already happily succeeded in Part, and which are still in Prosecution by his Majesty's New-England irregular Troops, with Conjunction with a few of the Regulars of that Province. I have no Inclination to distract from the acknowledged, Merit of Governor Lawrence; nor do I now dispute the Vigilance, Activity, and military Accomplishment of the Hon. Monchton," He gace one proof of his Activity and military accomplishments, while he was here in Boston. But the Part which Governor Shirley, Col. Winslow, and the Province of Massachusetts, had in the Affair, could not, I think, with any Propriety or Decency, be passed over with the slight, general Acknowledment of some "Countenance and Assistance," The Troops employed in this Expedition, irregular as well as regular, are, we know, in his Majesty's Pay: but the Expedition was, at least, as much Governor Shirley's, as Governor Lawrence's,

Nay; it might, with much more Propriety be said, That Governor Shirley had "the Assistance" of Governor Lawrence herein than that the latter had "the Assistance" of the former; Governor Shirley being plainly the Principal of it, and almost all the Troops employed, being raised in this Province under his Direction. It is well known that about 2000 of the Troops went from hence; who enlisted to go upon this Enterprize, under the immediate Command of Lieut. Col. Winslow, a New-England Man; whose Reputation as a Soldier, and a good Officer, was established amongst us. These Troops when they came to Nova Scotia were joined and assisted only by 250, or 280 Regulars, under Lieut, Col. Monckton: Tho' when they came to act in conjunction with the Regulars, the chief Command of the whole devolved (I suppose of Course) upon Col. Monckton, as being the superior Officer upon the Royal Establishment. This being a true, tho' brief Representation of the Case, I appeal to the World, whether it is just that the chief Honour of this prosperous Expedition, should be snatched from Governor Shirley, Col. Winslow, and our New-England Troops, and bestowed, by way of Compliment, upon those who had, comparatively speaking, so slender a Claim to it. This Address is a Specimen of the Returns made by those, when we have so often succoured and defended. Nova-Scotia must have long since fallen entirely into the Hands of the French, had it not been once and again befriended and supported by the Province of Massachusetts-Bay. But it seems that they, who have been from Time to Time both imploring, and receiving Protection from us, now envy us the Honour of affording it to them; and strangely arrogate to themselves the Credit of whatever is generously done by others for there Defence and Security, as if it were both more blessed and more surprized at the Address, as it comes from the Merchants and Traders at Halifax, who, 'tis said, are chiefly New-England Men; and who, as such, ought certainly to have had a greater Regard to the Credit of their Native Country, how little soever many of them had in it, when they made Halifax their Asylum.

BOSTON July 14. Extract of a Letter from the Hon. Alexander Lord Colvin, on board the Northumberland, at Sea. off Louisbourg to his Friend in Boston, dated June 22, 1755.

"We met with nothing remarkable in our Voyage, until we came on the Banks of Newfoundland, where we found ourselves surrounded with Islands of Ice, which appeared in various Shapes like mountainous Land, and on the 8th Instant we fell in with three Sails of the French Squadron from Brest, of which we took the Alcide of 64 Guns, and the Lys of the same Force, but fitted as a Transport for carrying Soldiers. The Dunkirk being our best sailing Ship, came first up with the Alcide, at which Time the Admiral made a Signal to engage; then Capt. Howe poured in his Broadside, and had a pretty smart Return; but the other Ships coming up, the Frenchman struck his Colours. The Defiance and Forguex continued to chase the Lys, and at sunset took her with little or no Resistance. The third Ship had greatly the Start of us, and got off. Admiral Holbourne who joined us three Days since, with Six Sail of the Line, and a Frigate just going to Halifax, gives me the Opportunity of writing to you. Yesterday we looked into the Harbour of Louisbourg, where there are only three Ships of the Line. All the rest must be gone to Quebec."

Extract of a Letter from Halifax, dated July 3, 1755.

"In the two 64 Gun French Ships, wich Admiral Boscawen has sent in, is contained their money Chest, with 50,000 Louisdores, besides all the Pick-Axes, Shovels, Spades and Wheel-barrows for carrying on their grand Design."

On Friday last, Capt. Cargill bro't up 12 Indian Scalps from the Eastward, which he and his Party kill'd at a Place called Owl-Head, near St. Georgr's River.

NEW-YORK July 14. Last Week Henry O'Brian, and Henry Huddle, the former taken with Col. Washington at the Great Meadow, and the Latter at Dartmouth, in Nova-Scotia, four Years ago, arrived here in 20 Days from Canada: By them we are informed, that the French were not in the least apprized of the Design of the English against Crown-Point, or Niagara, as the former garrison'd with only 45 Men, 20 Days ago, the greatest Part of their Force having been sent to the Ohio; that they were sensible a War must soon ensue, as our Northern-men were prohibited from Trading any more with Cape-Briton: That they had waited with Impatience for the Fleet from Old France, with a large Reinforcement of Men and warlike Stores; but imagined by their Delay. They were intercepted by some English Men of War; and 'twas reported, that immediately upon the Arrival of the Fleet 400 Men would be dispatched to attack Albany, 400 more to attack Oswego, and a large Detachment sent to the Ohio, and that the remainder of their Troops would be employed at the Situation of their Affairs should require.

We hear from Mount Johnson, in the Mohocks Country, that Major General Johnson had, on the Twenty-fourth past, a General Assembly of Indians at that Place, consisting of 1100 of 9 different Nations, who were consulting on the proper Measures to be taken on the present Conjuncture of Affairs; and there was great Hope that their Deliberation would end favourably for British Interest.

We hear from Kenderhook, that on Wednesday the 2d Instant, as 4 Men, 2 Boys, and a Negro, were hoing Corn in a Field near that Place, they were fired upon by 6 Indians and a Frenchman, which wounded one of the Men, a Boy and the Negro Fellow, when they, with the others, took to their Heels; the 7th, named John Gardineer, ran to their Arms, which were nigh at Hand, and having dispatched two of the Indians, a third closed in upon him, and in the Scuffle, the Frenchman came up, and seeing Gardineer get the better of the Indian, he knock'd him down with his piece, and afterwards scalp'd him, when the Indians made off, and carried their Dead with them. Soon after Gardineer came to hinself, and with Difficulty reached the Fort: He was so stunn'd with the Blow he received from the Frenchman, that he was insensible of his being scalped, until he was informed by the People, who discovered the Blood; but remembered the whole of their Proceedings before, and said he could have killed three of the Indians, had not the second Gun he took up, missed fired.

We hear, that on Monday last another Party of French and Indians consisting of 30 or 40, appeared at Kenderhook, and carried off a young Boy, and wounded a Negro Man; and that Robert Livingston jun. Esq; with about 40 Men, was gone in Pursuit of them.

A Letter from Philadelphia advises, That a Letter from Maryland, they learnt, that the advanced Part of General Braddock's Army discover'd a small Detachment sent out from the French Fort, who upon their Appearance retired, and let Monacatoocha, whom they had taken Prisoner, escaped.

BOSTON July 14. The beginning of last Week, we had by several Vessels just come in from the Sea, a considerable Number of very important Articles of News, (mostly relating to the Operation of the Fleet) which we feasted upon with great Delight till last Friday Morning, when Capt. Hall arrived in 4 Days from Halifax, and then it appeared by Letters and Oral Advices, that most of those articles were without even the Shadow of Truth to support them. However we have reason to believe the following Articles, brought by Capt. Hall, may be depended on, viz.

The Governor Lawrence having sent a Number of the Principal Neutrals (falsely so called) he informed them, that they must all either take Oath of Allegiance to the Britannick Majesty, or be transported to France; and they having desired leave to return and consult all their Friends and Neighbours on this important Affair, their Request was not consent to take the Oath required of them.

That upon the Approach of Commodore Rous, with his 3 Ships of War towards St. John's, the French Garrison blew up the Fort, spoiled the Cannon, and did what other Mischief they could, and then marched off to old St. John's, and abandoned Fort a few Leagues further up the River; and that after Rous was landed, 150 Indians came in, made their Submission, and desired to put themselves under the Protection of the English, on such Condition as should be agreed upon between Governor Lawrence and them, and in the mean Time they left a Number of their Chiefs in the Hands of the Commodore, as Security for the faithful Performance of their Promises.

We hear, that a Letter, from a Jesuit, directed to the French Inhabitants of Nova-Scotia, has been intercepted, and in it he conjures them not to come to any Agreement with the English, but to continue faithful Subjects to their lawful Prince; assuring them, that the Men of War and Troops (then expected) from France, were designed for their Protection, and would soon recover the whole Province out of the Hands of the English.

'Tis said the Flag of Truce lately sent to Louisbourg with the Garrison of the Forts at Chegnecto, &c. was Returned, and reported, that the Peope of Louisbourg were in great want of Provisions; and that the St. John's Indians had given the same Account of their Wants at Quebeck.

By Letters from Halifax we are told, that Governor Lawrence has caused a great Number of Cattle to be taken from the French inhabitants, and hundred Head which were arrived at Halifax, and more expected: There were all fatted and was designed for the French Fleet on its Arrival.

——— And, that Fifty Thousand Louis de Ors, (about the value of our Guineas) had been found on board the Lys Prize.

A few Days ago Capt. Cargill, Commander of a Company of Voluntiers against the Indian Enemy, brought to Town 12 Scalps, viz. 4 Men's, 6 Women's and 2 Children's, and expected the Bounty; but on Examination before his Majesty's Council, and View of his Journal, it was found that most of the Indians killed were of the Penobscot Tribe, who were exempted by Law, and his Excellency's Proclamation and who were then actually in Treaty with this Government, and 2 of the Tribe then in Boston for that Purpose: And after mature Consideration of his Office, he was committed to Goal.

NEW-YORK July 14. Capt. Van Schaick, from Albany, informs us, that about 12 o'Clock on

Thursday last, he met with his Excellency Major General Shirley, at Claverack, 28 Miles from that Place, that a Gentleman was arrived in 6 Days from Oswego, some Time before he sail'd from Albany, who acquainted him, that one of the Gallies of 36 Feet Keel, as planked and compleatly rigged on the Stocks, and that they intended to launch in 4 Days after the Arrival of the Pitch and Oakham, which he met with on the Road the Day after he left Oswego; that a Snow 56 Feet Keel and another Galley, were in great Forwardness, and would soon be launched; That 7 Men were deserted from Oswego, and were going to Niagara, (we suppose to inform the French of our Design) but that six of them, (three of whom belonged to Esopos) were brought back by our Indians, and severely punish'd; and that .25 Pound Currency per Man, is given for Apprehending all Deserters from either of the Armies.

PHILADELPHIA July 17. By a Letter of the tenth Instant from Fort Johnson we have Advice, that the conference between the Indians of the Six Nations and Major General Johnson ended the Fifth: That they have made an unanimous Declaration, that they would stand by their Brethren the English, and no way assist the French: That the whole Confederacy is better disposed towards us than they have been for Forty Years: And that more will join the General than the several Legislatures have provided for.

By several Letters from Cumberland County we are informed, that the present made by the Government of the Lower Counties to the Army, consisting of fat Oxen, Sheep, and several Waggons filled with Necessaries, we got safe to the Camp; but that the new Road now cutting, for Communication between the General and this Province, was Way-laid by French Indians, in order to cut off our Supply: That on the Fourth Instant, at Night, the Commissioners and road Cutters, tho' they had an escort of Seventy Men, were greatly alarmed, and the next Day Thirty of the People left them, and the Remainder were very uneasy for want of Arms: That Adam Hoops, and Company, who were guarding a Convoy of Provisions, were attacked by a Party of Indians

upon the Road, at a Place near Ray's Town, who
had killed nine, but Hoops, three of his Man,
and three Waggoners, made their Escape, as did
also thirteen Soldiers who were sent by Capt.
Hog to meet and guard the Provisions.: That a
Parcel of Flour, consisting of seven Horse Loads,
was left at a Store beyond Ray's Town, the Men
who guarded it thither being afraid to proceed
any further for fear of the Indians: that after
the Return of Mr. Hoops, the Inhabitants had
held a Meeting at M'Dowell's Mills, and on Saturday last Thirty one Oxen with Flour and Bread
answerable, went of under a Guard of Sixty-four
Men, well armed, who it was hoped would meet
and take back with them, the Thirty Men that
had left the Work on the Road, and likewise collect the Waggons and Provisions that had been
abandoned.
   It is fortunate that the Governor is now at
Carlisle, since by his Presence the Inhabitants
will be animated, and it is hoped form themselves into Companies. And Arms and Communication, of which they are in great Want, will be
sent from this City with the utmost Expedition.
   FROM The Fort Du Quesne, dated June 30.
   "We have about 1300 Men, and Col. Dunbar, with
700 more, is about the Great Meadow. The Indian
Scouts have killed three Batmen, a Waggoner,
and one Horse, belonging to us, Our Men are all
in high Spirits, and have Plenty of Provisions,
with which they are regularly served."
   Williamsburg July 21. Last Sunday an Express
arrived in Town with the Melancholy News of several more of our Inhabitants being cut off, on
Holston's River. Capt, Stallnicher and his Wife
were taken Prisoners, his Mother and four Children being in an Out-House made their Escape,
and concealed themselves in a Rye-Patch, till
the Affair was over; there were there more tak-
en Prisoners and killed. Col. Stewart & William
Long, on their Return from Fort Cumberland,
where they had been to supply Provisions for the
Army, were shot at three different Times, but
escaped unhurt to Augusta Court-House, from
whence they were about 45 Miles distant.
   BOSTON July 21. We hear from Westfield, that

about 3 Weeks ago, a Scout from Fort Massachussetts came upon a Party of Indians, one of whom they killed, and got his Scalp.

We have Advice from Nova-Scotia, that on the 17th of last Month, Col. Winslow with 500 Men took Possession of Fort Gasperiau, scituated on Bay of Verte, about 15 Miles distant from the English Camp. ——— That on the 19th he examin'd the Fort, and found it 180 Feet square, with four Block-Houses on each, one on each Angle, and in Miserable Order 8 Cannon and 2 Swivels, the Buildings very bad within, as well as the Water without: The Store consists of 700 lb. of Powder, a large Quantity of Cannon Shot, some Claret, 280 Barrels of Pork and 8 Hogsheads of Molasses, but no Bread nor Butter. In reconnitring the Country there about three Days they found the Soil barren, and but little Fish in the Bay. ——— At Bay of Vert is a Village of about 25 Houses, a Store-House a Chapel and a Priest's House well finished; and that the Inhabitants of the Village seemed to live in a better Form, and more after the English Manner than any of the Province, and have an open Communication on with the Isle of St. John's, and the Inhabitants of Cape Breton whom they furnish with Lumber, Indian Goods, &c. from whom they receive all the Conveniences of Life in Return ——— That they were clensing the Fort, by the French People, and were about to repair it.

By a Letter from Cumberland Camp at Chegnecto, dated the 3d Instant. We have the following authentic Intelligence, viz. That upon Capt. Rous's appearing before St. John's with the Ships under his Command and sending his boat to reconnoitre (from whence he was to send Word to the commanding Officer of the Troops, whether or no the French had any Ships there) that the Officer commanding in the Fort immediately set Fire to all the Magazines and Houses in the Fort; burst all their Cannon, and destroy'd every Thing in and around it. ——— That there were about 100 Indians, who all seem'd inclined to Peace, and offered to send four of their Chiefs for that Purpose. The French return'd upon the River, and by what can be learn'd are gone to Canada. ——— Thar the Commanding Officer has in Possession one Chief and another Chief's Son, whom they had sent to him before this happen'd, he having sent a Person to them to know whether they were for Peace or War; the first of which they wisely prefer'd.

Extract oF a letter from Fort Lawrence of the same Date as above.

"You will be gland to hear, that the French have burnt their Town of Ft. John's which have saved us the Trouble of a Voyage there. ——— Upon Appearance of Capt. Rous, with the four Men of War, they set Fire to the Fort, burst the Cannon, broke their small Arms, and march'd off to Canada, leaving the Indians behind them. ——— Capt. Rous landed, and was saluted by the Black Gentry, who desired to come to amicable Terms with the English, and accordingly four of their Chiefs went on board. ——— We have two Chiefs now at Fort Cumberland, who came up from St. John's to pilot us down; and we were just going to embark 1500 Men to reduce thar Place, (the Stores and Provisions being on board the Transports when the above Accounts arriv'd, which was Yesterday. ——— I think Providence has been remarkably favourable to us; the French being now entirely dispossess'd of Nova-Scotia, with the Loss of only four Men. (and three of them belonged to this Fort) ——— We have prospect of bringing the St. John's Indians entirely over to our Interest. ——— All the Inhabitants in this River, are disarmed and kept tightly to work. ———I wish they were exchanged for as many good New-England Husbandmen, who would improve the Lands hereabouts, for they are well worth it. ——— Our Success in these Parts, as they must give you great Satisfaction in New-England; I doubt not they will spirit up the Troops at the Southward; And I hope are happy Omens of the Downfall of the Interest of the French in North-America. ——— You see there is nothing like cutting off the Head: how soon, in such a Case the Limbs wither: Upon the surrender of Beausejour, all their mighty Forts and Possessions came to nothing; However, we must not boast to much: we have, 'tis true, made a good

Beginning, and I hope the End will correspond Therewith."

BOSTON July 21. From the Gazette and London Daily Advertiser, May 22, 1755. To The Printer.

Sir,

While the nation is in doubt whether we are to have peace or war and uncertain how the differences about limits in North America may be settled, I am glad to find the Amsterdam Gazette giving us a glimmering light into the affair, in a paragraph of News dated from Paris April 28, which runs thus:

"It is judged here that the pretentions of the English are too vast. To say nothing of the extent they would give to the limits of Acadia or Nova Scotia, they maintain the Ohio, or the fine river, belongs to them because the source of it in the lands of their allies the Iroquois. The French might likewise say it belongs to them, because it falls into the Missisippi, which runs through their dominions. But one reason which they (the French) take to be decisive in their favour, is, that they discovered that river, and were the first that settled on it. This discovery and priority of Settlement are the titles have the Europeans in America. Moreover, the Apalacian mountains are, and must always be, the natural boundaries of the English possessions. But the Virginians have passed those boundaries in erecting forts towards the Ohio; and we don't see that our Canadians have gone beyond them in building Duquesne fort, in order to hinder their rivals from proceeding further."

——— In the Utrecht Gazette of the same date I find a paragraph to the same purpose, only with some immaterial variation in the stile; by order or desire of the French ministry, to prepossess the world in favour of their claims, as they do not yet think it time to assert them in a Manifesto; for it cannot be supposed they have been published by order of any body here, to serve a certain turn.

Now, in answer to this French state of the case, we are to observe,

That the Six Indian nations, named Iroquois by the French, are subjects and allies of Great

Britain, and have been so declared in the treaty of Utrecht.

The five original confederate nations are the Senekas, Cayugas, Onondagas, Oneedas, and the Mohocks. The Tuscarros, Missasagos, and other tribes are since incorporated with them, therefore, as all the land south of St. Lawrence river is the original property of the five nations with their allies and tributaries, the French can have no shadow of pretence to any part of this country; and their settlement about Champlain Lake is meer depredation, contrary to our title, which is entirely derived from agreement and purchase.

By public Indian treaties our right is far beyond the great lakes. (i.c. the lakes called Superior, Huron, and Michigan) and south-west to the Chickisas nation by the branches of the Missisippi. And since many people among the said lakes are united 'tis an idle vanity, if not superlative insolence, to suppose a dotted line in a French map must exclude the English from all those nations where there trade and dominion so visibly extend.

By several treaties made and renewed with the Cherakees, the Chiksas, the Natches, and the three Creek nations, the subjects of his Britannic Majesty have a right of possession from lake Erie to the Chikasas at the river Missisippi: whereas, in many of those parts, the French have no other title but that of intrusion and force. Thus our limits westward extend not only beyond the Apalachian mountains, but very far beyond the Ohio. ——— See Monsieur Danville's map of North America corrected and improved by Mr. Bolton.

By pretending to make the Apalachian mountains the natural boundries of the British dominions in America, the French would seclude us from a tract of land, 300 miles in length, and about the same in breadth, in Carolina alone; and by settling themselves therein, they would be able to insult and invade the remainder of that colony, and Georgia and Virginia, all at once: in short, their method of settling limits would prove no less than an excision of half our settlements; they would not leave us an extent of above 300 miles from the sea, in the broadest places, while themselves would stretch away, from the back of our settlements, above two thousand miles, claiming and taking all the lands westward of the mountains that are not actually possessed by the Spaniards, and could be safely done. That the French would keep all the Indian nations under subjection and play them off against us, make themselves masters of the whole fur trade, beat us quite out of the fisheries, and at a little time drive us clear off the continent of North America. Then adieu to our island colonies, and indeed to all commerce. The shipping of France would increase in proportion with her trade: our floating castles would be no more; and instead of true religion, liberty and plenty, superstition and tyranny, hunger and nakedness, chains and wooden shoes, would be the potion for Briton.

On our conduct at this important crisis our future happiness or misery, our liberty or slavery depends. The contest is about trade, which includes every thing valuable and dear to the British empire; by it we have been enable to humble the proud Tyrants of the earth, to quell the disturbers of mankind, and set nations free; and if we lose it, our condition will be infinitely worse than if we had never enjoyed it. Let us therefore behave with steadiness and resolution; let seasonable and judicious parsimony become part of an encumbered nation's system of Politics; let a little more of the old English honesty be displayed in our domestic economy; so shall we be able to baffle all the efforts of our enemies, and come out of this quarrel with more honour and profit, than we have reaped from any of our wars since the days of the renowned Elizabeth.   Your's

Probus.

BOSTON July 21. We hear from the Westward, That about a Fortnight ago, three Indians arm'd went into a House about 7 or 8 Miles above Sheffield, in the road to Kenderhook, in which they found a Woman who was at Work, ironing Clothes; one of the Indians took hold of her

and said, You must come with us; upon which with
her Box Iron, she gave him a Blow on the Head,
which made him sally; whereupon another of the
Indians presented his Gun at her; but she, with
her Arm threw it up, and it went off over her
Head: The third Indian then fired, and wounded
her in the Side; and then they all went off,
and entering another House at some Distance,
seiz'd a young Man and a Woman in a lower Room;
but in carrying them off, made such a Bustle,
that a Man in the Chamber hearing the Noise,
and having his Gun loaded, fired at the Indians,
and laid one of them dead on the Spot. The other two thereupon march'd off leaving their dead
Companion. The Indian's body that was kill'd,
was seen by the Persons who gave this Information, as they were travelling on the Road ———
The Woman that was wounded was alive when this
came away.

NEW-YORK July 21. We hear from Cleverack that
on Wednesday the 9th Inst. in the Morning, a
Party of Indians came to the house of Joachum
Vankerberg, and carried off a young Woman and
two of his Children, and the Man himself lying
on a Bed unobserved by the Indians, went quickly up Stairs, and after loading his Gun with
Swan Shot, fired at one of them that remained
somewhat longer than the rest, in order to carry off his Wife, who was then big with Child
and kill'd him on the Spot, and at the same time
wounded his Wife, but so slightly that her Life
was not in the least Danger.

We are told, that on the receipt of the above
News at Albany, and the cruelties committed by
the Savages at Kenderhook, one Hundred brave
New-England Men were immediately dispatched
from the Army, with Orders to scout the Woods
for six Days; and, if possible to intercept the
Indians in their Return to Canada.

From Albany we learn that the General Shirley
and Johnson, moved with each of their respective Commands from the City on Friday the 11th
Instant, the former towards the West End of Lake
Ontario, and the later towards the South End of
Lake Champlain.

Extract of a Letter from a Gentleman at Oswego

to his Friend in Albany.

"In your Letter to me, you tell me of the Extraordinary Conduct, Activity and Dispatch of Capt. Bradstreet, at Albany and Schnectady, in preparing every Thing necessary to come here with his Troops under his Command; but was you now to view Oswego, in the daily growing State, and the Order and Discipline of the Troops, you would gaze with Astonishment. His Conduct confirms his Abilities; as well as an experienced indefatigable Prosecutor. His Behaviour in general, with his Speeches to the Indians, and the good regulation, in which he has set the Trade on, conspicuously testifies a through Knowledge of Indian Affairs, and the Power and Measurements of the French in these Parts; And clear I am, that his Hands must be tied, or else the General's Work would have been much less on the Troops under his Command, obtained great Honour.

Copy of a Letter from a Trader at Oswego to a Man at Schenectady, dated July 9 1755.

"The Activity, Judgement and Management of Capt. Bradstreet, who commands here, has been, since his Arrival, very extraordinary, and more than we Traders could hope for; but the Spirit he shewed last Night, when we were to be attacked by a great Body of French and Indians, the method he took, and the bold and resolute Message he sent to the Indians, then in Arms with the French, is worthy the Praise of all Men, as it did not only make the French withdraw directly, but had such a Effect on the Indians, that they would not act against us. This is a Death Wound to the French, as the Indians look on them as Cowards, and hold all the Troops here in the highest Esteem, and I must say with great Justice, for never did Officers and Men show a better Spirit.

P. S. Fortification and Vessels grow here.

ALBANY July 23. I am sorry to inform you that a Party of 20 or more French Indians come this Day to Aal Plaats, a Place about 4 Miles to the North-East of Schennectady, and took there of our People four Captives, viz. William Hall, Dirik Van Vurst and his Son, and John Potman; there are also more Persons missed; and our

People hear firing of Guns at several Places, so fear shall hear more mischief."

BOSTON July 24. Privince of Massachusetts-Bay, By the Honourable the Lieutenant Governor and Commander in Chief.

Whereas I have given out Beating Orders for raising a Number of Men for his Majesty's Service, and it being necessary that the said Soldiers should be forthwith enlisted;

I do hereby require the Persons that have taken those Beating Orders, forthwith to compleat their Enlistments, and give me a speedy information of their Proceedings herein.

Boston July 24, 1755.   S. Phips.

By a Letter from a Gentleman in the Camp with General Braddock, dated the 21st of last Month, we are acquainted that they expected to be before Fort Du Quense by the 10th of this Instant; that the General had taken 5 French Indians, and that there was a Party of 60 Indians and 90 French sent out to cut off the General's Waggon and Horses, which they came up with, but seeing what fine Fellows there were for a Guard, and with what Regularity they March'd, the Party retreat'd without making an Attack saying, They never saw such a Body of warlike Men before.

PHILADELPHIA July 24. Extract of a Letter from Annapolis dated July 20.

"I am told that our Governor intends up either to Frederick or Fort Cumberland, in a Day or two, with about 250 or 300 Men, of which have already offered to go voluntarily with him, at their own Expence, any where that he should think fit to lead them. A Subscription for raising Money to defend our Friends on the Frontiers, has been handed about, to which People have Subscribed liberally. We keep a military Watch in Town every Night; and in some Parts of the Country they muster every Day."

HALIFAX July 26. Capt. Nickels arrived here from Louisbourg, and has brought with him from thence about 20 British Subjects whom the French did not care should make any longer Tarry with them having left this Place at different Times, and generally for the same Reason; but we hear they have detain'd some Artificers, in hopes they may be Some Service to them.

We are inform'd the French have now in Louisbourg an Admiral with five Ships of the Line and a Frigate, and that Admiral Holbourn, with the Squadron under his Command, often come within Gunshot of the Island Battery, which makes Monsieurs Fingers itch to give them a Salute in a rough Manner, but that he remembers it is a Time of Peace.

We also hear that the French have sent home two Vessels with Dispatches, to inform their Master of the unpolite Behaviour of the English in taking and detaining two of his Ships, when only going to take, as 'tis thought, a peaceable Possession of the Metropolis of Nova Scotia, by which they could not possibly be tho't to mean any Harm —— to themselves, and that they did not doubt their Master wou'd resent it in a proper Manner and make himself ample Amends for the Affront.

BOSTON July 28. Extract of a Letter from Albany dated July 14.

"Three Days ago arrived here His Excellency Major-General Shirley, and was received at the Water-side by the Mayor and Corporation, General Johnson and all the Officers of this Corps, &c. —— Yesterday his Excellency reviewed the Forces destin'd for Crown-Point Expedition, and we hear was a very well pleased with their Appearance, and now we are told that one Division of them will move To-morrow. As the Niagara Expedition, every Thing is in the greatest Forwardness, there being at present near 1000 of the Forces gone to Oswego, and the Remainder are marching off as fast as they can get Battoes and Steermen to transport them."

We hear from Hartford, that the Committee of War there, order'd out 35 Men under a Lieutenant, the Week before last, to guard the Frontier; and last Saturday, on the News of more Indians being seen order'd 25 Men more under a Serjeant, all for the Province of Massachusetts.

NEW-YORK July 28. Extract of a Letter from Albany dated the 20th Instant.

"Yesterday the first Division of General Johnson's Army, under the Command of Major-General

Lyman, marched from this Place; but meeting with some Difficulty in passing the Shoals by the Unfitness of their Battoes, and want of Waggons One Hundred and Fifty of the most substantial Inhabitants of Albany, with their Slaves, Battoes, and 30 Waggons, voluntarily; without Pay or promise, went to the Assistance of their Neighbours of Connecticut, as far as the Carrying-Place. —— This is clear Instance of their Disposition to forward his Majesty's Service, the cultivating the friendship lately established between this Province and Connecticut, and shews the difference between good and ill Treatment, when an Expedition is carried on without the View of enriching Individuals, as was the case of One Thousand Seven Hundred and Forty-six, when the Country had the misfortune to labour under many ill Misrepresentations.

Governor Sharpe, in his Message to the Assembly of Maryland, on the 5th Instant says, (I have just received Advice from Frederick County, that besides the Eleven Persons, who were killed and carried away Prisoners from thence, by a Party of French Indians, on the 23d of June; Fifteen more of our Inhabitants have since met with the same fate. There were nineteen white People together, fearing the Incursions of the Indians, had left their Habitations, and were going for Security and Protection to Fort Cumberland; three only of the 19 escaped unhurt, but a Youth whom the Indians had Scalpt and left for dead, is since gone to Fort Cumberland, and is likely to recover. I am also informed, that some Day last Week, twelve Indians were seen to cross Toonaloway Creek, and that another Party were Discovered last Saturday about Twelve Miles from the Mouth of the Conococheague."

Extract of a Letter from Oswego July 9, 1755.

"I found the Sloop Oswego, in a great fowardness, and shall turn her off the Stocks Tomorrow. ----- We have been greatly alarmed for two or three Days past, with an Account that the French were coming with 1000 European Troops, and a large Body of Indians, to attack this Place, which, by all the Accounts, we can get from the French Indians, they intended, had not their Spies, who come in here daily, informed them of the Preparations Capt. Bradstreet had made to receive them. We have now great Reason to think they are gone to Niagara, but we can give no particular Account of their Number. I sent Mr. Dean out in a small Schooner, upon hearing they were nigh us, who soon discovered them encamped within 8 Miles of this Place; But as there was little Wind, he could not venture nigh enough in to form any Judgement of their Numbers. I sent him out the next Morning, in the same boat, but they had left their Encampment in the Night, which makes us conclude, they are gone to Niagara. It was very unlucky that one of the Sloops was not ready; if she had I think they might have been stopped."

BOSTON July 28. By Letters from Halifax dated the 14th Instant, we are informed, That they had certain Advice there, that about 13000 of the French Troops, and 4 of their Ships are got into Louisbourg Harbour, where they are blocked up by our Fleet; The Remainder one got either got into St. Lawrence's River, or returned to France. ⸺ That every Thing goes well at Chignecto: Col. Monckton is now repairing and Strengthening the 2 Forts at Beausejour and the River Gaspereau, both which may be easily made very strong. He has ordered an exact Survey of the Lands that have been cultivated both on the Isthmus and without it, which are said to be very rich and fertile. ⸺ That it is the Governor's fixed Resolution not to suffer the French Inhabitants to remain there longer than till the Forts are put into a proper State of Defence. ⸺ That Vice-Admiral Boscawen and rear Admiral Maston were come into Halifax to refit, that Admiral Holbourn was Crusing off Louisbourg. ⸺ That every Body at Halifax, but especially the Governor, are full of the highest Encomiums on the Behaviour of all the New-England Troops under Col. Mockton's Command. He has represented their good Conduct in such a favourable, and striking Light, as must certainly give the highest Satisfaction to the Publick in general, but more especially to those who are more nearly connected with them. ⸺ And, that the Live Stock is very much wanted at Halifax.

NEW-YORK July 28. By a Letter from Albany dated the 23d Instant, we learn, that his Excellency Major General Shirley, with all his Forces, were to depart from this Place the next Day; and that the greatest Part of the Troops commanded by Major General Johnson, were on their march; that a great Number of Men, with their Waggons, went from Albany, without Fee or Reward, to facilitate the March of that Division of the Army commanded by Major Leyman to a Place called Stillwater; and that all the Officers and private Men belonging to the New-England Regiments expressed the greatest Satisfaction for the kind Treatment they received during their Residence at Albany.

BOSTON July 28. To the Publisher of the Boston Gazette, &c.
Since you published the few short Remarks which I sent you upon the Address of the Halifax Merchants, &c. on the success of our Troops at Chignecto, I find that two other complementary Addresses have been made there upon the same Occasion, to the same Gentleman, and much in the same Strain. Only I cannot but observe, That in there last, there is no mention made of so much as a "Countenance or Assistance" from Governor Shirley; nor the least Allusion to our New-England Troops: in which respects, these addresses seem more complementary than that of the Merchants. In that Address, New-England is kept almost out of Sight, and tho' we actually furnished about seven Parts in Eight of the brave Troops employed therein: But in these other Addresses, we are wholly and studiously kept out of Sight, as tho' we had no Concern at all in this Matter, any more than the People of Madrass ——— How my Countrymen will relish such Treatment from those, whom they have more than once snatched from the Jaws of Destruction, I cannot tell: But to me, it seems that They, and They only deserve, who can silently and timely submit, to be treated in this ungrateful and disrespectful Manner ——— I shall take this Opportunity just to add, That whereas in my Remarks upon the former Address, there was one

Sentence relating to the Hon. Col. Monckton, the meaning of which was tho't dubious, I should be very sorry if any should interpret it to the Disadvantage of the Gentleman: And more so, because his late Conduct at Nova-Scotia has and gained for him their universal Esteem, as a brave and good Commander.

PHILADELPHIA July 31. The Speech of the Honourable Robert Hunter Morris, Esq; Lieutenant Governor of the Province of Pennsylvania, and Counties of New-Castle, Kent and Sussex upon Delaware.

To the General Assembly of the said Province, met at Philadelphia July 24, 1755.

Mr. Speaker, and Gentlemen of the Assembly, It is with the greatest Concern I now lay before you the melancholy Accounts of the Defeat of the Forces under the immediate Command of General Braddock, which you will find is attended with very shocking Circumstances; the General killed and most of his Officers that were in the Action are either killed or wounded, the bulk of the Men cut off, his whole Train of Artillery taken, and Colonel Dunbar is now retreating with the remains of the Army to Fort Cumberland.

―――― This unfortunate and unexpected change in our Affairs, will deeply affect every one of his Majesty's Colonies, but none of them in so sensible a Manner as this Province, which having no Militia, is thereby left exposed to the cruel Incursions of the French, and their Barbarous Indians, who delight in shedding human Blood, and who make no distinction as to Age or Sex

―――― as to those that are armed against them, or such as they can surprize in their peaceful Habitations ―――― all are alike the objects of their Cruelty ―――― slaughtering the tender infants and frightening the Mothers with equal Joy and Fierceness. To such Enemies, spurned on by the native Cruelty of their Tempers; encouraged by their late success, and having now no Army to fear, are the Inhabitants of this Province exposed; and by such we must now expect to be over-run, if we do not immediately prepare for our own Defence. Nor ought we to contend ourselves with this, but resolve to drive and confine the French to their own just Limits.

This, Gentlemen, however gloomy the appearance of Things may be, is certainly in the Power of the British Colonies to do, and this is not only their Truest and most lasting Interest, but their High Duty. The Eastern Governments have gone a great Way towards removing that faithless, but active People, from their Borders. Let us follow the noble Example they have set us, shew ourselves worthy the Name Englishmen, and by vigorous Execution of our Strength, dislodge the Enemy from our Frontiers, and secure the future Peace and Safety of the Province; for we may assure ourselves, that while they possess the Countries that they have unjustly seized, we never shall truly enjoy either.

Allow us therefore, Gentlemen, to recommend to your most serious Consideration, the present State and Condition of your Country, the Danger in which the Lives and Properties of all those you have undertaken to represent, stand exposed, at this critical and melancholy Conjuncture, and to desire that you would not by any ill timed Parsimony, by reviving any Matter that have been in Dispute, and from any other Motive, suffer the People to remain any longer undefended, or the Blood of the Innocent to be shed by the cruel Hands of Savages. ——— There are Men enough in this Province to protect it all against any Force the French can bring; and Numbers of them are willing and desirous to defend their Country upon the present Occasion, but they have neither Arms, Ammunition nor Discipline, without wich it will be impossible to repel an Active Enemy, whose Trade is War. ——— I therefore hope you will, without Delay, grant such Supplies as may enable me not only to secure the People of this Province, but by reinforcing and assisting the King's Troops, enable them to remove the French from this Encroachments.

If something very essential be not done at this Time for the Safety and Security of the Province, the Enemy, who know how to make the best Use of Victory, will strengthen themselves in such a Manner, that it will be next to impossible for us to remove them.

Upon the earliest Intelligence of the Defeat of our Forces, knowing the immediate Danger to which we were exposed, I summoned you togetner, that you might have a timely Opportunity of exerting yourselves, to the Service of your Country, and of setting a proper Example to the neighbouring Colonies, who will, doubtless, if we do our Duty, employ their utmost strength upon the present Occasion, and heartily join in any Measure that may be concerted for our common Safety. July 24, 1755.

Robert Hunter Morris.

To the Honourable Robert Hunter Morris, Esq; Lieutenant-Governor of the Province of Pennsylvania, &c.

May it Please the Governor,
We have deliberately and seriously considered the Governor's Speech of the 24th Instant together with the Letters and Papers he has been pleased to lay before us, by which we find "that the Defeat of the Forces under the immediate Command of General Braddock, and the Retreat of Colonel Dunbar to Fort Cumberland, are attended with very shocking Circumstances: Nevertheless, it gives us real Satisfaction under this unfortunate and unexpected Change, in our Affairs, that this Province has seasonably and chearfully complied with the Demands of the King's Forces, and that no Part of this unhappy Defeat can be laid to out Charge.

We think it our Duty on this Occasion to be nether parsimonious, nor tenacious of such Matters as have been in Dispute, and are now under the Consideration of our Superiors; but reserving to ourselves all our just Rights, we have resolved to grant Fifty Thousand Pounds for the King's Use, by a Tax on all real and personal Estates, whithin this Province in which we shall proceed with all possible Dispatch; hoping to meet in the Governor the same good disposition he so earnestly recommended to us.

The Governor's Call of our House at this Time is agreeable to us, as it impowers us to exert ourselves yet farther in the Service of our Country; and the like Opportunity given to the lower Counties, that's under the Governor's

Administration, we doubt not, will be acceptable to them, and add their Contribution to the common Cause before the Time to which they stand Adjourned.   Signed by Order of the House,
July 30 1755.   Isaac Norris, Speaker.

Extract of a Letter from an Officer; dated at Fort Cumberland July 18, 1755.

"The 9th Inst. We passed and repassed the Monongahela, by advancing first a Party of 300 Men, which was immediately followed by another 200. The General, with his Columns of Artillery, Baggage, and the main Body of the Army, passed the River the last Time about one a Clock. As soon as the whole had gone on the Fort Side of the Monongehela, we heard a very heavy and quick Fire in our Front; and Immediately advanced in order to sustain them; but the Detachment of the 200 and 300 Men gave Way, and fell back upon us, which caused such Confusion, and struck so great a Panick among our Men, that afterwards no military Expedient could be made use of that had any Effect on them: The Men were so extremely deaf to the Exhortation of the General, and the Officers, that they fired away, in the most irregular Manner, all their Artillery fired and then run off, leaving the Enemy, the Artillery, Ammunition, Provisions and Baggage; nor could they be persuaded to stop till the got so far as Geist's Plantation, nor their only in Part, many of them proceeding as far as Col. Dunbar's Party, who lay six Miles on this Side.

The Officers were absolutely sacrificed by the unparalleled good Behaviour, advancing sometimes in Bodies, and sometimes separately, hoping by such Example to engage the Soldiers to follow them, but to no Purpose.

The General had five Horses killed under him, and at Last received a Wound through his Right Arm into his Lungs, of which he died the 13th Instant. Secretary Shirley was shot thro' the Head; Capt. Morris wounded; Mr. Washington had two Horses shot under him and his Clothes shot thro' in several Places behaving the whole Time with the greatest Courage and Resolution. Sir Burton and Sir John St. Clair wounded; and enclosed I have sent a List of the Killed and

Wounded, according to an exact Account as we are yet able to get.

Upon our proceeding with the whole Convoy to the little Meadow, it was found impracticable to advance with Twelve Hundred Men, with the necessary Artillery, Ammunition and Provisions, leaving the main Body of the Convoy under the Command of Col. Dunbar, with orders to join him as soon as possible.

In this Manner we proceeded with Safety and Expedition, 'til the fatal Day I just related; and happy it was, that this Disposition was made, otherwise the whole must either have starved, or fallen into the Hands of the Enemy, as Numbers would have been of no Service to us, and our Provisions all lost.

As our Number of Horses was so much reduced, and those extremely weak, and many Carriages being wanted for the Wounded Men, occasioned our destroying the Ammunition and superfluous Part of the Provisions left in Col. Dunbar's Convoy to prevent its falling into the Hands of the Enemy.

As the whole of the Artillery is lost, and the Troops are entirely weakened by Deaths, Wounds and Sickness, it was judged impossible to make any further Attempts; therefore Col. Dunbar is moving to Fort Cumberland, with every Thing he is able to bring up with him.

By the particular Disposition of the French and Indians it was impossible to judge of the Numbers thay had that Day in the Field.

A list of Officers who were present, and those killed and Wounded in the Action on the Banks of the Monongahela, the 9th Day of July 1755.

His Excellency Edward Braddock, Esq; General and Commander in Chief of all his Majesty's Forces in North-America. Died of his Wounds.

Robert Orme Esq;	Aide de Camps	wounded
Roger Morris Esq;	Aide de Camps	wounded
George Washington Esq;	Aid de Camps	
William Shirley Esq;	Secretary,	killed
Mathew Lesly, Gent.	Assistance to Quarter Master General	wounded
Francis Halket	Major of Brigade 44th Regiment.	

Sir Peter Halket,	killed.	Lieut. Halket	killed.
Lieut. Col. Gage,	slight wound.	Allen, Treeby,	killed. wounded.
Capt. Tatton,	killed.	Simpson,	wounded.
Hobson,		Lock,	wounded.
Beckworth,		Difney,	wounded.
Gethins,	killed.	Kennedy,	wounded.
Lieuts. Falconer,	killed.	Lieut. Townsend.	
Litteler	wounded.		killed.
Preston,		Bailey,	
Nartlow,	killed.	Dunbar,	wounded.
Pennington,	wounded.		

48th Regiment.

Lieut. Col. Burton	wounded.	Lieut. Hathorn,	wounded.
Major Sparks,	slight wound.	Lieut. Edmeston,	wounded.
Capt. Cholmsey,	killed.	Cope,	
Capt. Dobson,		Lieut. Brecton,	
Capt. Bower,	wounded.		killed.
Capt. Ross,	wounded.	Lieut Hart,	killed.
Capt. Lieut. Morris,		Lieut. Montreseur,	wounded.
Lieut. Barbue,	wounded.	Lieut. Dunbar,	
Lieut. Walsham,	wounded.	Lieut. Harrison,	
Lieut. Crimble,	killed.		wounded.
Lieut. Wideman,	killed.	Lieut. McMullen,	wounded.
Lieut. Hansard,	killed.	Lieut. Crow,	wounded.
Lieut. Gladwin,	wounded.	Lieut. Sterling,	wounded.

Artillery

Capt. Orde,		Lieut. Hathorn,	
Capt. Lieut. Smith	killed.	Lieut. M'Cloud,	wounded.
Lieut, Buckhannon,	wounded.		

Detachment of Sailors.

Lieut. Spendelow	killed.	Mr. Talbot Midsh.	
Mr. Hanen, Midsh.			killed.
Captt. Floyer of Gen. Warburton's Regiment,			wounded.

Independent Companies of New-York.

Capt. Gates,	wounded.	Lieut. Soomain,	
Lieut. Miller,	wounded.		killed.
Lieut. Gray,	wounded.	Lieut Howarth	wounded.

                    Virginia Troops.
Capt. Sthephens, wounded. Lieut. Woodward,
Capt. Waggwnwe,   Lieut. Wright killed.
Capt. Polscn,   killed. Lieut. Spicorff,
Capt. Paronie,   killed.   killed.
Capt. Stewart,   Lieut. M'Neale,
  According to the most exact Return we can as yet get about 600 Men killed or wounded."
  Extract of a Letter from Berks County, dated July 27.
  "People on the West-side of Susquehanna, in the new Purchase, are coming away, two Families having been murdered on Juniata: some are gathering together to defend themselves, others are coming on this Side of the Mountains. The miserable Conditions most of these People are in, I cannot express."
  A Letter from Carlisle dated on the 22d Inst. mentions, "That the Inhabitants of Juniata are entirely come away, and our People in general in great Trouble and Confusion."
  In another Letter from Carsle on the same date, there the following Paragraph, "We are now in the utmost Confusion, not knowing what Hand to turn to being more afraid of the Indians, (who no doubt were the late Murderers on the new Road) than the French. Our back Settlers are in general fled, and are likely to be ruined for the less of their Crops and Summer's Labour; several of them on Juniata having left some Parts of their Household Furniture in their Flight, and since, going back to fetch or hide it, have found every Thing broken and Destryoed by the Indians, and found their Horses in the Corn-fields."
  ANNAPOLIS July 31. By letters in Town we understand that Col. Dunbar, with the remainder of two Regiments and three Independent Companies, under his Command were to march from Fort Cumberland on Tuesday last, for Ray's Town in Pennsylvania.
  The same Letters mention the arrival of one Staut, at Fort Cumberland, who gave the following Account: That about the middle of June last, he and his Family were carried off from the back Parts of this Province by a Party of Indians,

to Fort Du Quesne; that when he came thither the French had not above 400 Men in the Fort; then on the 2d of July about 1000 French an 1300 Indians, came down the Ohio, and in a few Days afterwards several other large Parties of both French and Indians, arrived also from the other Parts: That a small Party of French, with about 2000 Indians, were soon after sent out to harass our Army on their March, who understanding the rout the General had taken, determined to have disputed his Passage over the Monongahela, but coming to late for that purpose found him enter'd into the Valley, where the Action happened: That after the Engagement the Indians pursued our People to the Monongahela, scalped and plundered all that were left upon the field, except five or six, who not being able to keep pace with the Victors in their Return to the Fort, were all treated in the same Manner, one Virginian only surviving it.

He further says, that the same day after the Attack, all the Artillery, &c. was carried into the Fort, and the Plunder distributed amongst the Indians; a great Number of whom, the second Day Afterwards, took Leave, and set out for Canada, carrying this Staut with them a Prisoner, who the first Night afterwards made his Escape from them, and with much Difficulty arrived at Fort Cumberland, almost famished. He says the French have now about 3000 Men at the Fort.

AUGUST 1755

CHARLESTOWN SOUTH CAROLINA Aug. 2. We are at last beginning our Fortifications upon which we have about 100 Hands at Work; in a fortnight we expect to have 100 more, and in 3 or 4 Months to be in Condition to mount 100 Pieces of Cannon, where at present we have none, on White Point, facing the Channel that Vessels come up; an experience Engineer being present to direct the Works: From Granville's Bastion to Broughton's Battery, we are to have a Wall 60 Feet wide, Ditch 22 Feet, then another Wall 73 Feet, the Ditch 9 Feet deep, and the Ramparts within 9 Feet above it, &c.

BOSTON Aug. 4. Our candid Readers are desired to correct or pardon an Error in our last Monday's Paper and instead of 13000 French Troops said to be srrived at Louisbourg, read 1300.

NEW-YORK Aug. 4. The Advices from Albany since our last, are, that Major Lyman, with a Detachment of 500 Men, went safe arrived at Still Water, about 28 Miles from that Place, where they were conducted by a Number of the Inhabitants from Albany, that Major General Shirley with all his Forces, were on the March for Oswego; and that Major General Johnson, only waited the Arrival of some warlike Stores, before he set out; that a Company of about 30 Indians went from Dutchess County last Week, in order to join the Army at Albany; that on the 19th ultimo, the French Indians carried off one Groot, from Schenectady; and on the 24th following, William Hall, commonly called Squire Hall, and his Son, with Jonathan Stevens, Son of Nicholas Stevens, and one Potman, were all taken by the Indians, within a few Miles of Colonel Glen's at Scotia; and carried to Canada.

We hear from Oswego, that on the 12th of July

last, there was a considerable Number of Indians at that Place, amongst whom were several great Men of different Nations, and that after Capt. Bradstreet had made them a Speech relative to the Times, their Answer to him was, "He has especially open'd their Eyes, and that they would be no longer Tools to the French, but would live in strict Friendship and brotherly Love with the English; and, if necessary, die with them." He ended his Entertainment on the 13th, by Launching one of the large Vessels, and firing three Cannon as she went off, which gave great Pleasure to the Indians; and the Traders there agree, they were intirely ignorant of Indian Affairs till now.

BOSTON Aug. 4. By an Express return'd from Albany last Monday we learn, That His Excellency General Shirley set out from that Place last Thursday for Schenectady, and from thence, with the last Division but one of the Troops, were to proceed the next Day towards Oswego and Niagara.

By a Letter from Halifax we have Advice, That the Schooner, with the Live-Stock, &c. which was sent from this Government as a Present to Admiral Boscawen was arrived there, and was received by him in a very obliging Manner; and that he esteemed it very kind and genteel of us.

By Vessels from Chiegnecto which arrived here since our last, we learn, That our Forces at Nova Scotia were generally in good Health; and that Orders were expected every Hour from Halifax what further Service they should be destin'd to.

Last Tuesday was sev'nnight four Men belonging to New-Hampshire Government was kill'd by the Indians at Winchester, near Fort Dummer, and an other carried off.

We hear from Deerfield that on Monday the 21st ult. two Men were kill'd and Scalp'd near Bellow's Fort; and that the Inhabitants there and Towns adjoining, were greatly distress'd by the Indians, who were seen daily on their frontiers.

ANNAPOLIS Aug. 7. Captain Gate's Rutherford's and Demerce's Independent Companies have left Fort Cumberland, and are proceeding to new-York, where they will wait General Shirley's Orders. All Provincial Troops remain at Fort Cunberland under the Command of General Innes. If the Companies be immediately compleated (as it is said they will) to 50 Men each, we shall not have less than 500 Men left for the Protection of the Frontiers of Virginia and this Province, which properly disposed, will, it is hoped, be found sufficient to prevent any Incursion of Indian Parties, who may otherwise have been encouraged by the late unhappy Action to infest our Borders, and destroy the distant Inhabitants.

Col. Dunbar, with the remains of the European Regiments, with all that is left of the Train of Artillery, marched from Fort Cumberland last Saturday; he is expected next Saturday Evening at the Mouth of Donococheague, in his way to Philadelphia, where, we hear, the Regiment will take up their Residence till next Spring.

We hear, that the Inhabitants of Baltimore Town has purchased, by a Subscription, a Quantity of Carbines, Bayonets, and Cartough Boxes, which are to be preserved in a publick Repository, for the Defence of that Flourishing Place.

PHILADELPHIA Aug. 7. Extract of a Letter from Catlisle dated July 28,

"Since the late Defeat of our Army, we in these Parts lie much exposed to the Incursions of the Enemy. But if our Superiors would take Advantage of the Spirit that is at this Time among the People, all might be soon retrieved. I am confident that were Matters well plann'd and headed by Men of Importance in the different Colonies, they would be no want of Voluntiers sufficient to do the Work, and willing to bear great Parts of their own Expence, or at least would be very willing to pay such a Tax as would be sufficient; if it even amounted to Half their Estates. The single Question now with most People have seems to be, whether they shall go West, and take a chance of saving their Estates, or East, and lose all."

Tuesday Night last an Express returned here from Major General Shieley; by which there is reason to believe that his Excellency is now in Oswego.

WILLIAMSBURG Aug. 8. By an Express from Augusta County we have the melancholy Account of the murder of Col. James Patton, who was killed by a Party of Indians on the last Day of July, on the Head Branches of Roanoke, and eight more Men, Women and Children. Col. Patton was going with Ammunition, &c. for the Use of the Frontier Inhabitants, and stopping at a Plantation on the Road to refresh himself, the Convoy being about five Miles before, he was beset by 16 Indians, who kill'd and stripped him, and then made off with his Horse, &c. ——— We are also well assured, that the Indians have killed 7 People in the County of Halifax, near Smith's Mountains, and that at least 70 or 80 Families have left their Habitations in that County, and fled from it, some to North Carolina, and some further down into the Country, and the County of Lunen-Burg.

BOSTON Aug. 11. Wednesday last, in the Forenoon, the Great and General Court or Assembly met here; and in the Afternoon his Honour the Lieutenant Governor was pleased to make the following Speech to both Houses, viz.

Gentlemen of the Council and House of Represetatives, It would have been very agreeable to me, if the Meeting of the General Court at this busy Season of the Year might have been dispersed with; but there are some Affairs of Importance which require your Consideration, and which cannot be deferred until a Time of more Leisure.

I shall order to be laid before you several publick Letters and Papers which have been received in the Recess of the Court, and also divers Minutes of Council relating to them, which will shew you the Steps that have been taken in Consequence of those Advises. You will from thence, Gentlemen, be able to form the best Idea of the present State of his Majesty's Forces in the several Parts of the Continent, and also to promote his Majesty's Service, and to retrieve the loss which has been sustained. But I must recommend to you first and immediate Consideration, the Subject Matter of the last Letter received from the Governor, and especially that Part of which respects to five Hundred Men ordered to be enlisted and kept in readiness for the Service of the Expedition to Crown-Point. His Excellency's Arguments for the Destination and immediate Employment of this Additional Force, are so weighty and Conclusive, that I need not add nothing to induce you to express your Approbation of his Proposal.

I have no certain Account what Proportion of those Men are enlisted, but daily expect a return from the several Officers.

Our Frontiers have met with a little Disturbance from the Indian Enemy as we could well expect: An unhappy Affair has now increased the Difficulty of now retaining and securing the the Penobscot Tribe; but whilst there is any hope left of doing it consistent with Honour of the Government, it is Prudence to continue our Endeavours for it.

I desire, Gentlemen, that you will not admit of private Petitions and Affairs, but apply yourselves wholly to the publick Concerns, that the Sessions may be as short as possible.

Council-Chamber August 6th 1755.

S. Phips.

BOSTON Aug. 11. An Extract of a Letter from a Gentleman in New-York, dated July 27, 1755. to his Friend in Boston.

"After repeated Alarm, by the various contradictory Accounts relating to the Forces under General Braddock, what follows, may I believe, be depended upon. ——— The General hearing that a Party of French and Indians being about 500 strong, were marching to reinforce Fort Du Quense, determined to intercept them; and accordingly pressed forward with 2500 Men, 4 12 Pounders, 4 Hawizers, and several waggons of Artillery and Baggage. ——— On the 9th Instant he sent a Party of 300 Men a-cross Monongehela, a small Stream, which empties itself into the Ohio, near the Fort; these were reinforced with 200, and about Noon, he crossed over with 1000 more leaving Col. Dunbar, with the Remainder of the Army, Artillery, &c. about 6 or 7 Miles behind him. ——— He had no sooner got over the Stream, than he heard a very heavy Fire ———

instantly upon which, the foremost Parties retreated to Him, in prodigious Consternation; the strength of the Enemy is not yet known, but the greater Number of them were Indians, whose hideous Howlings, struck the English Soldiers with a most extream Panic. —— The General used the utmost Art to encourage his Men to advance upon the Enemy; and for that End, the Officers bravely formed the Front, but so ill did the Soldiers behave, that not a Man could be prevailed upon to stir an Inch. —— in Circumstances, the Enemy fired upon them at a prodigious Advantage, and 600 of the Body were either killed or wounded, Sir Peter Halket and his Son, with Mr. Shirley the General's Secretary, and all the Officers, except about 10, are among the former; the General, who rode about to animate his Men, had 5 Horses, shot under him, and at last was himself wounded in the Arm and Breast. —— He died at Fort Cumberland, to which he had retreated with the Rest of the Army.

This melancholy Defeat is generally charged upon the Cowardice of the British Troops, in whom the General was intirely dissapointed —— It is said, that he had no Indians with him, and the Reason of it, because he forbad them to Scalp.

The Western Colonies are in great Consternance and Turmult, the Mob were with great Difficulty prevented from pulling down the Mass-House in Philadelphia; the Papists having shewn some Joy upon the News of the Defeat. At Lancaster, where they abound, Night Watches are regularly kept —— Pennsylvania is truly in a hopeful Condition; these are early Proofs of the little Reason they had for boasting of their sudden Growth, by the Importation of Foreigners from Germany; and the Quakers are a blessed Ballance, Governor Sharpe, with 300 Men, gone to reinforce Fort Cumberland; and the People to the Westeard, talk of nothing but retrieving the Loss, by another Attempt against Du quesne this Season. The Assembly is sitting at Philadelphia. —— It is thought amongst us to be absolutely necessary to reinforce Messirs Shirley and Johnson up the River, who are still at Albany, tho' there Troops marched a few Days ago.

In all Military Matters, it seems to belong to the New-England Provinces, to set a proper Example ——— all agree, that you are better able to plan and execute than any other of the British Colonies. ——— We put no Confidence in any other Troops but yours, and it is generally lamented, that the British Virginians were not put into Garrison, and New-England sent to the Ohio. ——— Your Men fight from Principles, and always succed. ——— The Behaviour of the New England Provincials at Albany; is equally adnirable & satisfactory ——— Instead of the Devastations, committed by the Troops in 1746, not a Farmer had lost a Chicken, or even a Mess of Herbs ——— they have five Chaplains, and maintain the best Order in the Camp ——— Publick Prayers, Psalm-singing, and martial Exercise, ingrosses their whole Time at Albany: Twice a Week, they have Sermons, and are in the very best Frame of Mind for the Army, looking for success in a Dependence upon almighty God, and a Concurrence of Means, Would to God, the New-England Disposition in this Respect were catching.

NEW-YORK Aug. 11. A Letter from Albany of the 5th Inst. says, "We have News that Captain Bradstreet has sunk several French Canoes on Ontario Lake. And that two Companies posted at Saraghtoga, had happily discover's Cartridge Boxes not to have any Bullets in em; ——— an Old-England Man it seems, made their Charges up, and he is now in Irons."

NEW-YORK Aug. 11. We are told, that when General Johnson made known to the Indians under his Command, the Defeat of the British Forces on the Banks of the Monongelela, they received the Intelligence with little or no concern, and remain'd silent for some Minutes, when the whole Body, as one Man, rose up and told him in substance, That they were not at all surprized to hear it, as they were Men who had cross'd the great Water, and unacquaited with the Arms of War among the Americans; and as it had happened so, it could not be help'd; it only because us (continued the Indian) in our present March to walk with more Circumspection, and to redouble our Diligence in all our Attacks, that so we may convince King George we are his Friends, and redeem the Honour his Folks have lost.

By a Letter from Albany dated the 6th Instant, we learn, that Major General Johnson was, that Day to set out for the Flats, his Artillery being gone before; where he proposed to remain only 24 Hours, then to proceed with his whole Force, for intended Expedition; and that two of his Majesty's Sloops of War were gone on a small Cruize, in order to make some Discoveries on Lake Ontario.

New-York Aug. 11. From the New-York Mercury, Nothing so highly deserves the public and natural Attention, as the present State of these Northern Colonies. Their Importance to the Trade and Navy of Great-Britain, is universally known and confessed; but the Danger they are in, if we argue from the Conduct of the Colonies themselves, is little, too little suspected. Because we possess a long extended Country, abound with Inhabitants, and enjoy a profused Plenty of all substantial Blessings of Life, many are apt to despise the Enemy, and laugh at the present Orporations, as the Product of Ambition on Cowardice. As nothing can have a more baneful Influence upon our Affairs, than such a groundless Security, I shall, in this Paper, in a Manner suited to the most illiterate of my Readers: exhibit a general View of our State, and make a few Reflections on the present public Designs to convince my Countrymen, that their Safety is less secure than some may fondly imagine.

This Continent was at first settled by the private Adventurers of several Companies, and the Inhabitants, for the most Part, were, as might naturally be expected, to the last Degree, indigent. ——— In these Circumstances, unsupported by the Crown, and many of them, indeed, such as fled from the Rage and Persecution of the Stewarts, they confined their Settlements to the Sea-Coast. ——— Hence in Process of Time, they stretched along the Atlantic, upwards of a Thousand Miles, and to this Day but few of our inland Possessions, extend farther than Two

Hundred Miles. ——— Our Frontiers, is equal to our extent along the Sea-Shore, and those Possessions consequently exposed to the Ravage, of a merciless Foe.

The French, who have never been wanting in their kind Offices to our Mother Country, jealous of the Growth of the Colonies, have long since projected a Scheme to harass and confine us, to a narrow Strip along the Sea-Coast. ——— To this End, they have vigorously promoted the Settlement of Canada and Louisiana. ——— These two Provinces lie beyond the Extremities of our Frontier. ——— Canada on the North, and Loisiana on the South. ——— Tho' they are at a vast Distance from each other, yet Ontario, and the great Rivers St. Lawrence and the Missisippi, the former of which, disemborgues into the Atlantic Ocean on the North, and the latter into the Bay of Mexico on the South.

The principal Aim of the French is to possess all the Passes in the Back Country, and to secure them by strong Garrisons: The Design of their Conduct, is evidently to restrict the English, from penetrating the Continent farther than they already possess, to engross the Fur Trade wholly to themselves, and to engage the Indians to scalp and captivate our People, as often as they shall judge it expedient. In this Prosecution of this Scheme, they have actually built several Forts, in the most proper Places that could be pitched upon, for accomplishing of their Arms. During the Administration of Mr. Vandam, between the Years 1728 and 1731, the Canadians boldly erected the Fort at Crown-point, within the Province of New-York; and what is scarce credible, at no greater Distance than 110 Miles from Albany. ——— From this advanced Garrison, they can easily annoy (as they frequently have done) all the upper Parts of New-York and New-England, and thereby prevent the Settlement of Lands, lying on the Northern Part of Hudson's and Connecticut River. The Erection of Fort Du Quesne, a Transaction of but two or three Years ago, in an Incroachment upon Pennsylvania, and enables the French to harass that, and the Neighbouring Provinces of Maryland and

Virginia. —— Niagara is a Fortification at the Streight, between the Lake Erie and Ontario, secures the grand Communication between Canada and Louisiana, and was built since the Year 1721, in the Country of the Senaca's, the most distant of the Five Nations. Possessed by these Advantages against us, 'tis easy to see, that nothing but a great Army is wanting in Canada, and the Southern Province of Louisiana, to render it feasible for them to cut off our Frontier Plantations, and penetrate thro' several of our Colonies, down to the Sides of the Oceans; and with what awful, terrible, and Ruinous Consequences, such as Invasion might be attended, let the History of our other Nations suggest. —— Once already France had equipped a large Fleet, under the Duke of Anville, to sweep the Continent with the Besom of Distruction; and had not the God of Heaven; fought on our Side, we might perhaps at this Day, have been the ignominious, impoverished Vassals of a lawless, arbitrary Monarch. —— Unsubdued by the Dispensing of that Fleet, France is still jealous of the British Colonies, and so intend upon our Destruction, that in the midst of a profound Peace, without regard to the Laws of Reason and Nations, a vast Armament was lately fitted out against us from Brest.

To the eternal Honour of the present Ministry the utmost Attention has been bestowed upon the Designs of the French and the prodigious Fleet for our common Security prepared, with a Dispatch unknown to the Nation, since the Days of the renowned Queen Elizabeth. —— But still unhappy for us, the greater Part of the French Ships has escaped ours, and probably landed a large Body of Forces, long before this Time, at Quebec.

Our Danger is also further increased, by the melancholy Defeat of General Braddock. —— A Defeat which ought never to be remembered, without exciting us to review the Glory of the British Arms. What Englishman, what Protestant can bear the thought, that a brave General should by the Hands of a Savage from the wilderness? —— That Man, who dare to meet Death in

the Field, should be slain by an unseen Enemy.
———— That a whole Army should be discovered, and routed, and several Hundred cut off, by inhuman Brutes, perhaps, scarce a Tenth of their Number.

In Consequence of this shameful Defeat, the Frontiers of several South-Western Provinces, lay exposed to the Enemy, and how much innocent Blood may be inhumanly sacrificed to the Cowardice of the British Soldiers in that Action, before the Winter be passed, no Man can tell, tho' we have the highest Reason to fear the Worst.

A Great Confidence is reposed by some, in the Prospects of Success against Niagara, and Crown Point. No Man is more ready than I am, to acknowledge the superior Merit of Governor Shirley. ———— He is, doubtless, the original Projector of all the late Measures, that have been concerted for the general Security of these Colonies: and were it not for his Vigilance, and unwearied Industry, this Summer might have witnessed the most tragical Event before this Time. After all, let it be considered, that his Forces are but a few, scarce Twenty five Thousand Men; ———— That his March to Oswego, is long and dangerous in spite of every Precaution, exposed to the Ambuscades of the Enemy. The whole Body consists principally of Raw Recruits, unaquainted with any Kind of War, and may e'er long, repeat the Scandalous Bahavior of the Regulars upon the Ohio. ———— Their passage from Oswego to Niagara, under the Convoy of the Vessels lately built in the Lake, will probably secure them from any Attack by the Way; but is there not to much Reason to fear, that the French Forces, and Indians from Fort Du Quesne, flushed with their late Success, joined to those Bodies, which has so frequently passed by Oswego, will be an over-match for the English Army? Or suppose we should succeed in the Reduction of that Fortress, what Assurances have we, that the French Veterans from Frontenac, may not cut off his Retreat by besieging our Garrison at Oswego, which will doubtless be lost under a Guard of but two or three Hundred Men? Should this be the Event, ———— the General himself, as well as the whole Body of the Army, will necessarily fall into the Hands of the Enemy; and Schenectady, as well as Albany itself, be in the most imminent Danger of being burnt down. Oswego, which has cost this Province immense Sums for its Support, may never be regained, and both the Trade and Indian Interest lost forever.

With Respect to the Crown-Point Expedition, I confess we have less Ground of Fear. ―――Those Troops are more numerous: The Distance from our Settlements is but small, nor is there any great Danger of losing their Retreat. ――― The Forces are New-Englanders, who, of all others, are best qualified for American Wars. ――― They fight, not like Regulars, for Pay; but from the highest, and most powerful Motive. ――― to revenge the Blood of their nearest Friends or Relations or to redeem them from the Miseries of a Captive State. ――― They are inspirited with the hope of Success, from a peculiar Confidence in the divine Protection and Favour. ――― War to them is a Matter of Conscience, and never will they return without Victory. They are inspired also by a Love of military Glory, and by Motives both of Public and private Interest. ――― Add to all this, that they are acquainted with the Country, enured to Fatigues, and as well skilled in an Indian Indian Warfare as the Natives themselves. ―――And should they be opposed as probably they will be principally by the late imported Soldiers from Europe, we may almost certainly presume upon the Success.

The Season of the Year forbid our entering upon any other Enterprize, than those we have already began, and nothing, in my humble Opinion, seems more necessary for the Safety of this Continent, and particularly for the Preservation of the Indian Interest, than heartily to join in a Reinforcement of Troops, and particularly those under the Command of General Shirley. ――― Parsimony at this Juncture, is the foulest of Vices. ――― A Complication of Vices. and involves in it, the worst of Consequences. ――― Half the Money which Pennsylvania has lately voted for the public Defence, laid out in due Season, would have ensured us the

Conquest of Fort Du Quesne, —— And the Aid of a Million may prove ineffectual the very next Summer, to repair the Loss which may be prevented by Ten Thousand Pounds opportunely expended in this. --- Up then, my Countrymen, scorn to be made the Slave of a perfidious, papistical Monarch: Under the Reign of King George the Second, and his Royal Father, your Properties, your Religion, and your Liberties, have been inviolated. —— And can you suffer the Lustre of his Imperial Crown to be tarnished by his relentless, Treaty breaking Foe? Great Britain defends you with her Purse. —— Your King is concerned for your Interest. Your Coast has been honoured with an expensive Fleet for your Preservation. —— Let Gratitude then inspire you to return these Favours, by vanquishing the common Enemy of Mankind. ——Away to the Field of Battle. —— Your Country calls. —— Your Cause is just, and God will undoubtedly protect you. He can defend you in the Hour of Battle, as well as in the securest Retreat; and let even the Coward know, that he is always in Danger, unless in the Way of his Duty. —— For your King, your Country, your Rights, your Liberties, your Wives, your Children, and what is more, for your God, rise up in Arms then against the King, who drinks in the very Blood of his own persecuted Subjects, —— against an Enemy, bent upon the Abolition of the Protestant Religion, and the Extinction of the whole British Nation.

PHILADELPHIA Aug. 14. The British Troops under the Command of Col. Dunbar were last Saturday at Conacogig, in their Way to this City; which Troops are ordered to join Major General Shirley with all Expedition.

We are assured that the Assembly of New-Jersey have granted Thirty Thousand Pounds towards the present Expedition.

WILLIAMSBURG Aug. 15. We are advised from Lunenburg, that the Inhabitants of that County have enter'd into an Association for laying a Company of Light Horse, to consist of Fifty effective Men, to range on the Frontier of this Colony, to defend the Inhabitants from the

Incursions and Depredation of the French, and their Savage Indian Allies: which Association his Honor the Governor in Council has been pleased to approve of, as also to furnish them with Ammunition and Provisions, and has Appointed Mr, Nataniel Terry Captain of the said Company.

HALIFAX Aug. 16. Thursday last Capt. Cole arrived in about 8 Weeks from London, which whom came Passenger the Hon. Montigue Wilmot, Esq; Lieutenant Colonel of General Warburton's Regiment, whose Baggage arrived here a few Weeks ago. We hear Capt. Cole has bro't the Cloathing, Arms, and Field Equipage for the three Regiments here, for 1000 Men strong each Regiment.

A few Days ago three French Men were taken up and imprisoned, on Suspicion of having poisoned some of the Wells in this Neighbourhood. They are not tried as yet; and 'tis imagined, if they are convicted thereof, they'll have but a few Hours to live after they are condemned.

The two French Men of War seized and brought in here by Admiral Bosawen's Squadron June last, have now English Pendants flying, and all their Guns mounted; and the Command of the Lys of 76 Guns, is given to Captain Amherst, who lately Commanded the Mars; and that of the Alcide its supposed will be given to the first Lieutenant of the Torbay.

BOSTON Aug. 18. By a Vessel from Halifax, arrived here last Saturday Morning, we have Advice, That the French Neutrals at Chenectady had refus'd to take the Oath of Allegiance to his Britannic Majesty; and that upon their refusal the Hon. Col. Lawrence, Commander in Chief of Halifax, had determined to compel them to quit their present Possessions; for which Purpose Transports were accordingly taken up.

That the Admiral cruizing of Louisbourg, had taken a large Ship from France bound to Louisbourg, laden with Provisions. ⸺ That he had also taken another Ship [a Packet] bound with Dispatches from Canada to France; both of which were safe arriv'd at Halifax, before the above Vessel sail'd from thence.

Boston Aug. 18. From the London Magazine for

May of 1755.
Number of the British Subjects, Men, Women, and Children in the Colonies in North America taken from Military Rolls, Pole-Taxes, Bills of mortality, Returned from Governors, and other authentick Authorities.

The Colonies of	Inhabitants.
Halifax and Lunenburg in Nova-Scotia	5000
New-Hampshire	30000
Massachusetts-Bay	220000
Rhode-Island and Providence	35000
Connecticut	100000
New-York	100000
The Jerseys	60000
Pennsylvania	250000
Maryland	85000
Virginia	85000
North-Carolina	45000
South-Carolina	30000
Georgia	6000
Total Number	1,051000

Exclusive of military forces in the pay of the government, and Negroes.

Number of French Inhabitants in North-America, exclusive of regular Troops and Negroes.

The Colony of	Inhabitants.
Canada	45000
Louisiana	7000
Total Number	52,000

So the English are more than in the proportion of 20 to 1; but in the words of the memorial quoted by authors of the State of the British and French Colonies in North America "Union, situation, proper management of the Indians, superior knowledge of the Country, and constant application to a proposed, will more than Balance divided numbers, and will easily break a rope of Sand.

BOSTON Aug. 18. Extract of a Letter from New-York, dated Aug. 7 1755. Since received this particular Account brought from Camp.

	Killed	Wounded	Return	total
Staff Officers to Major	3	7	2	12

	Killed	Wounded	Return	total
Captains	6	4	8	12
Lieutenants	14	20	11	18
Serjeants	17	20	21	58
Corporals	18	22	21	61
Drummers	2	6	24	32
Metrosses & Private Mem	386	323	486	1195
Royal Artillery	4	7	10	21
American Troops	49	57	111	217
Midshipmen	1	1	0	2
Seamen	8	7	13	28
	508	474	707	1689

 Besides Pioneers, Waggoners, Suttlers and Gentlemen's Servants, about 250 killed and wounded; and out of 54 Women only 4 returned.
 The above Numbers was a Detachment from the whole Body.
 The Artillery with General Braddock left in the Field were 34 twelve Pounders, 4 six Pounders, 4 Hoyetts, and 3 Royalls, with every thing belonging to them: What remained with Col. Dunbar was destroyed by the General's Order before he died, only 2 six Pounders. There was upwards of one Half of Capt. Oates's Independent Company killed in the Action.
The latest Accounts from Philadelphia are. That it had been expected there that Col. Dunbar with the Remains of the Army would begin their March from Fort Cumberland on the 21st of July, and that he intended to leave a Garrison there of the two Independent Companies; but on the 31st an Express returned to Philadelphia which left Fort Cumberland the 27th, who says, that Col. Dunbar was still there, and that nothing new had occurred. ——— That the Secretary's Office, with all the general's Letters, Papers, Instructions, &c. were taken by the Enemy. ——— That it was talk'd of raising 3000 Men in that Province to join the Forces Col. Dunbar has at the Fort, and make a second Attack on the French. ——— And it is said, that the Bill for granting 50,000 Pounds was passed by the Assembly there, agreeable to the Governor's Instructions; and that the People there seem to be now rouzed, a great many Petitions having been presented to

the Assembly to double the above Sum; and that they would pay the necessary Taxes chearfully.

The last Advices from Albany, are of the 30th ult. which say, That they had received the bad News of our Defeat near Fort Du Quesne; but that the Indians there were not disheartened at the News, but promised to die with Johnson.

NEW-YORK Aug. 18. James M'Gregory, an Irishman, (and not an Old-Englishman) was the Person who fill'd the Cartridges with Powder only, for the two Companies posted at Saraghtoga. He has been many Years in the French Service at Quebec, in Canada, and two Years since deserted from them, and enlisted himself into the Connecticut Forces this Spring, to which he now belongs.

NEW-YORK Aug. 18. By the Master of a Sloop that left Albany on Friday last, we are informed that General Shirley was got to the Great Carrying Place, (160 Miles above Albany) Saturday se'nnight; that Major General Johnson left Albany on Friday the 8th, and had joined Col. Lyman at the Carrying Place, 60 Miles from Albany where they intended to build a Fort, that in case they were repulsed (which God Forbid) it may save a Place of Retreat; that the New-Hampshire Provincials, consisting of 500 Men, were just arrived 4 Miles above Albany, they having marched a-cross the Country: They intended to proceed immediately to join the Army commanded by Major General Johnson.

NEW-YORK Aug. 18. We are informed from Fort Cumberland, that Col. Dunbar arrived there the 22d of July last, with the Army, having about 300 wounded Officers and Soldiers, and that he intended, as soon as Circumstances would admit to March to the City of Philadelphia, for which he was, the latter end of the Month making the necessary Dispositions. The Removal of the Army from the Frontiers of Pennsylvania, will leave the back Settlements of that Province entirely exposed to Incursions of the French and Indians, who are flushed by their Victory and will be encouraged by the Retreat of the Forces, to penetrate deep into Pennsylvania, and the People being defenceless will undoubtedly quite their Habitations.

Extract of a Letter from Albany dated Aug. 14,
"The last Division of General Johnson's Army marched for Crown-Point on the 23th Instant.
—— The People of this City and County of Albany, shew the greatest Readiness to forward the Expedition: In short, old and young offer their Service to do what they can. The great fatigue these People have undergone in carrying up Batteaus to Oswego, in low Water, now five Times in a few Weeks, and their principal People assisting General Johnson, gratis, with Battoes and Waggons, through the most difficult Places, between Albany and the Carrying Place; and the great loss they have sustained in their Crops, even where they dare yet stay upon their Farms, by the Men, Waggons and Horses, &c. attending the Army of Niagara and Crown-Point, and the rest of the Inhabitant quite drove from their Farms, will, it's hoped, entitle the Inhabitants of this distressed County, to the Indulgence of the Legislature, that they may be eased of Quit-Rent and Taxes for some Years; and the City of Albany, walled with Stockades again, and again, at the great Expence of the very poor Inhabitants of that City, may be now walled with the Money raised for that Purpose, when Time will serve."

Extract from the Answer of the Six Nations to the Speech made to them by the Lieutenant-General of New-York, at Albany July 2, 1754.

"We have several Times attempted to draw off those of our Brethren who are settled at Osweegatie, but in vain; for the Governor of Canada is like a wicked deluding Spirit: However, as you Desire, we shall persist in our Endeavours.

"We made a strict Enquiry among all our People, if any of them have either hold or given the French Leave to build the Fort you mention, and we cannot find that either any Sale has been made, or Leave been given, but the French have gone thither without Consent of Approbation, nor ever mentioned it to us.

"Brethren, the Governor of Virginia and the Governor of Canada are quarrelling about Lands which belong to us, and such a Quarrel as this may end in our Destruction. They fight who shall have the Land. The Governor of Virginia and Pennsylvania have made Paths thro' our Country to Trade, and built Houses without acquainting us with it: They should first have ask'd Consent to build here, as was done when Oswego was built.

"This is the ancient Place of Treaty, where the Fire of Friendship always use to burn, and it is now three Years since we have been called to any public Treaty here; 'tis true, they are Commissioners here, but they have never invited us to smoke with them [by which they mean, the Commissioners had never invited them to any Conference] but the Indians of Canada came frequently and smok'd with us, which is for the sake of our Beaver; but we hate them [meaning the French Indians] Tis your Fault, Brethren, we are not strengthen'd by Conquest; for we would have gone and taken Crown-Point, but you hinder'd us: We had concluded to go and take it, but we were told, it was too late, and that the Ice would nor bear us; instead of this, you burnt your Fort at Saraghtoga, and ran away from it; which was a shame and a Scandal to you. Look about your Country, and see, you have, no Fortifications about you; no not even this City. Tis but one Step from Canada hither, and the French may easily come and turn you out of Doors.

"Brethren, you were desirous we should open our Minds and our Hearts to you; Look at the French, They are Men; they are fortifying every where; but we are ashamed to say it, you are like Women, bare and open, without any Fortifications." [A great Truth this.]

PHILADELPHIA Aug. 21. We hear from Virginia, that the Assembly of that Province met the 5th Instant and that 40,000 Pounds is voted for the Defence of the Country. It is said in the Account of the late unfortunate Battle published there, that "the Virginia Officers and Troops behaved like Men, and dy'd like Soldiers: for out of three Companies that were there that Day, scarce 30 came safe out of the Field; Captain Peyroney and all his Officers down to a Corporal was killed. Capt. Polson's Company (who was himself killed) shared almost as hard a Fate for only one of his escaped. Capt. Stewart, and his Light Horse, behaved gallantly having 25 killed out of 29 which was brought into the Field. But the Regulars were seized with such Panick, that their Officers lost all Command of them, and they would gather in Bodies of 10 or 12 deep, contrary to Orders, and then in their Confusion would level, fire and shoot down the Men before them; so that many of those killed and wounded received their Shots from our own Soldiers.

BOSTON Aug. 20. Mr. Fleet, If you will give the following Lines in your next Paper, you will greatly oblige your humble Servant,

Many of the Inhabitants of this Province, apprehending that it will be found necessary to raise strong Forces in order to suppress our French Enemies, and taking Notice what Backwardness there is in many Towns as to the Enlisting into his Majesty's Service, are humbly of Opinion, that if the many Male Slaves in this Province (since they are not suffered to bear Arms) were obliged by Law to do some publick Duty in lieu thereof, in working at the King's High-ways six or eight Days in a Year, or to pay a Sum of Money equivalent, that it would greatly encourage his Majesty's good Subjects to enlist, we can't but think it reasonable, since Gentlemen's Slaves have Hands and Feet, and earn us much or more Money for their Masters than other Servants do for theirs, that something be done: The Common People who have no Slaves, are a continual Safeguard to those that have, and they know it, were it not for them, or every Family Slaves, should we not be in as much or more Danger from our Slaves than we are from the French, unless we kept them in Ignorance, and treated them like Dogs. ——— Some Masters of Slaves are pleased to say, by Way of Objections that the Negroes cost a great deal more Money than the other Servants do; but they don't consider that a White costs as much to bring him up till he is able to work, and that they are brought up at Somebody's Charge.——— The Government has been pleased of late to consider Slaves a Personal Estate and have Taxed them accordingly; but that, including Women and Children too, don't amount to so much as the white Servant's Pole-Tax.

Inasmuch as this is a Matter of Justice, and as Prayers continually are made that our Exactors may be Righteousness, we would use our best Endeavours to have it so.

And further, we are humbly of Opinion, that it will not be for the Safety of his Majesty's American Provinces to go on importing Slaves as they have done, since we are upon a main Continent, near our own common Enemy, and not on an Island in the Sea. The French are very sedulous to settle and cover as much of their Lands in America as they can, even to an Encroachment upon the English, but not with Slaves.

If all the Slaves in the English Provinces in America were free Men, it is not likely that the French would attempt to trouble us. What vast Armies might presently be raised in our Southern Provinces, where Strength at this Time is so much wanted! —— We are sensible it is a pleasant Thing, as well as, probable, to have Slaves to do our Labour without Wages; and that many have been used to them won't like to have a Stop put to the Importation of them; yet nevertheless we had better be without them, than be exposed to Danger and fill'd with Terror by Reason of them.

It is credibly reported, that the Inhabitants of the Town near Salem at their last annual Meeting, voted, That the Substance of what is above inserted respecting Slaves, maybe presented to the Great and General Court for their Consideration, and made Choice of a Person for that Purpose, who as soon as the Governor shall return, and the Court can Attend it, intends to lay the Matter before them.

PHILADELPHIA Aug. 21. We hear that the Assembly of Virginia has voted 40,000 pounds to protect their Frontiers. And that the Assembly of New-Jersey have changed their Vote of 30,000 pounds to 35,000 pounds to keep their Troops full and affective.

CHARLESTOWN SOUTH CAROLINA Aug. 21. We seem in this Province to be entirely unconnected with the rest, no regular Accounts are sent to us, either of our Acquisitions or Losses. —— Our Governor is certainly used with great Contempt by all his Brethren. —— We have an irregular Account of General Braddock's Defeat and Death, which alarms us very much.

WILLIAMSBURG Aug. 22. An Express arrived in Town this Morning in 4 Days From Fort-Cumberland with Advice from Col. Innes informing us, that Lieutenant Savage was just come in from the Great Meadow, which he had been ordered with 18 Men; that he there met some friendly Indians, who acquainted him, that a Body of between 4 and 500 French and Indians were then within three Miles of him, and advised hin to retreat as fast as possible to the Fort, as it was uncertain whether they intended to fortify themselves there, or would march immediately to the Fort. Upon Receipt of this Advice, Colonel Innes, Immediately dispatched an Express to Colonel Dunbar, to acquaint him with it, and desire Assistance.

We hear from Hanover, that 50 Men have offered themselves to Voluntier, to range on the Frontiers of this Colony, and having recommended Mr. Samuel Overton to the Governor as their Captain, his Honor has been pleased to give him a Commission, and furnish the Company with Ammunition and Provisions.

NEW-HAVEN Aug. 23. We hear the Government of Connecticut are preparing to raise an additional Number of Men, to be sent forthwith to support and assist in the Expedition now carrying on against Crown-Point.

A Letter from a Connecticut Officer, dated at the Carrying Place the 16th of August, informs us, that the whole Body of Forces, with all their Artillery and Stores, arrived there well on the 14th: That General Johnson with 60 Indians were arrived at the Camp; and more were daily expected; and that the Army in general was very chearful and determined to push on with all possible Expectation. In the Carriage of Cannon, a young Man of Connecticut was unhappily run over, and had his thigh broke, and died soon after; and another's Gun going off by Accident, shatter'd his Arm so that it was oblig'd to be cut off, but the Man is like to do well.

BOSTON Aug 25. By Capt. Bacon, who arrived here last Evening in 8 Days from Cheignecto, we are informed, That the French Neutrals were lading a Schooner and a Sloop up the Bay Vert, with Provisions, in order to send to Louisbourg: That upon Intelligence thereof to Col, Monchton he immediately dispatched away 250 Troops to said Bay by Land, but when they got there would not find any Boats or Canoes; and upon asking the Neutrals whether they knew of any, they said they did (or would) not know; but the English threatening to hang two or three of them if they did not tell, they soon procur'd them two, which 13 of our Men took and went off to the above Vessels, but while they were going, they were constantly fired upon from the Vessels with swivels and Small-Arms, but those brave Fellows not minding their Firing boarded and took them, with 13 Head of Cattle on Board, and bro't them safe to Cheignecto, without receiving any Damage.

—————— That Col. Winslow had march'd with 400 Men to Pisquit in order to take off the Neutrals there; and from thence he was to proceed with them to Halifax.

By Express come to Town Yesterday from his Excellency Major General Shirley, we learn that His Excellency with all the Troops were well and in high Spirits; and that they were within 40 Miles of Oswego Fort when the Express came away.

BOSTON Aug. 25. From Albany we hear, that 200 of the New-Hampshire Forces under the Command of Col. Blanchard, were arrived there, but came some Days after the last Division of the Army had proceeded on their March; 250 more were Expected 9 Days after. These Troops were raised very early, all fine fellows, but what has thus retained them, is expected will in proper Time be Matter of Enquiry.

By a Vessel arrived here last Wednesday, and another the Day following, both 4 Days from Halifax, we are informed that a 50 and a 20 Gunship were arrived there from Virginia; and that 19 sail of Men of War were in the Harbour when they came away. —————— That a Number of Transports were preparing to sail for the Bay of Fundy, which were to be conveyed by Capt. Rous, in order to carry off the French inhabitants from Nova Scotia. ——— That a Schooner was arrived there in 6 Weeks from England; but bro't nothing material. War was not declar'd when he sailed.

We hear that two Men who belong'd to a Fishing-Vessel of this Place, went ashore, at the Eastward, they were fir'd upon by a Number of Indians, who kill'd one of them; the other we hear, with some difficulty got off.

BOSTON Aug. 25. A Letter from one of the Officers that was in the Action near Ohio, has these Particulars. That after a sharp and Bloody Action of three Hours and thirty five minutes, our Troops yielded Ground, chiefly owing to the Consternation the Indian Method of Fighting threw the British Men into, and the want of Officers, most of them being either killed or wounded by that Time; very soon after giving Way, the Panic became so great and General, That notwithstanding the utmost Effects of the few remaining Officers, to rally and return to the Charge, and that they had to retreat upwards of 60 Miles thro' a Wilderness, without one Mouthful of Provisions or Sustenance of any kind, before they could join the other Division of the Forces, yet all proved ineffectual. ——— The General having a Detachment of Light-Horse, that attended him, out of 29 had 25 killed. ——— Monocatucha, our Friend the Half King, behaved well, but his Son Killed. ——— Many of the Officers and Men contracted a Flux in the retreat, nor was it surprising as they marched on Foot for two Nights and Part of two Days, without taking anything but Water.

Wednesday Last Express returned hether from Albany; and by Letters from thence on the 14th & 15th Instant, we have Advice. That by the last Advice. That the Generals Shirley and Johnson were both on their March. ——— That by the last Advice they had from General Shirley, he was about half Way from thence to Oswego, with about 3000 English and Indians; and was supposed to be arrived there when the Express came away. ——— That General Johnson set off from Albany with the last Division on Sunday the 9th Inst. That the Cannon and Warlike Stores with the second Division under the Command of Col. Titcomb, went the Thursday before, and were all safe at the Carrying-Place —— That Col. Ruggles, who march'd with General Lyman, in the first Division, has been at the Carrying-Place some Time, where they have built a Store-House, and have been mending the Roads, and making preparations for the Army's Arrival, which consists in the whole about 3100 Men, besides 300 Indians.

NEW-YORK Aug. 25. As the Following Letter from Albany, dated Aug. 14th Instant, contain some remarks of the utmost Consequence, when well observed: It is therefore thought proper to let the Publick know them.

To The Printer.

Some Weeks ago as I passed by a Company of new Men who were exercising; commanded by an English Officer, with whom I had found little Acquaintance, waited to see them Exercise; the Captain told me for the Time they were pretty expert. —— I who have some Experience on the Indian Wars, looked on with the utmost Concern; and when the Men Retired, told the Captain we exercised our Men that were to fight against the French and Indians, in a different Manner. —— Pray Sir, said the Captain, how is that? Only to load quick, and hit the Mark, that is our whole Exercise. —— What! do you take Aim at the Enemy, said he? Yes, good Aim, or not Fire, said I, So if any Officer appears, said he, twenty shall aim at him —— absolute Murder! You're not in much Danger of that, said I; you will scarce find upon Attack six Indians together, and you must divide yourselves in small Parties every where, to oppose the scattered Enemy. —— Quite absurd, answered he; pray, do you think when a Body of Regular Forces keep Rank, and fire regular Platoons that any irregular Attack can defeat them? It cannot be, Sir, you're certainly mistaken, and here is my Orders, said he, (pulling out a Card) with on the Back, keep Rank and fire Platoons: Sir you see what I say is the Opinion of the Council of War

―――― It was so indeed. Witness Onto.

Pray let me acquaint these Gentlemen, who are Strangers to the French and Indians, that they require no Exercise, but to be perfectly acquainted with the Use of Arms, that is to lead quick and hit the Mark. ―――― And so military Discipline, but this one Rule; ―――― if they were attack'd by French and Indians, to rush to all Parts from whence their Fire comes, and if they can put their Guns to the Enemies Breast, so much the better. The Gentlemen Officers from Europe will better understand me, when I Inform them, they must fight the French and Indians in the same Manner they force Trenches in Europe.

I have found by Experience one smart Fire, and some Execution, well effectually disperse both French and Indians. ―――― It is an unpardonable neglect of Duty to be surpris'd by the French, when a few brisk Men scattered for two hundred Yards on each side, will prevent it; ―――― keep them from surprising you, and they are an easy Conquest.   I am, &c.

We shall add to the above Remarks a new Piece of Policy made use of by General Johnson, in his March to Crown-Point: ―――― He has made his Indians naked and painted: perform many mock Fights, with his other Troops, in the Manner of real Indian Fight, except Lead and Guns; by this Exercise he accustoms his Troops to be well acquainted with the Indian Manner of fighting. A most prudent thought indeed.

Our Intelligence from Oswego by Letters of the 6th Instant, and by several Persons arrived from thence last Saturday, are to the following Effect, viz. That Col. Shuyler with his division and Artillery, arrived there three Days before: That General Shirley was expected to be there as last Wednesday, having been met on the Road by some of the Persons come to Town, not far from the Fort: That they expect to be in motion for Niagara soon after his Arrival: That they have 200 Men Employed on the Works laid out, which were forwarded with surprizing Dispatch: And, That the Oswego Man of War, and one other of the Vessels built on the Lake, had been out on a Cruize for several Days; but had not met with any of the Enemy.

We hear from Oswego, that Capt. Bradley, and Aysough, were both returned from a Cruize on Lake Ontario having been out several Days, but could discover neither French or Indians.

BOSTON Aug. 25. Most of the Transports which carried the Troops from hence to Nova-Scotia, and returned, have brought with them about 80 Invalids, and some others who have been discharged. The Soldiers yet remaining there were generally in good Health, but uneasy for want of some military Employment. 'Tis said they tell their Officers that they entered into the Service to fight, and not to lie unactive in a Camp. Such Men will never be affrighted at the Faces or the yelling of their Enemies.

Notwithstanding what has lately been said of the Assembly of Pennsylvania's voting the Sum of 50,000 Pounds yet Letters from thence says, that it is now thought the Bill will hardly Pass, as the Proprietary Estate is propos'd to be taxed as well as private Estates: That it can't be concerned what confusion the People are in throughout the Frontiers of that and the neighbouring Colonies.

NEW-YORK Aug. 25. Extract of a Letter from Albany dated Aug 18.

"These are to acquaint you, that Major General Johnson, with his Train of Artillery, is got safe to the Carrying Place; from whence Capt. Gilbert came Yesterday, and is going to Boston, in order to solicit for 1000 more Oliverians, to assist those of their Countrymen now going against Crown-Point, as the Forces now under the Command of Major General Johnson, is not thought sufficient to reduce that Fortress, which, 'tis said, is now garrisoned by a large Body of Regulars from Canada. Major Lyman has cleared 8 Miles of a Road on the Carrying Place, and the remaining 16 will be cleared with the greatest Dispatch, at the End of which they intend to built a Fort, as well as to cover the Troops in transporting their Artillery, &c. over that important Pass, as to serve as a Place of Retreat. By the Time that the Fort is compleated; 'tis expected the Boston Men will arrive;

for to their Honour be it said, that Providence excells all others on the Continent, for Dispatch in military Affairs."

Friday last came in an Express from the Westward, and brought Letters informing that General Johnson having sent Indians to Canada to get what Intelligence they could, on their return they reported, that the Governor of Canada received the News of General Braddock's Defeat, he sent for all the Indians, and gave them a grand Entertainment, threatrning at the same Time, to come with Six Thousand Men to oppose our Army at Crown-Point. It seems his Account of Braddock's Defeat, was, that he lost Eight Thousand Men in the action.

PHILADELPHIA Aug. 28. By a Person arrived from Oswego we learn, that they are now 4 armed Vessels belonging to that Fort near finished, the 2 largest are a kind of Schooners of Brigantines, and carry eight 6 Pounders, and 24 Swivels each; the two smallest are of the Galley kind, carry 28 Swivels each. When General Shirley arrives, it is supposed they will be near 3000 Men at Oswego. He was met on the 11th Instant at the Carrying Place having with him about 300 English, and 50 Indians, and it was thought would not be at Oswego before the 19th, the Water being low. There are prepared for his Expedition near 600 Battoes. There is a great plenty of Provisions, and the Fortification of the Place are greatly inproved and enlarged. The French now pass all on the other side of the Lake.

We hear from Fort Cumberland, that Lieutenant Savage having bee out with a Scouting Party towards the Great Meadow, returned about the 10th Instant, and reported, that having met with some Friend Indians, he learnt from them, that the French were no sooner in Possession of General Braddock's Artillery, than the fell to work on it, and burst and destroyed the Hawbizers and 12 Pounders, not attempting to carry off any thing but two Six Pounders, as they imagined the Rear under Colonel Dunbar was but a small Distance, and that our People would return and attack them afresh, not imagining that they had obtained a compleat Victory.

By a Letter from Halifax we have Advice, that a Letter was found on Board a French Packet, taken by Admiral Boscawen's Fleet, from the French Admiral to his Court, acquainting that his Men were very bad with the Small-Pox, Fluxes and other Distempers, and were in great want of Provisions; and that if he could get clear of the English Fleet he would make the best of his Way back to old France.

PHILADELPHIA Aug. 28. Extract of a Letter from a Gentleman in the Army, dated at Shippensburg, August 17, 1755.

"It gave many here great Concern to see Colonel Dunbar reflected on in a Letter from Philadelphia, for Things he was not even acquainted with before executed: nor was there one Field Officer consulted in destroying the Artillery, Ammunition, Provisions, &c. at the Camp, where General Braddock joined the Rear Division: This and our March this Way, was by General's particular Order. The unhappy Action was on Wednesday the Ninth of July, and on Thursday Morning, by Five a Clock, the Account of a total Defeat was brought to the Rear Division; nay, it was said there was not one escape; notwithstanding we remained resolved to hear further. This day many that were wounded came up, and some who were not; their Account being more favorable, we resolved to keep our Ground till we heard further. In the Afternoon there came an Order from the General to send some Waggons to Gist's Plantation, where the General was coming to bring away the wounded Officers, and Soldiers, and to send some Refreshments for them; this was immediately done under a strong Guard. The next Morning another Order came, to send the only two Companies of the old Troops, with more Waggon's to Gist's, for the purpose before mentioned; This was complied with. All this Day Number of Wounded and others joined the Rear and in the Evening the General, with some wounded Officers and Soldiers joined us. Preperation were immediately ordered for setting out next Morning, by Order of the General; but the Time required to prepare the Ordinance, &c. to be demolished detained us; and the next Day, the Thirteenth, we marched, leaving People behind to see the Destruction made as Ordered; all this was done by the General's own Orders, as we are told; and certain it is, that not one of the Field Officers were consulted in it: Nor, on the Divisions of the Army at the Little Meadow, was either of the Colonels consulted, even in public Orders. And had the Gentleman reflected on, being in a Hurry, I think it very plain, he might have found Means to have got faster from the Enemy than he Did. He has heard what has been said of him, and only observed, that it was severe to reflect on a Man from common Report: That he desired no Favour; he was satisfied the world should say of him all they knew to be Facts; and that a little Time would shew (if any Faults were) were the Faults are to be laid.

The Soldiers are charged with running away. The Numbers killed and wounded, it is thought would plainly shew that was not the Case; since out of about 1270, 600 were killed, and wounded, and all on the Field of Battle. If I were to give my opinion, I would Advise the Public to be cautious how they reflect, as Reflections cannot be agreeable to either the Innocent or the Guilty (if any, of the latter.) Such Things may be productive of ill Blood. By the care taking on our Side, it seems to be resolved to cultivate and preserve a good Understanding between the Troops and Inhabitants wherever we go.

The thought by some, we might keep the Field some Months longer; they won't know the Condition we are in. All those that were in the Action, did not save any of the Baggage, and the whole now remaining are naked; there is not one who has a second Shirt , scarcely a Shoe or hose among them; nay, some without Breeches, and not Half the Number of Tents to cover them, in case of bad Weather."

We hear that Colonel Dunbar, with the Army under his Command, will be in this City on Saturday next.

A Letter from Reading dated the 25th Instant, there is Advice, that there were then several Families in that Town, on their way to New-Jersey, who had left their Habitations on our Frontiers; and that Forty more were expected some Time this Week, thinking it not safe to stay any longer, on Account of the Scalping Indians.

HALIFAX Aug. 30. On Friday come from Lawrence Town our new Settlement at Musqueduboit, that the same Day, as two Men were mowing, within about two Gun-shot of the Fort, they were fir'd upon by the Indians, who kill'd one of them and Scalp'd him, but in their Hurry took but half the Scalp and half the Scull, the other was wounded, but it is likely to do well. The other Men who were at Work at a greater Distance, hearing the Firing and suspecting the Occasion, held themselves for a while and saw the Indians, three in Number, cross the River in a Canoe, after which they got safe to the Fort. The Body of the Man they kill'd was bro't to the Town, and decently buried last Sunday Night.

Last Saturday Capt. Broom of the Royal Train of Artillery, with a Detachment from the Troops under his Command of the Hon. Col. Monckton, arrived at Pisguit, and has brought with him three French Priest and eight other Frenchmen, Prisoners, who had been taken by our Troops since the Surrender of the French Forts at Beausejeur, &c. and we hear they are now confin'd on board one of his Majesty's Ships in this Harbour.

On Tuesday last His Majesty's Ship Port Mahone arrived here from the Squadron under the Command of the Hon. Rear Admital Holbourn, now cruising off Louisbourg; bro't in with 3 French Snows, Prizes, one of which was taken by his Majesty's Sloop Baltimore, in her Passage from this Place to the Fleet and the other two were taken by Part of Admiral Holbourn's Squadron, just as they were entering the Mouth of Louisbourg Harbour; one of them was a Pacquet from France, laden chiefly with Wine, one from Martineco with Rum and Molasses, and the other from St. Estatia, with Provisions.

BOSTON August 31. Captain Gardner, of Major General Lafcelle's Regiment now quarter'd at Halifax, in the flourishing Province of Nova Scotia, hereby gives publick Notice to his Countrymen, that he is properly autoriz'd to raise Men for his Majesty's Service in the said Regiment: All Gentlemen Voluntiers, that incline to serve the King, by applying to him, shall meet with good Encouragement, shall enter into present pay and good Quarters; and on their joining the Regiment, shall receive new Cloathing, Arms and Accountrements, becoming a Gentleman Soldier. ——— The said Capt. Gardner may be spoke with at his Lodging at Mrs. Emerson's in Cornhill, Boston.

SEPTEMBER 1755

BOSTON Sept. 1. Last Friday, an Express arrived here from General Johnson, and by the Letters brought, we learn, That perfect Harmony subsist between the Officers of the Army. ──── that they were all in Health, and high Spirit, tho' determined to act with Caution; that a Division of the Army was marching to Lake Sacrament, where they intended to erect a Fort, which might secure them a Retreat, or enable them to make a Stand till further reinforc'd; ──── that four of the Indian Spies got back from Canada, who Report, that the Savages who defeated General Braddock's Army were return'd, cloathed wit English Regimentals; but no mention of any of their Canoes being stopt by our Boats and Vessels at Oswego, on their return from the Ohio; which from reported Activity of the Commanding Officer there, we supposed must be the Case, or otherwise its a Proof, that the Western side of Lake Ontario is passable; and that unless Fort Frontnack is taken, our securing Oswego, and having several Vessels of Force on the lake, will not give us the entire Command of these Waters. ──── The Spies report, That the French Mohawks (alias Cagnowagoe,) had, as was expected, taken up the Hatchet against the English, which may partly account for the backwardness of our Mohawks in joining the Army; ──── that the Canadians were all in Motion, who give out, that they are quite desirous of meeting us at Crown-Point, and that they purpose to do it with Six Thousand Men. ──── But altho this should not be a Gasconade, if the other Governments give a powerful and speedy Reinforcements to our Army as we are doing, it need not discourage us from proceeding. ──── several Hundred of our new rais'd Soldiers are already upon the March, and the greater Part of the Whole will follow this Week, ——— however, if the Advice does not stimulate New-York to act immediately and with Vigour, it is to be hoped, that the Government will order our Forces to return; for if we are to act only upon the Defensive, it may be presumed that we shall stand an equal Chance with that Province.

The Southern News-Papers inform, that when their Provincial Companies at Fort-Cumberland are filled up, they will amount to 500 ——— and be sufficient to defend Virginia and Maryland from the incursions of the Indians, ———(which is indeed the only Enemy they have to fear on this side of the Mountains) ——— that the Remains of the European Regiment had march'd from Fort-Cumberland, on their way to Philadelphia, where they were to take up their Residence till the Spring. ——— From these Articles, we may infer, that they have no Intention of another Ohio Expedition this Fall, and indeed they have not as yet rais'd a Man for that Service. We may also infer that those Troops while in Pennsylvania can be of no Service to the common Cause this Fall. ——— but whether it would have been prudent for the Officers who had the Destination of that Corpse, to have order'd them where he apprehended they might have been of immediate Service or whether he considers those Troops in light of a Mettlesome Horse, which having once taken a Fright, is apt to be so startled ever with the falling of a Leaf, as to endanger the Rider, we shall not presume to determine.

Extract of a Letter at the Camp at the Great-Carrying Place, near Crown-Point, dated Aug. 24,

"Yesterday at a Council of War, we had 4 of Col. Johnson's Indians before us to examine, in Regard to the Observations they have lately made, who were sent to Canada about 30 Days since, by General Johnson for Intelligence, and return'd the 21st Inst. who say, That the Canadians are all in Motion, for the Protection of Crown-Point; and as they came from Mount-Real to St. John's, the Roads was constantly crowded with Waggons, passing and repassing to convey Provisions, Ammunition, &c. There, and from thence to be conveyed over Lake Champlain to Crown-Point, in a Brig and one small Sloop, which are constantly employed in that Service: That from St. John's they went to Crown-Point, where they were kindly received by the Commanding Officer, who waited with Impatience to see General Johnson and the Army: and who said that he soon expected to have 8000 Men:" ——— (But this we are apt to think is a French Gasconade.)

NEW-YORK Sept. 1. Our Accounts from the two Camps to the Northward dated between the 20th and 24th of last Month, run thus, ——— That General Shirley arrived at Oswego the 20th of August past, in good Health, ——— That Col. Mercer passed the Carrying Place the same Day, with all the Baggage, save a few Pieces of Cannon, and were expected to join the General the 28th. ——— That two of the Vessels on the Lake had been out on another Cruize, one of which 'tis said, has gone within Sight of Niagara, and made her Observations. ——— That between 150 and 200 Indian Warriors went thro' Albany the 21st to join General Johnson, and that another Body of much above the like Number of Indians were met on the March for the General's Camp the 24th, ——— That the 500 New-Hampshire Forces left Albany on Wednesday last, ——— that certain Spies sent out were returned to the Camp, and reported, That a Large Body of French and Indians were at Crown-Point, and by their Preparations, seemingly expected an Attack; ——— That the French has stopt at Wood Creek to prevent our Forces passing that Way ——— That General Johnson proposed to make Lake Sacrament, instead as Wood Creek, being advised thereto by some of the Indian Chiefs; and for which Place he actually was to march the 25th of August, with 1500 Men, from Fort Nichols, and General Lyman with the Division under his Command, was to form a Rear, and march the Day after.

NEW-YORK Sept. 1. By a Letter from the Camp at the Carrying-Place, dated August 24, we have Advice, that General Johnson, with about 1500 Men, some Indians, and several Field Pieces, was to March from thence the next Day, for Lake Sacrament; and that Major General Lyman was to follow with the Rest of the Army, as soon as the New-Hampshire Regiment had joined them. And that it was expected upwards of 300 Indians of the Six Nations, would soon join the Army.

By Letter from Albany we learn that on Saturday the 23d of August, 170 of the Six Nation of Indians, all Warriors, set out from that Place, in order to join the Army under the Command of General Johnson; and that 500 New-Hampshire Men were some time before set out for the same Army.

Yesterday evening a Gentleman arrived here from Philadelphia, by whom we are told, that Colonel Dunbar, with the British Troops under his Command, arrived at that Place about 10 o'Clock on Friday last.

PHILADELPHIA Sept. 4. From Virginia we hear, that the Governor has passed an Act for giving Forty Thousand Pounds more, for Maintaining Twelve Hundred Men to defend the Frontier, and paying for Scalps, at ten Pounds each.

Extract of a Letter from Winchester, dated Aug. 28. 1755.

"Four Indians are killed at Augusta. Eight of them attacked a House and cut a Hole in the Door, to fire in upon the Inhabitants, who were beforehand with them, and killed one of the Savages through it; upon which they left the Door, and broke open a Place between the Logs through which one of them introduced his Firelock. The People within rendered it useless by a Blow, and killed the Fellow, upon which the rest Fled. The other two were killed in a distant part of the Country. Last Friday two young Women were carried off the South Branch of Potawmack by the Indians; there are 100 Men in pursuit of Them"

Friday last Colonel Dunbar with the Forces under his Command, arrived here, and encamped on Society-Hill.

BOSTON Sept. 8. From Canada, to Monsieur L' Maine, a French Officer, dated Montreal, April 10' 1755.

Sir. By my Latter, dated at Quebeck, Feb. 6, 1753. I Acquainted you with my Arrival, and his most Christian Majesty's Intentions concerning the Reduction of the English Provinces in

North-America, the Number of Regulars we had in Canada and Missisippi, with the Natives enlisted, and our Grand Monarch's Orders to Erect Forts all round the English Settlements, sufficient to receive Fifty Thousand Troops, which he determined to send when said Forts were Compleated. I also gave you an Account of the Correspondence we had with our Friends residing among the English, and the large Quantities of Provisions we were favoured with by the Way of Cape-Breton, &c. Since which I have further to add, that in July last arrived at Quebeck near three Thousand Soldiers, Part of which we immediately dispatched to the Ohio, who arrived in good Season to defeat the English Force last Fall; and in December last arrived in the River Missisippi, a large Number of Regulars, brought over in Merchant Ships, who were conducted to New-Orleans, tho' with great Difficulty, from whence, after a short Stay, were transported within forty Miles of our Fort Du Quesne (tho' it was April before they arrived there) and remained incon. to prevent the English from having any Intelligence what Force we had in those Parts, as we have certain Advice of two Regiments coming from Ireland to Virginia, who are to attack our Fort at the Ohio early this Spring, with some additional Forces to be raised to join them. We are daily sending Men from Canada to reinforce Fort Du Quesne, and expect by the middle of May to have at said Fort or near it, about Six Thousand Men, the Natives included. The main Body will meet with the English Army before they reach the Fort, and give them such a Reception as they have not been acquainted with.

We are impatiently waiting the Arrival of a large Number of Troops, which are to be sent to Canada this Summer, with Money, Stores, &c. As soon as they arrive, we are to attack Oswego Fort, Albany, &c. upon which we doubt not the Six Nations will openly join us. There is a Rumour here that our Grand Monarch is to send a large Fleet of his Ships with Troops, &c. to Cape Breton, this Summer, in Order to make a final Conquest of all Nova-Scotia, which will be a glorious Acquisition, and secure in our interest all the Indian Tribes Eastward, who with our Troops that Way will Harrass the New-England Men, and keep them at Home, while we are Subduing the Western Provinces. Our Military for seven Years past, have wisely been sending great Numbers of Veteran Troops and poor Families to settle the Land bordering upon the Ohio, on the Back of the English. The Soldiers are to be kept in pay, and have a Bounty with so many Acres of Land to Improve: The Males of the poor Families for this Encroachment, have also a Bounty, so much Land, and all Sorts of Utensils for Husandry, which has brought over great Numbers to Settle, and will soon fill that Part of the Country with Catholicks, so as to drive the Hereticks into the Sea. It is of infinite Advantage, Sir, to our Cause, that the Land Southward of Hudson's River, are principally peopled by Vertue of Patents granted to Penn, Baltimore &c. with Liberty for the Catholicks to carry on their Publick Worship, which gives our Court Opportunity, undiscovered, so send great Numbers of our Jesuits, and good Catholicks into those Parts (which they have lately done) in order to inspect into the State and Circumstances of the Inhabitants, and the Number of our hearty Friends, Penn's Disciples, and our good Friends the Moravians, you know, Sir, refuse to take up Arms against us; and our friends inform us, that they are almost half the Number of Inhabitants in those Parts, and that the other half consist of a variety of mongrel Protestants of different Nations, viz. Dutch, German, Palatines, intermixed with great Numbers of our own good Catholicks, who have from Time to Time fled into those Parts or been Transported from Scotland and Ireland, so that if they raise any Number of Men in those Parts to oppose our Troops, their Army must be made up chiefly of Catholicks, who if obliged to take Arms, will throw them down as soon as a Battle commences.

I must acquaint you, Sir, that among other particulars in the Grand Plan our Court formed for the Reduction of the English Settlements in North-America, one was to send a Number of

Missionaries into the Western Provinces for sundry Years past, who were to Transform themselves into any Shape be of any Religion, and become all Things to gain some. Into such as cannot be gain'd to act for us, they instill Principles not to act against us, and by this infatuating then we reduce their Numbers, and as it were kill one half of the Inhabitants with Jesuits Powder.

We have some Men in this great Authority, who conform to their established Religion, and others to the Religion of the Country, in order to get into Office, which will give them Opportunity sooner or later to help us bring about a general Revolution, by extirpating Heresy, and establishing the true Catholick Religion in those Parts. I must tell you, Sir, we fear no Army that can be raised by the English in North America, except the New-England Oliverians; they will die hard, all out Indians and Canadians seems to dread them, and say, if we ever get their Land it must be Inch by Inch. The whole Body of those Puritan Hereticks Eastward of Hudson's River, are like a formidable standing Army, that will one and all Sacrifice their lives before they will give us their Lands, their Religion and the Protestant Cause. However if our Army at the Ohio defeats the English Troops, which we are not in the least scrupulous of, the Day is our own, and the Western Provinces will become easy Prey to out Troops, and our Indian Allies. If there is not an Army sent into those Parts of old Britons, or New-England Oliverians to stop our Career, tho' the latter we most dread, they (esteeming us ravenous Wolves) would drive us out of our Burroughs and sculking Places; but as we design to harrass them Eastward, they will find Work enough to defend their own Territories.

But there is one Thing, the want of which amidst all our pleasing Prospects, would disappoint our deep laid Schemes, frustrate our design, and render the Measures we have already pursued quite abortive, I mean, a constant Supply of Provisions. The Inhabitants of Canada are already reduced to the utmost distress, having sent all our Army, and left themselves to feed almost upon Herbs and Roots; and the Provisions we sent were such an unsignificant Trifle, that if there had not been carried last Summer, a large Quantity of Pork, Beef, Flour, Rice, Bread, &c. up the River Missisippi, our Troops must have abandoned the Forts there.

Our Court suspected that as soon as we began to attack the English Settlements, they would not bring any Provisions publickly to Cape-Breton, therefore prudently form'd a grand Scheme to obtain Provisions from another quarter and wisely sent Commissaries to all the Neutral Ports, viz. to Surinam, St. Eustatia, St. Thomas, Curiacca, Carthagena, and also to the Havanna and St. Augustine, knowing these Places were profusely supply'd by the English from New-York, Philadelphia, South Carolina, and various other Parts, and at these before-named Ports our Commissaries are to reside to buy up all the Provisions they can come at, and send to Canada and Missisippi. Our Court have also sent into various Ports of North-America, Gentlemen of no small Figure to reside among the English; these have blank Permissions signed ready to fill up for all English Vessels, to trade in any French Ports, whose Owners will send so much Provisions. But all our deep laid Plots, Schemed and Artifices will be confounded, and we at last defeated, if the English Government on this Continent should take it into their Heads to lay an Embargo, and prevent the Exportation of Provisions to any Place where we could come at them: and finally, if the English Court should get angry, and send a Fleet of their Ships, and block up the River St. Lawrence and the Missisippi but one Year, We at Canada, and our Troops at the Ohio, must sell ourselves to them for Food, or perish. I do therefore intreat, Sir, that all our Jesuits, Monks, Friers, and Holy Fathers of our Mother Church, may put up Ten Thousand Pater Notre's and Ave-Maria's that they may invoke our holy Saints that the English might continue their former Charity towards us, and supply us with Provisions as heretofore and not block up the aforesaid Rivers, but that our Ships might go in and out without Molestation; then we shall accomplish all our deep laid Schemes, extirpate Hereticks, and enlarge the Dominions of our Grand Monarch.

I Am, Sir,
      your most obedient.
            De Rouche.

The foregoing Letter is printed by itself on half a Sheet of Paper, for the Benefit of such as do not take this News-Paper; and may be had at the Publisher, at the Heart and Crown in Cornhill, at the small Expence of two Coppers.

N. B. It ought to be read (for more Reasons than one) by every intelligent Man in North-America.

BOSTON Sept. 8. Our Advice from Halifax by several Vessels, That the Squadron cruizing off Louisbourg have taken 4 French Ships and 3 Snows, laden with Provisions, &c. three which were safe arrived there and the others were daily expected: That the Admiral had given Orders for the Fleet to take, sink or destroy all French Vessels they should meet: That it was tho't in three Weeks there would not be a French Neutral at Chiegnecto: And that a Party of Troops had escorted three French Priest from Pisguit to Halifax, where they were under Confinement.

BOSTON Sept. 8. Last Week several Vessels arrived here from Halifax, and by Letters from Gentlemen of the best Intelligence there, we are told, that in three Weeks Time all the French in Nova-Scotia, would be removed out of the Province, but to what Place not known. ——— That Col. Monckton had orders to destroy every French Vessel, Boat or Canoe, he could find in any Harbour, Bay, Creek or River in the Province, to prevent the Inhabitants from making their Escapes. ——— That nine Transports were gone to Minas, to take in many of the Neutrals as they could carry, and that 3 Priest had been taken and sent to Halifax, and were put on board the Admiral's Ship for Security in order to be sent to England. ——— That Capt. Rous and 2 other Ships, were gone to Newfoundland to break up the French Settlements there. and to take all their Vessels and Fishing Craft and bring them away. —— And that they daily expected the Commencement of a Bloody War.

NEW-YORK Sept. 8. On Tuesday Afternoon at 5 o'Clock arrived here his Majesty's Ship the Sphinx of 20 Guns. Capt. James Cambier, in 9 Weeks from Portsmouth, with whom came his Excellency Sir Charles Hardy, Knight, Captain General and Governor and Chief of this Province, and his Family as also his Excellency's Sister, and her Husband, Mr. Brown.

NEW-YORK Sept. 8. By a Gentleman who left Oswego last Friday Fortnight, we are told, That our Vessels on the Lake had blocked up and secured at a Place called Cadaroque, a French Brigantine loaded with Possessions, and bound for Niagara. —— Cadaroque is at the Entrance into the Lake of the River St. Lawrence, distant from Oswego about 20 Leagues, bearing N.E. by E.

Capt Bradstreet, is, by General-Shirley appointed Adjutant General —— Col. Schuyler to be Colonel of the Train of Artillery. Lieutenant Bartman (of the Grenadiers) to be Captain of the Train —— Lieutenant McKinnen, to be Lieutenant of the Train. —— Captain John Shirley, to be Aid de Camp. —— John Chesire, Esq; to be Judge Advocate. —— and Mr. Montague Brown, to be Lieutenant of Capt. Gates's Independent Company of Fusileers.

PHILADELPHIA Sept. 11. We hear from Virginia that two young Woman, Daughters of one Lanscisco, living on the North Fork of the South Branch of Potowmack, was taken by the French Indians, as they were looking for their Cown near the Plantation, and carried off. A Party under Capt. Cocks, followed the Track almost to Fort Du Quesne, in order to recover them; but could not come up with the Enemy.

BOSTON Sept. 15. All Gentlemen Voluntiers, who are willing to serve his Majesty's King George, for the Space of Five Years from the date of Inlistment, in his Majesty's Fortieth Regiment of Foot, now lying at Halifax in Nova-Scotia, Commanded by the Hon. Colonel Peregrine, Thomas Hopson, and in Capt, Paston Gould's Company, shall receive Seven Dollars Bounty Money, and a Dollar to drink his Majesty's Health, and enter into present Pay; and when they join the Regiment at Halafax, they will receive compleat Cloathing, &c. and all things necessary for a Gentleman Soldier, Over and above the King's Pay his Majesty gives them the same allowance of Provisions as on board his Majesty's Ships of War.

N. B. Captain Gould is to be spoke whith either at Mr. Wethered's, the Sign of the Bunch of Grapes in King-Street, or at the Widow Pelham's near the Town-House, in the same Street.

BOSTON Sept. 15. We hear that the Assembly of New-York has voted the sum of 8,000 pounds, towards Payment of the Connecticut Forces that are already raised, and now raising.

A Person who came from Roxbury Yesterday from Hartford in Connecticut reports, That several Letters were arrived there from Major Lyman, giving an Account of an Engagement between a body of French and Indians and a Detachment from General Johnson's Army, the Purport of which are as follows, viz. That Yesterday was 7-night, as the first Division of General Johnson's Army, consisting of about 1500 Men, were at the West end of Lake St. Sacrament, they were attack'd by about 1800 French and Indians when a bloody Engagement ensued, wherein the New-England Men, who well play'd the Man, gain'd the Field, with the loss of between 3 and 400 Men, as it is said, and the Enemy about 700; but we must patiently wait for a further Account, which is hourly expected.

The military Spirit greatly prevails in all Parts in this and other New-England Governments: As soon as Advice came from General Johnson that a Reinforcement was needful, our People have been daily inlisting into the Service. And this province alone will have upwards of four Thousand Men in the Expedition to Crown-Point.

—— We have the warmest Expectation of Success in that Undertaking —— Our Cause is just, and our Men inlist from Principle —— We are not asham'd to our own Dependence on the God of America, and we profess to go forth in His Strength.

The inglorious Defeat at the Southward has not Let in the least abated the Courage of our Men: On the contrary, it has enkindled the Fire of Resentment. —— The Blood of our Fellow-Subjects at the Ohio —— the Blood of our dear Brethren upon our own Borders, inhumanly Spilt from Time to Time, Cry aloud ——too loud not to be distinctly heard —— And we cannot but hope that those brave Men who are gone to Crown Point will be honoured by Providence to humble the Pride of our haughty French Enemy; and be made the Instrument to deal all the Vengeance upon them, which their Perfidy and Cruelty deserve.

NEW-YORK Sept. 15. Last Friday Evening, his Excellency Sir Charles Hardy Knt. our Governor attended by the Hon. James De Lancey, Esq; our Lieutenant-Governor and Oliver De Lancey, Esq; enbarked on board a Sloop for Albany: On leaving the Harbour, they were saluted by his Majesty's Ship the Sphinx and the Guns from Fort George, in this City.

We hear that several Chests of small Arms, as well as a large Quantity of Powder and Ball, and several other Necessities for General Johnson's Army, were yesterday put on board Captain Dowe, with whom his Excellency went to Albany.

His Excellency has carried with him some presents of Condolence for the Indians; and we hear that his Excellency purposed to stay at Albany some Time, in order to be ready on any Service that his Presence may forward, and is resolved to take the field if necessary.

Nothing can be more agreeable that the Accounts we have from Connecticut. No sooner did they receive Intelligence of a Conflict between our Forces and the French, at The Carrying Place, that they instantly determined to send recruits to the Army. The whole 2000 Men they lately voted for a Reinforcement, are actually gone, and 2000 or more, 'tis expected will join our Army in Ten Days Time. From the back Towns several Companies of these last Supplies are on their March, and on the Sea Side they are levying with astonishing Dispatch. Persons of all Ranks and Conditions enter into the Service of their Country. Surely the Conduct ought to shame the Southern Colonies, and animate them to give equal Proof of their Courage and Loyalty. 'Tis hoped this Province will make seasonable and ample Provisions for these brave Recruits at Albany: We also learn, that several hundred voluntiers are marching towards the Camp, from the Northern Part of this Government.

The Boston Post assures us, That Coming through the several Towns in Connecticut, he observed Multitudes of the Inhabitants of that Government preparing for a March towards General Johnson's Army, being spirited up by the just Resentment due to our common and perfidious enemy: And in particular he affirms, that one Captain Fairchild of Stratford, had, in the Space of three Days only, compleated a Company of one hundred Men, all Independents; Men that furnished themselves with every Thing necessary for the Expedition at their own private Expence, and marched away on Horseback for the Camp on Thursday or Friday last.

BOSTON Sept. 15. By last Saturday's Post, we had from Connecticut, a very uncertain and imperfect Account of an Action between a Division of our Army as they were on their March towards Crown-Point, and a great Body of the Enemy, and that great firing of Cannon had been heard from 12 o'Clock in the Morning till 5 in the Afternoon: ——— And Yesterday a young Man arrived here from Hartford in Connecticut, and informs, that just before he came away, they had an account from the Army, that on the 7th Instant 1600 Men, was attack'd by almost 1800 French and Indians near Lake Sacrament; that the Action was very sharp and Bloody, and lasted most part of the Day, but that at last the Enemy drew off, having lost 700 of their Men, and it is said we lost 300, among whom (we are sorry to mention it) are the brave Colonel Titcomb and Colonel Williams. An Express is hourly expected with the Particulars.

WILLIAMSBURG Sept. 15. The Troops in the Pay of this Colony, are ordered to be augmented to 1000 Men, under the Command of Colonel George Washington. The Officers have received their beating Instructions this Week, and immediately sent out to raise their several Companies.

Two great Warriors of the Cherokee Nation, with their Attendants, are come to Town, in Order to give a Proof of their Love and Friendship for their Brethren the English; and we hear are much pleased with their Entertainment at the Governor's, and the Cloaths and Presents he had made them.

NEW-YORK Sept. 15. A Letter the 9th Instant from the Great Carrying Place, says that we had the greatest Engagement that ever was fought in America: It began at 8 in the Morning and continued until 4 in the Afternoon; the Enemy charged us in the Front of the Camp with 1200 French and 700 Indians. Our Men fought with uncommon Bravery: We maintain'd our Ground with the Loss of some brave Officers, King Hendrick, and some brave Mohawks. We've got the Head-General in America now Prisoner, and mortally wounded his Aide de-Camp. We kill'd the Major-General, the same that fought Braddock: He died with these Words, "fight my boys, you've not Braddock here, but Johnson." Our brave General is wounded, but slightly; we have lost near 200, and it's thought we have kill'd near 500. I wish we had new supplies of every Thing.

The Express that came to Towm from General Johnson, even assures us, That he should have been in Town the Evening before, had not the different Bodies of People he met on the Road hither, bravely going to the Assistance of Mr. Johnson, prevented his Speed, by interrogating him about the Success of the Engagement, which did not a little contribute to the expedite their March.

And indeed we have received no less Assurance from Gentlemen of good Authority, That the City and County of Albany are since almost drain'd of the Inhabitants who are gone on the aforesaid Purpose, being excited thereto by a noble and exalted Spirit of justly vindicating their Sovereign's Cause.

On Thursday last, the General Assembly of this Province was prorogued till Tuesday the thirtieth Instant, his Excellency our Governor had been pleased to give his Assent to the following Acts, passed this Session, viz.

An Act for raising the Sum of Eight Thousand Pounds, to be contributed to the Colony of Connecticut, towards the Expence of a Reinforcement of Two Thousand effective Men, now levying in the said Colony, for the Army destined against Crown-Point under Major-General Johnson; and for emitting bills of Credit to the Amount of the said Sum of Eight Thousand Pounds, for making immediate Payment.

An Act to explain Part of a Clause of an Act, entitled, An Act for paying and subsisting Eight complete Companies of one Hundred effective Men, each, Officers included, to assist in Conjunction with the Neighbouring Colonies, in erecting one or more Forts nigh Crown-Point, within his Majesty's Dominions: for raising the sum of Ten Thousand Pounds, for and towards the said Service, and for making current Bills of Credit to the Amount thereof and other Purposes therein mentioned. And,

An Act more effectually to restrain the Exportation of Provisions and Warlike Stores from the Colony of New-York.

WILLIAMSBURG Sept. 19. Extract of a Letter from Norfolk, dated Sept. 15.

"I have the pleasure to inform you, that the Inhabitants of this Borough, have raised by subscription a considerable Sum of Money, which is to be disposed of for the Good of the present Expedition; by allowing every able-bodied Man, who shall enlist in this County, in his Majesty's Service, under George Washington, Forty Shillings Bounty over and above his Majesty's Allowance. The good Effect of which we have already experienced; several having enlisted and received the Bounty.

NEW-YORK Sept. 19. Yesterday arrived a Sloop from Albany, which left that City on Monday last: the Skipper whereof reports, that Number of Indians in Alliance with the English has come in there from the late Engagement, and every one brought in more or less Number of Scalps fixed on Poles, (it's said upward of 80) and that the Indians gave out, that when they left the Camp,

General Johnson was bravely recovered from the Weakness occasioned by his Wound, insomuch as to be able to walk about, and regulate the Army in order to follow up the Defeat: That the whole Body of our Indians were prodigiously inveterate against the French and their Indians, occasioned more particularly by the Death of the famous Hendrick, a renowned Indian Warrior among the Mohawks, and one of the Sachems, or King who was slain in the Battle, and whose Son, upon being told that his Father was kill'd, giving the usual Indian Groan, upon such Occasions, and suddenly striking on his left Breast, swore his Father was still alive in that Place, and that there stood his Son. —— That it was with the utmost Difficulty General Johnson prevented the fury of their Resentment taking Place on the Body of the French General, who they would have sacrificed without Ceremony, but for the Interposition of Mr. Johnson: That Numbers of the French Regulars, being disordered on the Defeat, unacquainted with the Country, and afraid of our Indians had come into Camp, and other of them Straglers taken Prisoners: That it was Rumour'd throughout the Camp, that the Balls made use of by the French, were chew'd and that when extracted from the Wound, appear'd surprizingly green: But upon the French General's being Questioned about it, he declared he gave no such Orders, and that if such Bullets were fired, they must have come from the Irregulars of Canada only, and not from the Eropean Soldiers.

His Excellency, just before he embarked for Albany, issued a Proclamation, appointing Thursday the second Day of October next, to be observed as a Day of publick Thanksgiving throughout this Province for the late Victory obtained over the French and their Indians.

Almost all Officers from France are Gentlemen of Distinction, and of great Families.

WILLIAMSBURG Sept. 19. By Express from Augusta we are assured, that about the last of August, 50 Indians, supposed to be Shannese, appeared on Green Briar River, in that County, and that they killed and captivated 15 People, burnt 11 Houses, and drove off 500 Head of Cattle, Horses,

&c. Several of the Inhabitants fled to a small Fort that they had built for their Security, and were there blocked up by the Enemy four Days. As soon as Captain Lewis, who was then on Jackson's River, about 70 Miles off had Intelligence of it, he marched with his Company on their Relief, but the Indians were gone off two Days before he arrived.

Last Saturday the Industry, Miller, From Cock, and on Sunday, the Nancy, Montgomery, from London, with Arms and Cloathing for the Soldiers, and a large Quantity of Cash, arrived at Hampton.

HALIFAX Sept. 20. There have already imported into this Place from New-England, since the arrival of his Majesty's Fleet (besides a large Quantity purchased in from the French Settlements in this Province) near a Thousand fat Cattle, and Five Thousand Sheep, besides Hogs, Goats, and vast Quantities of all Kinds of Poultry and other Refreshments, and more are Daily arriving.

HALIFAX Sept. Some Indians, in our Interest, having resolved, to revenge the Death of the English, who have been killed and scalped within this Province, by the Cape-Breton or, other Indians, through the Instigation of the French, from whom it is certainly known they have Constantly received a large Reward for each Scalp: a Party of these lately set out from their Head Quarters for that Purpose, and proceeding along the Eastern Coast of this Province as far as Isle Madam, near Canso, have killed and scalped some of their Men: And the Pilot Schooner is coming from the Fleet accidentally passing near that Place took them on board and bro't them in here with their Scalps. And we hear there is a considerable Body of Indians in the Interest of the English in this Province, who are determined to proceed in the same Manner, till they have effectually discouraged the French from giving Rewards for English Scalps.

We also hear, That on board one of the French Ships lately brought in here, there has been found a large Number of Scalping Knives which were sent out of France for the Indians.

BOSTON Sept. 22. Last Saturday was sev'night

we had a Rumour of an Engagement at Lake George, in the Evening it was confirm'd; the event uncertain till Monday Night, whenby an Express from General Johnson we receiv'd the News that our Forces had gain'd a compleat Victory. The Particulars are given in the General's Letter, which has diffus'd a general Joy —— It is a Conquest sensible and important; and tho' we cannot do to much Justice to the Bravery and Conduct of our General's, Officers, and Men —— we must yet acknowledge the singular Interposition of a Providence in our Favour —— his Hand is visible in the Honour and Advantage we have obtain'd —— The Enemy flush'd with their late Success Southward boldly attack'd our Army —— about 1000 of them were Slain during the Engagement and Pursuit —— more Canadians and Indians have fallen, than ever fell at one Time before; many of their principal Officers, among whom is the Chavalier St. Pierre, who commanded all the French Indians on the Continent, and had the greatest Influence over them —— General Dieskau who was under the Marshalls Saxe and Lowendall, was so often victorious in Flanders is now a wounded Prisoner in our Camp, together with his Aide-de-Camp and about 30 others —— On our Part, we have indeed lost some Officers and Men of distinguish'd Valour —— but they fell in a glorious Cause, and their Names will be dear to Posterity —— The Advantages we have gain'd must give fresh Spirits to those Men rais'd for Reinforcement —— We trust in God that all our Forces will be still enable to act up to their Character, and do valiantly —— That the Success already obtained at Nova Scotia and Lake George, are only Earnests of future and more important ones.

BOSTON Sept. 22. Last Monday Night an Express arrived here from Major General Johnson, Commander of our Army near Crown-Point, from whom we have the following Letter.

Camp at Lake George, September 9, 1755.

To the Governors of the several Colonies who raised the Troops on the present Expedition.

Gentlemen,

Sunday Evening the 7th Instant, I received

Intellegence from some Indian Scouts I had sent
out, that they had discovered three large Roads
about the South-Bay, and were confident a very
considerable Number of the Enemy were marched
or on their march towards our Encampment at the
Carrying-Place, where were posted about 250 of
the New-Hampshire Troops, and five Companies of
the New-York Regiment. ——— I got Adams a Waggoner, who voluntarily and bravely consented to
ride Express with my Orders to Col. Blanchard,
of the New-Hampshire Regiment, commanding Officer there. I acquainted him with my Intelligence,
and directed him to withdraw all the Troops
there within the Works thrown up ——— About
half an Hour, or near an Hour after this, I got
two Indians and two Soldiers to go on Foot with
another Letter to the same Purpose.

About 12 o'Clock that Night, the Indians and
Soldiers returned, with a Waggoner who had stole
from the Camp, with about 8 others, their Wag-
gons and Horses, without Orders. This Waggoner
says, they heard and saw the Enemy about four
Miles from this Side of the Carrying-Place. ———
They heard a Gun fire, and a Man call upon
Heaven for Mercy, which he judged to be Adams.
——— The next Morning I called a Council of
War, who gave it as their Opinion, that in which
the Indians were extremely urgent, that 1000
Men should be detached, and a Number of their
People would go with them, in order to catch
the Enemy in their Retreat from their Camp,
either as Victors or defeated in their Design.
——— The 1000 Men were detached under the Command of Col. Williams, of one of the Boston
Regiments, with upwards of 200 Indians ———
They marched between 8 and 9 o'Colck ——— In
about an Hour and a half afterwards we heard a
heavy firing, and all the Marks of a warm Engagement, which we judged was about 3 or 4 Miles
from us: We beat to Arms, and got our Men all
in Readiness ——— The Fire approached nearer,
upon which I judged our People were retreating,
and detached Lieut. Col. Cole with about 300 Men
to cover their Retreat ——— About 10 o'Clock
some of our Men in the Rear, and some Indians
of the said Party, came running into the Camp,

and acquainted us that our Men were retreating, that the Enemy were too strong for them: The whole Party that Escaped returned to us in large Bodies.

As we had thrown a Breast-Work of Trees round our Encampment, and planted some Field-Pieces to defend the same, we immediately hauled some heavy Cannon up there to strengthen our Front, took Possession of some Eminence on their left Flank, and got one Field-Piece there in a very advantageous Situation; the Breast-Work was manned throughout by our People and the best Disposition made through our whole Encampment, which Time and Circumstance would permit. About half an Hour after 11 the Enemy appeared in sight, and marched along the Road in very regular Order directly upon our Center: They made a small Halt about 150 Yards from our Breast-Work, when the regular Troops (whom we judged to be such by their bright and fixed Bayonets) made the grand and center Attack; the Canadians and Indians squatted and dispensed on our Flank —— The enemy's Fire we received first from the Regulars in Platoons, but it did no great Execution, being at too great a Distance, and our Men defended by the Breast-Work —— Our Artillery then began to play on them, and was served under the Direction of Capt. Eyre, during the whole Engagement, in a Manner very Advantageous to his Character, and those concerned in the Management of it.

The Engagement now became general on both Sides —— The French Regulars kept their Ground and Order for some Time with great Resolution and good Conduct, but the warm and constant Fire from our Artillery and Troops put them into Disorder, their Fire became more scattered and unequal, and the Enemy's Fire on our Left grew very faint: They moved then to the Right of our Encampment, and attacked Col. Ruggles, Col. Williams, and Col. Titcomb's Regiments, where they maintained a very warm Fire for near an Hour, still keeping up their Fire in the other Parts of the Line, tho' not very strong; the three Regiments on the Right supported the Attack very resolutely, and kept a constant and strong Fire upon the Enemy; This Attack failing, and the Artillery still playing along the Line, we found their Fire very weak, and with considerable Intervals: this was about 4 o'Clock, when our Men and Indians jumped over the BreastWork pursued the Enemy, slaughtered Numbers and took several Prisoners, amongst whom was Baron de Dieskau, the french General of all the regular Forces lately arrived from Europe; who was brought to my Tent about 6 o'Clock, just as a Wound I had received was dressed. The whole Engagement and Pursuit ended about 7 o'Clock.

   I don't know whether I can get the Returns of the Slain and wounded on our Side to transmit herewith; but more of the greatest lost we have sustained, was in the Party Commanded by Col. Williams, in the Morning, who was attacked, and the Men gave Way, before Col. Whiting, who brought up the Rear, could come to his Assistance: The Enemy who were more numerous, endeavour'd to surround them; upon which the Officers found they had no Way to save the troops, but by retreating, which they did as fast as they could. In this Engagement we suffered our greatest Loss, Col. Williams, Major Ashley, Capt. Ingersal and Capt. Puter, of the same regiment, Capt. Ferall, Brother-in-Law to the General, who Commanded a Party of Indians, Capt. Stoddert, Capt. McGin, Capt. Stevens, all the Indians say near 40 of their People, who fought like Lions, were all slain: Old Henddrick the great Mohawk Sachem, we fear, is killed: We have abundant Reason to think we killed a great Number of the Enemy; amongst whom Monsieur St. Piere, who commanded all the Indians: The exact Number on either Side, I cannot obtain; for tho' I sent a Perty to bury our dead this Afternoon it being a running scattered Engagement, we can neither find all our dead, nor give an exact Account. As fast as these Troops joined us, they formed with the rest in the main Battle of the Day; so that the killed and wounded in both Engagements, Officers excepted, must stand upon one Return.

   About 8 o'Clock last Night a Party of 120 of the New-Hampshire Regiment, and 90 of the New-York

Regiment, who were detached to our assistance under the Command of Capt. McGinnes, from the Camp at the Carrying-Place, to reinforce us, were attacked by a Party of Indians and Canadians, at that Place where Col. Williams was attacked in the Morning; their Engagement began between 4 and 5 o'Clock; this Party, who our People say were between 3 and 400, had fled from the Engagement here, and gone to scalp our People killed in the Morning. Our brave Men fought them for near two Hours, and made a considerable Slaughter amongst them: Of this brave Party 2 were killed, and 11 wounded, and 5 Missing. Capt. McGinnes, who behaved with the utmost Calmness and Resolution, was brought on a Horse here, and I fear his Wounds will prove mortal. Ensign Falsam of the New-Hampshire Regiment, wounded through the Shoulder.

I have this Morning called a Council of War, a Copy of the Minutes of which I send you herewith.

Monsieur La Baron de Dieskau, the French General, is badly wounded in the Leg, and thro' both his Hips, and the Surgeon very much fears for his Life. He is an elderly Gentleman, an experienced Officer, and a Man of high Consideration in France. From his Papers I find he brought under his Command to Canada, in the Men of War lately arrived at Quebec, 3171, regular Troops who were partly in Garrison at Crown-Point, and encamped at Ticonderogo and other advantageous Passes, between this and Crown-Point. He tells me he had with him yesterday Morning, 200 Grenadiers, 800 Canadians, and 700 Indians of different Nations ——— His Aid de Camp says (they being separately asked) their whole Force was about 2000 ——— Several of the Prisoners say about 2300 ——— The Baron says, his Major-General was killed, and his Aide de Camp says, the present part of their chief Officers also: He thinks by the Morning and afternoon actions, they had lost near 1000 Men, but I can get no regular Account. Most of our People think from 5 or 600. We have about 30 prisoners, most of them badly wounded; the indians scalped of their Dead already near 70, and were

Employed after the Battle last Night, and all this Afternoon in bringing in Scalps, and great Numbers of french and Indians yet left unscalped: They carried off most of their Dead, and secreted them. Our Men have suffered much fatigue for 3 Days past, and are constantly standing upon their Arms by Day; half of the whole upon Guard every Night, and the rest lay down armed and accoutred, that both Officers and Men, are almost worn out. The Enemy may rally, and we judge they have considerable Reinforcements near at Hand; so that I think it necessary we be upon Guard, and be watchful to maintain the Advantages we have gained: For these Reasons, I don't think it either prudent or safe to be sending out Parties in search of the dead.

I do not hear any Officers killed at our Camp, but Col. Titcomb, and some wounded but myself and Maj. Nichols of Col. Titcomb's. I cannot yet get certain Returns of our dead and wounded; but from the best Accounts I can obtain, we have lost about 130, who are killed, about 60 wounded, and several missing from the Morning and Afternoon Engagements.

I think we may expect very shortly, another and more formidable Attack; and that the Enemy will then come with Artillery. ——— The late Col. Williams had the Ground cleared for building a stockade Fort. Our men are so harrased and obliged to be so constantly upon watchful Duty, that I think it would be both unreasonable, and I fear vain, to set them at Work upon the Designed Fort.

I design to order the New-Hampshire Regiment up here to reinforce us, and I hope some of the designed reinforcements will be with us in a few Days: When those fresh Troops arrive, I shall immediately set about building the Fort.

My wound, which is my thigh, is very painful; the Ball is lodged and cannot be got out, by which Means I am, to my Mortification confined to my Tent.

This Letter was begun, and should have been dispatched Yesterday; but we had two alarms, and neither Time nor Prudence would Permit it. I hope Gentlemen, you will place the incorrectness hereof, to the Account of our Situation, I am, most respectfully, Gentlemen your most obedient Servant, Wm. Johnson.

NEW-YORK Sept. 22, Late Thursday at 11 A,M. arrived here a Sloop from Albany, which left the City at 12 o'Clock: the Skipper whereof reports. General Johnson's Letter sent by Adams, to Col. Blanchard, was found in the Aide de Camp's Pocket. Among other Papers, is found a new and current Map of Hudson's River, and all the Eastern Parts of North-America, which has been for Years making and correcting.

It is reported, that the French General said, when he left Quebeck, intended to go to Niagara; but on Intelligence received when he was at Montreal, of a numerous Army being design'd against Crown-Point, it was resolved he should march that Way.

It is also reported of an Indian, one called Corneliess (who Governor De Lancey made Sachem) that a White Man, standing near him, had his Gun split to pieces, and calling out, what shall I do, I have no Gun, the Indian gave him his, jump'd oner the Breastwork, run up and took a Gun our of a Frenchman's Hand, turn'd it, shot the Man he took it from, and returned to his Post.

We hear that the Indians will join General Johnson again, in about two Weeks after their Departure from his Camp; it being customary with them after an Engagement, to return home, with their Trophies of Victory, as well as to console with the Widows of those that fall in the Field of battle.

Monday last a Subscription was set on Foot here, in order to purchase Necessaries for the Sick and Wounded in the Army commanded by General Johnson; and by Wednesday Night the Sum of Five Hundred Pounds, was generously subscribed and paid into the Hands of Trustees appointed for that Purpose; when it was immediately laid out, in such necessaries as were thought most proper for them in their present Situation, and directly sent to Albany.

By several Persons that arrived here last week from Oswego, we learn, that General Shirley and all the Troops under his Command, in that Garrison, as well as 400 Indians, were in high spirits, the 3d instant, and that they only waited the Arrival of some Necessaries, before they set out on their Intended Expedition, which Necessaries must have arrived there a few Days after our Informants set out, as they met several Battoes, with Bread, &c. near the Carrying Place.

We are told, that soon after Mensieur Deiskau, the French General, was taken Prisoner, he acquainted Major General Johnson, that but a few Hours before, he had dispatched an Express to the Governor of Canada, to inform him, he had drove the English before him, like a flock of Sheep, and that he expected that Night, to lodge in General Johnson's Tent.

[The last Part of the Information proved true]

We hear from Elizabeth Town in New-Jersey, that the Inhabitants of that Borough only, has raised one Hundred Men, to be immediately sent to the Assistance of General Johnson.

We hear, that the Inhabitants of Queen's County on Long-Island, at their own Expence, raising 3000 sheep, for the use of the Army at Lake-George; and they are all be at Jamaica by Wednesday next, from whence they are to be drove to Albany.

By a Letter from Philadelphia, we learn, That Six Nation indians in the English Interest, have sent Word to the Indians, their Allies, to the Southward to sharpen their Arrows, for that they are determined to drive the French from their Forts on the Ohio.

HALIFAX Sept. 27. On Monday last arrived here the Jolly Bacchus (a Tender belonging to the Fleet) from Lunenburg; with the Inhabitants of a small French Settlement a little above that Place. they brought with them all except two, who we hear fled to the Indians for Succour and Assistance.

BOSTON Sept. 29. The following is the Extract of a Letter, from a Gentleman of Character in Connecticut to his Friend in Town, giving an Account of the Battle of Lake George, as he collected from Major General Lyman's Letter and is as follows.

That Sabbath Day the Sept. 7, The indians informed, that a large Army had marched along the the South-Bay Towards Fort Lyman at the Carrying Place: That an Express was sent to the Fort, who when he came within 4 Miles of it was shot, and also some Waggoners who set out from the Camp at the same Time without Leave: That, the News was bro't back by others sent for that Purpose, in Case of the Express should be killed: The next Morning 1000 of our Men and 170 Indians were sent to cut off the Retreat of the French Army, who when they had marched about 3 Miles were attacked by the Enemy: That Col. Williams, Major Ashley, Capt. Ingersol, and about 17 or 18 more were killed on the Spot: That the Engagement began about 40 Rods from the Place where the Enemy had encamped the Night before: That Hendrick was in the Engagement and fought valiantly, but was finally killed: That the enemy's endeavouring to surround our Men caused their Retreat; but they fought valiantly while retreating and killed, according to the French General's Account, more of his Men then they lost themselves: That they heard the Fight at the Camp and perceived it drew nearer; that they cast upon a Breast Work of Logs and placed a Cannon and Men ready for an Engagement, strict Command being given to all not to leave their Post without Order: That when our Men Appeared, they perceived the French near them, with their Bayonets fixed and their Arms glittering like the Sun, seeming as confident, of Success and of coming into the Camp, as ever an Army did: That the retreating Party came in, in a Body, and perfectly formed in with the rest of the Army: That in one Minute there was nothing but one continued Charge of Cannon and small Arms which lasted from a little before 11 o'Clock till about half after five, the Men behaving with the utmost Bravery: That they made their first Attack upon Connecticut Forces and fought 2 or 3 Hours, when they could not force them they attacked the other Wing, where the Province Forces were posted and met with the like warm Reception there: That the Battle continued very hot and obstinate about 6 Hours, and then the Enemy slackn'd and began to retreat, which our Men sprang over the Breast Work and pursued them like Lions, made terrible Havock, wounded and took the General Prisoner, killed the Second Officer, and a great many other Officers of Distinction, took a Number of Prisoners, brought in Arm-full of Guns, with laced Hats, Cartouch Boxes, &c. &c. That the Prisoners say we have now ruined their Army: That 300 Men chiefly New-Hampshire, and some Yorkers, coming from Fort Lyman, fell in with about 800 of the Enemy, chiefly Indians, whom they engaged and drove off, they killed a great Number, took some prisoners and got 1000 Packs: That the French General is a Swiss educated in France; he was commander of all the French Forces in Canada; he had in his Army 3117 Men, part of whom he left at Crown-Point, and on this Side, and that he engaged with 1800 of his best chosen Men. That we have lost but few Men considering the Fierceness of the Battle, among whom Col. Williams and Titcomb, Major Ashley, Capt. Ingersol, Howley, Porter, Keys, Lieut. Burt and Pumroy: And that the Indians are well pleased with the noble Victory.

NEW-YORK Sept. 29. Friday last a Number of Matrosses that have been procured by the Inhabitants of the City, embarked for Albany, in order to join the Artillery under the Command of General Johnson.

Impress Warrants were issued soon after his Excellency's Arrival at Albany, and dispatched with proper Officers, about the Country for waggons and Horses: of the former of which, hundreds have been already secured, and Numbers of other daily sent in, in order directly to convey Provisions and all Necessities to the Camp.

Mr. Dieskau, General of the French Forces in America, lies dangerously ill of his Wounds at Albany. ——— And, His Most Christian Majesty's Attorney General at Montreal, his son died of Wounds, a few Days ago in Confinement in Albany. BOSTON Sept. 29. Extract of a Letter from Halifax, Sept. 10th 1755.

"I have been here one Month; since which 13

Prizes have been brought in here, with Wine, Rum, Sugar, Bread, Flour, Silks, &c. &c. some have been sold very cheap in Vendue. Admiral Holburn, off Louisbourg, had taken 3 more Prizes, strip't one, and sent all the Men in her to Louisbourg; Also upwards of 20 Shallops, and burnt but one, and sent the Men into Louisbourg, to tell the Governor if he want fresh Fish, he may send the Men of War out to catch them. ——— This you may depend on. ———

P. S. There is in and out upwards of 20 Sail of Men of War; but every Thing very Plenty at present.

By a Vessel from North Carolina we have Advice from good Hands, That the Cherokee Tribe of Indians, encouraged by a Bounty of Three Pounds Sterling, and Seven Pounds for every Scalp of the Enemy granted by the Province of South Carolina, had, to the number of 1600, engaged to march against the French, and the Indians in their Interest, on the Ohio; and that, as a further Encouragement towards the Expedition, the Government of North Carolina had made a Present to them of 300 Steers. [A late Writer says, "the Cherokees are computed to be Three Times the Number of the Six Nations put together, They are a free and independent People, were never conquered, nor relinquished their Possessions, never sold them, never surrendered or ceded them".]

By the latest Vessel from Halifax we have Advice, that 200 of our Men having been put on board one or more Vessels with Orders to destroy some French Villages, about 70 of them landed, and burnt all the private Houses and barns without Molestation; but just as they were setting Fire to a Mass-House, they were fired upon by a large Body of French and Indians concealed in the Bushes, who killed and wounded 23 of our People: Among the former is Lieutenant (or Dr.) North, and Lieutenant Billings is badly wounded. 'Tis said our People have about 1200 of the Neutrals on board their Transports and that 1000 or 1200 Men, French and Indians, among which are 300 Regulars are escaped on a rising Ground, with a Flag of Defiance flying.

Wednesday last an Officer arrived here from General Johnson's Army near Lake George, with Letters from the General for the Government. He left the Camp the 17th Instant, and says, there had been no Engagement with the Enemy since the 8th ——— That Col. Blanchard was gone with a strong Detachment from the Army, to begin the building of a fort at the Carrying-Place.

——— That Parties from the Camp were daily sent on to discover the Enemy's slain and to pick up Arms, &c. and that they had found a great Number of Dead bodies in the Swamps and Holes, which they had carried off on Biers, Forty of which were found all bloody at the Side of a Pond ——— That the Body of Hendrick, the old Mohawk Sachem, had been found among our slain, and was buried with all the Honours of War.

And Thursday last another Gentleman arrived here from the Camp, which he left about the same Time that the other Gentlemen did, and has brought in an imperfect List of the killed and wounded on our side, in the Engagement on the 8th Instant, which is as follows viz. killed 126 wounded 94, missing 61. N. B. Several who had been missing, and tho't to be killed or taken, were since returned to their Duty. They quited the Field and fled on the first Attack in the Morning.

The French quitted the Field of Battle in such a Hurry and Confusion, that they left behind them above a thousand Weights of Powder and Shot, and many Waggon Loads of Provisions, besides their Arms, Baggage, &c.

BOSTON Sept. 29. Messieurs Edes & Gill, By inserting in your Paper, the following Copy of a Letter to a Gentleman in Halifax, you will oblige, at least one of your stated Customers,
Your's, &c. S. M.

Sir,

Not only your particular Friends here, but the best Gentlemen in Town, of every Rank, are surprized, and offended, at the Conduct of those at Halifax, who have sent their recruiting Officers into this Government to fill his Majesty's Regiments there. One would think the 2000 Troops transported from hence, last Spring, for your Defence and Security, might have been a sufficient supply from us. We did not suppose, after such extraordinary Exertment of ourselves that more of our Men would have been desired; especially, as it was known at Halifax, that we had engaged in several important Expeditions, which would for all the Strength we could spare. Under these Circumstances, it appears to us highly unreasonable in our Friends at Nova-Scotia, to send their Officers among us upon recruiting Designs; nor must they take amiss if we signify our Displeasure thereat, and plainly tell them, that we with their Labour may be in vain, and that we shall do all in our Power that it may be so.

It is probable the Governor of Nova-Scotia was not apprized of the true State of our Crown-Point Expedition; that it was a virtual fighting with all Canada; that we have been obliged to raise, and send, in support of the Enterprise, almost trible the Number of Men at first intended; and that we know not but we shall soon be called upon to supply still further Reinforcements. Had he been acquainted with these Things, it cannot easly be supposed he would have permitted any of his Officers to come here upon the Designs they are endeavouring to put in Execution. We have a better Opinion of him, than to think he would discover so little Regard to a Province that has once and again been the Salvation, under God, of those Territories over which he has the Honour to bear rule.

As our General Court is now sitting, it may justly be expected, they will ad the Part of Fathers to this People; not suffering any of our Men, at such a Time as this, when we may be in absolute want of them all, to be carried out of the Province; Or if they should set still, and not interpose on our behalf, (which can scarce be supposed without reflecting dishonour on them) it is to be hoped, our People will discover a true New-England Spirit, and not be inveigled, by any Pretence whatsoever, to leave the Province, when their Help may be necessary for its Protection against the French Enemy.

I think, we may be sure, if his Majesty, our

most gracious King, know how vigorously this Government were not exerting themselves, in Defence of his Rights, and to drive the French out of their Encroachments, he would instantly recall these Officers, and order them elsewhere.

The short of the Matter is, 'tis a downright Abuse of this Province to call upon us for any more Men. We are almost depopulated already.

—— We begin to be dispirited under the weight of the Burdens that are laid upon us; and if care is not taken we shall soon sink under them. This ought, in Point of Policy, be considered even by our Nova-Scotia Brethren; for if we sink, they will soon sink after us, and so will the other Colonies likewise.

I am with Great Respect, your affectionate Friend, and very humble Servant.

Boston, Sept. 24, 1755. S. M.

PHILADELPHIA Sept. 29. Assembly Chamber, at Philadelphia, September 29, 1755. P. M.

A Member of this House producing a Letter to himself, from the Honourable Thomas Hutchinson, Esq; a Person of great distinction and Weight in the Government of the Massachusetts-Bay, and a Member of the Council of that Province, mentioning the Application to the Government for Provisions and the Necessity of an immediate supply: And it appearing by the Resolution of the Council of War, held at the Carrying-Place, and on the 24th past (an Abstract of which is committed to the Speaker by the Honourable Thomas Pownal, Esq; Lieutenant Governor of the Jerseys,) that the Army will be in want of Blankets and other Cloathing, suitable to the Approaching Season; and this House being willing to afford what Assistance may be in their Power, under the present unhappy Circumstances of an exhausted Treasury, and a Total Refusal by the Governor of their Bills for raising Money.

Resolved, That a voluntary Subscription of any Sum of Money, not exceeding Ten Thousand Pounds, which shall be paid by any Person into the hands Isaac Norris, Evan Morgan, joseph Fox, John Mifflin, Reese Meridith, and Samuel Smith, of the City of Philadelphia, Gentlemen, within two Weeks after this Date, towards the furnishing

Provisions, and Blankets, or other warm Cloathing to the Troops now at or Near Crown-Point, on the Frontiers of New-York, will be of Service to the Crown, and acceptable to the Pubblick, and the Subscription ought to be thankfully reimbursed (with Interest) by future Assemblies to whom it is accordingly by this house earnestly recommended.

A True Extract from the Minutes,

           W. Franklin, Clerk of Assembly.

NEW-YORK Sept. 29. Jamaica in Queen's County, on Long-Island, Sept. 24.

This Day One Thousand and Fifteen Sheep, that was raised in about 3 Days in the County, were delivered at New-York Ferry, in order to be sent to Albany by Water, which were chearfully given for the Use of the Army now near, or at Crown-Point: 200 of which were shipped this Day, and the whole we expect will be on board Albany Vessels by Saturday Night.

While the Husbands at great-Neck in this county, were employed in getting Sheep, the good Matrons in the Neighbourhood, in a few Hours, collected near 70 good large Cheeses, and sent them to New-York, to be forwarded with the Sheep to the Army.

OCTOBER 1755

PHILADELPHIA Oct. 2. We hear that 500 new small Arms, with proportionable Ammunition, have lately been imported by the Committee of Assembly. and sent up to the Frontiers for the Defence of the Inhabitants.

WILLIAMSBURG Oct. 3. From Augusta we learn, that a Party of the Militia, under the Command of Captain Dickinson, met with and attacked a Party of the Northern Indians of whom one was killed, and several wounded. Two Indian Boys of the Catawba Nation, whom the Northern Indians had taken Prisoners, were retaken by our People. Capt. Dickinson had one Man killed.

Halifax Oct. On Thursday Last a Sailor belonging to the Fleet, was hang'd at the Yard-Arm, on board his Majesty's Ship Terible, Rear-Admiral Helbourn, for Desertion.

NEW-HAVEN Oct. 4. Several Persons who set out as Volunteirs from this Place, exclusive of the 2000 raised by the Government, in order to assist and relieve their Brethren on the News of the late Engagement returned from the Camp, there appearing no Necessity for their Help: They all agree, that the Army are brave and healthy, in good Spirit, and were busy in building flat bottom'd Vessels to carry the Cannon across the Lake; That the Officers of the Government are for pushing on with all Expedition while some of the others thought it full late for this Season. —— Indeed if we are allowed to think or speak on this Occasion; must it not appear strange, that tho' Forces began raising here for this Design in February last, yet the forwardnest of them have scarce proceeded 400 Miles, and the most of them not so far; whilst the French General could come from Old France since the first of May last, with the greatest

Part of his Soldiers, meet us upon our own Ground; and Mons. St. Pierre, who defeated General Braddock on the 5th of July, could proceed upward of 1000 Miles afterwards and be ready to attack our Forces by the 8th of September! —— It is the Opinion of many judicious Men, that it were better we had never began or at least that we had not defeated the French this Time, then not to push farther; for, say they, this must be attended with worse Consequences than the Defeat of General Braddock, as it will naturally excite the French Court to send over a large Force, and Experience shews us those People do not dally as we do; the effect of which will be strengthening of Crown-Point impregnably against us: And besides, it is more than probable, if our Army is disbanded, (or if they go into Winter Quarters, our Men whom don't love to be regular Soldiers, will desert) That it will be no easy Matter to get such a Number of willing People together again: Mean while, if we could once take Crown-Point, we should not only have comfortable Winter-Quarters, but long before next Spring secure to ourselves a Barrier sufficient to defeat all the Power the French could ever send against us. —— Will Englishmen never grow wiser! Or are we to be the eternal Dupers of the French, and their Adherents! And must we not think that those who are Accessory in duping of us, are French Adherents!

BOSTON Oct. 6. In the House of Representatives, Oct. 1, 1755.

Voted, That the seventy-first Section of the Act of Parliament, Entitled "An Act for Punishing Mutiny and Desertion, and for a better Payment of the Army, and their Quarters;" be printed in all Publick Papers; also, that a Number of the said Section of the Act be printed in separate Papers, and distributed in the several Towns through the Province.

Sent up for Concurence, T. Hubbard Speaker.
In Council October 1, 1755. Read and Concur'd.
      Tho. clarke. Dep. Secr'y.
   Consented   S. Phips.

NEW-YORK Oct. 6. Our last Account from Oswego between the 8th and 12th of September last, which say, that they talkt then in setting out very soon, but whither, even some of the Chief Officers knew not: ⸺ That there had not been above two or three Days for near a Fortnight before the Date of their Accounts, in which the Battoes could swim on the Lake, where the Surge rises almost as high an on the Beach of the Ocean: ⸺ That they did not abound with Provisions in the Camp, and in particular Rum and Articles necessary (if ever so) on Action, and cold Weather.

Several Vessels arrived here Yesterday from New-England, deep loaded with Provisions for Albany; and others are hourly expected.

BOSTON Oct. 6. Extract of a Letter from Albany, dated Sept. 24.

"Our Governor is now here, and we are all very busy in expediting Stores and Provisions to the Army under General Johnson; and indeed such brave Men deserve to be well taken care of. The late Victory must make a deep impression upon the French as well as all the Indians in their Interest: And as such powerful Reinforcements are continually coming up to out Army from New-England, we may hope soon to gain our Point at Lake George. The Mohawks are in an excellent Temper, being enraged at the Loss they have sustain'd in the late Battle, at the same Time elated with the Victory, and the Enemies Scalps, their dearest Trophy.

Tho' Affairs of our Army at Oswego have gone on deliberately, we doubt not the will end Happily. Our Forces in and near that Fort may be reckoned about 2400 ⸺ besides Carpenters, &c. and four Armed Vessels upon the Lake. There certainly was never a more lucky Season for making our selves Masters of all Passes on Ontario; a thing of prodigious importance to British Interest. By Papers and other Accounts since the late Battle we find, that the French alarm'd with the Sound of a great Army coming to Crown-Point, have turn'd their Chief Attention that Way. Not only their Regulars, but their Indians and Militia having been employ'd to oppose General Johnson, and doubtless their late Defeat will induce them to call more of their Forces from other Places to Lake Champlain. This looks as if the French were not very strong either at Frontinack or Niagara. Now then is the Risk of Time for striking a Blow at the Westward; by which we shall save a vast Expence of Blood and Treasury ⸻ We hear that General Shirley has sometime since ordered the two Regiments and Independent Companies, with Col Dunbar, to take up their Quarters in the City till Spring, from whence we conclude there is no Want of Forces at Oswego for the Intended Expedition."

BOSTON Oct. 6. By Letters from the Camp before Fort Cumberland in Nova-Scotia, of the 8th ult. we have advice, That on the 27th of August, Major Fry, with several Officers and 200 Men, embark'd on board the Sloop York, Capt. Cobb, and the Schooner Warren, Capt. Adams; and the same Evening landed at Chipoudie, a Village, about 8 Leagues up the River, having Instructions to bring off all the Inhabitants and set Fire to the Houses. ⸻ That upon the first Landing they march'd with an advance and two Flank Guards to the Village, but found all the Inhabitants were fled except 25 Women and Children, who were taken Prisoners. The next Morning the set Fire to the Buildings and burnt down 181 Houses and Barns, with all the Hay, Grain, &c. therein. ⸻ After this they proceeded to the Mass-House which, with what was therein, was burnt to Ashes. ⸻ then putting the prisoners aboard one of the transports which lay ready for that Purpose, they embark'd again; and next Morning two of the Officers with 62 Men were ordered to proceed to Pitcoundiack; and having landed, within sight of the Arm'd Vessels, they found the Houses entirely Evacuated; and by the first of September, they had the Buildings in Ashes for 15 Miles in length on the Northerly Side of the River, and about 6 on the other Side; and when they came in Sight of a Mass-House, they Discover'd Foot Tracks lately made, and soon after perceiv'd a Smoke; the Mass-House being close to thick Wood, they posted Guards, and they were preparing to fire the House, a Signal Gun was fired by the Enemy, and before the Guards and a few of the Men with them could repair to the main Body, they found themselves almost surrounded by them; upon which they were obliged to rush thro' them as they could, firing their Pieces, and receiving their Fire; and while thus retreating, the Indians gained Ground and shot Lieut March, and took and wounded some others —— But a Serjeant with 6 Men coming from a Corps of Wood, stop'd their pursuit so that the rest of the Men gain'd the Dyke, and secured their Retreat.. —— At this Time it was impossible for Major Fry to come to their Assistance, on Account of the Rapidity of the River, being driven by the Current 3 Quarters of a Mile below the intended Landing-Place; But landing the rest of his Men as soon as he possibly could, drew up the whole Body, and made a stand; upon which the Enemy haulted, and our Forces kept the Ground; the Enemy likewise drew up in a Body, besides the Dyke lined with Indians, and Parties scouting in the Woods, suppos'd to be upward of 300, but they were not inclined to engage our Forces in an Open Manner, tho' with such a Number they might have drove almost as they Pleased. —— At high Water the two arm'd Vessels got in as near the shore as they safely could, and covering each of the Flanks, sent their Boats ashore, and took our Men and carried them on board; the Vessels during the Embarkation, fired their Cannon and kept the Rebels off. —— Several of the Enemy were killed but how many is uncertain. —— Two Hundred and Fifty-three Houses and Barns besides the Mass-Houses have been burnt.

A List of Men Missing, and of the wounded returned of Major Fry's Party, since the Engagement at Pitcoundiack, in Nova-Scotia on the 2d of September past.

Lieutenant Colonel Winslow's Battalion.
Major Prebble's Company. William Mogaridge missing. Elisha Gitchell, missing. David Linsey, wounded.
Major Goldthwart's Company. Lieutenant Billings, wounded. Charles Babon, Missing.
Capt, Sampson's Company. Samuel Stoddard, missing. Samuel Chapman, missing.
Capt. Malcom's Company. David Pike, missing,

Joseph Poguite, wounded.
Capt. Speakman's Company. Joseph Gibbs, missing.
  Lieutenant Colonel Scott's Battalion.
Capt. Perry's Company. Lieut. March killed.
Lieut. Col. Scott's Company. Corporal Seth Miller, wounded. Nathaniel Stone, missing. Elijah Rich, missing. Joseph Bedunah, missing. Samuel Thompson, missing.
Maj. Fry's Company. Samuel Clark, wounded. Jeffe Marble, missing, James Chandler, missing. Samuel M'Shannon, missing. John Barker, missing.
Major Bourn's Company. John Hamilton, missing. David Reynolds, missing. Samuel Brackgross, missing, Elisha Sacham, missing.
Capt. Bayley's Company. Corporal James Emery, missing. Reuben Greenly, missing.
Capt. Willard's Company. William Hutson, missing. Hezekiah Stowell, wounded.
Capt. Gilbert's Company. Timothy Brown, wounded.

It is said, That above 2000 of the French Neutrals were already on board the Transports which were taken on Chignecto, and it was thought would sail about the latter end of last Week; and that Transports were arrived at Minas and Pisiquid, to take on board the Neutrals that were in those Places; —— That a large Body of French and Indians had rendezvous'd at the Spot where the old Fort of St. John's was, and hoisted a Flag there; it is said there is about 250 or 300 Regulars with them.

NEW-YORK Oct. 6. Last Saturday Evening, a Sloop touched here in her Way from Albany for Connecticut, with some sick People from General Johnson's Army: They left the Camp about ten Days since, when our People, to the Number of between 5 and 6000, were employed, until the arrival of some Waggons with necessities, in building a Fort at Lake George.

ANNAPOLIS Oct. 9. By a Person who arrived in Town last Monday from Col. Cresap's, we are told, that last Wednesday Se'nnight, in the Morning, the Indians had taken a Man Prisoner, who was going to Fort Cumberland from Frazier's Plantation, which is four Miles on this Side of Fort Cumberland. The same Morning they fell in with a Man and Wife, who had just left their

Plantation, and were retiring into the more populous Parts of the Country; They shot the Horse on which the Man rid, but as it did not fall immediately, he made his Escape; the Woman it was supposed fell into their Hands, as neither she, nor the Horse on which she was riding, have since heard of. The same Party of Indians have also killed or carried off Benjamin Maile of Fredrick County. On Patterson's Creek many Families have, within this Month, Been murdered, carried away, or entirely broke up that Settlement.

Another Person who left Stoddert's Fort last Sunday acquaints us, that the Inhabitants of that Part of the Country were in great Consternation; that near 80 Persons were fled to the Fort for Protection, and many more gone off in the greatest Confusion to Pennsylvania: This, it seems has been occasioned by an Express that was sent Lieutenant Stoddert and the Neighbourhood, by Col. Cresap, advising them a Party of Indians has passed by his House, and cut off some People who dwelt on the Town-Creek, which is a few Miles this Side Col. Cresap's: One Daniel Ashloff, who lived near the Creek, is come down towards Conocheague, and gives the same Account. He says also, that as himself and his Father, with several others, were retiring from their Plantation last Saturday, they were attacked by the same Indians, as he supposes, and all but himself killed, or taken Prisoners. It is said that Mr. Stoddert who has the command of 15 Men, invited a few of the Neighbourhood to join him, and go in Quest of the Enemy, but they would not be perswaded; whereupon he applied himself to Major Prather for a Detachment of the Militia, either to go with a Party of his Men in Pursuit of the Savages, or garrison his Fort, while he made his Excursion. We hope there will be no Backwardness in the Militia to comply with such a reasonable Request, especially as any Party or Person that shall take an Enemy Prisoner, will be rewarded with Six Pound Currency; and the Person who will kill an Enemy, with Four Pounds, provided he can produce Witnesses, or the Enemy's Scalp, in testimony of such Action.

PHILADELPHIA Oct. 9. Late Letters from London advise, that the War is thought unavoidable; and that the Insurance on London to America has risen to Eight per Cent.

Extract of a Letter from Fort Cumberland, of September 21, 1755.

"We are alarmed this Morning by two Indians, who shot a Couple Arrows into a young Man not a Musket Shot of the Fort. The Woods on Wills's Creek are not cut down. There were seen some Days ago, numerous Tracks of People, with Indian Shoes, at a Spring about three Miles off. This comment there came in a brisk Lad, who was taken Prisoner by two Frenchmen and five Indians, but made his Escape from them, after receiving a Blow of a Hatchet. I fear a great Deal of Mischief is coming; there is a Body of the Enemy round us.

WILLIAMSBURG Oct. 10. By an Express just arrived from Fort Cumberland, we are informed that 150 Indians have lately appeared in that Neighbourhood, and have killed and Captivated upwards of 20 Families: Colonel Washington, who was on his Way down hither when the Express overtook him, immediately returned to take upon him the Command of such of the Recruits as are already rais'd, in order to go in Pursuit of them.

BOSTON Oct. 13. By a Letter from Halifax, dated 22d of September, we learn, That Capt. Rous was returned there from a six Week Cruize, on the French Encroachments of Newfoundland, where he had laid waste all the Fisheries and Improvements and sent the Inhabitants off the Island to Louisbourg; and that he had likewise taken two Ships and two Snows laden with Fish, salt and Oil; also a Ship with Provisions from St. Maloo's for New-France, and that on his return to Halifax, he met with a Snow and a Dogger from France, with Provisions, which he has also taken, and got them safe in.

By a Letter from Halifax we are informed, the Admiral Boscawen, considering the advanced Season of the Year, and the Danger his Majesty's Ships would be in continuing longer on the Coast of Cape-Breton, &c. had called a Council of War to advise on that important Affair; and that the Commanders 23 in Number, had given it as their unanimous Opinion, that it was neither safe or for his Majesty's Service, to continue so many of his Majesty's Ships any longer in those Seas, and that, the Admiral had thereupon determined to sail for England with most of the Ships, in about a Fortnight, leaving a Squadron under the Command of Captain Spry, for the Protection of that and the Neighbouring Provinces.

BOSTON Oct. 13. Last Week the several Carpenters who went from here to Oswego returned here, having as we understand, compleated the Building of several armed Vessels, designed for the Security of Lake Ontario, in about 28 days from the cutting of the Trees. ——— By Letters brought by them, and an Express from Albany, we learn, that General Shirley's Spies had got back to the Army, and report, that the Fort at Niagara was in ruinous Condition, and defended by but 100 Frenchmen, and 60 Indians. ——— That near Fort Frontenack on Cattoracky River, they discover'd 31 Tents, from whence its concluded, that Troops at that Important Pass are not very numerous. ——— That our Army was in health, and the Indians with them, quite uneasy for Action. ——— that Governor Shirley had just received the joyful News of the Victory General Johnson had obtained over the French near Lake George, which has put his whole Army in high Spirits; and it may be reasonably expected, that the main Force of Canada will be now turned that Way, He determin'd as we hear, to attempt Both Frontenack and Niagara this Season, and we Impatiently wait the Event. We also learn that all the Warriors of the Six Nations have resolved to join our Army at Lake George, and to act with Vigour against the Enemy ——— That Governor Hardy was extremely active at Albany in expending the Waggons and Horses with Provisions and Necessaries for our brave Forces ——— and as the chief of our Recruits must have join'd the Army, we expect soon to hear that they are Advancing to Crown-Point.

We learn from Spencer, a small District, which

lately set off from Leicester, that on their hearing the Army (now encamp'd at Lake George) wanted a Supply of Provisions or rather a Change of Diet, and being willing to cast in their mite, at the Town-Meeting held there on Monday last, voted the Sum of 120 Pounds Old Tenor for that Purpose; which was immediately laid out in good Cheese, and forwarded by four Persons to that Part of the Army which went from that place Gratis: We doubt not this noble Example will animate those who have Friends and Brethren in that Part of the World, to go and do likewise.

By a Vessel from Halifax, we hear, that the Capts. Rouse, and Shirley, has sailed from thence as was supposed for St. John in the Bay of Fundy, that the French were repairing the Fort on that River, which they deserted in the Summer upon the Approach of Capt. Rous, the English having neglected to secure it —— Thar a considerable Body of French Regulars were arrived there, and great Numbers of the Neutrals and Indians had joined them, Encouraged no doubt from the Advice they had received of General Braddock's Defeat; so that our Troops in Nova-Scotia, may have still more Business on their Hands, that was expected; but as New-England Men inlist for Service, they are not commonly pleas'd with a State of Inaction.

NEW-YORK Oct. 13. Last Wednesday Evening, the Troops under the Command of Col. Dunbar, consisting of about 1500 Men, arrived here in 33 Sloops from Amboy, and next Day they sailed for Albany.

The same Day three Sloops arrived here from Rhode-Island with 150 Men, and sailed that Night for Albany, in order to join General Johnson.

NEW-YORK Oct. 13. By an Account from Lake George we are told, that on the 28th of September, a Scout of four Men who had been sent out to view the French at Tieronderaga, were returned, and reported, that the Enemy at that place, had a Camp and Fort as large as ours; And that on the other Side of the Streight, they had another of about 1000 Men —— That in the Morning after they had harboured at a small Island in their Rout, a Batteaux with ten Persons, one of which was a French Officer, came close by them; and would have taken the other four Prisoners, but saw at a Distance others coming off to their Assistance. They brought into Camp with them an Indian Prisoner who was wounded in the late Action.

A Scout of thirteen Men who have been at Crown-Point, were also returned, and brought in one of the Enemy's Scouts. They gave the same account as above.

BOSTON Oct. 13. We hear, That some of our Men who were lately sent out as Scouts from the Camp near Lake George, had been as far as within sight of the Fort at Crown-Point and, keeping themselves undiscover'd to make what Observation they could, saw a Number of French and Indians suppos'd to be 500 at work upon an Entrenchment at a small Distance from the Fort; and that upon their Return, in the Road thro' which the French retreated they saw a number of dead Bodies and Guns scattered about. —— And that likewise at Ticonderoga, they discover'd a Number, which they supposed to be 8 or 900, building a Blockade.

We are also inform'd, That the Mohawks had return'd, and were upon their March to General Johnson, in a very great Body, dress'd and painted in a warlike Manner with all the tokens of Resentment at the Death of Hendrick their Chief and other of their Friends, at the late Engagement.

PHILADELPHIA Oct. 16. We hear that General Shirley has goven Directions for the Settlement of Accounts of the Waggons, Carriages and Horses hired in this Province for the late Expedition, and for Payment of the same, And that he has been pleased to forbid the Enlisting of Servants or Apprentices by the Recruiting Officers. It is hoped that in grateful Return for this, the Inhabitants will be industrious in securing Deserters, and encouraging the Enlistment of Freemen.

Extract of a Letter from an Officer of Distinction belonging to Fort Cumberland, dated at Greenway Court, October 6, 1755.

"I am here on my Way to Williamsburg, and,

with the Assistance of my Lord Fairfax, and hurrying off the Militia to the Neighbourhood of Fort Cumberland. The Body of Indians, who, 'tis my Opinion, tho't of surprizing the Fort, but have been diverted from their purpose by several false Appearances made under their Eyes to deceive them, have, in the mean Time, cut off the Communication of the Garrison with the Inhabitants, and have destroyed the whole Settlement of Patterson's Creek, and are continuing their Outrage down Potomack. —— Nothing is to be seen but Desolation and Murder, hightened with every barbarous Circumstance, and new Instances of Cruelty —— They, at the Instigation of the French with them, burn up the Plantations, the Smoke of which darkens the Day and hides the neighbouring Mountains from our sight —— They acted with the greatest Conduct, until they discovered our Weakness; but having been assured of that by Deserters and Prisoners, they now appear openly at all Hours of the Day, and lay all waste before them. —— I was attacked on my way down and drove back to the Fort, with the loss of one of my Men. Notwithstanding this Havock, our Country People seem asleep, and nothing but Force will engage them to go against the Enemy. —— The Savages carry off all the young Women. There are about 100 killed and taken, and the whole back Settlements running before them. —— I alarmed the Country some Days before the Mischief began, but they were infatuated, and waited their Fate."

Extract of a Letter from Winchester, October 9, 1755.

"This Day we hear that the Indians have burnt some Houses within fourteen Miles of this Town, and yet the People seem quite easy. The whole Settlements of Patterson's Creek have left their Plantations, and the People on the South Branch of Potowmack are doing the same."

There are a Number of Letters in Town confirming the above melancholy Accounts, one of which says, that it is the Shawanese and Delaware Indians (our pretended Friends) that have perpetrated these horrid Cruelties in Virginia: That the Number of Indians, who lately went out from

Susquehannah against the French and their Indians, have returned, being frighten'd at hearing of the Number of the Enemy, and the Mischief they have done among the Virginians: And that some of the Inhabitants, on the Frontiers of this Province, were leaving their Habitations, for fear of falling into the Hands of the Bloodthirsty Savages.

In a Letter from Demfries in Virginia, dated also the 9th of October, it is mentioned, that above a Hundred Recruits were to march that Day from Fredricksburg and Alexandria, for Will's Creek, where they had about 130 Men, but that there were not above 50 of them fit for Duty.

ANNAPOLIS Oct. 16. From the back Parts of Fredrick County, we learn, that the People are constantly flocking in, in great Numbers, to the more thick settled parts of the Country.

NEW-HAVEN Oct. 18. The Printer think it is the inherent Right of every British Subject to speak his Sentiments public affairs, when there is Occasion, imagines he has the following or such-like Discourse, now in the Minds of every true Englishman in this Colony, viz.

As our Expedition designed against Crown-Point began early in the Spring, and no Attack made yet; and it now appearing doubtful whether it will proceed this Winter, What have we been doing all these eight Months past? Did our People go only to eat and drink, or with an Expectation not to Fight? Did they think Crown-Point would come to them, (as Part of the French Troops did to chide them from their Delay) or did they expect the Walls of the Fort would fall to the Ground at the Terror of their Name, as the Walls of Jericho did at the Sound of Horns? if they did, the ought to have surrounded them first. Now or never, was the Cry at setting out, and surely the Cry was just. What Advantage can we have next Year, that we might not have this? on what Disadvantages will the French lie under them, which they were not liable to this? Where or who was the Cause of our so long Delays? Did they want Provisions? ought not such to have been timely provided? Can any one say, they were not to be had? Did they want more Men? had they proceeded early, they were strong enough: And as soon as it was known, that they stood in need of more, did not the Country pour forth their embattled Numbers to their Aid? Has any Thing been wanting that could not have been procured, if proper Measures taken? Does it not Appear, that if they had followed their Blow after the late Action, they would have almost ruined the Enemy? and that almost all Events! why was it still delay'd? What wretched Complaisance in this, to give the Enemy Time to fortify and to strengthen themselves against us, whilt we just roused them, and them tamely look on! And is all this mighty Parade then to answer no other purpose but to distress, if not ruin our Country, by running us in Debt, in expanding upwards of 200,000 Ponnds Proclamation Money, and leaving us in a worse Condition that it found us? ——— O tell it not in Quebeck! nor publish in the Streets of Montreal! lest the Daughters of the popish Nunneries rejoice and the British Name had Derision by the Slaves of haughty Lewis!

If any one can give clear and satisfactory Answers to the Questions, agreeable to Reason, Truth and Justice they shall freely have a Place in this Paper. But may it not be humbly added, whether Commissioners ought not to be appointed by the Legislatures of the several Provinces concerned in the Expedition, to make a strick Enquiry into the Cause of those Delays, and where the Blame lies; and if happily they should discover it, to make Report thereof, by which Means the Innocent would be clear'd the Saddle laid on the right Horse, and the Publick in general satisfied; and by thus discovering the Errors of this Year, proper Measured might be taken (if not fatally too late for another) to apply a Remedy, before Our all, is Lost!

NEW-YORK Oct. 20. We hear that a German who pretended to be a deserter from the French Army, arrived at our Camp, at Lake George, about 14 Days ago, and begging Protection of General Johnson; but the General after some Interrogation, suspecting him for a Spy, protected him with a pair of Irons, and ordered him directly for Albany.

BOSTON Oct. 20. The following is assured here to be a verbal Extract of a Letter from a General Officer at Montreal to another in the Service on the Side of the Seneca's, Dated April 26. "You are desired to be particularly attentive to the General Resolution you are already advised of; the Situation of Things, since known, not permitting such Latitude to be given as to authorize every Thing that may prevail on the Spot as the most advantageous: The Enemy is up in the North, and provided to attack us where we most doubted his Resolution. We have paid an Inquisitive Englishman the Price of his Labour; his Name is O'Connor, formerly a Subaltern in our Brigades. The more Service of this Kind you can do, we imagine, is at present, the most acceptable Duty and the greatest Promotion in the publick Good. He is the fourth we have detected and executed since my last."

Last Saturday Evening, a Man attempting to get ashore from a Vessel at the Long Wharf, fell into the Dock and was Drowned.

NEW-YORK Oct. 20. We have many different Reports concerning our Army now Encamp'd at Lake George; some People imagine, the season is too far advances, for our Men to proceed; whilst others on the contrary affirm, that if our People are properly provided against the Inclemency of the Weather, they may attack with much greater Facility, that in the Summer Season, as well from our Enemy Indians being less serviceable to the French in their sculking Parties, as the difficulty the Canadians must be put to, in supplying a Body of Men at Crown-Point with Provisions, as they are to be transported the greater Part of the Way by Water and perhaps too at a Time when all Navigation in that Part of the World is entirely stop'd. On the other Hand our Forces can be supplied with great ease.

PHILADELPHIA Oct. 23. Extract of a Letter from Reading, in Berks County, dated Oct. 20.

"we hear this Day, that six people are Scalp'd near george Gabrill's Mill, on the other Side of the Susquehanna, about 82 Miles from this Town. It is told us by a creditable Person who came from the Neighbourhood, and we expect to have a Confirmation of the unhappy News soon."

NEW-HAVEN Oct. 25. By the Post from Albany, we are informed, that on Monday the 13th of this Instant, five French Soldiers came to the English Camp at Lake George, and surrendered themselves Prisoners; On their Examinetion, they said, they deserted from the French Forces at Ticonderoga, on the Strength, for want of Provisions, and had not had for some Time past above half a Bisket a Day: They added further, that the French had not above 500 Men at work at that Place in erecting a Blockade. and not one Piece of Cannon there.

The same Evening just at Dusk, one of the English Centinals was shot dead and scalped without the Breast-Work, as he was standing on Duty, and the bold Enemy got off, before he could be molested.

BOSTON Oct. 27. Last Week an Express arrived here from Oswego by which we learn that Major General Shirley Commander of all his Majesty's Forces in North-America had laid aside the intended Expedition to Frontenack and Niagara, and that the three Regiments under his immediate Command were to take up their Winter Quarters at Oswego. ——— We are not a little startled at this Advice, as we flatter'd ourselves that the three Regiments with him, together with the Indians and Rangers, were more than sufficient to have carried both Frontenack and Niagara, inasmuch as Col. Dunbar and his Regiments were not order'd up in Season to that Service ——— We presume not to pry into the secret Reasons of this Conduct, but are obliged to suppose from the acknowledged Wisdom and Resolution of those who framed and conducted the Expedition, and the great Charge to the Crown with which it has been attended, that they are very substantial Ones.

At the same Time an Express arrived from Lake George, by which we learn, that our Forces there, were not like immediately to proceed to Crown-Point ——— That our general Suspicion of this has for some Time prevailed, the Intelligence has thrown us into great Consternation, ——— And it is to be hoped that the several

N. E. Colonies concerned in this most important and expensive Expedition, will make the Reasons of this Strange Delay, the Matter of a most serious Enquiry.

By Capt. Dogget who arrived last Saturday in fifteen Days from Chiegnecto, we are informed, that the Capts, Rous and Shirley were arrived there. —— That Col. Winslow had taken and ship'd 1500 French Neutrals on board the Transports prepared for that Purpose. And the 86 Neutrals had dug out of Fort-Lawrence in the night, made their Escape, and gone over to the Enemy, who tis reckon'd are 5 or 600 strong. —— Also that a considerable Number of the Provincial Troops in the Pay of the Crown, had inlisted into the King's Regiments at Halifax, induced hereto from the Prospect of bring better provided for. —— If this is the Case, and we are not like to have our brave Country Men return'd at the Expedition of the Time of their Inlistment, no New-England Men in the future encourage any Inlistments for the Province tho' it's Salvation may, as it have more than once depended upon the Assistance we have afforded them.

NEW-YORK Oct. 27. Col. Dunbar with his Forces are safe arrived at Albany. And the Number of House-Carpenters have been sent to the Northward to build Barracks, &c. for the Use of the Forces during the cold Season.

His Excellency our Governor, and the Gentlemen with him, still continue at Albany; are in Health, and very assudious in the Publick Affairs.

Baron de Dieskau, the French General taken by General Johnson, and who by Lewis of France is allowed a Pension of 4000 Livres per Annum; was brought down Prisoner from Albany on Monday Afternoon last, to this City; and about nine o'Clock at Night, to avoid a Crowd of People assembled to see him, he was landed, and carried to Lodgings prepared for him in Nassau-Street where he lies dangerously ill of his Wounds. His Aid de Camp is with him.

Friday last, a Sloop from New-England, having on board a large Number of Sheep, passed by here for Albany.

PHILADELPHIA Oct. 30. Extract from Virginia, dated Oct. 24.

"About a Week ago the Militia of Domfries, Prince, William, and Fairfax Counties were draughted, on on Tuesday Evening marched (to the Number of 160) out of Winchester, towards the South Branch of Potomack where the late Murders were committed. At the same Time 200 of the Virginia Regiment (recruits) set out for the same Place, who were followed the next Day by Col. Washington: And 110 Recruits more, from James's River, crossed the Ridge Wednesday; so that in about a Fortnight we shall have (with 130 more at Will's Creek) about 500 Men fit for Duty at Fort Cumberland, exclusive of the Militia and scattered Parties, in the Pay of the Colony.

Our Back Inhabitants have left their Settlements in great Numbers, under all the Miseries of cold and Poverty, added to the Misfortune of being without any Hope of Reimbursement."

Extract of a Letter from Lancaster County, dated Oct. 28.

"I imagine you have been alarmed before this Time, with a great deal of bad News from these Parts, I think it my Duty to give you as much Light into the Affair as I can. ------ About the 20th Instant, News was brought that the French and Indians had actually massacred and Scalped a Number of our Inhabitants, not more than 40 Miles from Harris's Ferry. It is reasonable to think the Receipt of such News must put the Inhabitants in the utmost Confusion. About 45 of the stoutest of them got themselves mounted in Readiness the next Day, to go and bury the Dead: They reached the Place accordingly, and found no less than 14 Bodies most shockingly mangled ------ Whilst they were in the Place, some friendly Indians, who were flying to the Inhabitants for Protection, told them there was a large Body of French and Indians actuallly on their March to the inhabited Part of this Province, and were already on this Side of the Allegheny Mountains; upon this they concluded to go as far as Shamokin, to know whether the

Indians assembled there, were Friends or Enemies (for our People suspected those Indians had some knowledge of the Murders) and to get, if possible, further Intelligence about those they had heard were advancing towards them. ——— The Indians at Shamokin treated them with civility, but had several Councils and a good deal of Whispering among themselves, which made our Men suspicious of them, especially as some of them were missing soon after. However, in the Morning (for they staid with them all Night, not thinking it safe to sleep in the Woods) Andrew Montour, and Delaware George, advising them to avoid going a particular Road, in which they said there was Danger; but our Men suspecting their Sincerity, went their own Way which was the very one they were cautioned to avoid, and were fired on by a Party of Indians, about 40 in Number, some of whom they believed were with them Part of the Night before. Our Men returned the Fire in the best Manner they could, but one of them came off when the Engagement first began, and it was feared was the only one of them could escape, alive out of the whole. ———

The News soon spread all over our County, and we were in the utmost Consternation, till Yesterday Afternoon, we are told fifteen more of our Men returned: They all agree it was the the Delaware Indians that did the Mischief. ——— Our Court-House Bell has been ringing almost ever since, to call the Inhabitants to some Consultation for their Safety. ——— We hear there are above one Hundred Men already gone up to Harris's Ferry. out of Donnegal and Places adjacent."

Extract of a letter from Harris's Ferry on Susquehanna, Oct. 27.

"Out of near 50 who went up from hence to bury the Persons killed near Gabriel's Mill, only 23 are as yet returned, & It is supposed that John Harris is dead. There is an Account come here, that one Powell, who was in the Action, returned to Shamokin and soon after a young Indian Runner came there, and said that the French and their Indians to the Number of 1500 were very near. How the Account may be I will not undertake to say; but sure I am, if there is not some speedy Measures taken by Men of Weight that we shall be utterly ruined. There are gone up to Hunter's Mill, above Harris's upward of 500 Men, but they are in want of Ammunition. It is said the French and Indians were seen Marching into Shamokin."

We have a Number of Letters confirming the above melancholy Accounts; but as they are all to the same Purpose, think it needless to insert them.

The Women and Children in the Back Parts of Cumberland, Lancaster and Berks Counties, are all come or coming down, to the Townships that are thich settled, and some of them are come to this City. In short the Distress and Confusion our People in general are in on the Frontiers, is inexpressible.

Within these few Days, several additional Quantities of Arms and Ammunition have been purchased by a Committee of Assembly, and sent up in Waggons for the use of the back Inhabitants.

We hear that a place of some Strength is now building by the Inhabitants near Penn's Creek to retire to in case of an Alarm, and that some Swivels have been purchased for their Use by the Committee, and sent up together with two Cannon given by a Gentleman in this City.

NOVEMBER 1755

BOSTON Nov. 3. Province of Massachusetts-Bay, by his Honour the Lieutenant Governor.

The Right Honourable Sir Thomas Robinson, one of his Majesty's Principal Secretaries of State, having been pleased by a Letter of the 26th of July last, to inform me, That there was great Reason to apprehend that it might be the Intention of the Crown of France to proceed to an open Rupture; and having also been pleased to direct me to give immediate Notice thereof to his Majesty's Subjects within this Government;

I do therefore, in conformity to the Directions; I have received, make the said Advices Publick; and I recommend it to all concerned to proceed with all necessary Care and Circumspection in the present Conjuncture, and to be upon their Guard against any Mischief that may be apprehended, under these Circumstances, to their Navigation and Commerce.

Given under my Hand this 28th Day of Oct. 1755
By His Honours Command.   S. Phips.
　　　Theo. Clarke, Dep. Secr'y.

BOSTON Nov. 3. By His Honour Spencer Phips. Esq; Lieutenant Governor and Commander in Chief in and over His Majesty's Province of Massachusetts-Bay in New-England.

A PROCLAMATION.

Whereas the Tribe Penobscot Indians have repeatedly in a perfidious Manner acted Contrary to their solemn Submission unto his Majesty, long since made and frequently renewed;

I have therefore, at the Desire of the House of Representatives, with the Advice of His Majesty's Council, thought fit to issue this Proclamation, and to declare the Penobscot Tribe of Indians to be Enemies, Rebels, and Traytors to his Majesty King George the Second: And I do hereby require His Majesty's Subjects of this Province to embrace all the Opportunities of pursuing, captivating, killing and destroying all and every the afore said Indians.

And Whereas the General Court of this Province have voted that a Bounty or Incouragement be granted and allowed to be paid out of the Publick Treasury, to the marching Forces that shall have been employed for the Defence of the Eastern and Weastern Frontiers, from the First to the Twenty-fifth of this November:

I have thought fit to publish the same; and I do hereby promise, That there shall be paid out of the Province Treasury to all and any of the said Forces over and above their Bounty upon Inlistment, their Wages and Subsistence, the Premiums or Bounty following. viz.

For every Male Penobscot Indian above the Age of Twelve Years, That shall be taken within the Time aforesaid and bro't to Boston Fifty Pounds.

For every Scalp of a Male Penobscot Indian above the Age aforesaid, brought in as Evidence of their being killed as aforesaid, Forty Pounds.

For every female, Penobscot Indian taken and bro't in the aforesaid, and for every Male Indian Prisoner under the Age of Twelve Years, taken and brought in aforesaid, Twenty-Five Pounds.

For every Scalp of such Females Indian or Male Indian under the Age of Twelve Years, that shall be killed and brought in as Evidence of their being killed as aforesaid, Twenty pounds.

Given at the Council-Chamber in Boston this Third day of November 1755, and in the Twenty-ninth Year of the Reign of our Sovereign Lord George the Second, by the Grace of God, of Great Britain, France, and Ireland, King, Defender of the Faith, &c.

By his Honour's Command   S. Phips.
    J. Willard, Sec.

BOSTON Nov. 3. We hear, that some Time before Admiral Boscawen sail'd from Halifax, a Discovery was made of a Letter wrote by the Captain of the Alcide, done up in a Wash-Ball, and directed to the Governor of Canada, wherein, it's said a Proposal was made to send Body of Men in Halifax.

We learn by Captain McKey, who arriv'd here on Wednesday Evening last, in 4 Days from Chegnecto, That this Day fortnight, 12 Transports, with about 1500 French Neutrals on board sail'd from thence (suppos'd for South-Carolina) under the Convoy of 3 20 Gun Ships. ——— That our men in general were in good Health as could be expected. ——— And that Capt. Wilson of one of the N. England Companies lately died there.

Our last Advices from the Camp at Lake George, bro't by an Express which arrived here last Friday, are, that Capt. Rogers (who was sent as a Spy) with four Men, returned to the Camp last Thursday was s'nnight, and reported in his Opinion, that he tho't there were not above 500 Men in Crown-Point; ——— that he kill'd and Scalp'd a Frenchman within 70 Rods of said Fort; in the middle of the Day, and got off without any loss ——— By the above Express we learn that his Excellency our Governor was within about 60 Miles of Albany when he came away; so that it's tho't he may be got safe there by this Time.

Last Night arrived here three Sloops from Pisguit, with a Number of French Neutrals on Board.

We hear that the Third Person of Note of the Penobscot Tribe of Indians, was taken Prisoner by our Men, after the late Engagement near Lake George.

BOSTON Nov. 3. By a Vessel from Chinecto in Nova-Scotia we are informed that some Thousands of French Inhabitants have been Shipped off for our Southern Colonies; That about five Thousand more at Annapolis, and were shipped fast as Vessels could be procured for transporting Them.

By a Letter from Halifax, dated October 21st. we are informed, that the Night before the Fleet sail'd for England, a most horrid Scheme was discovered, that had been laid by some of the principal French Officers, with a Plan of the Town and Batteries, and was done on exceeding thin Paper, and extreme fine Writing, and was folded and pressed as close as possible, and put up in a middle of a Wash-Ball to go to

Canada by way of Louisbourg. It was to take Halifax this Winter, with a Number of Canadian, Indians and Regulars, and when they had taken the Town, they were to fire the Batteries upon the Ships; the Inhabitants all to be shut up in Church, and Fire put to it, and the Troops were all to be put to the Sword without Quarters —— The Admiral put it to the chief Person conserned, (viz. the Captain of the Alcide) who firmly denied it, upon which the Admiral shewed it to him in his own Hand writing to his horrible Confusion.

Yesterday several Transport Vessels arrived in our Harbour from Nova-Scotia, with French People from that Province, who are to be disposed of among us, but in what Way or Manner, we cannot yet say.

NEW-YORK Nov. 3. We are informed by a Gentleman from Suffolk County, the People of the County have sent a Present of Sixty Head of fat cattle to General Johnson and his Army, of which a Yoke of good Oxen are for (the late Famous) Hendrick's Son, and his Indian Adherents. And they have contributed 127 Pounds of York Money, to defray the necessary Expence of their being convey'd alive to the Army.

General Shirley is hourly expected at Albany, with a Company of Grenadiers belonging to his Regiment, which are, we are told, to be Quarter'd in Fort George in this City, during the Winter Season.

From Oswego, we have Advice of the Death of Captain Descury, first Captain of the Regiment under General Pepperrell.

A general Congress of all the English Governors on the North Continent of America, is appointed to be held here on the 10th or 15th of this Inst. November.

PHILADELPHIA Nov. 6. Extract of a Letter from Lancaster, dated Nov. 3.

"The News that is most to be depended on is, that about 3 Weeks ago, the French and Indians left Fort Du Quesne, under the Command of the Marquis Du Quesne, with a determined Resolution to Invade the Province with 1500 Men. They got to our Frontier about 10 Days ago, and 'tis said are now building a Fort at Shamokin. This Intellegence comes from Andrew Montour. The Country is now assembling at Harris's Ferry, in order to oppose the Enemy should they advance so far. Tomorrow 400 Men will march from this to the Place of general Rendezvous, and by Wednesday Night it is tho't there will be 2000 Men at Harris's. All that is wanting, is a proper Law for conducting the whole."

ANNAPOLIS Nov. 6. We are now about entreaching the Town. If the Gentlemen in our Neighbourhood of Annapolis would send their Force to assist in it, a few Days would compleat the Work.

BOSTON Nov. 10. Province of the Massachusetts Bay. In the House of Representatives, Sept. 27, 1755.

Voted, That all needful and necessary Support be allowed such sick and wounded Soldiers as shall have Liberty to return Home from General Johnson's Army (who belong to this Province) and shall desire Relief, until they shall get to their respective Homes; and that each and every Person that shall supply such sick or wounded Soldier shall keep a fair and particular Account of each and every Man's Name, and what Company he belongs to, and of what he receives; and return such Account, which shall be certified by the Person relieved, to the Commissary-General some Time before the Master-Rolls shall be made up, that so Payments thereof may be made in such a Way and Manner so this Court shall hereafter Order.

Sent up for Concurence, In Council, october 3, 1755.   T. Hubbard Speaker

Read and concurr'd. Tho. Clarke, Dep. Secr.

Consented to, Copy examined, per Tho' Clarke Dep. Secr.   S. Phips.

NEW-YORK Nov. 10. Extract of a Letter from a Gentleman at Oswego, dated 16th October last.

"Ever since I wrote you, we have been employed in building new Forts and Barracks. Indian Affairs, which have been the Subject of great Consideration, begin to wear an agreeable Appearance; and I flatter myself, that the Generals Attention to the Matters, will have a Powerful Influence on the next Campaign, and the

Onondagaes, who were most in on the French Interest, of any of the Five Nations, declare their Attachment to us. Many of the Confederate Tribes seated at Oswagatie, I hope soon to see here at Oswego. Among the Messasacs and Chippawees, residing on the North Side of the Lake, and in the Country, extending thence to Lake Huron, we have sent trusty Messages. The Ontawaes, who were active against General Braddock, resent the Conduct of the French, both in the Action and Division of the Spoils, and declare they will abandon their Interest, and fall upon their Settlements this Winter, if we will forgive their past Conduct, and supply them with Necessaries. We doubted this Sincerity, till our Messenger had returned from their Country. The Senecas, heretofore to little known to the English, gave us great Satisfaction. Joncuer, a French Man, who has resided among them several Years past, was driven away from their Country, about a Fortnight ago; and they assure us, they will never admit him again. The general sent a Message about a Month ago to the Senacas, and in Consequence of it, 50 Men engaged to meet us at Niagara. Besides double that Number, which they promise for our Assistance the next Campaign, they have engaged to inhabit the Indians, from aiding the French over the Carrying-Place at Niagara. I do assure you, sir. that our Indian Affairs, are altered much for the better. If the means we have begun be pursued, 'tis really not a hard Task, to gain all the Indians who inhibit the Countries, on this, and the Lakes Huron and Erie. I am astonished, that we should have had, so slender an Acquaintance with the Indian Natives. The Mohawks indeed we know, but tho' they are a brave People, yet their Numbers are very small. The Oneidas too, with whom we have had a Connection, are but a handful of dastardly Thieves. As to the Onondagaes, Their Chiefs as I said before, were mostly of the French Interest, till secured this Summer by the Industry and Art of General Shirley.

    Unless an expected Accommodation between the two Crowns disappoint us, the Preparations already made, give us Reason to hope, that the Frontiers of these Colonies will be perpetually secured from the future Invasions, and the French driven out of all their Encroachments.

NEW-YORK Nov. 10. Four of the French Men that deserted from Crown-Point and surrendered to a Party of our Men coming down to Albany, were brought to town a few Days since from that City, two of them his Excellency our Governor has ordered to be provided for in the Fort, the other two our late Lieutenant Governor takes care of in his House in the Bowry. These Men say, that Mons. Dieskau could not be prevailed upon when he left Crown Point, to take more than 1500 Men with him, being confident of Success against our forces.

PHILADELPHIA Nov.13. A Letter from Lieut. Col. Stephen of the Virginia Regiment, at Winchester November 9, 1755.

"The proper Steps to be taken to secure your Frontiers, are to set about a Chain of Forts directly. One at Ray's Town, another in the Fork of the North and South Branch of Juniata, some others up Susquehanna, at the proper Passes. Unless this is done, the pacific Gentlemen, our Colony will either from Necessity change their Principles, or have their Throats cut. I have reason to believe, from undoubted Intelligence, that a grand Design is formed against your Province by the Enemy, and nothing but Unanimity and vigorous Measures can prevent the Success of their Design. It is very practicable yet, let us therefore redeem lost Time."

PHILADELPHIA Nov. 13. A Letter from Conegochieg, dated Nov. 3 says that the People of the Great Cove are in the greatest Distress imaginable, nothing being to be seen but Houses burning, most of the Cattle shot down, the Roads full of the unhappy Sufferers, flying with their Children to save their Lives; many of them having nothing to subsist on, no bed to lie upon, not hardly any Cloaths to defend them from the cold, being obliged to leave every Thing behind them, or run the Risque of being murder'd by the merciless Savages."

Extract of a Letter from Winchester, Nov. 5.

"Two Presbyterian Clergymen in Cumberland County, have marched in quest of the Enemy, at the Head of two considerable Parties of their Hearers. ——— The People in your back Counties seem to have a fine Spirit, and are willing to do any Thing for the Defence of their Country, and Safety of their Families, but want Order and Discipline, and complain of the want of proper Persons to directs."

We hear that two Persons have made Oath before a Magistrate in Cumberland County, that the Party from Fort Cumberland had fallen in with the Indians, and killed a great many of them.

Just now we hear an Express is arrived with a Confirmation of the Indians being all cut off at Ray's Town by our Men.

BOSTON Nov. 17. By an Express arrived here last Saturday Night from Albany, we are informed, That his Excellency Major General Shirley arrived there from Oswego, on the 4th Instant: ——— That the Indians had burnt a small Place called Scatacook, a few Miles above Albany.———

That Captain Rogers with a Party of Men who were sent out as a Scout from the Camp, had been attack'd by a considerable Number of Indians, who finding our men resolute, were oblig'd to quit the Field with the Loss of Eight or Ten: And Captain Rogers having Intelligence that a Number of French and Indians had come over the Lake and were building a Kind of Breast-Work in order to defend themselves, he sent to Camp for a Reinforcement, when 500 Men were immediately dispatch'd to his Assistance; and the next Day a very heavy fire was heard, 'twas tho't the two Parties must have engag'd. ——— We impatiently wait the Arrival of an Express to bring a further Account of the above Affair.

NEW-YORK Nov. 17. Monday last a Sloop arrived here from Albany, in whom came Passengers the Capts. Shirley and Morris of Shirley's Regiment and Capt. Ascough, Commander of one of the Vessels of War on Lake Oswego, where, we are told, Col. Mercer is left Commander in Chief for the Winter Season, with a Garrison of six Hundred Men.

The Governor, Council, and General Assembly of North Carolina, on the 15th of October last, passed an Act for granting a further Aid of Ten Thousand Pounds Proclamation Money, to be appropriated in raising three Companies of 50 Men each, to be sent to the Assistance of the Northern Colonies, in Support of the Common Cause against the barbarous and perfidious Enemy. Governor Dobbs, after he had given his Assent to the Bill, told the other Branches of the Legislature, That their having granted as great a Supply as the Circumstances of that Province could bear, it could not but be most agreeable to his Majesty, especially when other rich and flourishing Colonies kept up a continual bitter Spirit of Party, regardless of their Religion and Liberties: and was glad to find the People of North Carolina kept up the Spirit of Resentment against the common Enemy of the Country.

BOSTON Nov. 17. The Government of Nova-Scotia having judged it necessary to remove the French Inhabitants from thence, and to dispense them among the British Colonies in North-America, have decided to send about 200 Families to this Province; and as in Consequence of the Resolution, one Vessel with about 50 Families is already arrived in the Port of Boston, and others are daily expected: The Inhabitants of the Province who are inclined to take any of the same French Families or Persons into their Service; or to accommodate them with Settlement, are hereby notified, that there is a Committee appointed by the General Court, to place them out in such Manner as shall be most for the Interest of the Province, and that said Committee may be spoke with every Forenoon from Tuesday to Friday inclusive, at the Town-House in Boston, and will be ready there to treat with any Person willing to employ or accommodate them as aforesaid, until they shall be disposed of.

PHILADELPHIA Nov. 20. Some Vessels are in the River from Halifax with French Neutrals, one of which came up to Town on Tuesday Night, but is since ordered down again.

BOSTON Nov. 24. Wednesday last his Honour the Lieutenant Governor was pleased to issue a

Proclamation, for the further proroguing of the Great General Court or Assembly of the Province to Thursday the Eleventh of December Next.

PHILADELPHIA Nov. 27. By Letters from Oswego we have arvice, that the Onondago Indians that returned from Oswegarche, say, that the French have built 5 Vessels at Fort Frontenac, and that while they were there, they had got their Masts in.

One of the Vessels had 2 Masts, the other one each. The Indians judged them as large as those built at Oswego.

It is said that a Bill for granting sixty Thousand Pounds to the King's Use, sent up Yesterday by the Assembly, will this Day be passed by the Governor, to the great joy of all that wish well to this of late unhappy Province. The honourable Proprietors have on their Part, made a free Gift of Five Thousand Pounds for the Defence of the Country. ——— Tuesday was passed the Military Law ——— It is hoped that the Spirit of Party, which for some Time past raged so violently among us, will now, subside, and that we shall no longer, by our Dissentions, continue Enemies to our Friends, or Friends to our Country's Enemies.

WILLIAMSBURG Nov. 28. The Five Vessels that are arrived with the French Neutrals in this Colony have on board near 900 Souls, who are disposed in the following Manner, viz. One Vessel with about 170 is sent to the Falls of James River; two with about the same Quantity each, are sent to Norfolk, and the two remaining at Hampton. They are provided with Houses, Provisions, &c. at the Expence of the Government, with Leave to hire themselves as Labourers, or to any other Employment, 'till such Time as something be resolved on, with regard to their Settlement among us. They appear to be quite, sober, and industrious People well acquainted with Agriculture and othe useful Employment of Life, and as they have long ago, and now do acknowledge themselves to be English Subjects, we hope not the least Danger is to be apprehended from them, and that they may in Time prove of great Benefit and Service to the Country.

DECEMBER 1755

Boston Dec. 1. We hear from New-York, that Yesterday Morning sen'night, about Six o'Clock, departed this Life, Mr. John Shirley, youngest Captain in the Regiment under his Father General Shirley, and one of his Aid de Camps.

By Express which arrived here last Saturday, from Albany, we are inform'd, that the Expedition against Crown-Point was to be laid aside for this Season.

NEW-YORK Dec. 1. Saturday Evening last an Express arrived here from Goshen, in Orange County, in this Province, by whom we are inform'd, that the People of that Place having received Advice that two Men were scalped by the Indians at Minisink, they dispatched our Informant on Order to know the truth of the Matter; that he had not proceeded far before he was met by a Man on Horseback, who acquainted him, that the Day before, which was Thursday, the French Indians had set Fire to a small Village at Minisink, about 30 Miles from Goshen; that he heard many Guns go off, and several bitter cries; and that he was of Opinion, he alone was the only Inhabitant that escaped, the Rest being either put to the Sword, or carried into Captivity.

NEW-YORK Dec. 1. Wednesday Morning last, his Excellency Sir Charles Hardy, Knt. our Governor, attended by the Honourable James De Lancey, Esq; our Lieutenant Governor, and several of his Majesty's Council of this Province, arrived here in good Health from Albany.

And we are told, his Excellency Major General Shirley, is daily expected here.

ANNAPOLIS Dec. 4. Sunday last arrived here the two last of the Vessels from Nova-Scotia, with French Neutrals for this Place, which makes four within this Fortnight; who have brought upward of Nine Hundred of them. While they have lain in this Port, the Town have been at considerable Charge in supporting them, as they appear very needy, and quite exhausted in Provisions; and as it cannot be expected that the Charge or Burden of maintaining such a Multitude can be supported by the Inhabitants of Annapolis (a small Part of the Publick Society when compared to the People of the whole Province, and who, upon this Occasion have been very liberal) it will be necessary soon to disperse them to different Parts of the Province. As the poor People have been deprived of their Settlements in Nova Scotia, and sent here (for some very political Reasons) bare and destitute, Christian Charity, nay common Humanity, call on every one, according to their Ability, to lend their Assistance and help to those Objects of Compassion. We are told that three of these Vessels are to sail with the first fair Wind (which we heartily wish soon to happen) one for Patuxent River, another to Choptank, and the third to Wicomico, there to wait the Orders of his Excellency our Governor.

PHILADELPHIA Dec. 4. We have Advice from Virginia, that a Ship is arrived there from England, having on board a train of Artillery, 6000 Muskets, and 14000 Pounds in Cash.

BOSTON Dec. 8. Extract of a Letter from Halifax. dated November 27, 1755.

"LAST Week arrived here the Otter's Prize, she is a large Ship and a fine Prize: Next Week we have a Thanksgiving: ——— Col. Winslow is arrived with a Party of 50 Soldiers; There is 1200 more expected in Town every Day."

By a Courier which arrived here on Saturday last from Albany, we are informed, That the Army was disbanded, saving a sufficient Number of Men left to Garrison the two Forts there, under the Command of the Colonels, Bagley of this Province and Whiting of Connecticut.

NEW-YORK Dec. 8. Extract of a Letter from Albany dated November 18, 1755.

"Last Week we were alarmed, by the coming in of Rykert Bovie, from Schacticook, who was in high Flight wounded in the back and Thigh, with Swan Shot; He informs us a Party of Indians being there; and the next Day we heard that they burnt the Church and two Houses, &c.

PHILADELPHIA Dec. 11. We hear that on Tuesday the 2d Instant, one John Rhoads, who lately lived beyond the Blue Mountains, on Lizard Creek, near Gnadenhurren, and had removed his Family for their greater Safety to this Side of the Mountain, was returning, with a Servant Man and a Cart and Horses, to his old Plantation, to bring off part of his Goods he had left behind him; and as he passed over the Mountain he made some Stay with the Men who were stationed there as Watch, sending his Servant with the Cart, and Horses before him. In a little Time after, they heard four Guns discharged, and judging the Servant to be in Danger, they made up to him in a Haste, and found him shot dead; but they had not Time to scalp him. They shot also three Horses almost two or three Miles further up the same Creek, at the Plantation of one Leycock, the Indians killed his Wife and Son, and scalped the latter. It is supposed the Son made a stout Resistance, his Gun lying by him broke in Pieces; and then they arrempted to have scalped the Woman, she having a small incision of a knife just above her Eye-brow, but had been scared away: Her Arm was ript open from the Wrist to the Shoulder.

NEW-YORK Dec. 15. Edmond Broadstreet, a Soldier in this Garrison, who on the 3d Instant, was Sentenced at a Court Martial to be shot on Wednesday last for Desertion, was on the Day of his Excecution pardon'd by General Shirley.

BOSTON Dec. 15. Last Thursday the Great and General Court or Assembly of this Province met here, being the Day to which it stood Prorogued.

A Vessel from Halifax with French (falsely called) Neutrals, is arrived at Maryland.

Since our last a Number of the discharged Soldiers arrive in Town from the Army at Lake George.

PHILADELPHIA Dec. 18. In several Affidavits Mention is made of Broadhead a Barracks and Barns being seen on Fire; and that very great Firing, and screaming was heard about his House in which, it is said, there were fifty Women and

Children: And we hear, that unless it is his House, or that of Mr. Dupuy, which both Places are of some Strength, there are none of our back Inhabitants to be seen.

BOSTON Dec. 22. By several Letters from Nova-Scotia we have agreeable Accounts of the gallant Behaviour of many of our New England Men, particularly of Lieut. Billings, (on the List of the Wounded inserted in the Paper the 6th of October last) who behaved very greatly to his Honour and Reputation both with the Officers and Soldiers, who were all extremely surprized, considering Mr. Billing's hazardous Situation, considering his great share in the Action, and the true Intrepidity and Wisedom of his Conduct tho' the whole, not to see his Name mentioned in our Paper with peculiar Marks of Honour and Distinction.

We hear General Shirley is expected in Town the latter End of this Week or the beginning of next.

BOSTON Dec. 22. Friday Captain Foss arrived here in 6 Days from Chignecto, in Nova-Scotia who informs, that about a Week before he sailed, 7 of his Majesty's regular Troops being about some Business in the Woods at some Distance from the Fort, without Arms, they were suprized and taken Prisoners by the French and Indians: and that a little before 3 other Soldiers had been Captured by the Enemy who are seen almost daily lurking in the Woods near the Fort, and vastly exceeds our People in Point of Sagacity and Stratagem.

PHILADELPHIA Dec. 25. Extract of a Letter from Virginia, dated Dec. 11, 1755.

"We on the South End of Potomack in Hampshire County, Virginia, are now safe from the horrors of the Indian Enemy, under the protection of Providence, and Capt. William Baylis, a brave active young Gentleman, from Prince William County, with eighty Men, all single Persons, who strictly do their Duty, in scouting the Woods, and endeavouring to fall in with the Indians. We have also Captains Strother and Brown, from Colepepper County, with sixty Men, who with Capt. Ashley and Capt. Cock's Companies, make about 220 active and effective Men, which is pretty good Security at present."

On Sunday the 14th Instant Robert Caston, who lived at the Head of Hunter's Settlement, on the Forks of Delaware, was shot and scalped by some Indians, as he was foddering his Cattle. And soon after one Alexander Galbreth, and another Man, were shot at by the same Indians, when Galbreth, was wounded in the Side, and the other had his Horse shot under him, but both escaped on Galbreth's House.

The barbarous and bloody Scene which is now opened in the Upper Parts of Northamton County, is the most lamentable that perhaps ever appeared; ——— There is no Person who is possessed of any Humanity, but would commiserate the deplorable Fate of these unhappy People: There may be seen Horror and Desolation; ——— populous Settlements deserted; ——— Villages laid to Ashes; ——— Men, Women and Children cruelly mangled and massacred; ——— some found in the Woods, every nauscous for want of Interment: Some just reeking from the Hands of their Savage Slaughterers some hacked and covered all over with Wounds.

THE BRADDOCK MASSACRE

FULLNAME INDEX

----, Lewis 332 Lydia 124
ABUTHNOT, Capt 156
ADAMS, 305 310 Capt 322
ALBEMARLE, Earl Of 103
ALLEN, 252 Judge 151
AMHERST, Capt 268
ANSON, Adm 176
ANVILLE, Duke Of 264
ASCOUGHH, Capt 346
ASHLEY, Capt 352 Maj 307 313
ASHLIN, Lee 13
ASHLOFF, Daniel 325
B---R, Mr 50
BABON, Charles 323
BACKER, Robert 89
BACON, Capt 277 John 105
BAGLEY, Col 350
BAILEY, 252
BALTIMORE, 292
BARBUE, Lt 252
BARKER, John 324
BARNET, Abraham 65
BARONET, William P 196
BARRINGTON, Capt 168
BARTMAN, Lt 296
BAYLEY, Capt 324
BAYLIS, William 352
BECKWORTH, 252
BEDUNAH, Joseph 324
BELCHER, Gov 61 J 48 67 Jonathan 46 60 118 216
BILLINGS, Lt 314 323 352
BLANCHARD, Col 277 305 310 315
BOLTON, Mr 238
BOSAWEN, Adm 223 268
BOSCAWEN, Adm 176 202-203 229 256 283 326 340 Vice Adm 245

BOURN, Maj 208 324
BOVIE, Rykert 350
BOWER, Capt 252
BRACKGROSS, Samuel 324
BRADBURY, John 225
BRADDOCK, Edward 251 Gen 155 158 168 171-172 176 180 184 192 195-196 202 217 224 231 242 247 249 259 264 270 276 282-283 287 300 320 328 344 Maj Gen 166
BRADLEY, Capt 281
BRADSTREET, Capt 205 241 245 256 261 296
BRAMM, Mr 28
BRATT, Berent 94
BRECTON, Lt 252
BROADSTREET, Edmond 351
BROOM, Capt 285
BROWN, 201 Capt 352 Commodore 143 Montague 296 Mr 296 Timothy 324 Vendall 101
BUCKHANNON, Lt 252
BURRINGTON, Geo 166
BURT, Lt 312
BURTON, Lt Col 252 Sir 250
CALL, Mr 90 Philip 89
CALLENDER, Mr 79 Robert 78
CAMBIER, James 296
CARGILL, Capt 229 232
CARLISLE, Maj 166
CASTELIO, James 194
CASTON, Robert 353
CHANDLER, James 324
CHAPMAN, Maj 194 Samuel 323
CHARLEVOIX, Father 54
CHESIRE, John 296

CHEVALIERES, 54
CHOLMSEY, Capt 252
CLARK, Abraham 61 Samuel 324
CLARKE, Capt 77 Theo 339 Thomas 168 200 206 320 343
CLOCKLAN, James 26
COBB, Capt 181 322
COCK, Capt 352
COCKS, Capt 296
COLE, Capt 268 Lt Col 305
COLVIN, Alexander Lord 229
CONTRECOUR, 151
COOK, Alexander 89
COOKE, Capt 37
COOPER, Mr 6
COPE, 252
CRESAP, Col 224 324-325
CRIMBLE, Lt 252
CROFT, Childerman 155
CROGHAN, Mr 9
CROW, Lt 252
CURRIN, Barnaby 25 Barneby 12
D'AVILLES, Duke 222
DANVILLE, 238
DAVISON, 15 John 13
DEAN, Mr 245
DEBELLEGER, 223
DEDIESKAU, Baron 335 Le Baron 308
DEISKAU, 311
DEJONVILLE, Capt 69
DELAGE, David 166
DELANCEY, Gov 310 James 65 174 176 180 298 349 Lt Gov 38 Mr 47 Oliver 298
DEMERCE, Capt 256
DEMIROPOIX, Duke 134
DENISON, Robert 199
DEROUCHE, 295
DESAINTPIERE, Legardeur 24
DESAINTPIERRE, Legardeur 170-171
DESCURY, Capt 342
DEVILLIER, Capt 79
DICKINSON, Capt 319
DIESKAU, 345 Gen 304 Mr 313
DIFNEY, 252
DIGGS, Dudley 65

DINBAR, 144
DINWIDDIE, Gov 51 81 95 170 176 Lt Gov 60 Mr 46 Robert 1 7-8 12 183
DIVINALL, Michael 166
DOBBS, Capt 184 Gov 158 184 347
DOBSON, Capt 252
DOGGET, Capt 335
DOGWORTHY, Capt 105
DONAHEW, Capt 51
DOWE, Capt 298
DRUILLON, 85 105
DUNBAR, 252 Col 195 234 247 249-251 253 257 259 267 270 276 283-284 290 322 328 334-335 Lt 252
DUPUY, Mr 352
DUQUESNE, 50 Marquis 342
EDES, 315
EDMESTON, Lt 252
ELIZABETH, Queen Of England 264 Quuen Of England 239
EMERSON, Mrs 286
EMERY, James 324
ENGLAND, King Of 138 164 177 249 286
EYRE, Capt 306
FAIRCHILD, Capt 299
FAIRFAX, Thomas 215
FALCONER, Lt 252
FERALL, Capt 307
FLEET, Mr 274
FLOYER, Capt 252
FOOT, Isaac 199
FORTY, John 104
FOSS, Capt 352
FOX, Joseph 317
FRANCE, King Of 46 57 79-80 145 195 220 227
FRANKLIN, Benjamin 65 W 318
FRAZIER, Mr 2 12 18 29
FRY, Col 52 69 84 Joshua 68 Maj 110 323-324
GABRILL, George 333
GAGE, Lt Col 252
GALBRETH, Alexander 353
GARDINEER, John 230
GARDNER, Capt 285-286
GATES, Capt 252 256 296

GAY, Capt 168
GEORGE, 2nd King Of
  England 46 71 91-92 168
  194 197 202 262 267 296
  339-340
GETHINS, 252
GIBBS, Joseph 324
GILBERT, Capt 281 324
GILL, 315
GIST, 9 Christopher 69 Mr
  10 12 14 23 28-29 96
GITCHELL, Elisha 323
GLADWIN, Lt 252
GLEN, Col 255 Gov 124 J
  126 James 154
GOLDTHWART, Maj 323
GOODRICH, Elihu 199
GOULD, Capt 297 Paston 296
GRAY, H 127 153 Lt 252
GREENLY, Reuben 324
GROGAN, Mr 191
GROUT, 217
GULFORD, Richard 166
HALKET, 144 Francis 251 Lt
  252 Peter 195 252 260
HALKETT, Peter 194
HALL, Capt 231 Squire 255
  William 241 255
HAMILTON, Capt 209 John
  324
HANCOCK, Mr 60-61
HANEN, Mr 252
HANSARD, Lt 252
HARDY, Charles 296 298 349
  Gov 327
HARRISON, Capt 190 Lt 252
HART, Lt 252
HATHORN, Lt 252
HAWKE, Adm 176
HAY, Mr 212
HELBOURN, Rear Adm 319
HENDRICK, Daniel 87
HENMAN, Benjamin 199
HOBSON, 252
HOGG, 95 Peter 94
HOLBOURN, Adm 245 Rear Adm
  228 285
HOLBOURNE, Adm 229
HOLBURN, Adm 314
HOLDERNESS, Earl Of 46
HOLDERNESSE, Earl Of 135
  138

HOOD, Capt 183
HOOPS, Adam 233 Mr 234
HOPSON, Thomas 296
HOW, Caleb 217
HOWARTH, Lt 252
HOWE, Capt 229
HOWLEY, Capt 313
HUBBARD, T 122 200 204 206
  320 343
HUDDLE, Henry 229
HUTCHINSON, Thomas 83 317
HUTSON, William 324
INCHES, Joseph 75
INDIAN, Anagarondon 88
  Andrew Montour 337
  Corneliess 310 Custaloga
  20 Delaware George 337
  Half King 11 14-16 18-20
  22 25 53 60 66-68 79 152
  278 Hendrick 73 302 312
  329 Hendricks 315
  Henndrick 307 Jeskakake
  20-21 John Shickealami
  224 King Hendrick 300
  Monacatoocha 13 19-20
  231 Monocatucha 278
  Montandre 88 Shingiss 13
  18 20 Susquehanna Jack
  82 White Thunder 21 27
INGERSAL, Capt 307
INGERSOL, Capt 313
INNES, Col 71 78-79 81 83
  105 202 276 Gen 85 257
  James 82
JACKSON, Capt 65
JENKINS, William 12
JOHNSON, 260 271 Abraham
  215 Col 288 Gen 199 240
  243 261 272 276 278 280
  282 287 289 297-300 302
  304 313 315 321 324 327-
  329 332 335 342-343 Maj
  Gen 230 233 246 255 262
  281 301 311 William 180
  310
JONCAIRE, 23 27 Capt 19
  21-22
JONCUER, 344
JONES, Capt 203
JUMONVILLE, Ens 68
KELLER, Commodore 168
KENNEDY, 252 Archibald 55

KEPPLE, Commodore 175-176 184
KEYS, Capt 313
KIRKWOOD, Capt 181-182
L'MAINE, 290
LACHASSE, Father 33
LAFCELLE, Maj Gen 285
LAFORCE, 9 23 69 85
LANSCISCO, 296
LANVERAIT, Father 33
LASOL, [la Salle] 21
LAWRENCE, Charles 206 Col 268 Gov 203 227-228 231-232 Lt Gov 226 Mr 60-61 Robert 120
LEFORCE, 67-68 95 102
LEGG, Julian 116
LEGRAND, Lewis 169
LESLY, Mathew 251
LEWIS, Capt 303 [louis] King Of France 335
LEYCOCK, 351
LEYMAN, Maj 246
LINSEY, David 323
LITHGOW, Capt 32
LITTELER, 252
LITTLE, Mr 218
LIVINGSTON, Robert 231
LOCK, 252
LONG, William 234
LOUIS, 14th King Of France 163
LOWENDALL, Marshall 304
LYMAN, Gen 289 Maj 255 281 297 Maj Gen 243-244 311 Phinehas 199
LYON, Lt 105
M'CLOUD, Lt 252
M'GERTY, Alexander 87
M'GREGORY, James 271
M'KAY, Capt 81-82
M'LOUD, Lt 252
M'NEALE, Lt 253
M'SHANNON, Samuel 324
MACCAY, Capt 75 77-78
MACQUIRE, John 12
MAILE, Benjamin 325
MALCOM, Capt 323
MARBLE, Jeffe 324
MARCH, Lt 323-324
MASTON, Rear Adm 245
MCCARTY, Mr 211

MCGIN, Capt 307
MCGINNES, Capt 308
MCKEY, Capt 341
MCKINNEN, Lt 296
MCMULLEN, Lt 252
MERCER, Col 346
MERCIER, Lt 77
MERIDITH, Reese 317
MIFFLIN, John 317
MILLER, Lt 252 Seth 324
MOGARIDGE, William 323
MONCHTON, 227 Col 277
MONCKTON, Col 207-208 245 247 285 295 Lt Col 228
MONTEUR, Andrew 79
MONTOUR, Andrew 343
MONTRESEUR, Lt 252
MORGAN, Evan 317
MORIN, 50-51
MORRIS, Capt 250 346 Capt Lt 252 Gov 129 140 150 174 Robert Hunter 176 180 247 249 Roger 251
NARTLOW, 252
NEWELL, 124
NICHOLS, Maj 309
NICKELS, Capt 242
NORRIS, Isaac 65 250 317
NORTH, Lt 314
NOYES, Rev 200
O'BRIAN, Henry 229
O'CONNOR, 333
OATES, Capt 270
ORDE, Capt 252
ORME, Robert 251
ORNE, Capt 168
OSBORNE, John 163
OVERTON, Samuel 276
PARONIE, Capt 253
PATTEN, Joseph 11
PATTERSON, William 199
PATTON, James 258
PAYSON, Nathan 199
PEBBLE, Col 212
PELHAM, Widow 297
PENN, 292 John 65
PENNINGTON, 252
PEPPERELL, Col 171 Gen 183 217 Maj Gen 216 William 144 175 178
PEPPERRELL, Gen 342
PEREGRINE, Col 296

PERRY, Capt 324
PETERS, Richard 65
PEYRONEE, Mr 76
PEYRONEY, Capt 273
PHIPS, S 226 242 259 320 340 343 Spencer 339
PIERCE, Ezekiel 199
PIKE, David 323 Joseph 212
PITCHER, James 156 Mr 153
PITKIN, John 199
POGUITE, Joseph 324
POLSON, Capt 194 253 273
PORTER, Capt 313
POTMAN, 255 John 241
POWELL, 337 William 87
POWNAL, Thomas 317
PRATHER, Maj 325
PREBBLE, Col 91-92 Maj 323
PRESTON, 252
PROBY, Capt 168 171
PUMROY, Lt 313
PUTER, Capt 307
RALLE, Father 33
RANDALL, Mr 37
RATIASEN, Thomas 138
REYNOLDS, David 324
RHOADS, John 351
RICE, Capt 201
RICH, Elijah 324
RIPARIT, Capt 24
RIPARTI, Capt 25
ROBINSON, Thomas 113 153-154 339
ROGERS, Capt 341 346
ROSS, Capt 252 John 83 Mr 193
ROUS, Capt 235-236 278 295 326 328 335 Commodore 231
ROUSE, Capt 328
RUGGLES, Col 279 306
RUTHERFORD, Capt 194 256
SACHAM, Elisha 324
SAINTCLAIR, John 155 250 Sir 156
SAINTPIERE, 307
SAINTPIERRE, 320 Chavalier 304
SAMPSON, Capt 323
SANFORD, Samuel 199
SAUNDERS, Capt 104-105
SAVAGE, Lt 276 282

SAXE, Marshall 304
SCHUYLER, Col 88 296 Myndert 87 Peter 193
SCOT, Col 211
SCOTT, Lt Col 324
SHARPE, Col 130 Gov 155 157 176 244 260 Horatio 118 131 133-134 158 Mr 164
SHIELEY, Maj Gen 257
SHIRLEY, Capt 328 335 Col 175 Gen 217 240 256-257 266 271 278 282 289 296 310 322 327 329 342 344 349 352 Gov 91-93 144 171 180 207-208 226-228 246 265 351 John 91 296 349 Maj Gen 213 233 243 246 255 267 277 334 346 Mr 94 168 260 Secretary 250 W 71 116 122 172 200 205-206 Washington 174 Wiliiam 36 William 30 44-46 69-70 120 168-169 174 176 196-197 201-203 251
SHUYLER, Col 280
SIMPSON, 252
SINCLAIR, John 157 224
SMITH, Capt Lt 252 Samuel 317
SOOMAIN, Lt 252
SPAIN, King Of 218
SPARKS, Maj 252
SPEAKMAN, Capt 324
SPENCE, Peter 192
SPENDELOW, Lt 252
SPICORFF, Lt 253
SPRY, Capt 156 202-203 327
STALLNICHER, Capt 234
STANFORD, Capt 177
STEPHEN, Lt Col 345
STEPHENS, Lt Col 157
STERLING, Lt 252
STEVENS, Capt 307 Jonathan 255 Nicholas 255
STEWARD, Henry 12
STEWART, 262 Capt 253 274 Col 234 Mr 10
STHEPHENS, Capt 253
STOBE, Robert 81
STOBO, 105

STODART, 189
STODDARD, Samuel 323
   Thomas 224
STODDERT, Capt 307 Lt 325
STONE, Nathaniel 324
STOWELL, Hezekiah 324
STROTHER, Capt 352
TAGGART, Capt 203
TALBOT, Mr 252
TASKER, B 134 Bemnjamin 65
TATTON, Capt 252
TERRY, Nataniel 268
THOMPSON, Samuel 324
TITCOMB, Col 299 306 309 313
TOWNSEND, Lt 252
TREAT, Capt 182
TREEBY, 252
TRENT, 9 Capt 52 67
TROTTER, John 26
VANARNEM, 94
VANBRAAM, Capt 76 Jacob 12
VANBRAAN, 105
VANDAM, Mr 263
VANDERHEYDEN, 94
VANKERBERG, Joachum 240
VANSCHAICK, Capt 232
VANVURST, Dirik 241
VASSEL, Henry 180
WADDIL, Capt 102
WAGGWNWE, Capt 253
WALSHAM, Lt 252

WARBURTON, Gen 252 268 Maj 225
WARD, Ens 72 Mr 52
WASHINGTON, 127 Col 69 74-75 77 81-82 103 229 326 336 George 30 251 299 301 Maj 2 9 12 52 67-68 72 78-79 170 Mr 1 250
WATERBURRY, Lt 177
WETHERED, Mr 297
WHITE, Capt 200
WHITING, Col 200 350 Samuel 199
WIDEMAN, Lt 252
WILLARD, Capt 324 J 71 122 197 204 206 340 L 46
WILLIAM, 3rd King Of England 163
WILLIAMS, Col 299 305-307 309 313 Israel 114
WILLIAS, 215
WILMOT, Montague 268
WILSON, Capt 341
WINSLOW, Col 208 211 227-228 235 277 335 350 Gen 84-85 91 103 Lt Col 228 323 Maj Gen 75 104-105 110
WITHING, N 199
WITMARSH, Sallen 166
WOODWARD, Lt 253
WRIGHT, Capt 92 Lt 253

Other Heritage Books by the author:

1767 Chronicle

Boston, the Red Coats, and the Homespun Patriots, 1766-1775

Central Colonies Chronicle: The Freeman, the Servants, and the Government, 1722-1732

French and Indian War Notices Abstracted from Colonial Newspapers
Volume 2: 1756-1757
Volume 3: January 1, 1758 to September 17, 1759
Volume 4: September 17, 1759 to December 30, 1760
Volume 5: January 1, 1761 to January 17, 1793

Jolly Old England

Journal of Occurrences: Patriot Propaganda on the British Occupation of Boston, 1768-1769

Newspaper Datelines of the American Revolution
Volume 1: April 18, 1775 to November 1, 1775
Volume 2: November 1, 1775 to April 30, 1776
Volume 3: May 1, 1776 to November 1, 1776
Volume 4: November 1, 1776 to January 30, 1777

Pontiac's Conspiracy and Other Indian Affairs: Notices Abstracted from Colonial Newspapers, 1763-1765

www.ingramcontent.com/pod-product-compliance
Lightning Source LLC
Chambersburg PA
CBHW072132220426
43664CB00013B/2219